5000
73U

D1596291

THE BYZANTINE TRADITION AFTER THE FALL OF CONSTANTINOPLE

THE BYZANTINE
TRADITION AFTER
THE FALL OF
CONSTANTINOPLE

Edited by John J. Yiannias

DJK
24
B98
.1991
seab

UNIVERSITY PRESS OF VIRGINIA

Charlottesville and London

The United Library
Garrett-Evangelical/Seabury-Western Seminaries
2121 Sheridan Road
Evanston, IL 60201

The University Press of Virginia
Copyright © 1991 by the Rector and Visitors
of the University of Virginia
First published 1991

Library of Congress Cataloging-in-Publication Data

The Byzantine tradition after the fall of Constantinople / edited by
John J. Yiannias.
    p.   cm.
    Includes index.
    ISBN 0-8139-1329-2
    1. Europe, Eastern—Civilization—Byzantine influences.
    2. Byzantine Empire—Civilization.   I. Yiannias, John James.
DJK24.B985   1991
947—dc20   91-8474
                                                               CIP

Printed in the United States of America

CONTENTS

Contents

PREFACE

TRANSLITERATION out of Modern Greek has posed its usual vexing editorial problems. Complete consistency, not only between papers but within most of them individually, has proved to be out of the question. But readers of Modern Greek should have little trouble in reconstructing the Greek spellings. In the text proper it has been possible to make sparing use of a Greek font. For Slavic titles and names the system used fairly consistently is that of the Library of Congress, but without most of the diacritical marks; also, exceptions have been made in the case of proper names already made familiar to scholars through the "linguistic" system of transliteration. Readers of the original languages will have no difficulty in reconstructing the Cyrillic spellings.

The editor expresses his gratitude to the other contributors for their labors and for their patient cooperation in the course of the editing, and to Mr. and Mrs. Gus W. Pappas of Charlottesville for their encouragement and generous financial assistance.

INTRODUCTION

John J. Yiannias

CONSTANTINOPLE fell to foreign invaders only twice in its long history, if we leave aside its occupation by Allied forces after World War I: in 1204 to the knights of the Fourth Crusade and in 1453 to the Ottoman Turks. The fall of 1204 and the subsequent sacking of the city by the Crusaders did long-lasting damage to the relations between the Western and Eastern churches, but the feudal state that the conquerors hastily put in place, the Latin Empire of Constantinople, had an even shorter life than some of its counterparts in the Holy Land. Its inherent weaknesses and the Byzantines' powers of recovery enabled Michael VIII Palaeologus to take back the city in 1261.

The fall of 1453, on the other hand, was not reversed. The Byzantine state had been moribund for the entire Palaeologan period and was now consigned to extinction. The Ottomans went on to enjoy additional military successes; in their new capital, as throughout the formerly Byzantine domains, minarets replaced belltowers; Constantinople became and remained Istanbul. Nevertheless the culture for which the city had been the crucible for over a millennium, and which in the final days of the empire had displayed one of its finest flowerings,[1] continued to provide the "nation" of Orthodox Christians subject to the sultan, and to some extent even the Turks themselves, with models that commanded respect and emulation. The Byzantine tradition of statecraft, thought, spirituality, and artistic expression was rendered only partially obsolete by the new order.

It may be debated how much a historical entity must change before it merits or requires a new name. The problem does not arise in the case of individual human beings, who give every appearance of subsisting continuously from the womb to the grave despite their cycles of cellular replacement and their personality changes. But in the case of cultures and civilizations the matter is less simple. Can the term *Byzantine* be justifiably applied to historical phenomena of the period after the fall of the Byzantine Empire?

In the view of Arnold Toynbee, writing sixty years ago, a "Byzantine," or "Orthodox Christian," society (he used the terms interchangeably in this context) was one of a few living societies, which he distinguished on the basis of culture, some of the others being the Western, the Islamic, the Hindu, and the Far Eastern. All of them had a larger extension in space and time than any one of their constituent political communities; and he considered as belonging to the Byzantine society, despite modern political developments, Russia and the countries of southeastern Europe. Applying a biological metaphor in which societies are the "specimens" of a "species," Toynbee spoke of "apparentation" and "affiliation," and described the Byzantine and Western societies as being the morphologically differentiated descendants of a single society, the now extinct Hellenic.[2]

Whether one thinks in terms as broad as these or resolutely avoids doing so, it is safe to say that the forms under which life has been experienced in most parts of the world, at least until recently, have been remarkably constant from one generation to the next, except in times of cataclysmic social or environmental upheaval. While the Turkish overrunning of Byzantium presented most of the features of a true cataclysm to the peoples who were subjugated, it did not result in the eradication of their way of life.

The survival of some salient elements of this way of life is symbolized by the common use, in the Ottoman period, of the Turkish *Rumlar* and the Greek ῥωμαῖοι or ῥωμιοί to refer to Greek-speaking Orthodox Christians.[3] These terms, based on the Byzantines' officially preferred name for themselves ("Romans"), surely betoken the awareness of an appreciable degree of cultural continuity between the earlier and later populations, a shared identity. In English there seems to be no adjective but "Byzantine" that can be applied to both historical phases of that "Roman" (more properly, Greek Christian) culture. To describe the phase occurring after 1453, modern scholars have had recourse (as will be seen often in the present volume) to the term *post-Byzantine*—a name predicated on the termination of Byzantium as a political organism, not as a culture.

Our main concern in this volume, however, is not the name to be given the tradition in question but the tradition itself, the ideas and practices that were inherited from the days of Byzantine sovereignty and handed down (or in some instances revived) within the Orthodox Christian world after the imposition of Ottoman rule. It has not been the goal to determine how far into the modern period the Byzantine tradition has extended (although some of the papers allow inferences on this point) or to attempt a comprehensive survey.[4] Attention has been directed to a necessarily limited but fairly representative sampling of topics, which, it is hoped, will bring some important aspects of the tradition into sharper focus.

The contributions by Steven Runciman, Speros Vryonis, Jr., Miloš Velimirović, Charalambos Bouras, Gary Vikan, Thalia Gouma-Peterson, and the present writer reproduce, in widely varying degrees of revision, the papers delivered at a symposium organized by the present writer and held at the University of Virginia on April 15 and 16, 1988, under the title now used for the book. The positive responses to the symposium by those who attended it engendered the belief that the papers in collected form would make a welcome addition to the sparse literature on the subject in English. They are presented here with that idea in mind, accompanied by two contributions written especially for this volume by John Meyendorff and Aglaia E. Kasdagli.

The single institution most committed by its very nature, as well as by circumstances, to keeping viable the Byzantine tradition after the fall of the empire was the Orthodox Church; and ecclesiastical power, along with the civil privileges and responsibilities that it entailed within the Ottoman system, resided ultimately in the Ecumenical Patriarchate of Constantinople. Sir Steven Runciman's narrative takes us through the opening days of the Ottoman presence in Constantinople and portrays the conditions, some favorable and others oppressive, under which the ecumenical patriarchs and their flock managed subsequently to survive as a distinct community. The persistence and in some cases the resuscitation of characteristic elements of Byzantine formal culture in this community's legal concepts and practices, visual arts, calendrical observances, monastic life, and literary conventions are the topic treated by Speros Vryonis. His discussion suggests how pervasive were the patterns of thought and conduct inherited from Byzantium; but it has the added importance of drawing attention to the continued multiethnic composition of the Byzantine cultural world after 1453.

The diffusion and long-term potency of Byzantine ideas and norms outside the historical political boundaries of the Byzantine Empire are perhaps most dramatically illustrated in Russia. John Meyendorff provides a reassessment of Russia's "Byzantinism" in the period immediately preceding, and in the centuries following, the Turkish conquest of Byzantium, pointing out the stresses to which certain elements of the Byzantine tradition were subjected as Muscovite Russia proceeded along its unique political course, and correcting the misperceptions to which the all-too-convenient formula of the "Third Rome" has given rise. The recent (1988) millennial celebration of the introduction of Byzantine Christianity into *Rus'* makes such an analysis particularly timely.

To the older motivations of social history has been added in recent years the desire to rescue from obscurity the realities experienced historically by women. Basic to the background against which gender discrimination in any society must be examined is the legal status of its women. Tapping a huge number of archival and other written sources reflective of daily life on the island of Naxos and in other localities in post-Byzantine Greece, Aglaia E. Kasdagli establishes Naxos as an instructive case of marked disparity between, on the one hand, the low social position of women and, on the other, their legally protected access to property. Some parallels with, as well as divergences from, Byzantine practice emerge in the course of her discussion.

In the latter part of our volume, the arts take center stage. The distinguishing characteristics of Byzantine music and its influence on the music of the Slavic world, particularly that of the South Slavs and Russians, are sketched by Miloš Velimirović. In this field of creativity as in so many others, the rich liturgical life of the Orthodox Church provided the main impetus. Velimirović's conspectus gives an idea of the obstacles to research, as well as the opportunities for it, that are presented by the manuscripts in which the achievements of this brilliantly cultivated but elusive art are encoded.

The visual arts are probably the most accessible components of the Byzantine tradition after the fall of Constantinople; yet, except for the icon-painting of this period, they are not widely known. Students of Byzantine art at one time routinely included in their purview the works produced by Eastern Christians after the Turkish conquest, but in this century Byzantinists, especially those writing in English, have tended to confine themselves to the art of the centuries before 1453. Unquestionably the fall of Constantinople sapped much of the artistic creativity of the Orthodox world; but it did not, by any means, stifle it.

The building of churches even remotely approaching that familiar symbol of Byzantium, Justinian's Hagia Sophia, in scale and structural daring had ceased in the empire long before the Ottoman conquest, and after the conquest even the less ambitious experiments of late Byzantine architecture in planning and surface articulation became largely a thing of the past. But as Charalambos Bouras's paper makes clear, churches continued to be built in impressive numbers, when conditions permitted; and so long as they were conceived as symbols of the Orthodox community's ties with its own past, rather than as attempts at modernization along Western lines, almost all of these structures were dependent on Byzantine models. The scope of Bouras's survey and of his citations is indicative of the increased interest taken in the post-Byzantine period by architectural historians in the Balkans since the Second World War.

The art form through which the Byzantine tradition after the fall of Constantinople has gained the most exposure in the West is no doubt the icon. Thalia Gouma-Peterson describes the persistence of the Byzantine concept of sacred imagery through the times of social change and artistic evolution that followed the fall of Constantinople. The power of images to conjure up the values thought to be essential for the preservation of a community's identity has never been more clearly demonstrated than in the case of post-Byzantine icons, and to see them in this light is to understand better the significance of their distinctive visual qualities.

The manuscript described and analyzed by Gary Vikan, the Walters 535, attests to the revival in the late sixteenth century of a type of Byzantine illustrated book—the lectionary, or collection of liturgical Gospel readings—that had flourished over half a millennium earlier. We also learn, from Vikan's unraveling of its complex history, which involves his examination of some other manuscripts of the period, that the Walters lectionary bears eloquent testimony to the permeability of ethnic boundaries in the Orthodox world of the time, having been written by a Greek Cypriot hierarch resident in Wallachia, taken by him to Moscow possibly as a gift of the Rumanian voevod to the tsar, illustrated there by Russian artists, and eventually transported to the Holy Land.

If Byzantine culture continued after 1453 to be spread over a wide territory, it also had a place of concentration, a "clearing house" (in Speros Vryonis's words) in the Holy Mountain, Athos. The cultivation there of a tradition of monastic refectory decoration that had its roots in the pre-Ottoman period but can be seen at its flourishing in the post-Byzantine monuments, is the subject of the present writer's paper. No less than the church, of which it is in some ways an extension, and with which it is here compared, the refectory provided a setting for a selection of images owing its logic and inspiration to the religious vision of Byzantium.

The modern cult of nationalism, with its reordering of facts, and rephrasing of myths, to facilitate the formation and advancement of nation-states, has not been conducive to the preservation of a balanced memory of Byzantium's role in the history of southeastern Europe, Russia, and the Near East. Nor have the surprisingly ephemeral (as it now seems) political ideologies and alignments of the recent Cold War, which, whether for better or worse, imposed new divisions on the map of the world in place of the old. It is hoped that the papers in this volume will contribute to a fuller definition of that role, by conveying collectively an impression of the considerable momentum that the Byzantine tradition proved itself capable of maintaining after the fall of Constantinople in 1453.

Notes

1. Steven Runciman, *The Last Byzantine Renaissance* (Cambridge: Cambridge Univ. Press, 1970).

2. *A Study of History*, 2d ed., vol. 1 (Oxford: Oxford Univ. Press; London: Humphrey Milford, 1935), Introduction; cf. vol. 12, *Reconsiderations* (New York: Oxford University Press, 1961), esp. 458. More recently Dimitri Obolensky has introduced as a working concept the idea of a "Byzantine commonwealth," in many respects like Toynbee's Byzantine society, but coterminous with the empire; yet he also stresses the survival of the Byzantine tradition past 1453 (*The Byzantine Commonwealth: Eastern Europe, 500–1453* [1971, 1974; rpt. Crestwood, N.Y.: St. Vladimir's Seminary Press, (1982)]).

3. This may be an oversimplification of the intricate history of these usages, but I believe my underlying point to be valid.

4. For a thoroughly stimulating popularized discussion of Byzantine civilization and its cultural traces in present-day Southeastern Europe and Russia, see the article by Merle Severy, "The Byzantine Empire, Rome of the East," in the *National Geographic Magazine* 164 (July–Dec. 1983): 708–67.

"RUM MILLETI": THE OTHODOX COMMUNITIES UNDER THE OTTOMAN SULTANS

Sir Steven Runciman

THE LOSS OF FREEDOM is the cruelest fate that a people can suffer. To the Greeks the fall of Constantinople in 1453 has always been an unparalleled tragedy, marking the end of Byzantium, the Christian empire of the East, and their entry into captivity. With historical hindsight we can see that Byzantium was doomed, too sick to recover. Even if the gallant defenders of the city had succeeded in 1453 to force the Turks to raise the siege, it would only have been for a short respite. The Turks would soon have made another effort. And in the long run was the coup de grace so great a disaster? The Greek world was already fragmented, with far more Greeks living under alien domination, Turkish or Italian, than were still free. Would it not be a better thing for it to fall under a power that could reunite it, even though it would be reunited in captivity? What was the alternative?

There were some in Byzantium who hoped that Western powers might intervene to save the Christian empire. But would the Western powers ever bring themselves to cooperate in the task? And if they did, would they be effective? The so-called Crusades of Nicopolis and of Varna had shown that their troops were no match for the highly efficient and up-to-date Turkish army. Besides, Western help would only come if the Church of Constantinople submitted itself to the authority of the Church of Rome. Some statesmen thought the price worth paying; and a number of intellectuals believed that Byzantine culture should be merged with that of the West. But the average Byzantine, with memories of 1204 still vivid in his background, would never endure that. If Byzantium was to perish, let it perish with its Orthodoxy unblemished.[1] Many of them knew that their empire was doomed, piously seeing it as the punishment of its sins and its apostasies. It was an age, too, of chiliastic notions. The coming doom was the beginning of the reign of Antichrist, to be followed by Armageddon and the end of the world. That final event, it was generally thought, would take place seven thousand years after its creation, which the pundits now dated at 5508 B.C. Maybe they were right. Simple arithmetic shows that the world thus ended in 1492, the year when Columbus discovered America.[2] There were just a few Byzantines, such as the historian Kritovoulos, who thought that the only solution now was for the Greek people to accept the sultan's rule.[3]

Yet when the climax came, the citizens of Constantinople, whatever each might think, came together as one in their brave, hopeless attempt to save their liberty. They fought in vain. By the end of May 1453 the city was in the power of the conquering sultan, Mehmet II.

Mehmet was a remarkable young man. He was able and farsighted beyond his years, self-reliant, secretive and devious, trusting no one, and utterly merciless when it suited him. But at the same time he had a respect for culture, an interest in philosophy and the arts, and a genuine concern for the general welfare of his subjects. He should not be regarded as a savage oriental tyrant but should, rather, be compared with the Italian princes of the time or with monarchs such as Henry VIII of England. He was not unfriendly to the Greeks. He had grown up at a time when Constantinople, decayed though it was politically, was still a renowned cultural center. He almost certainly spoke and read Greek; and he was interested in Greek philosophy. With the great city in his power he saw himself as the heir to the emperors. He ruthlessly eliminated any Greek layman of prominence. But once that was done he was ready to give his Greek subjects a guaranteed legal status.[4]

It was anyhow necessary to organize the Christian communities within the Ottoman dominions. Hitherto when Christian towns had been conquered and the lay officials dismissed, the Christian population had been leaderless except for the local bishop. But he had been appointed by the authorities in Constantinople. He was always tempted to remain there; and the Turks might not allow him to go to his diocese. If he was there he had no official sanction when he tried to deal with the Turkish governor. Now all this could be reordered. In the East nationality was usually considered to be synonymous with religion. Under the Muslim caliphs, who followed a system started by the Persian kings, the Christians according to their various sects, along with the Jews and the Zoroastrians, formed self-governing communities within the state, each under its religious head, who was responsible for seeing that order was kept and taxes were paid, and that there was no disloyalty towards the ruler. Mehmet extended this system to his empire. The head of the Orthodox communities in Ottoman territory was the patriarch of Constantinople. He should be put in charge of the *Rum Milleti*, the Orthodox nation.[5]

There was, however, no patriarch of Constantinople at the time. The last patriarch, Gregory Mammas, had favored union with Rome and found himself so unpopular that he had fled in 1451 to Italy and was generally held to have thereby abdicated. The sultan made inquiries and decided that the best man for the job would be George Scholarios, who had been the leading Aristotelian scholar of the time. He had attended the Union Council of Florence and there had supported the union with Rome, but then changed his mind and retired to a monastery under the name of Gennadios, and had become a leader of the anti-Unionists. But he could not now be found. At last it was discovered that he had been captured at the fall of the city and been sold to a rich Turk of Adrianople, who was somewhat embarrassed to find that he had acquired so learned a slave and treated him more as a friend. Gennadios was redeemed and brought before the sultan. Before he would accept the patriarchate he worked out with the sultan the constitution under which the church and the whole Orthodox *millet* were to be governed.[6]

According to the terms arranged between them, the patriarch, in conjunction with the Holy Synod, had complete control of the whole ecclesiastical establishment. It must be remembered that the patriarch had never been more than the president of the Holy Synod, which officially elected him and could by a unanimous vote depose him were he proved to be unworthy of his office or to have been elected uncanonically. In practice in Byzantine times the lay suzerain could and did nominate the candidate for the patriarchate and could press for his deposition; and the synod seldom dared to disobey the sovereign's wishes. The sultan certainly expected to exercise a similar influence, should he so wish. No bishop could be appointed or dismissed except by permission of the patriarch and the synod; but episcopal appointments had to be confirmed by the sultan, as by the emperor in previous days. The patriarchal lawcourts alone had jurisdiction over the bishops. The lay authorities could not arrest anyone of episcopal rank without patriarchal permission.

This all followed traditional lines. What was new was that the patriarch was to be in control of the Orthodox laity. He was the ethnarch, the ruler of the *millet*. He was responsible for its orderly behavior and for ensuring that it paid its taxes. These were very heavy, in theory because non-Muslims had to pay for being excused—in fact, debarred—from being called up into the sultan's armed forces. The taxes were collected by the lay headman of the local community; and it was the duty of the church authorities to punish him if he did not do so fully and promptly. As clerics were officially excused from paying taxes, this did not make for good relations between the clergy and the laity. In fact the clergy were not wholly exempt. It was often suggested to them that they might like to make a voluntary contribution to the sultan's treasury; and it was unwise to ignore the suggestion. At the same time the patriarch could levy what taxes he pleased from his flock; and he needed large sums of money to keep his administration in working order.

Patriarchal lawcourts had for centuries dealt with cases that had a religious element, that is, not only matters of heresy and church discipline but also marriage and divorce, the guardianship of minors, testaments and successions, all according to Byzantine canon law. Now they had to take on also civil cases between members of the *millet*, according to Roman-Byzantine codified law and a growing volume of customary law. It was possible to appeal from their judgments to a Turkish court or to demand that the case be heard in the first instance before a Turkish court. But as such courts were slow, expensive, and often corrupt and judged according to Koranic law, no Christian would go before them unless he had influential Turkish friends. The patriarchal courts were generally thought to be remarkably free from corruption. Criminal cases and civil cases between a Christian and a Turk went before the Turkish courts.[7]

It is doubtful whether this constitution was ever written down. It conformed so generally with the traditional constitution for a *millet* within a Muslim state that it may have been thought unnecessary to record it. The general evidence of history makes clear that it was accepted; and we have further evidence provided by the survival of many of the *berats*, which every bishop received from the sultan on his appointment, and which stated his privileges and duties. We are told, however, of two definite documents signed by the sultan. One was a *firman* given to Gennadios, guaranteeing to the patriarch personal inviolability, exemption from paying taxes, freedom of movement, security from deposition, except by the unanimous vote of the synod, and the right to transmit these privileges to his successors. The *firman* may also have mentioned the patriarch's special right, alone among the Christians, to ride on horseback. His coreligionists all had to make do with a donkey or at best a mule.

The other document promised that the church's customs with regard to marriage and burial ceremonies should be legally sanctioned, that the Easter Feast should be officially recognized, that Christians should have freedom of movement during the three Easter feast days, and that no more churches should be converted into mosques. Unfortunately when, some seventy years later, the document was needed to halt the conversion of a church, it was found that it had perished in a fire at the patriarchate.[8]

With the constitution settled, Gennadios accepted the patriarchate. Presumably he was elected by such hierarchs as could be collected to form the Holy Synod. Then, on January 6, 1454, he was received in audience by the sultan, who handed him the insignia of his office, the robes, the pastoral staff, and the pectoral cross. The original cross had been lost, or, more probably, taken by the ex-patriarch Gregory Mammas when he fled to Italy. So Mehmet himself provided a new cross, made of silver-gilt. As he invested Gennadios he pronounced the words close to the formula used by the Christian emperors: "Be patriarch, with good fortune, and be assured of our friendship, keeping all the privileges that the patriarchs before you enjoyed." One privilege Gennadios could not enjoy. He could not be consecrated in the great church of Hagia Sophia, as it had been converted into a mosque. Instead he was taken to the second great cathedral of the city, the Church of the Holy Apostles. There he was consecrated by the metropolitan of Heraclea, whose traditional duty it was to perform the rite, and then enthroned. He emerged to mount on a fine horse, presented by the sultan, and rode in procession round the city. He returned to set up his residence and offices in the buildings attached to the church, enriched by a handsome gift of gold from the sultan.[9]

On the whole, once the horrors of the city's sack were over, the Greeks had not fared as badly as might have been expected. The Conqueror seemed to be eager to see them contented and prosperous, and to treat their church with respect. He was determined to revive Constantinople itself and for that purpose transported population there from other parts of his dominions, including large numbers of Greeks from Anatolia. Forced transportation is never pleasant; but many of these Greeks came from districts where they were surrounded and often outnumbered by unfriendly Turks. They were not sorry to come to Constantinople, where large areas were set aside for them. There they could lead their lives and conduct their crafts and businesses in some security and could worship without interference. Even in the provinces they now enjoyed better security; and in areas such as Greece itself, where the Turks were only a thin veneer, they were probably more comfortable than they had been in the previous turbulent centuries. Moreover, with the Ottoman Empire still advancing, the Greek world was soon to be united, except for the Ionian Islands, Cyprus, and Crete, where the Venetians still held sway; and Cyprus and Crete would soon be conquered by the Turks, freeing the Greeks there from the hated domination of the Roman Church.[10]

It might have been worse. But it was not all well. The Greeks were made to realize that they were now second-class citizens. They had to wear a distinctive dress and the laity could not sport beards. In lawsuits against Turks they had little chance of success. Even a decree of the sultan that favored them might be annulled by Muslim legal authorities as being contrary to Koranic law. Still, the sultan's good will was valuable. The Conqueror, once he had eliminated their leaders, was gracious towards the Greeks. But his son and heir, Bayezit I, had grown up at a time when the intellectual greatness of Byzantium had been forgotten. He was no intellectual himself and saw the Greeks merely as a subject people, unworthy of respect. His son, Selim I, actively disliked the Christians and even thought of converting them all forcibly to Islam. When told that this was impracticable he demanded that they should at least surrender all their churches. The horrified grand vizier warned the patriarch, who, in default of documents, was able to produce two octogenarian janissaries, who swore on the Koran that they had witnessed the Conqueror receive the keys of various quarters of the captured city and promise in return that the Christians should retain their churches. Selim gave way.

The great sultan Süleyman the Magnificent, or, as the Turks called him, the Lawgiver (d. 1566), was a just and conscientious ruler who saw that the rights of the minorities were respected. But after his death rot set in from the top.[11] Few subsequent sultans were men of real ability. There were several distinguished viziers, such as the members of the Köprülü family, who were consistently fair to the minorities. But usually no one intervened if local governors or other officials chose to be oppressive. In particular, high officials and even sultans continued to convert churches into mosques, until in modern times only one Byzantine church in Constantinople, St. Mary of the Mongols, had remained in Christian hands, saved because the Conqueror himself had signed a *firman* guaranteeing its preservation, as a reward to his favorite Christian architect.[12]

Gennadios himself had been aware of the difficulties. The Church of the Holy Apostles, which the sultan had allotted to him, was in a very poor condition and would be costly to restore. It was moreover placed in a district occupied by immigrant Turks who resented its presence. Within a year he handed it over to the sultan, who pulled it down and built a mosque on the site. Gennadios then moved to the convent church of the Pammakaristos. The nuns were moved to nearby buildings, and he took over the convent building to be his residence and offices. Sultan Mehmet used to visit him there to discuss theology with him, carefully never entering the church itself, lest later Turks would use the excuse of his entry to take it over from the Christians: which was, in spite of this precaution, exactly what Sultan Murad III did in 1586. The patriarchate was obliged then to borrow the little church of St. Demetrios Kanavou from the patriarch of Alexandria, till, early in the next century, it was allowed to build its present church of St. George, with offices around it, in the Phanar quarter, then entirely inhabited by Greeks. Like all churches built under the sultans till the nineteenth century, it was not allowed to have a dome visible from outside.[13]

There were two particularly cruel burdens that the Christians had to bear. First was the practice called by the Turks the *devshirme* and by the Greeks the παιδομάζωμα, which permitted the Turks to take one boy from each Christian household and bring him up as a Muslim, to serve as a janissary, either in the armed forces or in the sultan's secretariat, or as a master craftsman, according to his ability; and naturally it was the most promising boy of the family who was taken. Occasionally the janissary remembered his Christian family and might be in a position to help it in various ways. Süleyman the Magnificent's distinguished vizier, Mehmet Söküllü, who was by birth a Serbian Christian, used to have his Christian nephews stay with him and sometimes even accompanied them to Christian services. But such cases were rare.[14]

The second burden concerned education. The Turkish authorities discouraged Christian schools. They did not interfere with the Patriarchal Academy in Constantinople, which had had a high reputation in Palaeologan times and has survived to this day, having been periodically reformed by progressive-minded patriarchs. But attempts to found schools or academies in the provinces seldom succeeded. In Anatolia the local governors closed them down almost at once. In the European provinces, where the officials were on the whole more tolerant, they usually lasted on until some suspicious governor accused them of teaching sedition. An excellent academy was founded in Athens towards the end of the sixteenth century but was closed in about 1615, to be refounded in about 1717. It lasted, though with a diminishing reputation, throughout the eighteenth

7

century. There were short-lived academies at Thessaloniki, at Arta, at Nauplia, and at Yannina, and in some of the islands. An academy founded in the late seventeenth century had a high repute. Six patriarchs of the eighteenth century were educated there. Till the later seventeenth century it was possible to obtain a good theological education on Mount Athos. But then the monks turned obscurantist. When in 1753 the patriarch Cyril V tried to found an academy on the Holy Mountain, the professor whom he sent there, Evgenios Voulgaris, so shocked them by his modernist taste for German philosophy that he fled, lucky, he thought, to have escaped with his life. In the Ionian Islands, under Venetian rule, there were some good schools in Corfu and Zante. But boys from the Turkish provinces were not encouraged to go there.[15]

Venice was more helpful over higher education. A boy having some connection with a member of the Greek colony there who would finance him could go to the University of Padua, then one of the best in Europe, especially for philosophy and medicine; and no one there would try to convert him to the Roman church. The Greek hierarchy would also pay for a number of boys of humbler origin to study there. After 1577 there was also the College of Saint Athanasius at Rome, run by the Jesuits for young Greeks. It provided an excellent education. Orthodox pupils were admitted; but great pressure was put on them to go over to the Roman church. A wider choice was provided after the early eighteenth century when the Greek-born princes of Wallachia and Moldavia founded academies at the capitals of Bucharest and Jassy. These maintained high standards; but many pious Greeks found them a bit too modernistic.[16]

Perhaps the church could have done more for education. But schools are expensive to run, especially when it is necessary to bribe the authorities. Lack of money was to be the church's main problem; and it was enhanced by the Greek passion for politics, which now could only find an outlet in ecclesiastical affairs. The new responsibilities of the patriarchate involved an enlarged secretariat, to include lawyers and financiers, all of whom wanted good salaries. Soon the higher lay officials, such as the Protekdikos, the head of the judiciary, the grand logothete, the keeper of records, and the later created grand orator, the official spokesman of the church, were given places on the Holy Synod. Eminent laymen joined the episcopate in intriguing to secure such posts, which commanded prestige as well as power and often a chance of personal enrichment. The expansion of the Ottoman Empire had brought the eastern patriarchates, Alexandria, Antioch, and Jerusalem, as well as the autonomous archbishoprics of Cyprus and Sinai, under the sultan's sway; and their dealings with the central government were handled by the patriarchate of Constantinople, because it was on the spot. All this added to its labors and expenses. The patriarchate, and many of the bishoprics and monasteries, had large endowments; and the patriarch could tax them as he pleased. But there were limits to the sums that the faithful could pay. And the Turkish authorities demanded more and more in the way of bribes.[17]

This was largely due to the patriarchs themselves. Gennadios seems to have retired in 1465. His successor, Mark Xylokaravas, had only been on the throne for a few months before an ambitious prelate, Symeon of Trebizond, collected the sum of 2,000 gold pieces, which he offered to the sultan's ministers if they would order the Holy Synod to depose Mark and elect him in his stead. The sultan's Christian stepmother, the Serbian princess Mara, whom he greatly respected, heard of this and rushed to see him to get the transaction annulled. But she herself prudently brought 2,000 pieces of gold with her. Though her wishes were granted, henceforward every would-be patriarch had to produce a sum of money, generally known as the *peshkesh*, or gift, to have his candidature ratified by the sultan. Symeon managed to secure the throne a few years later, but then was outbid by a Serbian prelate, Raphael, who offered to pay in addition a yearly sum of 2,000 gold pieces to the Sublime Porte.[18] By the middle of the seventh century the *peshkesh* was usually 3,000 gold pieces, and the annual tribute roughly the same. By then the patriarch was also expected to pay a varying number of "voluntary" taxes; and he had to provide the mutton consumed by the palace guard, men of voracious appetites.[19]

It was thus to the interest of the sultan to appoint new patriarchs or to reappoint deposed patriarchs as frequently as possible. Süleyman the Magnificent was the only sultan to disapprove of this. Thanks to him the patriarch Jeremiah I enjoyed an unbroken reign of twenty-one years, by far the longest in patriarchal history. In the century from 1495 to 1595 there were nineteen patriarchal reigns. From 1595 to 1695 there were sixty-one changes on the throne, though only thirty-one individual patriarchs, as many were reappointed after deposition. Some reigns were short. Matthew II reigned for twenty days in 1595, then for four years, 1598 to 1602, then for seventeen days in 1603. Cyril I had seven different spells on the throne. His rival, Cyril II, reigned first for one week only, though later he reigned for twelve months. The climax was reached in 1726, when Calixtus III paid 5,600 gold pieces for his election and died of joy, from a sudden heart attack, the following day. After that even the Turks realized that things had gone too far. The *peshkesh* and the annual tribute were fixed. In the century from 1695 to 1795 there were only thirty-one patriarchal reigns and twenty-three individual patriarchs. After 1765 patriarchs were forbidden to try to pay for the *peshkesh* from the revenues of the church. They had to raise the sum from their own pockets.[20]

This was just as well, because the debts of the patriarchate were steadily rising. By 1730 they were estimated at 100,769 piasters, while the annual revenue was seldom enough to pay for regular expenses. By the eve of the Greek War of Independence the debts were said to approach 1,500,000 piasters.[21] It was fortunate for the church that it had rich friends who were ready to come to its aid. The rulers of the wealthy principalities of Wallachia and Moldavia had submitted voluntarily to the sultan and so were allowed to keep their thrones under Ottoman suzerainty. They were willing now and then to help the patriarchate with its money problems. Further to the north there was the tsar of Muscovy. As he considered himself, after the fall of Byzantium, to be the head of the Orthodox Christian commonwealth, it was his duty to concern himself with the welfare of the Great Church of Constantinople. But the generosity of these potentates, though great at times, was spasmodic. In the first half of the seventeenth century Muscovy was in no position to send aid. Patrons nearer at hand were needed.[22]

An unforeseen result of the Ottoman conquest had been the rebirth of Greek mercantile life. The Italians, who had dominated the trade of the Levant in the later Middle Ages, lost their privileges, and their colonies dwindled away. Few Turks had any liking or aptitude for commerce; so trade within the large and expanding Ottoman dominions passed into the hands of their subject races, Jews, Armenians, and, above all, Greeks. Unable to indulge in their favorite pastime of politics, except as regards the church, the livelier Greeks took up commerce and banking, thus being of use to powerful Turks who did not bother themselves with such matters. Other Greeks took up doctoring, there being few Turks with any knowledge of medicine. This gave them an entry into Turkish homes.

Soon a rich class of Greeks emerged. Discretion was necessary. A Christian who showed off his wealth was liable to have it all confiscated owing to some trumped-up charge of treason or some other misdemeanor, and maybe to lose his life as well. This was the fate of the first Greek millionaire of the captivity, Michael Cantacuzenos, whom the Turks surnamed *Shaitanoglu*, the son of the Devil. In the mid-sixteenth century he acquired the monopoly of the fur trade from Russia. He lived at Anchialos, on the Black Sea, a city that was almost entirely Greek, where his wealth would not attract Turkish envy. He was able to marry the daughter of the prince of Wallachia; and he could exercise so much influence in the church that he was able to have a worthy patriarch deposed for ruling that one of his family marriage schemes was forbidden by canon law. To gain favor with the sultan, he fitted out at his own expense sixty galleys for the Ottoman navy. Even so the sultan put him to death in 1578, appropriating and selling off his estate. Most of his magnificent library was bought by monasteries on Mount Athos.[23]

His slightly younger contemporary, John Karadja, made a vast fortune as caterer to the Ottoman army, a post in which he was succeeded by his son-in-law Scarlatos, surnamed Beglitsi, who acquired a fortune even greater than Shaitanoglu's. When he was murdered by a fanatical janissary in 1630, the bulk of his wealth was inherited by his youngest daughter, Roxandra, widowed princess of Wallachia and Moldavia. There were by now a number of rich Greek merchant and banking dynasties, based in the Phanar quarter of Constantinople, but seeking to invest their money in Wallachia and Moldavia, where alone in the Ottoman dominions lay Christians could own land. There they intermarried with the local nobility and with the ruling family of the Bassaraba, while maintaining their financial connection with Constantinople.[24]

In the mid-seventeenth century a young Chiot, trained in medicine at Padua, called Panayoti Nikoussios Mamonas and nicknamed "the green horse," from a saying that you could as easily find a green horse as a wise man from Chios, was appointed by the great Albanian-born grand vizier Ahmet Köprülü to be his family doctor. His linguistic gifts and his general ability so impressed Köprülü that in 1669 he created for him the post of grand dragoman of the Sublime Porte, that is, interpreter-in-chief and head of the secretariat in the Foreign Ministry. As such, Mamonas was allowed to grow a beard, to ride on horseback, and to wear a bonnet trimmed with fur. So well did this work that when Mamonas died in 1673, Köprülü appointed another Greek to the post.[25]

This was Alexander Mavrocordato, the son of Beglitsi's heiress Roxandra and her second husband, a Chiot who claimed descent from the Greco-Venetian family of Mavros or Moro (to which the general known to us as Othello the Moor actually belonged) and from the Greco-Genoese family of Cordato, and whose mother belonged to a branch of the old Roman family of the Massimi. Alexander had been educated first at the Greek College in Rome, without, however, becoming a Catholic convert, then at the University of Padua, from which he was sent down for riotous behavior, then at Bologna, where he obtained a doctoral degree with a remarkable thesis on the circulation of the blood. At the age of twenty-four he was appointed grand orator of the Great Church and director of the Patriarchal Academy, while continuing his medical practice, with the sultan as one of his patients. He was thirty-one when he became grand dragoman. He held the post till 1698, apart from a few months in 1684, when he was unjustly cast into prison as a scapegoat for the Turkish failure before Vienna. In 1698 a still higher post was created for him, that of Exaporites, Keeper of the Secrets and chief secretary to the sultan, with the titles of prince and illustrious highness. He died in office in 1709.[26]

No other Greek reached such eminence in the sultan's service. But many of them in the eighteenth century were employed by the Ottoman government, profitably for themselves; and they used their positions to help fellow Greeks as well. When the native dynasty of the Bassaraba died out in the Danubian principalities, the sultan appointed Greeks from the Phanar as princes of Wallachia and Moldavia. As with the patriarchate, candidates for the posts had to pay a large bribe to secure the appointment, as well as a heavy annual tribute; and the Turks therefore made frequent changes. No princely reign was allowed to last for long. Rich though the principalities were in natural resources, few princes returned to Constantinople financially richer for their experience. Yet many of them sought the post. It carried prestige and a princely title for the family, as well as a brief enjoyment of power. It cannot be said that the princes, in their eagerness to recoup themselves, did much for their subjects, though some, such as Constantine Mavrocordato, the Exaporite's grandson, were enlightened rulers. He reformed taxation, to make it more equitable, and he planned to liberate the serfs. But the princes did a great deal for Hellenism. The academies that they founded at Bucharest and at Jassy became centers of classical learning, where the Greeks were reminded of their intellectual heritage.[27]

The Phanariots were also generous to the Church. But there their influence was not so happy. In return for their generosity they demanded for their relatives the top lay posts in the patriarchal organization and a voice in the choice of patriarch. They valued modern education and wished to modernize the church. But the church was not ready for the benefits of the eighteenth-century Enlightenment. It still produced some well-educated clerics. But standards were declining. Till the middle of the seventeenth century the monasteries of Mount Athos were still adding to their libraries. By the end of the century the books were usually unread. Moreover the patriarchate with its political and financial troubles could no longer satisfactorily supervise the provinces. It lost touch with the faithful there. This became all too clear when in the eighteenth century the fashionable stirrings of nationalism began to affect the Greeks, especially in Greece itself. While the monks in Greece rejected the attempts of the patriarchate to improve their education, they supported rebellious movements, and even banditry, urged on by anticlerical Greeks such as Adamantios Korais, living safely in Paris.[28]

The movement for Greek independence posed terrible problems for the patriarchate. Each patriarch had on his appointment to swear allegiance to the sultan and to undertake that his flock would be loyal to the Ottoman government. Could he break his solemn oath? Besides, living in the center of things in Constantinople, he knew that though the Ottoman administration might be sinking into chaos the Ottoman army was still formidable. Every recent Christian rising, in the Peloponnese, in Cyprus, in the principalities, had been savagely put down. Could he encourage his flock to take such a risk? Would it not be better to follow the advice of the older Phanariots? They hoped to work their way further and further into the tottering Ottoman bureaucracy, so that when it collapsed they could take it over. But such an attitude was not to the liking of impatient young nationalists, even among the Phanariots and the hierarchy. When in 1821 the flag of rebellion was raised, in the principalities by a young Phanariot and in the Peloponnese by an archbishop, the fears of the patriarch, Gregory V, were justified. But he could not bring himself to denounce and excommunicate the rebels, as his Turkish masters demanded. He paid for it with his life.[29]

It is not possible in one brief article to give more than an outline of the story of the *Rum Milleti*. But I have tried to show that the Greeks in that dark period of the Tourkokratia deserve a better treatment than most historians like to give them. Despite all their difficulties, despite the unworthy behavior of many of them, they managed to keep Hellenism alive. For that the basic credit must go to the great patriarch Gennadios; and some of it, indeed, to Sultan Mehmet the Conqueror, who had no wish to see Hellenic culture perish. Subsequent sultans were less enlightened; and it must be admitted that several subsequent patriarchs were unfitted for their task. Credit must be given, too, to the much maligned Phanariots, who stimulated a renascence of Hellenism in the eighteenth century, making a far more solid contribution to it than did that overpraised anticlerical Korais. The story of the Tourkokratia displays few obvious heroes; but it is a heroic story all the same, the story of an oppressed people who refused to lose its identity and to forget its high traditions. And it was, above all, the church that kept the light burning.

Notes

1. Joseph Gill, *The Council of Florence* (Cambridge: Cambridge Univ. Press, 1959), 349–52, 366–68; Steven Runciman, *The Great Church in Captivity: A Study of the Patriarchate of Constantinople from the Eve of the Turkish Conquest to the Greek War of Independence* (London: Cambridge Univ. Press, 1968), 109–11; Joan M. Hussey, *The Orthodox Church in the Byzantine Empire* (Oxford: Clarendon Press, 1986), 283–86.

2. Ihor Ševčenko, "Intellectual Repercussions of the Council of Florence," *Church History* 24 (1955): 291–323, esp. 296–300.

3. This theme underlies the whole of Kritovoulos's work: *History of Mehmed the Conqueror*, trans. Charles T. Riggs (Princeton: Princeton Univ. Press, 1954).

4. Franz Carl Heinrich Babinger, *Mehmed der Eroberer und seine Zeit* (Munich: F. Bruckmann, 1953), 265–69, 449–53; Steven Runciman, *The Fall of Constantinople, 1453* (Cambridge: Cambridge Univ. Press, 1963), 55–56, 149–52, 186–87.

5. Runciman, *Great Church*, 167–68.

6. Kritovoulos, 94–95; *Historia Politica et Patriarchica Constantinopoleos; Epirotica* (Bonn, 1849), 78–80.

7. Runciman, *Great Church*, 170–72, giving references. See also the documents published in Theodore H. Papadopoullos, *Studies and Documents Relating to the History of the Greek Church and People under Turkish Domination* (Brussels: N.p., 1952).

8. Runciman, *Great Church*, 170–72.

9. *Historia Politica et Patriarchica*, 27–28, 80–82; Runciman, *Great Church*, 169–70.

10. See N[icolae] Iorga, *Byzance après Byzance: Continuation de l'"Histoire de la vie byzantine"* (Bucarest: Institut d'Etudes Byzantines, 1935), 45–56, for a general conspectus.

11. Runciman, *Great Church*, 186–91, giving references.

12. The story of the preservation of St. Mary of the Mongols is told by Demetrie Cantemir, *The History of the Growth and Decay of the Othman Empire*, trans. N. Tindal (London, 1734–35), 105.

13. Runciman, *Great Church*, 186–91; Manouel Ioannes Gedeon, *Patriarchikoi pinakes: Eideseis istorikai biographikai peri ton patriarchon Konstantinoupoleos apo Andreou tou Protokletou mechris Ioakeim G' tou apo Thess[a]lonikes, 36–1884* (Constantinople, 1890), 530.

14. Stephan Gerlach, *Stephan Gerlachs dess aeltern Tage-buch* (Frankfurt, 1674), 88. Gerlach was the Lutheran chaplain to the Holy Roman Empire's ambassador at Constantinople and had many friends among the Orthodox ecclesiastics.

15. Runciman, *Great Church*, 208–25.

16. For the Greek colony in Venice and its educational facilities, see Deno J. Geanakoplos, *Greek Scholars in Venice* (Cambridge: Harvard Univ. Press, 1962), esp. chaps. 4–6. For the College of St. Athanasius at Rome, see Martin Jugie, *Theologia dogmatica Christianorum Orientalium ab Ecclesia Catholica dissidentium*, 5 vols. (Paris: Letouzey et Ane, 1926–35), 1:522–24. For the academies in the principalities, see below, n. 27.

17. Papadopoullos, 48–50, 86–89; Iorga, 72–77.

18. *Historia Politica et Patriarchica*, 39–44, 102–15.

19. For a full discussion of the patriarchal finances see *Dictionnaire de théologie catholique*, s.v. "Constantinople (Eglise de)"; Runciman, *Great Church*, 200–202, with references.

20. "Constantinople (Eglise de)," listing the patriarchal reigns; Runciman, *Great Church*, 200–202.

21. Papadopoullos, 132, 160. The figure for the patriarchal debt in 1821 is given in Maxime Raybaud, *Memoires sur la Grèce, pour servir à l'histoire de la guerre de l'indépendance, accompagnés de plans topographiques* (Paris, 1824), historical introduction by A. Rabbé, 80.

22. Runciman, *Great Church*, 195–96, 322–32.

23. For Shaitanoglu, see Iorga, 114–21. The ambassador Gerlach knew him well and believed him to be the illegitimate son of an English ambassador (Gerlach, 55, 60, 223–25). M. Crusius, *Turcograeciae, libri octo* (Basle, 1584), 509, tells of the sale of his books, his informant being Gerlach.

24. Runciman, *Great Church*, 363–66.

25. Ibid., 364, with references.

26. There is no satisfactory life of the Exaporite. The fullest is to be found in Alexandre A. C. Stourdza, *L'Europe orientale et le rôle historique des Maurocordato, 1660–1830; avec un appendice contenant des actes et documents historiques et diplomatiques inédits* (Paris: Plon-Nourrit, 1913), 25–91, based on a vast number of documents, published and unpublished, but somewhat carelessly compiled. See Runciman, *Great Church*, 366–69, with other references.

27. Runciman, *Great Church*, 371–76.

28. Ibid., 392–93.

29. The most vivid account of the patriarchate on the outbreak of the Greek War of Independence is given by the English chaplain Robert Walsh, *Residence at Constantinople during a Period Including the Commencement, Progress, and Termination of the Greek and Turkish Revolutions*, 2 vols. (London, 1836), 1:299–333. He witnessed the hanging of the patriarch.

THE BYZANTINE LEGACY IN THE FORMAL CULTURE OF THE BALKAN PEOPLES

Speros Vryonis, Jr.

THE SUBJECT OF our symposium, "The Byzantine Tradition after the Fall of Constantinople," is as vast as it is important. Both the title and the subject recall another such conference, held at Dumbarton Oaks in the spring of 1968, entitled, "After the Fall of Constantinople."[1] But the years that have elapsed between the two conferences have brought a virtual revolution in our understanding and conceptualization of the period itself and of its importance. There is now much more concern with the history of the ongoing rhythms of Byzantine civilization, and a realization that the political and military events that led to the demise of the Byzantine Empire did not terminate Byzantine civilization in eastern and southeastern Europe. Indeed the older and narrower academic divisions of the disciplines, which attached decisive importance to political and military history, have collapsed before a broader understanding of human historical experience.

Although most Byzantinists today are still encapsulated in their chronological cocoons, they are slowly, often vaguely, becoming aware that Byzantium did not die on the fateful morning of May 29, 1453, and that its civilization remained a potent force in the lives, mentalities, and cultural creations of Greeks, Bulgars, Serbs, Rumanians, Albanians, and others. But a difficulty is presented by the matter of languages. All those who wish to chart or study the *Nachleben* of Byzantium in this later period must master not only the classical languages, but also a bewildering array of Balkan languages: modern Greek, Rumanian, Serbo-Croatian, Bulgarian, and eventually even Albanian; and in addition they must turn to the oriental languages: Turkish, Arabic, and, it is hoped, Persian.[2] All of these languages are rich in primary source materials, but in addition, no one can successfully pursue Byzantine or post-Byzantine studies without reading the voluminous modern scholarship in them. One begins Byzantine studies by becoming a classicist and then becomes, successively, a Slavist, Orientalist, and Neo-Hellenist.

Whereas the interest in things post-Byzantine is new to Byzantine studies in the Western hemisphere, the Balkan peoples have a long and well-developed interest in this period in their respective national histories. The postwar era has seen not only extensive and detailed monographic scholarship on the history and culture of the various inhabitants of the Balkans, but also several excellent multivolume series on the national histories, in which great attention is given to the Ottoman period and to the survival of the Byzantine tradition. The sixteen-volume Ἱστορία τοῦ ἑλληνικοῦ ἔθνους, which came out in the 1970s, dedicates two volumes (10 and 11) to what the Greeks call the *Tourkokratia*. These volumes display a very high level of scholarly sophistication and represent, in most cases, the sum total of the most recent scholarly conclusions in the realms of politics, institutions, religion, the economy, society, the arts, education, literature, and popular culture. On a similarly high level is the fourth volume of the *Istoriia na Bulgariia*, a series currently appearing under the auspices of the Bulgarian Academy of Sciences. In the two-volume *Istorija Naroda Jugoslavije*, a combined effort on the part of Yugoslav scholars and their respective academies, most of the second volume summarizes the latest researches on the history of the Yugoslav peoples under Ottoman rule. Impressive also are the volumes in the *Istoria Romeniie*, which the Rumanian Academy of Sciences published after World War II. In short, no scholar can avoid consulting these massive research tools when dealing with the subject of the Byzantine legacy after the fall of Constantinople.

My own interest in this subject was stimulated by three factors. First, I could not derive from my university textbooks or teachers any satisfactory explanation of what happened to the millennial, vigorous cultural tradition of Byzantium after the establishment of the Ottoman Empire. Second, I was aware, simply from speaking modern Greek, that such fundamental words as *kaiki* (boat), *çiş* (urine), and *habaria* (news) were Turkish and not Greek; yet all three words would have been essential to the lives and societies of the ancient and Byzantine Greeks. What then was the relation of Ottoman culture to the cultures of the conquered peoples? Finally there was my interest in, and wonderment at, learning new, so-called exotic, languages. Having begun in classical history and literature, I had moved through the curriculum of Byzantine studies and then realized that in order to come to grips with these fundamental questions I had to become familiar with Balkan and oriental languages, and that only then could I begin to probe the nature of Byzantine culture and the extent of its survival after 1453.

I have turned to this last question in three articles over the past twenty years, in which I have tried to work out for myself the answers to questions related to the degree of survival and the form of the Byzantine legacy during the Tourkokratia. In the first essay I attempted to discern the boundaries between Byzantine and Ottoman cultural institutions.[3] Therein I concluded that the inextricable union of religion and the state in the Middle Ages, and indeed in early modern times for the geographical area in question, determined that the formal aspect of Turkish society would be Muslim: sultanate, bureaucracy, "church," literature, and a great deal of the art. Conversely the *basileia* and Orthodoxy had determined the formal institutions of Byzantine society, and so the influence of Byzantine formal culture could only follow the large-scale adoption of the Byzantine style of theocracy, as occurred in Serbia and Bulgaria, and to a lesser degree in Russia and Rumania. At a second level, however, it was obvious that Ottoman folk culture was profoundly influenced, and in some cases was even determined, by that of Byzantium. At the same time, Ottoman institutions reduced much of Byzantine culture to the level of popular culture. I concluded this first study as follows: "The effect of Turkish forms on the Byzantine legacy was decapitation on the formal level and isolation on the folk level."

A few years later I attempted to analyze the historico-cultural experience of one Balkan people, the Greeks, under Turkish rule.[4] I concluded that the Tourkokratia constituted one of the major periods of Greek historical experience and that Turkish rule brought eight far-reaching developments in the culture and society of the Greeks: political disenfranchisement, the simplification of class structure, economic impoverishment, ethnic dilution, religious retreat, legal disenfranchisement, the popularization or deformalization of culture, and cultural isolation.

Most recently, in the conference "The Byzantine Legacy in Eastern Europe, 1500 to the Twentieth Century," in which a panel of speakers dealt with the *Nachleben* of Byzantium in formal rather than in popular culture, I returned to the general subject with a communique entitled "The Byzantine Legacy in Folk Life and Tradition in the Balkans."[5] In this third incursion into later Byzantine culture I returned to an analytical categorization that I had always found useful in examining Greek historical experience—namely, the separation of the popular and formal elements in culture. This distinction has proved extremely convenient in my efforts to understand the processes that affect continuity and change in Greek culture throughout its four millennia of identified existence.

In this third essay I began by pointing to the different approaches of two great scholars, Nicolae Iorga and Phaidon Koukoules. The former, in attempting to trace the survival of Byzantine culture after 1453, found it in a relatively small number of ghost institutions. Koukoules, on the other hand, traced the rhythms of cultural survival in popular institutions and accordingly found it necessary to write eight volumes, whereas Iorga found that he could cover his own subject in one thin volume. I posited as a heuristic device the existence of horizontal layers of popular culture among the various Balkan peoples, together with a vertical structure of historical events and processes placed one layer atop another. Further, given the fact that folklore studies, or I should say studies of the popular culture, of the Balkan peoples are well developed in the Balkans, I employed a comparative approach by examining Greeks, Bulgars, Serbs, and Turks. Six topics were studied: Byzantine Constantinople and Turkish Istanbul; religion, or man's relation to others and to the unknown; the agrarian and pastoral cycles and calendars; the *panegyris*, or festival; and the popular legend of Alexander the Great. This comparison revealed a profound continuity of the Byzantine legacy in the popular culture of the Balkans and underlined the fact that despite great linguistic and ethnic variety, this popular culture had a pronouncedly Byzantine spinal cord.

In the present essay I wish to turn to the second facet of the general problem of the fate of the Byzantine legacy, that of the formal culture of the Balkan peoples under Ottoman rule. This is a far more complex phenomenon than the Byzantine legacy in the popular culture of the Balkans. First, the nature of the Ottoman conquest was such that it largely, but not completely, destroyed the Balkan dynasties and aristocracies, the very patrons of Byzantine formal culture. Second, the primary beneficiaries of the new political order were the Muslims and their society, so that it was their formal cultural institutions that now gained from the wealth of the land. One need look only at the splendid network of mosques, medresses, hospitals, imarets, libraries, and palaces with which the Ottoman ruling class adorned the Balkan peninsula.[6] Third, the urban centers were, to varying degrees, converted to Islamic rhythms of social and cultural life.[7] Thus the Byzantine legacy in the formal culture of the Balkan peoples was truncated, and often led a strange half-life. Finally, we are dealing with a large area, one that displayed a certain regional variety, and with a period that endured for over four hundred years, with the life and culture of the Christians undergoing a fundamental change in the eighteenth and nineteenth centuries. Because my subject is vast I shall restrict myself to a few topics: law, the religious calendar, religious painting, Mount Athos, and literature.

Law

Byzantium, as the conscious heir of Rome and unconscious heir of the Hellenistic kingdoms and ancient Greece, had a very elaborate legal system, which was divided on the one hand between secular law and canon law, and on the other between formal legal codes and acknowledged customary law. The diffusion of Byzantine legal codes, customary law, and practices, particularly to the Syriac Christians and medieval Bulgars, Serbs, and Rumanians, has long been the subject of investigation. The closer the medieval Balkan states drew to Byzantine civilization, the more did their legal structures reflect the influences of Byzantine law. The shock of the political decapitation of these medieval states at the hands of the Ottoman conquerors undoubtedly relaxed the hold of the Byzantine legal system.

I should like to begin by underlining the importance of the land and the sea in Byzantine legal codes and customary law. The economic exploitation of the land and sea lay at the basis of Byzantine economic life and accordingly the emperors were constantly exercised to regulate it, in works as early as the *Digest* and the *Novels* of Justinian,[8] and then through their various reworkings, until the abridgments of Armenopoulos and Vlastares.[9] Perhaps the two most spectacular bodies of law that deal with the regulations on land and sea are the agrarian laws of the Macedonians and the Rhodian Sea Law.[10] I shall examine certain provisions from each and try to trace their history during the Ottoman period. This will give us the opportunity to look at the question of legal survivals in very important areas.

Protimesis and *Protime*

In the extraordinary corpus of Macedonian agrarian legislation dedicated to blocking the land expansion of the magnates, the tenth-century emperors attempted to protect the fiscal, social, and territorial integrity of the free peasant village by restricting land purchases and exchanges among peasants, relatives, and neighbors. Utilizing a much older principle known as *protimesis* (προτίμησις), or preemption, this body of legislation, as is well known, established an elaborate, calibrated hierarchy of peasants who had preemptive rights in the purchase of peasant lands and farms. The peasants' right to exercise this preemptive purchase, granted first to relatives and then to neighbors, was known in the Byzantine texts as *protimesis*.[11]

By the eleventh century the efforts of the central government to halt the inroads of the wealthy into peasant lands through the application of *protimesis* had largely failed. But the later Byzantine legal compendia retain a clear understanding of the nature of *protimesis* and either quote or give the contents of some of this Macedonian legislation, especially the law of Romanus I, and occasionally that of Constantine VII. Such are the decisions of Demetrios Chomatianos, the *Procheiron Auctum* (ca. 1300), and the *Hexabiblos* of Armenopoulos (1345). Although these texts indicate a clear knowledge of the fact that the Macedonians had promulgated these laws to halt the depredations of the aristocracy at the expense of the peasantry, the laws were no longer applied with this socio-political aim in mind. That some aspects of *protimesis* were still being applied in late Byzantium emerges from two documents of sale dated 1375 and 1392, where an individual exercises a protimetic right to buy property on the basis of being a neighbor.[12]

We know that the texts and vernacular Greek paraphrases of Armenopoulos and Vlastares circulated in Greek lands under Ottoman rule. Indeed the *Nomokriterion* of the seventeenth century, composed in vernacular Greek, covers the subject of *protimesis* in chapters 53 and 55, and refers to the *Novels* of Romanus I and Manuel I (?) on the subject.[13] What does this all mean? Was *protimesis* still a living legal principle regulating the sale of land in the Ottoman Empire?

The answer to this question is to be ascertained by analyzing two bodies of documents, the so-called insular constitutions and the notarial records. Recently I analyzed and translated a large number of these constitutions, which describe the law and custom that were proclaimed by the local governments of Mykonos (1647), Syros (1695, 1700, 1812), Poros (1829), Santorini (1797), and Pholegandros (1808) under Ottoman rule and which refer to a legal institution and practice known as *protime* (προτιμή).[14] These constitutions vary in length on this matter, and often differ on specifics; but they agree in proclaiming one unifying principle in the sale of property. This is the principle that whatever the cause for the sale (except in the case of monastic property), an entire category of preferred persons has prior rights to purchase. These documents vary in their definitions of the "preferred" persons. The *Tarifa* of Mykonos of 1647 simply differentiates between relatives and strangers.[15] In 1695 the constitution of Syros refers to persons who have protimetic rights in the purchase of property but does not describe them, whereas in 1812 it identifies them as "close relatives."[16] The authorities of Poros refer to them as consisting of, in descending order, brothers, relatives, neighbors, and finally any citizen, whether local or not. Santorini and Pholegandros provide the most specific definition of preferred purchasers, identifying them as the first relatives, from the most immediate down through the first cousins and their children (second cousins and their children are not included), and then neighbors.[17]

The rights of the preferred purchasers differ from island to island, often in regard to the statute of limitations within which the right of preemption had to be exercised. In the case of property sold at public auction, the constitutions of Syros (1695, 1812) provide that the preferred residents on the island itself have a period of ten days in which to exercise their option to purchase, whereas in Santorini (1797) they have but three days.[18] The island of Poros provides a general, nonspecified period of six months for the preferred to appear and make their claims.[19] In cases of sale other than by public auction Santorini provides a fifteen-year period for those who are abroad to return and to claim their rights.[20] On Pholegandros the period is only five years.[21]

Extremely important was the seizure of property for debt and its sale at public auction to pay the debt. This is particularly important in the case of a citizen's failure or inability to pay the sultanic tax of the *haradj*, as well as other taxes. In such cases the rule of preemptive purchase was always upheld and enforced (Mykonos, Syros).[22]

The constitution of Santorini underlines a most important principle that lies at the basis of land sale and of land confiscation by the authorities. This states that the ownership of the land is inviolably yoked to the payment of the *haradj* and other imperial taxes to the sultan. So long as an islander remained domiciled abroad, the authorities of Santorini removed him and his immediate family from the category of the "preferred" purchasers.[23]

These references to *protime* in the constitutions of the Cyclades are a striking proof of the continuity of the Byzantine legal practice and concept of *protimesis* in the legal codes and custom of these small islands. Particularly notable is the occasional application of *protime* when the insular authorities confiscate the property of delinquent taxpayers and then sell these lands, along with their tax obligations, to the preferred category of preemptive purchasers, either at public auction or otherwise. This recalls the oldest Byzantine practices and legal forms, which associated land ownership with taxes and with preemptive purchase.

Remarkable as they are, our samples are from a restricted group of small islands. Do these constitutional provisions represent a freak, isolated survival, or are they part of a general pattern? And were they actually implemented?

Here one must turn to the notarial archives. Petropoulos has edited several thousand of these documents from Mykonos, Siphnos, and elsewhere. I have chosen one of them, at random, which deals with the institution of *protime:* it is dated September 14, 1666, and is from Mykonos.

> "In praise of Christ, Amen, September 14, 1666. Today Kera
> Kourtesa appeared in the office of the chancellery and says that her
> first husband, the late Georges as he was called, had a piece of land
> bought from Nikolos Delatolas for 24 reals, as appears in the doc-
> ument of this same first purchase recorded in 1649. Today the son
> of Ioannes Papagiakoumos came from Chios [and asserted] that
> the above property was dowry of his aunt by the name of An-
> nousa, daughter of the late George Papagiakoumos. Since this son
> was absent at the time that the above property, which is located in
> the land called Demetrakes, was sold, coming today he "contra-
> dicted" [the sale] as [being] the closest relative and the nephew of
> the above Annousa. And he took the property by giving the above
> payment of the 24 kurush. In this [matter] the above Kera Kour-
> tesa is taken [i.e., bought out] and she acknowledges that she re-
> ceived the payment of 24 kurush and that the property belongs to
> the above Giannoules in the future. For confirmation of the truth
> the summoned witnesses sign—George Santorineos witness. An-
> tones Tzeretanos witness. Papagerasimos Vidos chancellor of Myk-
> onos."[24]

The young man Giannoules was able to invalidate the sale of his aunt's property some seventeen years later on the grounds of preemptive rights—*protime*. The practice of *protime* in the Tourkokratia was thus directly modeled on and descended from Byzantine legal practice. We see it in documents from not only Mykonos but also such islands as Patmos,

Syros, Hydra, Naxos, Melos, and Nisyros. Further it has been recorded in the Peloponnesian towns of Gargalianoi, Kyparissia, and Philiatra. Kampouroglou noted it in Ottoman Athens as well.[25] But all of these citations come from territories under Ottoman control, and there are enough cases of its invocation in tax-related matters to suggest that *protime* may have been preserved or reinstituted by the Ottoman authorities to safeguard their fiscal interests.

That this was not the case, however, emerges from an examination of the partially published notarial documents from Cephallenia and Paxoi, islands in the Ionian Sea that escaped Ottoman rule and were governed for centuries by the Venetians. Here too the principle of *protime* in the purchase of property appears to be the established legal practice.[26] We may conclude that the *protime* mentioned so copiously in the insular constitutions and in the notarial documents of regions under both Ottoman and Venetian rule constituted a Panhellenic legal phenomenon that enjoyed an uninterrupted life from the earliest Byzantine times until its formal abrogation by the modern Greek kingdom in the mid-nineteenth century.

I have not yet inquired further into the diffusion of this Byzantine legal concept and practice outside the Byzantine homelands. It was, however, introduced into the legal systems and agrarian practices of the Danubian principalities in the seventeenth century as the result of the influx of Greek influences.[27] The lack of complete uniformity in the actual exercise of the preemptive rights of purchase in the Greek-speaking lands that we have examined must originate in the destruction of the centralized Greek political authority, which gave ample opportunity for the development of local variations.

Maritime Law of Byzantium and of the Tourkokratia

Just as the disposition of the land remained crucial to the everyday life of the Balkan Christians under Ottoman rule, so the regulation of sea exploitation remained particularly important for the Greeks, who continued to be the Balkan seafarers par excellence during the Tourkokratia. As in the case of *protime*, the matter of maritime law is richly illustrated by the insular constitutions and the notarial archives, and it is to these that I once more turn to make sondages regarding the possible survival of Byzantine legal forms. The Justinianic *Digest*, the *Basilica*, the later legal handbooks, but above all the Rhodian Sea Law provide considerable material for establishing the legal base of maritime regulations in the period before

1453; and these documents, when taken together with the insular constitutions and notarial archives, make it possible to discern the patterns of survival of Byzantine maritime regulations in the Ottoman period. Having completed a lengthy discussion of this matter in a recent work, I shall refer only to its conclusions here.[28]

In the later Greek customary law dealing with the sea we observe the following:

(1) Most remarkably, the captain and the crew share in both the profits and loss of a commercial voyage.[29]

(2) When only the capital and interest are attained at the completion of a voyage, the crew is entitled to a portion of the interest.[30]

(3) When the capital is either lost or diminished the creditors lose their interest, and the captain and ship (crew?) must contribute to the full restoration of the capital.[31]

(4) Maritime loans differ from land loans in that they are not fully and completely secure. They are valid maritime loans when they finance a maritime commercial venture and there is a maritime risk involved, that is, "rizigo maritimo." Thus it is possible for the lender/venturer to suffer damage to his investment while being entitled to a higher rate of interest (usually, but not always, 20%) if the voyage is successful.[32]

(5) For the maritime loan to be fully collectible there must be a safe journey and return of the ship, a fact stated explicitly in the notarial records but also implied in the insular constitutions.[33]

(6) Commercial journeys that are disrupted or in which the ship is damaged or destroyed by storms or by piratical or foreign ships do not fit into the above category (no. 5), and so the responsibility of the captain and crew is either negated or diminished.[34]

(7) Aside from their share as participants, members of the crew can also invest capital (βλυσίδια) in a commercial voyage.[35]

(8) If a ship is wrecked and its goods are scattered, both ship and goods remain the property of the original owner(s). This interesting fact, not mentioned in the surviving insular constitutions, appears in the notarial notices, again illustrating the inadequate and incomprehensive nature of those written constitutions.[36]

(9) Notarial documents indicate that the jettisoning of cargo during storms, necessary for saving the crew and ship, mitigates the responsibility of captain and crew for the attendant loss.[37]

These nine provisions in later Greek maritime custom and law are in effect also found in the Rhodian Sea Law and in other Byzantine legal documents. In the Rhodian Sea Law the captain and crew share in the profit, just as they do in post-Byzantine maritime custom: "A master's pay two shares; a steersman's one share and a half; a master's mate's share one share and a half; a carpenter's one share and a half; a boatswain's one share and a half; a sailor's one share; a cook's half a share."[38] As for the loss, the constitution of Hydra (1793) ordains, "Where there is a loss, each member of the crew and [each] companion shall pay in proportion to that which he takes, again because it coincides with their share. Similarly they shall contribute toward the loss a sum commensurate with their share."[39] The Rhodian Sea Law has a similar provision: "If there is an agreement for sharing in gain, after everything on board ship and the ship itself have been brought into contribution, let every man be liable for the loss which has occurred in proportion to his share of gain."[40]

The Rhodian Sea Law distinguishes markedly, as does the later Greek customary law of the sea, between maritime and other types of loan: "The law ordains: let them not write moneys lent at sea to be repaid out of property on land without risk. If they do write them, let them be invalid under the Rhodian Law."[41] This difference is reiterated: "Captains and merchants, those among them who borrow money on the security of ship and freight and cargo, are not to borrow it as if it were a land loan . . . let them pay back the loan from the property on land with maritime interest."[42]

Full repayment of the maritime loan depends on a successful termination of the sale of goods and safe return to the home port, and this is so in both the Rhodian Sea Law and the later customary law.[43] Damage or destruction to vessel or cargo that is not the fault of the captain and crew either negates or diminishes their fiscal responsibility.[44]

The reference to capital investment ($\beta\lambda\upsilon\sigma\acute{\iota}\delta\iota\alpha$) by sailors in post-Byzantine maritime custom[45] seems to be referred to in the Byzantine legal code of the *Basilica*: "The captain is not responsible for the commercial exchanges of the sailors."[46] This provision is repeated in the *Hexabiblos* of Armenopoulos.[47]

As in later customary law of the sea wherein wrecked ships and goods remain the property of their original owners, so in Byzantine times they remain in the possession of their original holders. "Goods taken from a shipwreck or from jettison cannot become [someone else's] property by the passage of time. For they are not unowned."[48] The *Basilica* condemns those who take such goods: "He who takes away the jettisoned goods from the ships is guilty of theft."[49]

This brief comparison of provisions in Byzantine and post-Byzantine maritime law and custom proves, beyond any doubt, a very strong continuity in the regulation of the sea. Although there is undoubtedly some immixture from Italiote practices, as one sees from the *termini technici*, much of the legal structure of maritime regulation is of Byzantine origin. Particularly striking is the fact that captain and crew share in the profit and loss, a condition that did not exist in Venetian maritime ventures.

This concludes the investigation of the continuity in agrarian and maritime law from Byzantine into Ottoman times. The fact that such Byzantine concepts as the *protimesis/protime* and that of the sharing of the profits and losses by captain and crew not only survived but remained Panhellenic phenomena during the Tourkokratia indicates how indebted to Byzantine law were the later ages. The law of *protime* was not abolished until 1856, and the local Greek maritime codes remained vital until they were replaced by the French codes in the later eighteenth and nineteenth centuries. This corroborates an observation holding true for almost every aspect of the cultural domain—namely, that many Byzantine institutions and practices survived the Ottoman period only to succumb to Western influences.

The Seasonal and Religious Calendar

More recently I have examined the seasonal and religious calendar of the Serbs, Bulgars, and Greeks as a device contributing to the perpetuation of their popular culture and incorporating many elements from the pre-Christian popular religious culture of the Balkans.[50] By way of example it was shown how the celebrations of the feast days of the Prophet Elijah (July 20), St. George (April 23–24), and St. Tryphon (February 1) were something more than the commemoration of these saints. The celebration of the Prophet Elijah, which usually took place on mountaintops or other high locales, was associated with divination, with the sacrifice of a rooster, and with thunder, one of the attributes of Zeus.[51] The feasts of St. George and St. Tryphon coincided with important events in the pastoral and agricultural cycle. In the case of the former a young lamb was sacrificed, and the pastoral celebrants partook of a communal meal and conducted magical practices associated with the assurance of healthy flocks.[52] On the feast of St. Tryphon the peasants went to the fields to prune the vines, drink wine, and eat kollyva (κόλλυβα: boiled wheat).[53] These and other annual events indicate a considerable pagan underpinning in the life of the Orthodox Christians of the Balkans.

In the broader sense, however, the calendar is a complex and highly organized routine of seasonal life, formulated by the church. As such it was the ultimate programming of the life of the Balkan Christians, and since it was sanctioned by church and state it became the official axis of social life. This finished seasonal and religious timetable was the creation of Byzantium. It survived the Ottoman conquest and rule virtually unchanged, ensuring the continued cultural homogeneity of the Orthodox Christians and providing them with another strong tie to Byzantine (and indirectly to pagan) culture. Among the feasts that it marked, in addition to those already mentioned, were Christmas and the Duodecameron; thereafter the viticultural feast of St. Tryphon, the great carnival inaugurating the Lenten season and thus combining pagan seasonal and Christian celebrations; Easter, the Sunday of the Rosalia; the leaping over fires on June 24 (day of St. John the Baptist); the Feast of the Dormition on August 15; and All Saints on November 1, when meals for the returning souls were placed on the tombs of the departed. This seasonal calendar gave the Balkan Orthodox Christians one of the most striking institutions of cultural homogeneity and continuity. A calendrical system is much like a standard of measurement: it is primary in the cultural orientation of any society. In a sense a culture is its calendar, and vice-versa.[54] The calendar of the Orthodox Church may be reckoned among the most important manifestations of Byzantine formal culture, and it endured long after the Byzantine state had disappeared and the church had been reduced to inferior and impoverished status.

Traditions of Byzantine Painting and the *Ermeneia tes zographikes technes* of Dionysios of Fourna

The formal tradition of Byzantine painting in the Ottoman period has increasingly drawn the attention of art historians. One may refer to the late Andreas Xyngopoulos and to Manolis Chatzidakis, whose writings have established the broad lines of artistic development between the fall of Constantinople and the final victory of Western painting in the nineteenth century.[55] The tradition's variations in Serbia, Bulgaria, and Rumania have also attracted more study. Authorities have traced the life of the Cretan school, which, beginning as one of the two major currents in late Byzantine painting, culminated in the works of Theophanes the Cretan and certain of his compatriots. In the fifteenth, sixteenth, and seventeenth centuries Crete saw the rise of a Greco-Venetian aristocracy and middle class, which patronized this art and so contributed to its flourishing. The

Byzantine traditions continued to be pursued even as Italian styles and taste began to intrude into both style and iconography. The final conquest of Crete in 1669 destroyed the socioeconomic basis and patronage of this art; the Cretan school declined, and many Cretans sought refuge and work in the Ionian Islands, which remained Venetian possessions until the destruction of the Venetian Republic at the end of the eighteenth century. The Cretan tradition, with its refined style and rich colors, was preserved until a comparatively late period in the Ionian churches. But it remained largely a regional phenomenon, as the Ionian Islands had neither the wealth nor the social prominence to project it beyond their own narrow confines.

In the eighteenth century, however, the economic conditions of the Greek mainland and islands improved considerably, bringing a revival in the building of provincial churches and an attendant increase in the need for painters to decorate them. Chatzidakis has pointed out that we know of more than 750 Greek painters active in the eighteenth century, two and one-half times the number known for the previous century, and that the numbers for the second half of the eighteenth century are four times greater than those for the first half.[56] This sudden rise in the number of painters, most of whom were of rural origin, meant a certain decline in the quality of the art. Further, noticeably more details from contemporary everyday life are evident in the paintings.

The early eighteenth century is witness to two distinct tendencies within this upsurge of painting, tendencies represented in the writings of two contemporary painters. The first is the Ἑρμηνεία τῆς ζωγραφικῆς τέχνης, written between 1728 and 1733 by the monk and painter Dionysios "ὁ ἐκ Φουρνᾶ," on Mount Athos, and the second is the work Περὶ ζωγραφίας, by Panayiotes Doxaras, written on the Ionian Islands in 1726. The history of these two works is the history of a bifurcation in Greek culture in Turkish times. The Greeks were torn between the old, authorized Byzantine culture and the new, revolutionary cultures of the Italian Renaissance, Baroque, and Enlightenment. Dionysios urged a return to the pure Byzantine forms and subjects of Manuel Panselinos, while Doxaras instructed his readers on how to paint in the manner of Veronese. To add insult to injury, Doxaras also translated into Greek Leonardo da Vinci's treatise on painting.

Of concern to us here is the decision of Dionysios to codify painting as it had been practiced by the Byzantines. What is noteworthy is the intentional archaism of his views: whoever wishes to paint should return (claims Dionysios) to the norms of the fourteenth-century painter Panselinos. Even if the manner of painting he attributed to Panselinos was not still practiced, the Byzantine artistic legacy was everywhere to be seen, and Dionysios found his models in churches, in which were preserved a variety of styles and subjects. Further, the very practice of utilizing painters' handbooks was a tradition known to Dionysios from the earlier manuscripts that he used in composing his own. Thus after the eclipse of the Cretan school in the seventeenth century, just when much Orthodox art was being subjected to popularization or Westernization, we see in the writings of this monk an insistence on a return to the traditions of Byzantine painting.

Dionysios's manual is of great interest to the art historian, inasmuch as it instructs the student on the preparation of paints, gypsum, wood, plaster, and other materials, as well as on the iconography of individual scenes, their arrangement in the various types of churches, the proportions of the body, and other matters. But this is a domain which, though of interest to me, I must leave to art historians to analyze. Here I propose, first, to examine the text for indications of Byzantine inspiration, and then to describe briefly the dispersal of the text throughout the Balkans.

From the first invocation to the Virgin Mary to the last section, which gives the epigrams proper to certain iconographic subjects, Dionysios's *Ermeneia* is committed to maintaining the tradition of Byzantine painting, which he treats as a sacred art.[57] The *Ermeneia* begins with three prologues and is then organized as follows. Part One deals with such technical matters as how to copy paintings and how to prepare the materials used in painting. In Part Two Dionysios describes how to illustrate over one hundred events in the Old Testament, and in Part Three he describes the Gospel illustrations. Part Four is devoted to depictions of the parables, the Divine Liturgy, the psalms, and the Apocalypse; Part Five to the festivals of the Virgin, the apostles, saints, ecumenical councils, and martyrs; and the sixth and final part to miscellanea.

The *Ermeneia* is thus intended to be a comprehensive guidebook. But the author acknowledges that he has had access to older manuals, and Papadopoulos-Kerameus has identified and published five of these. None seems to go back further than the sixteenth century.[58] Dionysios states not only that he relied on older guides, but that he went about to various churches, studying the paintings of Panselinos himself. Undoubtedly he also incorporated oral tradition, as well as knowledge gained from his personal experience in working with or under various painters.

Thus Dionysios's *Ermeneia* is very strongly retrospective. In his second prologue Dionysios cites Panselinos but also the Cretan painters, thereby placing himself consciously in the mainstream of late Byzantine and post-Byzantine art. Indeed the first of the earlier manuals, which Papadopoulos-Kerameus has identified as one of Dionysios's primary sources, is entitled *Ermeneia of the Painter's Art, Containing the Proportions and Colors of Panselinos and of "Naturale," and the Flesh Tones of Theophanes, and Certain Other Matters Useful for This Art.*[59] Clearly Dionysios chose to go back to the traditions of Byzantium at a time (ca. 1730) when the Cretan school had collapsed and painting had been diverted from its source.

This Byzantine inspiration and spirit are reflected in two of the prologues he composed for his work. In the first, addressed to painters' apprentices, he resorts to Scripture to justify his book and to stress the sacred nature of the art:

> Heeding, O apprentices of the toil-loving painters, who are eager for learning, the Lord in the holy Gospel, wherein he condemned the one who hid the talent and said to him, "O evil and idle slave, you should have entrusted my silver to the bankers, so that on my return I would have received it with interest," I feared lest I too be condemned as lazy. Thus I was stirred to increase this small talent that was entrusted to me by the Lord, that is, this my meager art, which I learned with great effort and time, from childhood, by imitating, to the degree that I could, Kyr Manuel Panselinos of Thessaloniki, who shone like the moon, and the holy icons and beautiful churches which he painted on the holy-named mountain of Athos. And he who once shone in this art of painting like the golden, shining and moving moon, surpassed and eclipsed with his wondrous art all the ancient and modern painters, as his paintings on icons and walls most clearly demonstrate. And anyone who in any way participates in [the art of] painting will comprehend this clearly when he sees and studies these [paintings] carefully.
>
> And it is his art—which, as I said, I learned with great labor from childhood—which I desired, with all my will, to increase on behalf of you my fellow artists, interpreting this [art] in the present book, recording all his measures and forms, flesh tones and colors, with all accuracy.[60]

His justification for writing the book is thus scriptural. The third and last prologue, entitled, "Preliminary Training and Instruction for Him Who Wishes to Learn the Painter's Art," is thoroughly Byzantine in character. He first sets out the stages through which the apprentice must progress, almost as if he were describing the procedures of a Byzantine guild:

> Let him who wishes to learn the painter's art be introduced first to the fundamentals, and let him carry out exercises of a simple nature, without drawing proportions, so that he may show himself prepared. And then let there be carried out on his behalf the prayer to Jesus Christ and the petition before the icon of the Theotokos Hodegetria. Giving the blessing, the priest, after [having recited the prayers] the "Heavenly King," and so on, the megalynarion [short hymn] of the Theotokos, "The lips are speechless," and the troparion of the Metamorphosis, and having signed his [the apprentice's] forehead with the cross, should say aloud, "Let us beseech the Lord." The prayer:
>
> "O Lord Jesus Christ our God, who is uncircumscribed by nature of his divinity and who, for the ultimate salvation of man, was incomprehensibly made flesh through the Virgin Mary Theotokos and deigned to be circumscribed; You who impressed the holy features of your immaculate face on the holy towel, with which you healed the illness of the toparch Abgar and enlightened his soul in the knowledge of you our true God; You who through your Holy Spirit brought understanding to your divine apostle and evangelist Luke, [enabling him] to draw the form of your blameless mother holding you as an infant. . . . Do you, Lord God of all, enlighten and bring understanding to the soul, the heart and the mind of your servant ——— and guide his hands so that he may draw without blame and superbly the form of your likeness and of your most immaculate mother and of all your saints; for your glory and for the brilliance and beautification of your holy Church and for the remission of the sins of those who accord them [the images] relative veneration and embrace them with piety and send up honor to the prototype. Save him [the apprentice] from every diabolical influence so that he will progress in all your commands by the intercessions of your most immaculate mother, of the holy and glorious apostle and evangelist Luke, and of all the saints, Amen."[61]

Only after the initial period of teaching and the religious ceremony is the apprentice to be taught proportions and forms. Dionysios exhorts the neophyte:

Know, therefore, O eager pupil, that when you desire to undertake this science [ἐπιστήμην] you must search to find some competent teacher, whom quickly you must evaluate to see whether he will teach you as I have indicated. But if you should happen upon someone who is ignorant and artless, do you then just as we did, and look to find some archetypes by the famous Manuel Pan- selinos, and labor over them, drawing in the manner that we shall explain to you further on, until you comprehend his proportions and forms. Next go to a church that he has painted so that you can make copies in the manner that we shall explain to you. Take care not to work simply and in any which way, but with the fear of God and with piety, for the labor is sacred. Take care when you have re- moved the copy, whether from the wall or icon, to wash well the original with a clean sponge, to clean all the black [which you have left], for if you do not clean it immediately and the black remains atop [the painting] and later can no longer be cleaned, you will thus fall into the crime of impiety and be condemned as a despiser of the icons, since, as the great [St.] Basil has said that the honor of the icon proceeds to the prototype, so also the reverse. I give this small advice and order to you, O friend, in godly love and true brotherly regard, in fear of the [last] judgment. For I also found in many places where the painters had raised copies, that, I know not whether from ignorance or from impiety and without fear of judg- ment, they did not clean the icons immediately but left them black- ened. And these I tried in every way to clean and to wash but was not able. If the icon from which you wish to take a copy happens to be ancient and the strokes are not clear, or the gypsum is feeble and you are afraid to wash it lest you destroy it, do as follows: First, wash it carefully, then repair it and coat it with varnish, then make the copy, and after that wash it again just as I have explained to you.[62]

Toward the end of this prologue Dionysios exhorts the reader to learn the art with great care and diligence, "for this labor is divine [θεῖον] and descended from God [θεοπαράδοτον]. And this is clear to all from many other signs, but particularly from the *acheiropoietos* [not-made-by-hand] and revered icon which He himself the God-man Jesus Christ, having wiped His all holy face, sent to the toparch of Edessa Abgar [as] the imprint of His divine image on the holy towel."[63]

Not only is the art of the painter divine, but it was praised by the Mother of Christ herself when "she prayed on behalf of and blessed the holy apostle and evangelist Luke for this art."[64] Further, that the art is blessed is evident "also from the countless miracles which the icons of Christ and the Mother of God and of the remaining saints have performed and still perform."[65] Because of this all those who labor piously and carefully receive God's grace and blessings. But all who labor impiously and carelessly, being greedy out of love of money, let them have a care and let them repent before the end, calling to mind . . . the punishment in the fire of hell."[66]

The author describes a system of teachers and apprentices, as well as a graduated, simple system of instruction involving a religious ceremony. All of this recalls the system of apprenticeship in the guild of the *taboullarioi* described in the tenth-century *Book of the Eparch*, where also the candidate, before his induction, goes to church for the appropriate ceremony. Dionysios cites a special relation between the painter and Christ, the Virgin, and St. Luke, thus giving religious sanction to the art and the system of training. Also imbued with religious significance, for Dionysios, is the copying of paintings. He says that any damage inflicted on an older icon during the making of a copy subjects the painter to the charge of criminal impiety. Here Dionysios employs a corollary of the idea, used by St. John of Damascus, that the reverence paid to an image passes through the image to the prototype. Dionysios knew well the christological basis of Byzantine painting as defined by the Seventh Ecumenical Council, and he invokes it by referring to Christ as "uncircumscribed by nature of his divinity and . . . incomprehensibly made flesh through the Virgin Mary Theotokos and . . . thus [he] deigned to be depicted, for the ultimate salvation of man."

With these remarks I complete my analysis of the Byzantine inspiration and character of the *Ermeneia*. It remains to discuss the diffusion of the text to the other Balkan peoples. The Rumanian scholar Vasile Grecu has studied the diffusion and translation of the text and has edited the translation into Rumanian by the cleric Macarie (which dates to 1805).[67] Bulgarian translations also began to appear in the nineteenth century, although in some cases the possibility of the mediation of a Russian translation has been raised.[68] As Dionysios's *Ermeneia* was intended to be a practical handbook, there was no canonization of the text, and therefore some Bulgarian *Ermenii* do not reproduce exactly the contents, details and order of the Greek text. It is interesting, however, that these manuals bear, in Bulgarian, the Greek title of *Ermenii*.

Athos

The text of Dionysios's *Ermeneia* and its emanation from eighteenth-century Mount Athos to the Orthodox peoples of the Balkans, Asia Minor and Russia, brings to our attention one of the most important sources of Byzantine influence on the formal culture of the Balkan peoples. This is, of course, Mount Athos, with its rich and living Byzantine traditions and its Greek, Serbian, Bulgarian, Rumanian, Russian, and Georgian monks and monasteries.

According to Joseph Georgirenes, archbishop of Samos (1666–71), there were approximately six thousand monks living on Athos in his day, including about eight hundred in the Serbian monastery of Chilandar and two hundred in the Bulgarian monastery of Zographou, revealing that in the late seventeenth century there was a considerable Slavic presence on the Holy Mountain.[69] The eleemosynary activities of Rumanian and Russian rulers further strengthened Athos as a central meeting ground and clearing house of Byzantine religious, literary, artistic, and other traditions for the entire Orthodox world during Ottoman times. Athos was both a living organism in the culture of what has been termed the Byzantine Commonwealth and a rich repository of its artistic and literary treasures. Icons, frescoes, and manuscripts figured actively in the ongoing Byzantine culture of this unique monastic community. In their liturgical and ascetical life the monks were surrounded and guided by manuscripts, books, and icons produced in the Byzantine tradition. These shaped and refined their consciousness of that tradition, as well as of its enemies, Islam and the Latin Church. Further, these literary and artistic treasures offered a rich variety of choices, which on occasion led the monks to revert to one or another text/ideal or artistic style and to revive cultural forms from the Byzantine past, as in the case of Dionysios and his *Ermeneia*. The influence of Mount Athos was such that it radiated, at times, far beyond the Athonite peninsula to Asia Minor and to Greek, Serbian, Bulgarian, Russian, and Rumanian lands. This radiation was facilitated not only by the strength of the Byzantine tradition on the Holy Mountain, but also by the pan-Orthodox and multinational character of its community, and by the fact that Byzantine formal culture had already put down roots in those lands.

Literature

One of the correspondents of Dionysios of Fourna was the Greek priest, teacher, and author Anastasios Gordios (1654/5–1729). Although born of a poor peasant family in a small mountain village in the district of Agrapha, he went early to the local monastic school and thereafter sought teachers successively at Karpenisi, Athens, and Yannina, returning to teach at the monastic school of St. Paraskevi, where he had had his first schooling. Ordained a priest, he went to Italy twice (1686–89, 1698–1701) to continue his schooling at Padua, Florence, and Rome, studying ancient Greek, Latin, medicine, and pharmacology, and coming into contact with Roman Catholic theology. On his return he dedicated himself to teaching (at schools in Karpenisi, Patras, Aetolikon, and finally from 1711 to 1729 at the monastic school of St. Paraskevi) and literary composition.[70] Of interest to us here are the personality of Gordios and his writing entitled, *Composition concerning Mohammed and against the Latins*, composed between 1717/18 and 1723, and therefore contemporary with the *Ermeneia* of his compatriot Dionysios (also from Agrapha). Just as Dionysios took Byzantine artistic traditions as his inspiration and guide, so Gordios derived his ideas, literary genre, and theological and historical principles from Byzantine antecedents.

Gordios meditated long and hard in the light of his personal experience and observation, as had his Byzantine predecessors, on the hardships of the Greeks, and indeed of the Orthodox peoples as a whole, under Muslim rule. Despite his education in the West and his work in translating classical Greek texts into demotic Greek, Gordios comprehended the enslavement of the Orthodox by the Muslims in religious, not secular, terms. Although earlier Byzantine etiological traditions on the subjugation of the Orthodox world by the forces of Islam (first Arab and then Turkish) presented two fundamentally different explanations, secular and religious, it was only the latter that absorbed this Greek priest of the Tourkokratia.[71]

To explain the military defeat and political oppression of the Orthodox world by Islam, facts from which he was convinced there was no salvation, Gordios turned to Scripture, and specifically to the Book of Revelation. His work is therefore an attempt at a historical exegesis of the Apocalypse and an apocalyptic explanation of the historical vicissitudes of the Orthodox peoples.[72] Briefly stated, the four kingdoms in the dream of Nebuchadnezzar were Babylon, Persia, Greece/Macedonia, and Rome, but, Gordios observes, the greatest of all kingdoms is that of Muhammad, which has outlasted the others. Since it is not mentioned in the Apocalypse, this is the kingdom of Antichrist, a preparation for the Second Coming and the end of the present world. As he develops his theme Gordios states that the pope and Muhammad represent the two faces of the Antichrist and are identical with the two beasts in the Apocalypse. He then applies traditional Byzantine expositions of the two Latin "heresies" of papal primacy and the filioque and analyzes the hardships that Islam has inflicted on the Orthodox.

Whatever the novelties of his treatment, the genre (exegesis of the Apocalypse), the spirit (religious), and the polemic (against Latin Christianity and Islam) are Byzantine in origin. The archbishop of Thessaloniki, Symeon (d. 1429), had found himself in a very similar historical dilemma as Gordios some three centuries earlier, caught between the Latins (Venice) and Muslims (Turks). Though he excoriated both as diabolical evils, Symeon urged his flock to remain faithful to their Venetian rulers.[73] Gordios relates that the Orthodox live much as a shepherdless flock (that is, without an emperor) between two ferocious beasts. No sooner do they fall into the jaws of the one than they are snatched by the jaws of the other, continuing thus until that day when there will be no Orthodox Christians remaining. In contrast to the Thessalonian Symeon, Gordios felt that of the two "beasts" the more dangerous was the pope, for he endangered the souls of the Orthodox, whereas Muhammad endangered only their bodies. This is obviously a reflection of a man of the cloth, for Gordios himself states that in his day the converts to Roman Catholicism were few and represented the better educated and upper social class, whereas those who were constrained to convert to Islam in large numbers were of the lower class, poorer and less educated.

This medieval and very pessimistic Byzantine-inspired literary composition had a considerable success, as we learn from the editor of the text, who has identified thirty-seven manuscripts without exhausting the possibilities. Thirteen of these manuscripts are in the libraries of eight Athonite monasteries, and others were to be found at Patmos, Agrapha, Cyprus, the Peloponnese, Jerusalem, Constantinople, Bucharest, and Smyrna.[74] The work of Gordios is representative of only one aspect of the dynamic life of Byzantine literary traditions in the Greek literature of the Ottoman period. I shall not go into the main body of homiletics, epistolography, archival style, hagiography, theology, and rhetoric.

What of the literary traditions among the other Balkan peoples? The first of these to come under the influence of Byzantine literature were the Bulgarians, particularly in the reigns of Boris (852–89) and the great Symeon (893–927).[75] The religious literature of Byzantium was decisive not only in this first golden age of Bulgarian literature but also later, in what has been called the "Second South Slavic Influence." Euthymios of Tirnovo, as a result of his extended stays in Constantinople and on Mount Athos, took with him a knowledge of Byzantine literature and founded the school of Tirnovo, which became a new center of Bulgarian literary activity, and where in 1375 he became patriarch of the Bulgarian Church.[76] With the conquest of Tirnovo by the Turks in 1393 the scholars there scattered, taking the manuscripts and the Slavo-Byzantine tradition with them to Serbia, Russia, and the Rumanian lands.

Although Bulgarian literary activity suffered a disastrous blow in the Ottoman conquest and did not attain a high plateau again until the Bulgarian *Vuzrazhdane* (renaissance) in the nineteenth century, it did not disappear. The last flickering light of the Tirnovo school is seen in the hagiographic activity of the two sixteenth-century authors Pop Pejo and Matei Grammatik. Both authors were active in Sofia, which by the latter sixteenth century is said to have had twelve Christian churches and two schools for the preparation of priests.[77] The primary compositions of these authors were two hagiographic-martyrological texts. Pop Pejo composed the life of Georgi Novi Sofiiski, burned to death for the faith in 1515 by the Turks in Sofia. Matei Grammatik composed his piece on the martyrdom of Nikola Novi Sofiiski, who was stoned to death for his faith by the Turks in Sofia in 1555. The genre, hagiography/martyrology, is of Byzantine origin, and the literary style is to some degree in the tradition of the Byzantino-Slavic school of Tirnovo.[78] Contemporaneously, Bulgarian scribes were copying the standard religious and liturgical manuscripts that the Orthodox rites required.

Among the most widespread of the Bulgarian texts in the seventeenth and first half of the eighteenth century were the so-called *Sborniks*. Written in a simpler language and therefore comprehensible to a larger audience, the Sborniks were of two types. The first usually contained miscellaneous texts or excerpts that included, among other things, lives, edifying tales, sermons, historical works, apocrypha, legends, prayers, and questions and answers on natural phenomena. Such materials were taken, by and large, from older, Byzantine and Slavo-Byzantine, literature, including the apocryphal tales of Adam and Eve, and the tales of Solomon and Baruch. Included also were lives from Euthymios, of Cyril and Methodius, Clement, Ivan Rilski, materials from the cycle of the Trojan War, Akir the Wise, the *Fall of Tsargrad*, and the *Alexandrida*. In addition there were sermons of John Chrysostom, Gregory the Theologian, Damaskenos Studites, selections from the *Physiologos* and from the Byzantine chronicles of George Amartolos and Manasses. This first type of Sbornik was thus a florilegium, in a sense, drawing on earlier Slavo-Byzantine literature and reflecting the traditional moral and aesthetic values and Weltanschauung of the Byzantine cultural tradition.[79]

The second type of Sbornik, also very popular, is known in Bulgarian as the Damaskini. Appearing in the late sixteenth century, it became widespread throughout the Bulgarian-speaking lands. Whereas the contents of the first type of Sbornik represent an older Slavo-Byzantine tradition, those of the Damaskini reflect a contemporary Greek influence. The name derives from the author himself, Damaskenos Studites, a sixteenth-century Greek cleric of Thessaloniki, who brought together forty-three of his sermons in a text called the *Thesaurus*.[80] These sermons, or some part of them, were translated into Bulgarian in the latter half of the sixteenth century. The popularity of the text in Bulgarian is to be seen not only in its wide diffusion but also in the fact that it was translated at least ten times from the Greek, in various places, including Mount Athos and Bačkovo.[81] Thus the sixteenth-century hagiographies/martyrologies and the later Sborniks demonstrate that the Byzantine and Slavo-Byzantine literary traditions, with their contents, genres, and moral-aesthetic values, remained important and vital among the Bulgarians in Ottoman times.[82]

Notes

1. See *Dumbarton Oaks Papers* 23–24 (1969–70).

2. By way of example, see Speros Vryonis, Jr., "Islamic Sources for the History of the Greek People," *Indiana Social Studies Quarterly* 32 (1973): 56–68; reprinted in idem, *Studies on Byzantium, Seljuks and Ottomans* (Malibu, Calif.: Undena Publications, 1981).

3. "The Byzantine Legacy and Ottoman Forms," *Dumbarton Oaks Papers* 23–24 (1969–70): 251–308; reprinted in Vryonis, *Studies*.

4. "The Greeks under Turkish Rule," in *Hellenism and the First Greek War of Liberation (1821–1830): Continuity and Change*, ed. Nikiforos P. Diamandouros et al. (Thessaloniki: Institute for Balkan Studies, 1976), 45–58; reprinted in Vryonis, *Studies*.

5. Lowell Clucas, ed., *The Byzantine Legacy in Eastern Europe* (Boulder, Colo.: East European Monographs, 1988), 107–45.

6. See Ömer Lûtfi Barkan, *Süleymaniye cami ve imareti inşaatî (1550–1557)*, 2 vols. (Ankara: Türk Tarih Kurumu, 1972, 1979), which discusses in detail the expense, labor, and laborers in the building of the mosque complex of Süleyman the Lawgiver. One may also

consult the massive architectural survey of Ekrem Hakkı Ayverdi, *Osmanlı mi'mârîsinin ilk devri: Ertogrul, Osman, Orhan Gaziler Hudavendigar ve Yıldırım Bayazid 630–805 (1230–1420)* (Istanbul: Baha Matbaası, 1966); *Osmanlı mimarisinde Celebi ve II. Sultan Murad devri 806–855 (1403–1451)* (Istanbul: Baha Matbaası, 1972); *Osmanlı mi'marisinde: Fatih devri 855–886 (1451–1481)* (Istanbul: Baha Matbaası, 1973); *Avrupa'da osmanlı mimarisi eserleri: Romanya Macaristan*, 1 cild, 1 ve 2 kitabi (Istanbul: Baha Matbaası, 1977); *Yugoslavya*, II cild, 3 kitap, (Istanbul: Baha Matbaası, 1981); *Yugoslavya*, III cild, 3 kitap, (Istanbul: Baha Matbaası, 1981); *Bulgaristan, Yunanistan, Arnavutluk*, IV cild, 4, 5, 6 kitap, (Istanbul: Baha Matbaası, 1982). On the pious foundations of Istanbul, see Ömer Lûtfi Barkan and Ekkrem Hakkı Ayverdi, *Istanbul vakıflarî tahrîr defteri 953 (1546)* (Istanbul: Baha Matbaası, 1970).

7. On the establishment of the Ottomans in the towns, see *Encyclopedia of Islam*, new [2d] ed., s.v. "Istanbul"; Heath W. Lowry, "Portrait of a City: The Population and Topography of Ottoman Selanik (Thessaloniki) in the Year 1478," *Diptycha* 2 (1980–81): 254–93; Speros Vryonis, Jr., "The Ottoman Conquest of Thessaloniki in 1430," in *Continuity and Change in Late Byzantine and Early Ottoman Society*, ed. Anthony Bryer and Heath Lowry (Birmingham and Washington, D.C.: University of Birmingham and Dumbarton Oaks Research Library and Collection, 1986), 281–322; Heath W. Lowry, *Trabzon şehrinin islamlaşma ve türkleşmesi: 1461–1583* (Istanbul: L'Université Boğaziçi, 1981); Speros Vryonis, Jr., "Religious Change and Patterns in the Balkans, Fourteenth-Sixteenth Centuries," in *Aspects of the Balkans: Continuity and Change*, ed. Hendrik Birnbaum and Speros Vryonis, Jr. (The Hague: Mouton, 1972), 151–76; reprinted in Vryonis, *Studies*.

8. Speros Vryonis, Jr., "Mikra Asia," in *Istoria tou ellenikou ethnous*, 16 vols. (Athens: Ekdotike Athenon, 1971–78) (hereafter cited as *IEE*), 7:426–39.

9. Herbert Hunger, *Die hochsprachliche profane Literatur der Byzantiner*, 2 vols. (Munich: C. H. Beck, 1978), 2:400–476.

10. On the agrarian laws of the Macedonians, see George Ostrogorsky, *History of the Byzantine State*, trans. Joan Hussey, rev. ed. (New Brunswick, N.J.: Rutgers Univ. Press, 1969), 217, 272–76, 280–82, 306–7; idem, "Agrarian Conditions in the Byzantine Empire in the Middle Ages," in *Cambridge Economic History of Europe*, 2d ed. (Cambridge: Cambridge Univ. Press, 1966–), 1:205–34, 774–79; Paul Lemerle, *The Agrarian History of Byzantium from the Origins to the Twelfth Century: The Sources and Problems* (Galway: Officina Typographica, Galway Univ. Press, 1979). On the Rhodian Sea Law, see Walter Ashburner, ed., *The Rhodian Sea Law* (Oxford: Clarendon Press, 1909).

11. Ostrogorsky, 273.

12. The evidence has been brought together in Speros Vryonis, Jr., "Local Institutions in the Greek Islands and Elements of Byzantine Continuity during Ottoman Rule," to appear in the *Izvestiia* of the Ivan Dujčev Institute in Sofia. See also Demetrios Chomatianos, in Ioannes D. Zepos and Panagiotes Ioannes Zepos, *Jus Graecoromanum*, 8 vols. (Athens: G. Fexis, 1931; rpt. Aalen: Scientia, 1962) (hereafter cited as *JGR*), 8:325–26, 330–34; Konstantinos Armenopoulos, *Procheiron nomon e Hexabiblos*, ed. Konstantinos G. Pitsakes (Athens: Dodone, 1971), III, iii, 103–12; and Franz Dölger, *Aus den Schatzkammern des Heiligen Berges*, 2 vols. (Munich: Münchner Verlag, 1948), 1: nos. 20, 1147.

13. Demetrios S. Gines, *Perigramma istorias tou metabyzantinou dikaiou* (Athens: Grapheion Demosieumaton Akademias Athenon, 1966), no. 100.

14. See above, n. 12.

15. Gines, no. 134.

16. Gines, no. 221.

17. *JGR* 8:504–7.

18. *JGR* 8:522.

19. Gines, no. 802.

20. *JGR* 8:504–7.

21. *JGR* 8:522.

22. Gines, nos. 134, 237.

23. *JGR* 8:504–7.

24. Georgios Andreas Petropoulos, *Notariakai praxeis Mykonou ton eton 1663–1779* (Athens: N.p., 1960), no. 25.

25. *JGR* 8:458–59; Georgios Andreas Petropoulos, *Nomika engrapha Siphnou tes sylloges G. Maridake (1684–1835) meta symbolon eis ten ereunan tou metabyzantinou dikaiou* (Athens: Grapheion Demosieumaton Akademias Athenon, 1956), 232–33.

26. Georgios Andreas Petropoulos, *Notariakai praxeis Kephallenias tes sylloges E. Blessa ton eton 1701–1856* (Athens, 1962), nos. B96, B97; idem, *Notariakai praxeis Paxon diaphoron notarion ton eton 1658–1810* (Athens: N.p., 1958), nos. 508, 520.

27. Vladimir Georgescu, *Bizanțul și instituțiile românești pînă la mijlocul secolului al XVIII–lea* (Bucharest: Editura Academiei Republicii Socialiste România, 1980), 199–206.

28. See above, n. 12.

29. Gines, no. 647; *JGR* 8:559.

30. Gines, no. 580.

31. Gines, no. 647.

32. For the basic rates of interest, see Gines, no. 580.

33. On the nature of the maritime loan and maritime risk, see the two cases in Petropoulos, *Praxeis Kephallenias*, nos. 123, 124, 126.

34. Petropoulos, *Praxeis Paxon*, nos. 354, 499.

35. Gines, no. 580.

36. Petropoulos, *Praxeis Paxon*, no. 354.

37. Ibid., no. 499.

38. Rhodian Sea Law, pt. 2, chaps. 1–7 (Ashburner, 1–2; trans. 57).

39. Gines, no. 498.

40. Rhodian Sea Law, pt. 3, chap. 9 (Ashburner, 16–17; trans. 87). See also pt. 3, chaps. 31, 35 (Ashburner, 29, 31; trans. 108, 110).

41. Rhodian Sea Law, pt. 2, chap. 17 (Ashburner, 3–4; trans. 65).

42. Rhodian Sea Law, pt. 3, chap. 16 (Ashburner, 21; trans. 96).

43. Rhodian Sea Law, pt. 3, chaps. 16, 17 (Ashburner, 21–22; trans. 96–97) and Ashburner, ccix–ccxxxiv; *Basilica*, 53.3.8.

44. Rhodian Sea Law, pt. 2, chap. 18; pt. 3, chaps. 9–11, 17, 22, 30, 33, 38 (Ashburner, 4, 16–19, 22, 25, 28–29, 30, 32–33; trans. 67, 87, 91–92, 97, 102–3, 107, 109, 112).

45. Ibid.

46. *Basilica*, 53.1.15, which refers to "synallagmata."

47. II.ii.5.

48. *Basilica*, 53.3.22; Armenopoulos, II.ii.19. Rewards are given to sailors who salvage such goods, but the salvagers do not acquire title (Rhodian Sea Law, pt. 3, chaps. 45–47 [Ashburner, 37–38; trans. 117–19]).

49. *Basilica*, 56.3.19.

50. Speros Vryonis, Jr., "Byzantine Legacy in Folk Life and Tradition" (see above, n. 5), 133–35.

51. Georgios A. Megas, *Greek Calendar Customs* (Athens: Press and Information Department, Prime Minister's Office, 1958), 142–44; Edmund Schneeweis, *Serbokroatische Volkskunde* (Berlin: De Gruyter, 1961), 142.

52. Megas, 113–16; Schneeweis, 136–37; Christo Vakarelski, *Bulgarische Volkskunde*, trans. N. Damerau, K. Gutschmidt, and N. Reiter (Berlin: De Gruyter, 1969), 320–22.

53. Megas, 55; Schneeweis, 125; Vakarelski, 319.

54. For well organized and structured surveys of the calendars of the Greeks, Serbs, and Bulgars, see Megas, Schneeweis, and Vakarelski.

55. Andreas Xyngopoulos, *Schediasma istorias tes threskeutikes zographikes meta ten Alosin* (Athens: Archaiologike Etaireia, 1957); Manolis Chatzidakis, "Les debuts de l'Ecole crétoise, et la question de l'école dite italo-grecque," in *Mnemosynon Sophias Antoniade* (Venice: Ellenikon Institouton Benetias Byzantinon kai Metabyzantinon Spoudon, 1974), 169–211. See also the short essays by various authors in the exhibition catalogue, *From Byzantium to El Greco: Greek Frescoes and Icons* (Athens: Greek Ministry of Culture, Byzantine Museum of Athens, 1987), reprinted with some changes as *Holy Image, Holy Space: Icons and Frescoes from Greece* (Athens: Greek Ministry of Culture, Byzantine Museum of Athens, 1988).

56. Manolis Chatzidakis, "Techne," in *IEE* 11:243–66, for an excellent detailed analysis.

57. *Dionysiou tou ek Phourna Ermeneia tes zographikes technes kai ai kyriai autes anekdotoi pegai, ekdidomene meta prologou nun to proton pleres kata to prototypon autou keimenon*, ed. A. Papadopoulos-Kerameus (St. Petersburg: B. Kirschbaum, 1909). For an English translation of the whole treatise, see *The "Painter's Manual" of Dionysius of Fourna*, trans. Paul Hetherington (London: Sagittarius Press, 1974). The translations that I am giving here are my own.

58. *Dionysiou tou ek Phourna Ermeneia*, xxv–xxxii.

59. Ibid., 237.

60. Ibid., 3–4.

61. Ibid., 5–6.

62. Ibid., 6–7.

63. Ibid., 7.

64. Ibid., 7–8.

65. Ibid., 8.

66. Ibid.

67. Vasile Grecu, "Byzantinische Handbücher der Kirchenmalerei," *Byzantion* 9 (1934): 675–701; idem, *Cărţi de pictură bisericească bizantină* (Cernăuţi, 1936).

68. Asen Vasiliev, *Erminii: Tekhnologiia i ikonografiia* (Sofia: Izdatelstvo Septemvri, 1976).

69. Philipp Meyer, *Die Haupturkunden für die Geschichte der Athosklöster* (Leipzig, 1894; rpt. Amsterdam: A. M. Hakkert, 1965), 67–68; Ch. Patrineles, "Oi mones tou ellenikou chorou," in *IEE* 10:133 for earlier figures, according to the sixteenth-century Zygomalas, at around five thousand. For the earliest Ottoman figures, see Heath W. Lowry, "A Note on the Population and Status of the Athonite Monasteries under Ottoman Rule (ca. 1520)," *Wiener Zeitschrift für die Kunde des Morgenlandes* 73 (1981): 115–35, who gives 1,442 monks from the Ottoman *defter* of 1520, for the twenty monasteries.

70. For details see the excellent study and edition of Asterios Argyriou, *Anastasiou tou Gordiou (1654/5–1729) syngramma peri Moameth kai kata Latinon* (Athens: Association Scientifique d'Etudes sur la Grèce Centrale, 1983).

71. On the two explanations, see Speros Vryonis, Jr., *The Decline of Medieval Hellenism in Asia Minor and the Process of Islamization from the Eleventh through the Fifteenth Century* (Berkeley and Los Angeles: Univ. of California Press, 1971), 403–43.

72. For what follows, consult the clear analysis of Argyriou (above, n. 70).

73. Speros Vryonis, Jr., "Crises and Anxieties in Fifteenth-Century Byzantium and the Reassertion of Old, and the Emergence of New, Cultural Forms," in *Islamic and Middle Eastern Societies: A Festschrift in Honor of Professor Wadie Jwaideh*, ed. Robert Olson (Brattleboro, Vt.: Amana Books, 1987), esp. 107–8, 113–14, 115–17; David Balfour, ed.,

Politico-Cultural Works of Symeon Archbishop of Thessalonica (1416/17–1429) (Vienna: Verl. d. Österr. Akad. d. Wiss., 1979).

74. Argyriou, 10 and Annex 1.

75. *Istoriia na bulgarskata literatura*, vol. 1, *Starobulgarska literatura* (Sofia: Izdatelstvo na Bulgarskata Akademiia na Naukite, 1962), 23–253.

76. Ibid., 286–88.

77. Ibid., 381–84.

78. Ibid., 380–401.

79. Ibid., 404–5.

80. A. Angelou, "Poikilomorpha erga tes logias paradoses," in *IEE* 11:382–83.

81. *Istoriia na bulgarskata literatura*, 1:405–6.

82. I do not go here into the question of Byzantine and Byzantino-Slavic traditions in the literary activity of the Serbs and Rumanians in Ottoman times. This tradition is also noteworthy, but the literature of these two peoples was both more extensive and more influenced by the outside world than that of the Bulgarians. See *Istoria literaturii române*, vol. 1 (Bucharest: Editura Academiei Republicii Populare Romine, 1970); *Srpska knjizhevnost u knjizhevnoj krititsi*, 2d ed., vol. 1, *Stara knjizhevnost*, ed. Jovan Hristić (Belgrade: Nolit, 1972); and Milorad Pavić, *Istorija srpske knjizhevnosti baroknog doba (XVII i XVIII vek)* (Belgrade: Nolit, 1970).

WAS THERE EVER A "THIRD ROME"? REMARKS ON THE BYZANTINE LEGACY IN RUSSIA

John Meyendorff

Several East European countries adopted Orthodox Christianity from Byzantium and thereby accepted as the foundation of their literary and spiritual culture the entire corpus of the Byzantine liturgy, translated into Slavic, as well as the idea of a universal empire responsible for the unity of the Christian world. Of these countries, Russia alone remained untouched by the Turkish conquest. Historically, therefore, the problem of "Byzantium after Byzantium" is different when applied to Russia than when applied to the Balkan states.[1] The conversion of the princess Olga (957) and, later, of her grandson Vladimir (988–89), established the "land of Rus'," extending from the Carpathian mountains to the Volga and from Novgorod to the steppes, which were inhabited by Khazars and Pechenegs, as part of the "Byzantine Commonwealth," without making it ever a part of the empire. Russian princes recognized the universal moral supremacy of the Eastern Roman emperor, but not his political domination.

The Church of Russia, however, was administratively dependent upon Byzantium for centuries, from 988 until 1448. The metropolitan "of Kiev and all Russia" ($K\iota\acute{\epsilon}\beta\sigma\upsilon$ $\kappa\alpha\grave{\iota}$ $\pi\acute{\alpha}\sigma\eta\varsigma$ $'P\omega\sigma\acute{\iota}\alpha\varsigma$) was generally a Greek, always appointed from Constantinople. Only in the later period,—in the thirteenth and fourteenth centuries,—was there a regular alternation of Greeks and Russians as heads of the church, but the Russian candidates made the voyage to Constantinople in order to obtain consecration to the office of metropolitan.[2] The prestige and influence of the church were great, because it represented the only administrative structure extending over the entire country. Indeed, Kievan Russia was divided between warring principalities. Later, following the disastrous Mongol conquest

(1237–40), the northeastern principalities became a part of the Mongol empire centered in Peking, whereas the parts that were later known as the Ukraine and Byelorussia fell under Lithuanian and Polish domination.

The Council of Florence and the Fall of Byzantium: Aftermath in Russia

The weak Byzantine empire of the Palaeologan emperors (1261–1453) was not able, by itself, to determine events in Russia, but it exercised indirect influence through its diplomatic ties with the Mongol Khans (who were enemies of the Turks), and through its alliance with the Genoese, who controlled commerce with the Far East through the Black Sea. This Mongol-Genoese-Byzantine "axis" explains, at least partly, the diplomatic favors extended by Byzantium, through the church, to the great principality of Moscow, which began its political ascent as an ally of the Mongols. But religious factors also played a role: the western principalities, under Polish and Lithuanian domination, were more susceptible to fall under the spell of Latin Christendom. In fact, in 1386 Poland and Lithuania—with their numerous Orthodox population—were united under a Roman Catholic king. Even before that date, the Ecumenical Patriarchate had felt that Orthodoxy was more secure under the Mongols, and had supported the transfer of the metropolitan's see from Kiev to Moscow.

Paradoxically, as the empire was shrinking more and more, the ties between the Ecumenical Patriarchate and the Russian metropolitanate were strengthened. This was due to the activity of strong metropolitans like Cyprian (1375–1406)—a Bulgarian and close friend and disciple of the hesychast patriarch Philotheos Kokkinos—and Photius (1408–31), a Greek from Monemvasia. The famous embroidered *sakkos* of the latter, an episcopal dalmatic, featuring prominently the images of the Byzantine emperor John VIII and Grand Prince Basil I of Moscow, with their wives, represents the clear political and religious program which he was sent to fulfill as metropolitan: to assure the continuous membership of Russia in the Byzantine Commonwealth.[3] This mission was spelled out quite explicitly also in the often-quoted letter of Patriarch Anthony to Basil I, written in 1393, a few years before the appointment of Photius: the Byzantine emperor is emperor "of the Romans, that is of all Christians. . . . For Christians, it is not possible to have a Church, and not have an emperor." But the patriarch added: "Christians reject only the heretical emperors, who were raging against the Church and introducing doctrines that were corrupt and foreign to the teachings of the Apostles and the Fathers."[4]

When Metropolitan Photius died (1431), the Byzantine authorities were deeply involved in preparing a Union council, intended to secure direct Western help against the advancing Turks. In order to secure Russian support and commitment, a well-trained diplomat, Isidore, was appointed as metropolitan of Kiev and All Russia, while the grand prince's candidate, Bishop Jonas of Ryazan'—who had already come to Constantinople to receive the appointment—was rather humiliatingly rejected (1437–38). But Russian loyalty to Byzantium was not shaken: Isidore received money and a large retinue from Grand Prince Basil II, "the Blind," and traveled to Florence for the council, representing the metropolitanate of Russia.

In reading some modern historians of the period, one gets the impression that the Muscovite grand prince was eagerly awaiting the opportunity to supplant Byzantium and to assume the position of emperor of a "Third Rome." The facts reported above speak strongly against that view. The grand principality was still under Mongol rule. It had just gone through a long and bloody dynastic struggle, during which Basil II was blinded by a competitor before recovering his throne. The national—and somewhat "messianic"—self-affirmation of the Russians came later. It occurred as a reaction to Florence and to the subsequent fall of Constantinople, and it came about gradually, never taking the form of an official *translatio imperii* from Constantinople to Moscow.

Isidore returned to Moscow from Florence in 1441, as a cardinal of the Roman Church, after traveling through Italy, Hungary, and Poland. The Russians had been informed, both by their own delegates to Florence and by connections in Constantinople, of the resistance of Mark of Ephesus to the conciliar decrees and of the subsequent recanting of a majority of the Greek signatories. The grand prince's decision to reject Isidore was not an anti-Byzantine revolt; rather it was based on the expectation of an Orthodox restoration in Byzantium. In a highly respectful letter to the newly elected patriarch Metrophanes—who supported Florence in principle but was not in a position to proclaim officially a union of the churches—the grand prince requested permission to elect a metropolitan locally: "We beg your most holy lordship to examine your holy and divine Greek canons . . . and authorize the appointment of a metropolitan to be effected in our own country."[5] No reply came, and the Russians waited for seven years before performing in 1448 the independent appointment of the formerly rejected candidate, Jonas of Ryazan', as metropolitan of Kiev and All Russia. The appointment was recognized as legitimate not only in Muscovy but also in the dioceses located in the Polish-Lithuanian domain, through a formal investiture of Jonas by King Casimir IV. In another letter, addressed in 1451 to the new Byzantine emperor Constantine (there was not a patriarch that year in Constantinople, since the Uniate incumbent, Gregory Mammas, had left for Rome), the grand prince promised that, once there was an Orthodox patriarch, "it will be our duty to write to him . . . and ask his blessing in all things."[6] The subsequent events in Constantinople are well known: the Union was formally proclaimed at Hagia Sophia in December 1452 and the city fell in May 1453.

Rejection of Florence, but also politeness and reserve towards the desperate and wavering authorities in Constantinople, had been, therefore, the official attitude of the Russians in 1439–53. Unofficial reactions, however, often took a different bent. They came, first, from the Russian clerics who had accompanied Isidore to Italy and had followed his leadership in recognizing the Union. The Russian bishop Avraamy of Suzdal had indeed signed the decree. The Greeks, who had also signed, but eventually recanted, blamed psychological and material pressures exercised upon them by the Latins. The Russians put the blame on the "deviousness" of Isidore and the "betrayal" of the Greeks. Patriarch Anthony, in 1393, had called the Russians to be loyal to Orthodox Byzantium but had recognized the need to "reject heretical emperors."[7] The argument was now seen as fully applicable to the situation after 1439: "Oh great sovereign emperor," wrote one polemicist, addressing John VIII Palaeologus, signatory of the Union, "why did you go to them? . . . You have exchanged light for darkness; instead of the divine law, you have received the Latin faith; . . . Formerly you were the agent of piety, now you are the sower of evil seeds."[8] Under the circumstances, it was the grand prince of Moscow who had to be seen as a "new Constantine," savior of Orthodoxy.[9] But the same argument was used to exalt, not only Moscow, but other Russian centers, for instance Tver, whose prince Boris had also sent a representative to the council and now, after rejecting the Latin faith, was said by one polemicist to deserve an imperial diadem.[10] Furthermore, in Novgorod, under Archbishop Gennadios (1484–1509), there appeared a curious Russian variation on the Donation of Constantine, the Legend of the White Cowl. According to this legend, a white cowl (*klobuk*; Gr. ἐπικαλίμαυκον) was donated by Constantine the Great to Pope Sylvester following his bap-

tism; the last Orthodox pope, foreseeing Rome's fall into heresy, sent the
cowl for safekeeping to Patriarch Philotheos of Constantinople, who eventually (also foreseeing the betrayal of Florence) sent the precious relic to
the archbishop of Novgorod.[11] Thus not only Moscow, but also Tver and
Novgorod, were somehow claiming to be the heirs of "Rome" and centers
of the true Christian faith.

But of course, the destiny of becoming an imperial capital belonged
to Moscow. It is to its grand prince that the monk Filofei of Pskov (ca.
1510–40) addressed his famous letter: "All Christian realms will come to
an end and will unite into the one single realm of our sovereign, that is,
into the Russian realm, according to the prophetic books. Both Romes
fell, the third endures, and a fourth there will not be."[12] But, as Georges
Florovsky and others have shown, the theory of Moscow the "Third
Rome" was formulated in an apocalyptic context: for Filofei, Moscow was
not only the "third," but more importantly the "last," Rome, and he was
calling the grand prince to repentance and Christian virtue, motivating his
appeals by the imminence of the Second Coming. Politically the appeal
had little practical application. The Muscovite sovereigns were in the
process of building up a national empire, inspired largely by Western
Renaissance models and ideas, and had little use for apocalyptics. The
theory of the "Third Rome," or that of a *translatio imperii* from Constantinople to Moscow, was never accepted as official state theory.

In 1472 Ivan III married the niece of the last emperor of Constantinople, who had lived in Italy and received a Western education.
Although the marriage undoubtedly enhanced his prestige, it did not
imply the assumption of the imperial title,[13] and the practical effect of the
marriage consisted in increasing substantially Italian influence in Muscovy: the Kremlin was then rebuilt *more italico* by Italian architects. In
1547 Ivan IV, grandson of Ivan III, was crowned tsar (the Slavic equivalent of "emperor") according to a modified Byzantine ceremonial, but he
did not assume the title of "emperor of the Romans," as a *translatio imperii*
and the theory of a "Third Rome" would require, but that of "tsar of all the
Rus'." Furthermore, he requested the formal recognition of his title from
the patriarch of Constantinople, sending lavish gifts to the ecumenical
throne. The reply came in the form of two letters of Patriarch Joasaph
(1555–65). In the first, the patriarch expressed reservations: only the
Roman pope and the patriarch of Constantinople, he wrote, have the right
to crown emperors legitimately, so that the tsar should be crowned anew
by the patriarch's delegate, the metropolitan of Evripos, carrier of the

letter. The second document had the form of a synodal act, sanctioning the crowning, once it would be performed by the aforementioned metropolitan, and proposing an original scheme, proving Ivan's legitimacy: he was a descendant of Princess Anna, wife of St. Vladimir, and sister of the Byzantine emperor Basil II.[14]

No second crowning of Ivan ever took place, but the episode illustrates the continuous respect of the Muscovite authorities for the traditional ties between Russia and the mother church of Constantinople, in spite of the painful break of 1448–53. The same loyalty would be expressed in the procedures connected with the establishment of the patriarchate of Moscow in 1589.

Being in desperate need of material support, Ecumenical Patriarch Jeremiah II traveled to Moscow in 1588. This was an unforeseen opportunity for the Russian authorities to consider the possibility of proclaiming the establishment of a "Third Rome." Indeed, they offered Jeremiah permanent residence in Russia, with his see in the ancient city of Vladimir, which would thereby become the center of the Orthodox world. Jeremiah's refusal of this offer led to an alternative: the establishment of a new patriarchate in Moscow. The act was peformed by Jeremiah and later confirmed by synods, including the other patriarchs, particularly the intelligent and influential Meletios Pegas of Alexandria, in 1590 and 1593.[15] The meaning of these texts clearly implies the restoration of a "pentarchy" of patriarchs, which had been reduced to a "tetrarchy" by the defection of the bishop of Rome. The new patriarchate of Moscow was not seen to be an equivalent of the distant patriarchate of Georgia, or those of Pec or Ohrid, or of the archdiocese of Cyprus (all of which churches were still, at least nominally, in existence, but were neither consulted nor mentioned in the acts). Together with Constantinople, Alexandria, Antioch, and Jerusalem, Moscow was to become one of the five sees recognized in the legislation of Justinian as the "five senses" of world Orthodoxy. Patriarch Job, with the title of "patriarch of Moscow and all Russia, and of the Northern parts," ($\tau\hat{\omega}\nu$ $\dot{\upsilon}\pi\epsilon\rho\beta\sigma\rho\epsilon\acute{\iota}\omega\nu$ $\mu\epsilon\rho\hat{\omega}\nu$), was to be the "fifth patriarch," "counted" with the other four and sharing their dignity. He was to recognize "the apostolic throne of Constantinople as its head and its primate, as the other patriarchs do." It was also proclaimed that Constantinople and the other patriarchates had their positions and rights defined by councils "for no other reason than their place within the imperial system."[16] The motivation of the rights of Moscow resided, therefore, in the existence of the Russian "empire," so that the name of the "most pious *basileus* of

Moscow and *autokrator* of all Russia and the Northern parts" was now to be included at the required moments of imperial commemorations in the liturgical books everywhere.[17]

There is no doubt therefore that the establishment of the patriarchate of Moscow was, in itself, a most solemn reaffirmation of Byzantine traditions. The Byzantine "spirit" remained even in the fact that the new patriarchate was granted the fifth, and not the first, place among the patriarchates. Was not the same sense of established tradition and custom preserved as Constantinople, the "New Rome," refrained (until the schism) from claiming the first place above the "old imperial Rome"? Similarly, the "Third Rome" did not overtake the "second." However, there was also an aura of unreality around the events of 1589, not because Russians, or Greeks, did not *want* to preserve the Byzantine tradition in Russia, but because, at the very end of the sixteenth century, so many historical and cultural developments occurred that the political and legal aspects of that tradition were largely bypassed by existing political realities.

I mentioned earlier that, already in the fifteenth century, the grand principality of Moscow had begun building a national empire. Tsar Ivan IV the "Terrible" (1533–84)—his popular name, *groznyi*, is actually better translated as "awesome"—was an avid reader of Machiavelli. The focus of his cultural and political interests was Europe, not Byzantium. In the seventeenth century, "Europe" intervened in the very fabric of Muscovite national consciousness in the form of Polish and Swedish invasions during the so-called Time of Troubles (1598–1613), and also a greatly increased cultural and ideological influence coming from the West. All of this provoked a real crisis of Byzantinism in Russia, which occurred in the seventeenth century but was already in the making much earlier.

A Crisis of "Byzantinism"

The tragedy of the Council of Florence and the fall of Byzantium were interpreted by some Russian polemicists as an ultimate betrayal, followed by divine punishment. But at the same time, Russian contacts with and support for the Orthodox faithful under Turkish domination, travels to holy places by Russian pilgrims, visits to Middle Eastern monasteries— particularly Sinai, Mar Sabba in Palestine, and Mount Athos—served as strong assurances that Orthodoxy and the Byzantine tradition were still alive among Greeks, Arabs, and Balkan Slavs. The assumption by the metropolitanate of Russia of a de facto ecclesiastical independence in 1448 did not imply any break of communion with the Eastern patriarchates, restored in Constantinople after 1453.

Furthermore, the Russians were always aware of the fact that Orthodoxy had come to them "from the Greeks," and therefore almost automatically looked for Greek sources of the true faith. The most conservative among them feared Western threats against the purity of the tradition received through St. Vladimir from Byzantium.

It is impossible to present here a complete history of the intellectual, spiritual, and personal contacts between Greeks and Russians in the late medieval and early modern periods.[18] A few remarks about the great figure of Maximus "the Greek" should suffice to illustrate both the importance and the ambiguity of the cultural and religious relations between Russians and Greeks in the sixteenth century and explain in advance the tragedy of the seventeenth.

Ecclesiastically independent and self-conscious in its role as stronghold of Orthodoxy, Muscovite society was intellectually and spiritually nourished by what Russian writers referred to as the "Books" (*knigi*)—essentially the great body of liturgical, hagiographic, canonical, and theological writings translated from the Greek over the years. There were valuable local writings as well—especially *Lives* of saints and sermons—but these were closely connected in their style and content to Byzantine models. This Byzantine and South Slavic impact had been particularly strong during the rise of the monastic hesychast movement in Greek and Slavic lands in the fourteenth and fifteenth centuries. And yet by 1516 it was discovered that no one in Russia knew Greek, and therefore no one possessed the ability to make more translations of useful patristic texts, or to correct accumulated errors in existing Slavonic manuscripts. The Russians were rapidly entering a new and "modern" era of their history, but being also fully committed to the preservation of the Byzantine religious and cultural legacy, they lacked the means to use it meaningfully and critically.

In 1516, therefore, an embassy of Grand Prince Basil III traveled to Mount Athos and Constantinople, requesting that a Greek scholar be sent to Moscow, to help with translations and corrections. But there was no "Cyril" or "Methodius" among the Greeks either: the man who went to Muscovy was the monk Maximus, from the Athonite monastery of Vatopedi, and he knew no Slavic.

This last limitation, however crucial in view of his specific new mission, did not prevent Maximus from being one of the most extraordinary and talented men of his age.[19] Born in Arta around 1470 as Michael Trivolis, he became attracted, as other representatives of the surviving Greek intelligentsia also were, by the cultural atmosphere of Renaissance Italy. Traveling first to Florence—where he read Plato under the guidance of Marsilio Ficino—and then to Bologna, Padua, and Milan, before spending two years in Venice as an associate of Aldus Manutius, the publisher of Greek classics, he finally worked four years in Mirandola for the Hellenist Gianfrancesco Pico. The last stage of his stay in Italy was even more remarkable: for two years (1502–4), he may have lived at San Marco in Florence. His religious vocation was spurred by the example of San Marco's prior, the famous Girolamo Savonarola, who had been executed in 1498 for his denunciations of corruption and immorality.

In 1504, however, Michael Trivolis abandoned Italy to become an Athonite monk under the name of Maximus. During the rest of his life, he remained discreet about his past in Italy, but there can be little doubt that his curriculum vitae was known not only on Mount Athos but also by the Russian authorities. It might have been seen as an additional asset for his mission to Muscovy, for the mother of Basil III, Zoe-Sophia Paleologina, had been educated in Italy and had contributed to Italian tastes at the Muscovite court.

Sent to Moscow but hoping to return eventually to his Athonite retreat, Maximus would remain there, much against his will, for over thirty years, until his death in 1556. After a while he learned the Slavonic language, but his work as a translator began through the curious method of translating first a Greek patristic commentary on the Psalter into Latin, with a Russian diplomat, Dimitri Gerasimov, making a translation from Latin into Slavonic. Some misinterpretations were inevitable. Furthermore, Maximus, a man of wide international horizons and strong critical opinions, expressed unconventional views, which were embarrassing to many. Invoking the preaching of Savonarola, he castigated the wealth of monasteries and received, on this point, the support not only of Russian hesychasts (the "Transvolgan elders"), but also of a powerful party at court. When this party lost the battle against the spokesmen of the socially oriented abbot Joseph of Volotsk and metropolitan Daniel, Maximus's prestige at the court suffered also. As he was also calling the Russian metropolitanate to return to the canonical obedience of the ecumenical patriarchate (as was originally intended when Jonas was consecrated by Russian bishops in 1448), and as he was suggesting that the Muscovite grand prince should undertake an anti-Turkish crusade to liberate Constantinople (an unrealistic project, since Moscow was quite absorbed by its struggle against Poland and the Tatars), he fell out of favor completely. Arrested, repeatedly tried (in 1525 and 1531), accused of heresy and political treason, he remained in monastic confinement until around 1548. Freed by Ivan IV, he spent his last years writing and meeting many high-placed personalities. From the seventeenth century on, he was locally venerated as a saint, and he was officially canonized in 1988.

Around 1540, in one of his writings, he used an allegory that reflects not only the tragedy of his personal life, but also the fate of the Byzantine tradition: he remembered once encountering an old woman, sitting near a road, dressed in black, surrounded by menacing lions and bears, wolves, and foxes. She spoke to Maximus and gave her name: *Vasileia* ("empire," or "kingdom,"), and explained that the road, bare and desolate, is this "last" cursed age.[20]

However, the bitter nostalgia and understandable pessimism of Maximus did not represent the concluding motif of Russian Byzantinism. There came the tragedy of the seventeenth century.

The century began with a dynastic crisis, with the curious appearance of several pretenders to the throne under the name of Ivan IV's murdered son, Dimitri, and with a Polish occupation of Moscow itself. On the confused Russian political and ecclesiastical scene, there appeared Greeks, whose personalities—quite different from the venerable figures of Patriarchs Jeremiah II and Meletios Pegas, or from the wise and holy Maximus—tended to compromise the Byzantine "cause" in the eyes of the Russians. Among them was Ignatius, who usurped the patriarchal throne following the forced deposition of Patriarch Job. One generation later, a man called Paisios Ligarides, metropolitan of Gaza, was accepted as a major authority in ecclesiastical affairs in the restored Muscovite tsardom of Alexis Romanov (1645–76), but proved eventually to be a shady adventurer.

And yet the patriarch Nikon of Moscow (1652–58), with uncommon energy, tried to restore what he thought to be the Byzantine traditions and to reform the Russian Church by making it ritually and organizationally identical with the contemporary Greek Church.[21] The reform was actively supported by the tsar, who, in a gesture highly unusual in Muscovy, pledged obedience to the patriarch.

The motivation for the reforms came from the necessity of correcting liturgical books and practices—the very reason for which Maximus the Greek had been earlier invited to Russia. However, just as in the time of

Maximus, Russia lacked experts able to define what was the "right" way of worshipping. Everyone agreed that the "right" faith had been received by the Russians from the Greeks at the time of St. Vladimir, but what was the right way to restore that original ideal? Was it not by consulting ancient Greek and Russian manuscripts? A special envoy, Arseny Sukhanov, was sent to ecclesiastical centers and monasteries of the Balkans and the Middle East to acquire such manuscripts. He did obtain hundreds of them, which he brought to Moscow, making the patriarchal (later the synodal) library there one of the richest in the world for Greek codices. But there was nobody in Russia, in the seventeenth century, to make competent use of these books.

It was then that the powerful patriarch decided to adopt a simpler, but—as he soon found out—controversial solution. He decided to correct all Russian books and practices by making them identical to the contemporary Greek printed editions, as these were used under Ottoman occupation, ignoring the fact that they were not necessarily "Byzantine." The changes that he introduced were actually few, but some concerned every single person among the faithful. Thus instead of crossing themselves with *two* fingers (as they did before, and as was customary in Byzantium in the thirteenth century), the Russians were ordered to use *three* fingers. Russian clergy were required to dress like contemporary Greeks, with καμη-λαύκια (Russ.: *kamilavki*), whose form was roughly that of the Turkish fez, and with ample-sleeved black *rasa*, borrowed from Turkish fashion. Long hair—a sign of *civil* power in Byzantium, adopted by Greek clergy, as the patriarchate of Constantinople was invested with civil responsibilities in the Ottoman Empire—was also to be grown by Russian priests and monks (who previously used the early Christian and Byzantine practice of the tonsure [Russ.: *gumentso*], having their hair cut as they entered either clerical or monastic life).

There is no doubt that Patriarch Nikon and Tsar Alexis were still inspired by the "Third Rome" idea. "I am a Russian," the patriarch is reported as saying, "but my faith is Greek." However, their decision to follow contemporary Greeks as models, and the authoritarian and despotic methods used in imposing the reforms, backfired badly. Millions of faithful rebelled. The rebels were headed by former personal friends of Nikon, notably the famous archpriest (*protopop*) Avvakum. Unenlightened as they might have been, the schismatics used arguments that carried weight. The Orthodox faith, they said, might well be "Greek," but are the seventeenth-century Greeks the same as the ones who taught St. Vladimir? Were not the later Greeks delivered by God to Turkish slavery because of their betrayal at Florence? Did not Russia then become the last refuge of Orthodoxy? Are not the newly printed Greek books—which Nikon had adopted as originals for Russian reprinting—actually edited in Venice, that is, under Latin rule, where they might have been corrupted "by Jesuits"? Did not St. Paul write that it is shameful for a man to pray with a covered head, and to grow long hair as women do (I Cor. 11:4, 7, 14)? If church reforms are needed, are adventurers like Paisios Ligarides (eventually condemned not only in Russia, but in Constantinople too) the right advisors?

Eventually, Tsar Alexis tired of Nikon's authoritarianism and had him deposed. This deposition was confirmed by the Eastern patriarchs, but the same patriarchs—at a "great council" in Moscow (1666–67)—sanctioned all of Nikon's reforms.[22] But there were millions of rashly persecuted dissenters, the *Raskolniks*, or "Old Believers." Their leadership insisted on fanatic ritualism, and their rebellion was indeed a cultural and religious dead end: the fact that they were eventually split into a multitude of sects proves the point. Nevertheless, in seventeenth-century Russia they represented that part of the population that was religiously most committed and most unwilling to accept state and church authoritarianism.

The schism was an ultimate crisis of "Byzantinism." The reforms introduced by the official church assured Orthodox unity: even today, the Russian Church preserves, with utter exactness, the seventeenth-century Greek practices adopted by Nikon. But this was a formal Byzantinism, one of externals. The impact of many Western ideas was obvious. In aspiring to have the church rule over the state, Nikon was in fact inspired by papal ideology. The religious art of the period (in Russia, as in occupied Greece) was a pseudo-Byzantine art, giving signs of ultimate decadence. Liturgical music followed Western (particularly Ukrainian) forms in Russia, and increased oriental and Turkish patterns in Greece. The forced Westernization of Russia by Peter the Great—Tsar Alexis's son—was forthcoming, and was in many ways the logical consequence of what happened in the seventeenth century. In some sense, the dissenters were more faithful to the spirit of Byzantine Orthodoxy. Some of their traditions—iconography, music, and the very spirit of medieval Eastern Christianity—were most authentically Byzantine. But their absolutization of the Russian ways, as they knew them, and their secession from the hierarchical and sacramental life of the church, were a misinterpretation of the great, "catholic" Tradition in terms of "local traditions" only.

A Word of Conclusion: What Is Byzantinism?

My remarks concerning the Byzantine tradition in Russia seem to call for a rather negative conclusion. On the level of political ideology, the Muscovite tsars never seriously intended to follow the example of the medieval sovereigns of Bulgaria (Tsar Symeon in the tenth century, the tsars of the thirteenth and fourteenth centuries) or Serbia (Tsar Dušan) and establish a new "Roman" empire. It appears to me that the role of the theory "Moscow the Third Rome" as an inspiration of Russian politics in the postmedieval age is much too often given an exaggerated importance. Whenever it was used in Muscovy it served as a subsidiary element in the building up of a national state, not as an ideological focus. Indeed, as I noticed earlier, the Muscovites created a "tsardom of all Russia," not a "Roman empire," and they were doing so in the spirit of their age. The imperial idea had lost its contents in the West as well, and Europe had become a Europe of "nations." The Greeks too were to use Byzantine ideas and terminology to justify calls to national liberation from the Turkish yoke, but the "Great Idea" that would inspire them would also be a "national" idea. If my sketchy review of relations between Greeks and Russians were to be extended to the eighteenth century, I would have to speak of the two Greek prelates, Eugenios Voulgaris (1716–1806) and Nikephoros Theotokes (1731–1800), who fared better at the court of Catherine the Great than did Maximus the Greek at the court of Basil III. But their vision was clearly dominated by the spirit of the Enlightenment, that of a "Greek" renaissance to be helped by Russian military and political might.[23]

Yet there is a sense in which Christian Byzantinism remained very much alive in Christian Russia. This Byzantine continuity can be discovered primarily on the level of religious experience. First of all, the perpetuation in Russia of the Byzantine liturgical tradition—preserved with the meticulous ritual conservatism of which the Russians alone were capable—established a vision of the faith and of Christian culture that theologians call "eschatological." The realities of the kingdom of God are seen as *different* from the concrete realities of the "fallen" world: the kingdom, therefore, is to be experienced sacramentally, ritually, mystically, and not by exercising political power, or engaging in social activism, to make the world better than it is. Besides, and somewhat beyond, the liturgical tradition, there is monastic mysticism, rooted in early Eastern Christianity, but actively perpetuated in the Byzantine world. This mysticism had been well understood by the Slavs, particularly the Russians. In

Russia, as in Byzantium, the saint was given a particular prophetic authority, with a certain priority not only over the state, but over ecclesiastical institutions as well. This explains not only the continuous "philokalic" tradition—essentially the tradition of the "Jesus prayer" and contemplative monasticism—but also the emergence in nineteenth-century Russia, as in contemporary Greece, of "lay theology" (or theology done by laymen), and the general acceptance, in the entire Orthodox world, of the belief that communion with God, and therefore responsibility for the faith, belongs to all the members of the church, so that the charisma of teaching, with which bishops are endowed, is an authority within the church, and not over it.

This attitude to Christianity, which is common to the entire Orthodox world, is reflected in culture as well. Whether in Greece, or in the Balkans, or in Russia, or in missionary countries in Asia or North America, people—including the uneducated and culturally immature— are immersed, through the liturgy, into a highly sophisticated world of Hellenistic poetry, patristic theology, and biblical symbolism. Religious art—music and iconography—also play an important role in communicating this "liturgical" vision of the kingdom of God, created in Byzantium. Of course, the level of understanding and participation are not the same for everybody and everywhere, but the basic models and criteria are the same for all. Transcending centuries and nationalities, this religious "Byzantinism" is, indeed, the major legacy of Byzantium.

As a civilization, as a political system, Byzantium died long ago. But the religious vision, created at the time when the empire existed, still inspires millions. It survived the political, economic, and ideological realities, which today are the concern of learned Byzantinists alone. The "vision" is only obscured when it is confused with either Byzantine political ideology, or the pseudo-Byzantine caricatures of that ideology, used later by nation-states and their secularized politicians.

Notes

1. See the pertinent remarks by Antonios-Emil Tachiaos, "Byzantium after Byzantium," in John Meyendorff et al., *The Legacy of St. Vladimir* (Crestwood, N.Y.: St. Vladimir's Seminary Press, 1990).

2. On this period, see John Meyendorff, *Byzantium and the Rise of Russia: A Study of Byzantino-Russian Relations in the Fourteenth Century* (Cambridge: Cambridge Univ. Press, 1981).

3. For illustrations of the *sakkos*, see Alice Bank, *Byzantine Art in the Collections of Soviet Museums*, enl. ed., trans. Lenina Sorokina (Leningrad: Aurora Art Publishers, 1985), pls. 300–304.

4. Franz Ritter von Miklosich and Josef Müller, eds., *Acta et diplomata Graeca Medii Aevi sacra et profana collecta*, vol. 2, *Acta patriarchatus Constantinopolitani* (Vienna, 1862), 188–92; relevant passages are translated in John W. Barker, *Manuel II Palaeologus (1391–1425): A Study in Late Byzantine Statesmanship* (New Brunswick, N.J.: Rutgers Univ. Press, 1969), 106–9.

5. *Russkaia istoricheskaia biblioteka*, 39 vols. (St. Petersburg, 1872–1927) (hereafter cited as *RIB*), vol. 6, ed. Aleksei Stepanovich Pavlov (1880), cols. 525–36.

6. *RIB* 6: cols. 583–86.

7. See above, n. 4.

8. "Slovo izbrano," in Andrei Nikolaevich Popov, *Istoriko-literaturnyi obzor drevnerusskikh polemicheskikh sochinenii protiv Latinian* (Moscow, 1875), 372–73.

9. The argument appears in letters of Metropolitan Jonas in 1451 (*RIB* 6: cols. 559–60) and other documents; see a review of the texts in Michael Cherniavsky, "The Reception of the Council of Florence in Moscow," *Church History* 24 (1955): 347–59.

10. Monk Thomas, "Slovo pokhval'noe o blagovernom velikom Kniaze Borise Aleksandroviche" (Praise of the Pious Grand Prince Boris Alexandrovich [of Tver]), ed. N. Likhachev, in *Pamiatniki drevnei pis'mennosti i iskusstva*, 168 (Moscow, 1908): 1–15.

11. On this legend, see N. N. Rozov, "Povest' o Novgorodskom belom klobuke kak pamiatnik obshcherusskoi publitsistiki XV veka," in *Trudy otdela drevnerusskoi literatury* 9 (Moscow and Leningrad: Izdatel'stvo Akademii Nauk SSSR, 1953): 178–219; extracts translated in Serge A. Zenkovsky, ed. and trans., *Medieval Russian Epics, Chronicles and Tales*, rev. and enl. ed. (New York: E. P. Dutton, 1974), 326–32. Following the annexation of Novgorod by Muscovy, the white cowl became distinctive of the metropolitans (later the patriarchs) of Moscow. Peter the Great, following his suppression of the patriarchate, bestowed the right to wear a white cowl on all of the metropolitans of the Russian Church—quite a devaluation of an initially papal distinction!

12. Text in Vasilii Nikolaevich Malinin, *Starets Eleazarova Monastyria Filofei i ego poslaniia: Istoriko-literaturnoe izsliedovanie* (Kiev, 1901), app. p. 45. Among the historical studies concerned with the theory of Filofei, the best is probably that of Hildegard Schaeder, *Moskau das dritte Rom: Studien zur Geschichte der politische Theorien in der slawischen Welt*, 2d ed. (Darmstadt: H. Gentner, 1957), 82–117.

13. Interestingly, a *translatio imperii* was suggested to Ivan, not by Russians, but by the Venetian Senate: "Quando stirps mascula deesset imperatoria ad Vestram Illustrissimam Dominationem jure vestri faustissimi conjugii pertineret" (quoted in Aleksei Iakovlevich Shpakov, *Gosudarstvo i tserkov' v ikh vzaimnykh otnosheniiakh v Moskovskom gosudarstve* [Kiev, 1904], 1:43–48).

14. Text recently reprinted with commentary by Antonios-Aimilios Tachiaos, *Peges ekklesiastikes istorias ton orthodoxon Slavon* (Thessaloniki: Athon Kyriakide, 1984), 161–64. It has been shown by Vasilii Eduardovich Regel (*Analecta byzantino-russica* [St. Petersburg, 1891–98], LI–XCVIII) that the signatures of the metropolitans under the *Act* are forgeries. The document is therefore a personal composition of Patriarch Joasaph, lacking synodal approval. Eventually Joasaph was deposed for overstepping his prerogatives.

15. Texts recently reprinted in Tachiaos, *Peges*, 210–20, together with the ideologically important letters of Meletios Pegas to the new patriarch Job of Moscow and to the tsar.

16. "Oude . . . di'allon tina logon . . , ei me pros ta ton basileion axiomata," *Tomos* of 1593, Tachiaos, *Peges*, 218; and for the preceding quotation 210–11.

17. Tachiaos, *Peges*, 219. There is no special study in English on the events and conditions

of the establishment of the Russian patriarchate. The most authoritative Russian study is by Aleksei Iakovlevich Shpakov, *Gosudarstvo i tserkov' v ikh vzaimnykh otnosheniakh v Moskovskom gosudarstve: Tsarstvovanie Fedora Ivanovicha: Uchrezhdenie patriarshestva v Rossii* (Odessa, 1912); see also an account in Anton V. Kartashev, *Ocherki po istorii russkoi tserkvi*, 2 vols. (Paris: YMCA-Press, 1959), 2:10–47. The original versified description of the events by the Greek archbishop of Elasson, Arsenios, who accompanied Patriarch Jeremiah on his trip to Russia, has been reprinted in Tachiaos, *Peges*, 168–209.

18. There are fundamental pre-Revolutionary Russian studies on the subject; see particularly Vladimir Stepanovich Ikonnikov, *Opyt izsliedovaniia o kul'turnom znachenii Vizantii v russkoi istorii* (Kiev, 1869), Andrei Nikolaevich Murav'ev, *Snosheniia Rossii s vostokom po delam tserkovnym* (St. Petersburg, 1858), and Nikolai Fedorovich Kapterev, *Kharakter otnoshenii Rossii k pravoslavnomu Vostoku v XVI i XVII stolietiiakh* (Sergiev Posad: Izdanie Knizhnago Magazina M. S. Elova, 1914). The first part of Georges Florovsky's *Ways of Russian Theology*, trans. Robert L. Nichols (Belmont, Mass.: Nordland, 1979), is also full of interesting observations concerning the intellectual history of Russia's relations with the "Christian East."

19. There is an abundant secondary literature on Maximus, which is referred to in the brilliant portrait of him drawn recently by Dimitri Obolensky, *Six Byzantine Portraits* (Oxford: Clarendon Press, 1988), 201–19. See also Jack V. Haney, *From Italy to Muscovy: The Life and Works of Maxim the Greek* (Munich: W. Fink, 1973). Maximus's writings and translations include over 365 titles (see A. I. Ivanov, *Literaturnoe nasledie Maksima Greka* [Leningrad: Izdatel'stvo "Nauka," 1969], 39–215), of which only half are published, in an uncritical edition (*Sochineniia prepodobnago Maksima Greka*, 3 vols. in 2 [Kazan, 1859–62]).

20. *Sochineniia prepodobnago Maksima Greka*, 2:319–37.

21. The study by Kapterev (see above, n. 18) contains the most complete information about Nikon's policies. See also Pierre Pascal, *Avvakum et les débuts du Raskol* (1938; rpt. Paris: Mouton, 1963).

22. Texts in Tachiaos, *Peges*, 227–31 and 234–64. The council was attended by the patriarchs Paisios of Alexandria and Macarius of Antioch, as well as by several other Greek prelates.

23. See the excellent recent study by Stephen K. Batalden, *Catherine II's Greek Prelate: Eugenios Voulgaris in Russia (1771–1806)* (Boulder, Colo.: East European Monographs, 1982).

GENDER DIFFERENTIATION AND SOCIAL PRACTICE IN POST-BYZANTINE NAXOS

Aglaia E. Kasdagli

Problems and Sources

IN JUNE 1689 a public warning was posted "in all usual and prominent places" of the capital of Naxos, an island of the Cyclades, in the Aegean Sea. It was signed by mastro Vasilis Lemonitis, a craftsman, and was directed to his wife. His complaint was that, without consulting her husband, she had secretly settled her entire dowry property on her daughter by a first marriage and had not left anything aside for the two children she had had by him. She had no right to do this, the furious husband declared, because "I am the head of my wife and I am the master of her property and I am the one who will go to collect her share of the harvest and it is for this property that I married her."[1]

The end of the story is not on record, but this unique direct contemporary testimony of how the woman's place was perceived is of particular importance for the theme of this paper. The surviving written records reflecting some important aspects of the life of women on Naxos in the seventeenth century provide us with the opportunity to reconstruct, albeit partially and tentatively, the social realities that confronted women in the Greek world of that period, and to note certain links between these realities and those of the Byzantine past.

The problems attending such an investigation are well known. Since the proper place of women has traditionally been considered to be far from the public limelight, their role has been consistently depreciated, constrained, and given accessory status. Until recently historians did not question these biases. Today attempts to redress the balance are often frustrated by the historical records themselves, most of which present the experiences and characteristics of women as subordinate to those of the men, who dominated the scene and compiled the documents.[2]

The case of Naxos is no exception. The source material reflects primarily the interests of males acting for themselves or as representatives of the female members of their families. None of the extant notarial acts was composed or even signed by a woman. On the other hand, the male bias in these documents is a reflection of actual conditions and attitudes, not the prejudice of individuals. It should also be noted that, in principle at least, the women of Naxos enjoyed legal rights of a wide range and thus appear in the sources in a systematic way.

The Byzantine material presents its own problems, with the consequence that the position of women in Byzantium is one of the many aspects of Byzantine social history that are very inadequately known. Some recent monographs offer valuable information about female activities that are linked to a specific time and place. Generalizations are meaningless, however, since these would only result in the fictitious portrait of a timeless and classless Byzantine woman, in which the significant variations between town and country, and between the Asiatic and European provinces, would be ignored.[3]

It is probably safe to assume that many features of the Naxian society were broadly characteristic of other Greek communities existing under comparable geographic and economic conditions. They had in common a Byzantine inheritance, but in the post-Byzantine period we observe significant variations, partly explained by their different historical experiences (whose impact, however, gradually diminished). Even so, one should not lose sight of the common themes that have run through preindustrial Greek communities since at least Byzantine times.

Regrettably, regional comparisons cannot be taken far, because hard evidence from the early centuries of Turkish rule is extremely scarce, and most scholars have concentrated on the last decades before the Greek War of Independence of 1821. The exceptionally rich archives of certain regions (including the Cyclades, Crete, and the Ionian Islands) have not been explored systematically, but two recent articles about women in Venetian Crete give a tantalizing glimpse into the potential of these sources. Not much is revealed about peasant women—even though they were by far the largest group—but urban life surfaces with liveliness and vigor.[4]

Very few Greek urban centers of that time can be compared with the cosmopolitan and sophisticated towns of Venetian Crete, with their substantial commercial and artisan elements and comfortable middle and upper classes, who followed Italian fashions. Nevertheless the Cretan woman of every class had much in common with her contemporaries elsewhere. She was similarly subjected to her parents and, later, to her husband; she might lose several of her children, or have to face the all too common hardships of widowhood, or the risk of death at childbirth. And along with the rest of the Greek population throughout the Ottoman period, she was a frequent victim of epidemics, piracy, and warfare.

One type of source offering an overview of social life in post-Byzantine Greece is the accounts written by Western European visitors to the Levant. In the absence of other readily available information, parallels drawn from these travel records may be illuminating, if we keep in mind their limitations. For one thing, their geographical range in the early period is confined largely to the islands, Athens, and Constantinople. Most travelers were not particularly accurate as reporters, and even those who had some interest in the everyday life of the local populations lacked the time and means of communicating with people who inevitably viewed and treated them as outsiders.

It is therefore not surprising that some of their stories give conflicting evidence. A notable example is their treatment of the women of Chios; their beauty, grace, and winning manners were generally acknowledged, but comments on their morality range from the sweeping claim that Chian husbands were regular pimps, offering their wives to any stranger, to high praise for the women's "inner beauty and virtue."[5]

Generally the travel accounts abound in stereotypes and present women mostly in terms of their physical beauty and moral virtue. Nevertheless they provide some evocative glimpses into their daily lives. We can see the wrinkled and emaciated old women of fifteenth-century Paros as they climb, heavily loaded but with apparent ease, the steep hill leading to the fortress of Kefalos;[6] the magnificent wedding of a wealthy Greek merchant in Galata, with the bride seated on a gilded throne among smart and bejeweled women who listen to the solemn wedding songs in complete silence and immobility;[7] the women of the islands lamenting their dead;[8] or the women of Chios passing an evening on their doorsteps, chatting with their neighbors, singing and observing the passers-by.[9] An incident that impressed an English visitor to Kea in 1670 is characteristic of the conditions in which Greek peasants lived until recently. One morning a woman, pregnant and with a child in her arms, went to the fields to gather acorns; there she gave birth, and in the evening she brought home both children.[10]

Naxos in the Seventeenth Century

The links of the Cyclades with the Byzantine Empire had been formally severed at an early date, in the aftermath of the Fourth Crusade. The Duchy of the Archipelago, founded by the Venetian Marco Sanudo in 1207, comprised a dozen islands, with Naxos as its capital. It lasted for three and a half centuries, a period marked by the growing infiltration of Venice into the Levant, the counteracting Ottoman expansion, and the final collapse of Byzantium. The Cyclades were integrated into the Ottoman Empire only in 1566, but in the course of the seventeenth century the region was once more thrown into disorder by two long Turco-Venetian wars (1645–69 and 1685–99); for much of that time the islands were virtually under Venetian control.[11]

The population of Naxos during the seventeenth century is estimated at between six thousand and seven thousand, of whom a small minority (about 5%) were Latins, the Catholic descendants of Western Europeans. There were also a few Muslims, never more than seventy, most of them recent converts to Islam, and a few Turkish officials. The common language was Greek.

The inhabitants were dispersed among some forty villages or hamlets, most of them on the hilly interior of the island, and the town of Naxos, whose inhabitants included craftsmen, merchants, and mariners, as well as landowners and direct agricultural producers. All peasants and the majority of townspeople were Greek Orthodox. Almost all Latins lived at the Kastro, the fortified old part of the town; from this group came the so-called lords and ladies—big landowners, many of whom exercised seigneurial rights over extensive areas of land.

The economy was based on mixed arable and livestock farming. The main products were barley and wheat, wine, legumes, figs, and olives, along with some cotton, flax, silk, honey, nuts, and acorns. Owing to the lack of a good harbor, Naxos was not as prominent a commercial center as some of the other Cyclades. Nevertheless the relatively high customs duties of the island highlight the importance of its exports of agricultural and livestock surpluses. There is evidence of regular contacts with the outside world—principally with Constantinople and Smyrna, but also with Crete and other parts of the Aegean.

Information about the economic and social life of the island in the period under examination comes mainly from more than three thousand notarial acts, most of them unpublished. They include records of sales and of donations of real property, contracts for the cultivation of land, wills, marriage contracts, mortgages, settlements of debts and of disputes, testimonies about a great variety of incidents, and a few contracts of service, apprenticeship, and commercial partnership.

The legal system in force in seventeenth-century Naxos is of major importance for our investigation, but limitations of space permit no more than the briefest outline of its main features as they emerge from notarial sources. It is of further interest in that it offers some insights into the broader cultural inheritance of Naxian society.

A Byzantine descent is easily discerned in legal matters and may be partly explained by the common customary basis of the two systems. Another decisive influence, which reinforced and updated the Byzantine legal tradition, was the Orthodox Church.[12] It should be noted, however, that the judicial role of the Orthodox clergy was not as important in Naxos as in most parts of the Greek-speaking world, because their authority was seriously checked by a powerful landowning class, whose members were overwhelmingly Latins and in alliance with the Catholic clergy and missionaries.

Very little evidence survives from the ecclesiastical courts, and this concerns mostly cases referring to family law. Parallel to canon law, and prevalent for the regulation of most social relations and for the decisions taken by both communal judges and arbitrators, was customary law, as it had developed over the centuries, continuously modifying and readapting itself. The influence of Islamic law seems to have been minimal in the Cyclades. Although the islanders at times had recourse to Ottoman justice, one of the important privileges granted to them through successive charters (*ahdname*) was the freedom "to follow their own erroneous law."[13]

The possibility of the influence of Western European law must also be taken into account. Before the Ottoman conquest the Assizes of Romania were applied in the Duchy of Naxos. This Frankish code, however, expressed the law of the feudatories and had little to do with their Greek subjects, for whom old laws and local customs had been largely upheld. Thus it is not surprising that any direct impact the Assizes might have had at the time of the dukes did not long outlive their rule. But inevitably some Western elements found their way into the body of oral customary law.[14]

The Ideological Background

Direct information on the ruling beliefs affecting social relations, and in particular the position of women, in Naxos is scarce, but there are many signs of the strong influence exercised by the teachings of the Orthodox

Church, upheld and perpetuated throughout the Byzantine period, teachings that arguably "played a key role in defining the female image and bolstering the values incorporated in the social and economic structures which discriminate against women."[15] If nothing else, everybody would have been familiar with St. Paul's description of the proper role and status of women, and in particular with his injunctions that were (and still are) an integral part of the Orthodox marriage ceremony: "Wives submit to your husbands as to the Lord. For the husband is the head of the wife as Christ is the head of the Church. . . . Now as the Church submits to Christ, so also wives should submit to their husbands in everything. . . . And the wife must respect her husband" (Eph. 5.22–33).

A similar source of inspiration must have been contemporary religious tracts and homilies, which in turn reflected current attitudes. An example is the *Salvation of the Sinners*, a didactic book by the Athonite monk Agapios, first published in Venice in 1641. Even though references to books are extremely rare in our sources, we learn from them that at least two copies of this popular edifying work had found their way onto Naxos.[16]

The book's treatment of women is often colored by the author's predictable attitude to sexual intercourse, which he calls "a brief pleasure, lewd enjoyment" (p. 32) and an abominable crime if not aimed at procreation. The only way to avoid the deadly sin is to avoid women altogether. "Never look a woman in the face, never speak to her with familiarity and sympathy . . . because it is impossible for anybody to be near a woman and remain collected," Agapios advises (p. 34). Such admonitions, however, refer to the nature of the relationship between women and men, rather than to any inherent female wickedness.[17] As a matter of course the author provides examples of saintly, as well as sinful, individuals of both sexes, but inevitably he lapses into well-worn stereotypes. Thus in one of his stories he seems to agree with Satan, who maintained that even though men cheat one another, women are generally more sinful, for four reasons: first, by making up their faces they pretend to be better-looking than the Lord made them to be; second, they nourish all sorts of prejudice and engage in witchcraft and fortune-telling; third, they clatter and are loud not only at home but also in church; and finally, out of ignorance or guile they often do not confess fully (p. 196).

Aspects of Everyday Life in Town and Countryside

Male perceptions do not provide the best means of approaching the reality of women's lives. The attempt to reconstruct this reality will be better served through the use of "objective" evidence, which can tell us something about female property and other legal rights, and about women in the family, in the community, and at work.

The picture that emerges from sporadic glimpses into the everyday lives of women is a familiar one. Loquacious accounts of witnesses describing various incidents serve to define the separate spheres within which women and men functioned. In the town, for example, male activities and social life were concentrated near the harbor and in or near the workshops-cum-shops in the marketplace. Women apparently spent most of the time in their neighborhoods, whether in the house or outside.

The women of the upper—Catholic—classes, if we are to believe an account written in 1643 by a Jesuit, led a secluded and rather dull existence. Remarkable for their purity, chastity, and sweet sobriety, these pious ladies hardly ever left the house when in town, except to go to church or pay the prescribed social visits. With a single exception, they could neither read nor write, and their main occupation was sewing and embroidery.[18]

Female confinement indoors is mentioned by many travelers to Greece. We hear that in Crete women went out only on feast days or when the weather was very hot; that in Rhodes young women were never seen in public, not even in church; that the Greek girls of Pera in Constantinople rarely went out, and that even prostitutes were difficult to talk to.[19] Nevertheless a careful examination of the evidence reveals that such confinement was a partial, urban and upper-class phenomenon. It has a close parallel in the Byzantine tradition of $\theta\alpha\lambda\acute{\alpha}\mu\epsilon\upsilon\sigma\iota\varsigma$, which was also far from universal.[20] In the case of Naxos, moreover, the great ladies led a much freer life when out of town—which was often, since they and their families spent several months of the year in their countryside "towers," near their estates.

Lesser townswomen are regularly encountered in the streets, sitting on doorsteps, chatting with passers-by. Much socializing took place in the open, and quarrels were an inevitable part of it. While men would fight with fists, swords, and firearms, women would resort to slandering each other, to great effect. We hear, however, of a furious townswoman who attacked a neighbor's servant girl and cut off her plaits, and this was undoubtedly not the only case of female violence. Close contact between neighbors played a major role in social life: one female witness was able to provide detailed testimony about another woman's marital quarrels, as well as about her chattels, which she listed individually, asserting that she knew what she was talking about because as neighbors they used to see each other daily.[21]

Domestic servants were quite common in town, but, with or without their help, most women had to perform a wide variety of specifically "female" duties, including domestic chores, child rearing, looking after the old, the infirm and the dying, and attending the dead.[22]

Women in town must also have spent much time preparing their own and later their daughters' trousseaux, which involved weaving and plain sewing, as well as fine embroidery. By contrast, the trousseaux of peasant women (containing minimal furnishings and items of clothing) suggest that women in the countryside were not confined to the home and domestic labor but played an important role in the subsistence economy and the production of economic surplus. It is evident that rural women helped with all types of agricultural work and were not occupied only with traditional "female" tasks such as fetching water and firewood, looking after the yard animals, or tending the kitchen garden. In a peasant economy in which the family as a whole formed the unit of production, economic roles were only broadly defined by gender.[23] Thus we hear of a poor woman hired to help at harvest time, of women involved in harvesting beans or in grape picking and pressing, and of plowgirls (and boys) twelve years of age.

Women only rarely figure in contracts of sharecropping as the person in charge, and then, with one exception, it is jointly with a male. In practice, if they were widows or if their husbands were working abroad they were quite often left to cope on their own. Seasonal or long-term absences of men were a regular feature of Greek communities throughout the Ottoman period. Many males emigrated in search of employment, others became sailors or merchants, and others were conscripted into the Ottoman navy. The women of Santorini cultivated the land while their husbands were away in Chios or Venice, while the male Cretan peasants were frequently required to leave their holdings and work either on fortifications or as rowers in Venetian galleys.[24] The high rate of male mobility suggests that despite the widely accepted social ideals and stereotypes, women were very frequently required—and able—to bear the entire responsibility for the family and even be its sole provider for long periods.

Female wage earners seem to have been common, but there are few references to a woman's profession other than that of domestic service. We know only of a couple of midwives, a female baker, a charcoalmaker, a woman who was paying off her debts by embroidering for the lender's family, and another who took in washing. In fact there is hardly any information on wage earners of either sex, and absolutely none for retail traders, making it impossible to find out whether women played an important role in retail trading, as they did in Byzantium and in the medieval West.[25]

Evidence from other parts of contemporary Greece testifies to the wide range of women's economic activities. From Chios specifically female handicrafts (cotton and silk textiles, knitted stockings and purses, embroidered shawls, belts, and silk ribbons) were exported throughout the Levant, and we are told that on the arrival of foreign ships the women went to the port to display and sell their products. The Greek women of Romylia sold foodstuffs in the streets to the passing caravans; their wares included fruit and eggs but also prepared food such as bread, drinks of hot sweetened milk, and roast meat. The women of Icaria could swim for over a mile to reach the ships anchored off their island, carrying above the water basketfuls of fruit for sale.[26]

Notarial evidence from Venetian Crete reveals that women were active in various trades. Weaving is the most commonly encountered occupation, and as early as the fourteenth century we see two female silk-weavers running their own business and taking in a young girl as an apprentice. Other women were tailors, tanners, cobblers, or tavernkeepers, or followed traditional female trades as midwives, practical doctors (as well as witches), wet nurses, or domestic servants (whose wages were two to three times lower than those of their male counterparts).[27] Large numbers of urban women were involved in prostitution as brothel owners, prostitutes, or procuresses.[28]

Whenever they had enough property and some control over it, women appear to have been as business-minded as men. In Naxos no woman involved in long-distance trade appears in the few commercial documents that survive, but the Jesuit chronicler mentions a Latin lady shipping her wine to be sold abroad. In Crete we find women investing money in commercial ventures and lending cash or agricultural products such as wheat and wine to peasants whose supplies had run short and who undertook to return the loan after the harvest.[29]

Marriage and Family

Marriages were commonly arranged by the two sets of parents, or by other relatives if the intended spouses were orphaned and young. The consent of both partners was necessary and is often explicitly mentioned. Examples of open abuses, however, suggest that the common formula found in contracts from Venetian Crete, in which the fathers of the partners promise to *make* the daughter or son accept the proposed spouse, is probably indicative of how such consent was perceived.[30]

The arranging of children's marriages was often part of a general family strategy, a practice not confined to families at the highest social level.[31] Clearly the personal preferences of the prospective partners were not taken into account as a matter of course, and women often appear in the sources as passive while business matters and conflicts centering on them were debated and settled by the male members of their families. Thus in the detailed account by an eye witness of an attempted abduction by a young man and a band of his companions, the intended victim hardly figures; not even her name is on record, let alone her reaction or possible involvement. She is simply referred to as "the girl," who during the imbroglio was sent away by her father, to be hidden by a friendly neighbor.[32]

Obviously the parents' power as dowry-givers was of crucial importance for the relations between the generations and the smooth functioning of the social system. Property settled on young people before marriage was always given on condition that the female beneficiaries would not "suffer misfortune" ("shaming her body," as a father explains the euphemism), and that, whether male or female, they would be obedient to the parents (or other property-giver) and marry with their consent.

That this was not always an idle threat is illustrated in the case of the notary Pandoleon Miniatis, who was determined to disinherit his "accursed daughter" Marieta, "because she married without my consent and proved disobedient and I do not confirm the contract she has and says her mother made for her." From other testimony we learn that Marieta had eloped with a French soldier who deflowered her and married her only later; after his departure she had a string of lovers and later settled down with yet another soldier. Notwithstanding his customary obligation to give a share of the patrimony to each of his children, Miniatis makes it clear that his daughter, having overstepped the social norms by her unrestrained behavior, could no longer claim their protection.[33]

Only two (less than 2%) of the female testators seem to have been single. This may be because women who had no property, and who therefore may not have been able to afford to marry and set up house, were the ones not likely to leave any record. Such seems to have been the case with certain servants. Some women of propertied families also never married, especially if there were several daughters, for whom it could be difficult to provide adequate dowries and husbands of suitable status.

For many poor girls the only outlet was emigration, and even married women at times went abroad with their husbands in search of seasonal or other temporary employment. Unmarried women who stayed in Naxos had fewer options than men, and the problem was particularly acute since female monasticism hardly existed on the island. Throughout the seventeenth century very few Greek nuns are mentioned. An equally small number of Latin women kept vows of chastity while living at home, or were sent to the Dominican convent at Santorini.[34]

The minimal role played by religious establishments for women was obviously at variance with the Byzantine tradition but was typical of the Ottoman period.[35] At a time when ecclesiastical institutions were virtually the sole providers of learning on the elementary level, the absence of women's monasteries in Naxos may partly explain why female illiteracy was apparently universal in a society in which literacy was not confined to an exclusive elite, at least not in town.[36]

A large percentage of the women appearing in the sources were widows. Up to a point this is because married women were more likely to leave the management of their affairs in the hands of their husbands. But it is also true that marriages were frequently disrupted by premature deaths, and that 37 percent of all female testators were widowed, as against 16 percent of the males.[37]

The situation of widows is commented upon in the Jesuit chronicle. We are told that according to local custom, people in mourning for a close relative, particularly if they were women ("who are the most obstinate"), did not enter the church for years, and that consequently the Fathers had to conduct special services at daybreak, which the mourners could attend without being seen. Although he disapproved, the author allowed that there was some justification for this practice, since there would always be a bystander ready to tattle that a widow—especially if she was young—was eager to remarry.[38]

Widows were conspicuous in traditional Greek communities, and their plight is masterfully represented in a folk song: "The widow stays indoors but there is talk of her without. If she walks humbly they tell her that she is proud, and if she walks fast they tell her that she is out of her mind; if she speaks to anybody they tell her that she is looking for a man; if she spins with her distaff they tell her that she makes preparations for her trousseau; and if she ever becomes ill they tell her that she is expecting a child."[39]

Illicit liaisons do not seem to have been extraordinary, even if socially unacceptable. Most known instances are established by implication, through references to illegitimate offspring. "Natural" or even "bastard" children are often mentioned as accepted members of the community, but a women sexually active out of wedlock was not viewed without censure.

The Jesuit chronicler noted with some complacency that the ladies of the town were paragons of purity and chastity; bastards (and there were many of them) were found only among servants and other low-class females. In applying typical double standards, he failed to mention that Latin aristocrats (including priests) had fathered many of those children.[40] Moreover, illicit love was by no means confined to women of the lowest classes: it reached as high as the Koronellos family, at the top of the Latin social hierarchy. The same author relates that Benetina Koronellou eloped with a Turk, cohabited with him, and gave birth to his daughter. The ending of this story betrays a different set of double standards; being a Koronellos was presumably enough to erase any blot, for some years later Benetina is seen respectably married to a Catholic of good family.[41]

The one recorded instance of extramarital activities in the villages demonstrates that moral standards could give way anywhere. Our source is a string of testimonies concerning the sexual feats of a Greek priest, the σακελλάριος of the villages of Drymalia, who had a neglected wife (we hear of her starving downstairs while her husband feasted with another woman upstairs) and three long-term mistresses. One of these was the wife of a fellow priest, and her conduct was said to have brought her husband such shame and grief that he became ill and died; another was "the village whore," a stranger with no family in Naxos, who had a child by him; the third, whom her father and other relatives had rejected and left to go hungry, also had a child by him.[42]

The woman's honor was highly prized everywhere in the Greek world and strictly guarded—at least in theory. In Naxos a jealous husband threatened to bring to justice a French visitor who had had an inordinately long conversation with the Naxian's wife.[43] In Athens, Greek women convicted of adultery either paid a high fine or were put in the pillory and forced to ride a donkey through the streets of the town facing backwards (a lenient punishment, considering that in the same place Turkish adulteresses were condemned to death by drowning). Girls suspected of having illicit affairs were subjected to physical examination by a midwife, and if found deflowered were sold as slaves, unless their parents gave a generous bribe to the Ottoman official.[44] In Zakynthos the nuptial bedsheets were put on display as a proof of the bride's virginity, and the custom of Chios demanded a tax on sexual inactivity from widows who did not remarry.[45]

Divorce does not seem to have been very difficult to obtain from the Greek Church so long as there was a valid reason—including even incompatibility and mutual unwillingness to continue the marriage. If need be, legal reasons could also be devised. For instance, a parent's acting as godparent to his or her own child (which created a spiritual bond between the spouses and made their marital relationship incestuous) seems to have served as an excuse for divorce regularly since Byzantine times. Other recorded grounds for divorce include a man's absence of more than five years (during which he had sent neither a letter or message nor a remittance); a husband's wish to become a monk; a marriage contracted while either partner was minor or unwilling; a husband's permanent extramarital relationship; adultery committed by the wife; male impotence lasting for more than four years; insanity.[46]

The financial arrangements following a divorce were not usually spelled out, as each partner had definite and inalienable rights to his or her own property. The only information on the maintenance of children in such an event occurs in the annulment of a marriage by the ecclesiastical court for reason of affinity within the prohibited degree. The woman was pregnant, and it was decreed that both parents should contribute equally to the upkeep of the child.[47]

The central social importance of the family is obvious from the sources. It is much more difficult to establish how people perceived the role of the woman within the family, how she was treated, and what authority she exercised on a daily basis, since attitudes and emotions usually elude documentation. Undoubtedly the way in which the spouses treated each other, and the balance of power between the sexes, varied considerably.

A portrait of the ideal wife is given in the will of Zuanes Girardis, a Catholic gentleman who left all property still in his hands to his second wife because she had raised his five orphaned children, waited on him in every illness and other need, looked after him, and supported him with her labor, her wise housekeeping, and the revenues of her lands. Conversely, a rare example of direct negative judgment on a partner is found in the will of Katerina Theologiti, a widow from the town. She attributes the diminution of her dowry and the deprivations suffered by her children to the misdeeds of her late husband, who, among other things, sold six of her rings and used the proceeds to enjoy a holiday on Paros with his chum.[48]

There are further indications of love and harmony, as well as of misery and discord. We even hear of a battered husband, a villager who brought his complaint before the ecclesiastical court after three years of marriage.[49] Wives of course would have been less likely to make an issue of such incidents, but they did not always accept them meekly. One gentle-woman, infuriated at some cuffs she had received from her husband, locked him out of the house and subsequently sent away his belongings. Separation was avoided only through the good services of intermediaries, and we are told that both Latins and Greeks were greatly shocked—apparently not by the beating but by the wife's violent reaction to it.[50]

It can hardly be accidental that this particular woman belonged to the upper class. There are indications that wealthy women were often more assertive than their humbler sisters in regard to their property and its disposition, if for no other reason than because such issues were likely to subside when the main concern was the family's subsistence.

Dowry and Inheritance

Since the women of Naxos are best documented as property holders, a detailed examination of their activities in this respect may give valuable insight into their life and position.

Dowry contracts were the main instrument for the transmission of property, because marriage was the critical point at which both women and men received their share of the family inheritance. This process of premortem bilateral inheritance affected females, males, and their respec-tive families in exactly the same way, other things being equal. The term *dowry* (πουρκί or προύκα) was used for the marriage portions of both partners, and this is not surprising, for they had the same fundamental characteristics.[51]

The fact that both partners received marriage portions consisting of movable and immovable property does not mean that there were no differences of emphasis between the sexes. The content of dowry not only differed according to the economic and social status of the beneficiary but also conformed to the functions that society assigned to each sex.

The first item given to a bride in most instances (90% of the total) was a dwelling place, while many bridegrooms (about 62%) were also endowed with a house that could serve as chief residence. The young couple was in the vast majority of cases to set up an independent house-hold; but significantly this was more often than not in the wife's house and locality, even when both partners were provided with a dwelling place. This meant that a woman was likely to live near her parents, sisters, and other relatives and thus have a network of her own relations at hand; concomitantly, it was the daughter who looked after the aged parents.

Land was a necessity for everybody who could afford it, and we find it in about 96 percent of both female and male contracts. In contrast, money characterized a new, rising class, and it is mostly among the towns-people of middling social status that one in three women and men pre-sented cash or credit in their dowries.

Livestock is a more sensitive economic and social index, as it reflects a marked difference between the sexes, as well as occupational differences between the middle and lower classes. On the whole, animals figure in over one half of all marriage contracts, but the proportion of the receivers is 52 percent of all women and 67 percent of all men, presumably because animal husbandry and the closely linked agricultural labor were considered predominantly male concerns.[52]

Some chattels were indispensable for the brides of all social classes, although with great variations in both quantity and quality. A man's movables might not differ from the trousseau given to a bride of similar status, but this was not the norm; his chattels were directly related to the existence or absence of sisters, who enjoyed preferential treatment in this respect.

The fund established at marriage was family property, in the sense that all members of the nuclear family were entitled to a share for mainte-nance and the means to set up in life, as well as to a portion in the event of division. It was managed by the husband while he was living, but he was not to dispose of it at will—a notion emphatically reinforced in regard to the wife's contribution to it.

A woman's legal possession of her dowry was recognized by both Byzantine and later canon law, and the principle is so common that it has been claimed that "the regime of separation of goods [is] implicit in the dotal marriage."[53] The status of female property in Naxos is amply illus-trated. A case in point is the will of a widow who divided her property among her children and left to the son only a parcel of land coming from his father. The accompanying statement suggests that she considered the son—presumably as representative of the male line in the family—to be morally responsible for his father's excesses, which had reduced the patri-mony: "If the male child sets up a quarrel [with his sisters for a fairer redistribution of the property], let him first give the money for what his father sold, since a woman's dowry is protected" (τὸ προυκὶ τῆς γυναίκας εἶναι σιδεροκέφαλο).[54]

In this and other examples one sees that, despite the apparent similarities between female and male dowries, there is a preoccupation with the woman's protection and financial security—a response no doubt to the vulnerable and dependent position of women in the family and in society. Thus it should not come as a surprise that a cobbler and his wife in straitened circumstances gave a token dowry to each of their sons (who would be better able than the daughters to fend for themselves—one at least seems to have followed his father's craft) and asked them to waive any further claims in favor of their sisters.[55]

The woman's consent was necessary for the alienation of any part of her dowry or other patrimony, even if such assets were to be settled on one of her children. If the wife was not present when a contract of alienation was drawn up, the husband had to present witnesses, produce a written document giving him power of attorney, or make a declaration to the effect that she was in agreement. This is what Zuanes Yustinianis, a wealthy Latin aristocrat, confirmed twice when settling a dowry on his daughter; four years later, however, he stated formally that the contract—which included property belonging to his wife—was drawn up while she was away in the country and knew nothing of his plans. In a subsequent deed his lady stressed that, since the dowry had been given without her prior consent, she had the right to annul the contract and would do so should her grandson (heir of the deceased daughter) prove disobedient.[56]

There might be the odd reverse case, too, like that of the woman who dowered her daughter with both maternal and paternal property while her husband was away. What followed was apparently marital hell, and the injured husband would have won his case and taken back his possessions had not his wife been the lover of a Turkish official, who intervened and forced him to confirm the contract. Even in this instance the solution was to be imposed by males holding power—namely, the judges or the lover.[57]

This was perhaps an exceptional case, but we find many references to similar actions by men, and, whatever the laws and formulas say, one can never find out with what means a man might have persuaded or even forced his wife to give her consent. A last case in point concerns mastro Stefanis Lemonitis, a craftsman, whose attitude is suggestive of male high-handedness. According to the testimonies of several women, not only did he appropriate some of his wife's clothes after her death, but he also bartered—while she was living—the wine of her vineyard for an orchard which he kept for himself. "They quarreled all the time because he was buying property in his name, while the money came from the revenues from her land," the women reported.[58]

The idea that dowry forms "part of the conjugal estate to be enjoyed by husband and wife and transmitted in time to their children"[59] is accurately reflected in the formula of marriage contracts whereby the givers promise the dowry to the groom, the bride, and the children they are going to have together. An unequivocal term of settlement is that "if [the couple] have legitimate children of their body everything will go to [the children]."[60] But "if it chance—God forbid—that they die without issue," some variation might be possible, even though the overriding principle was that the property reverted to the next of kin (πρόξιμοι, σιμότεροι ἐδικοί), not of the deceased but of the dowry-giver (which two coincided in the majority of cases).

A diachronic examination of dowry arrangements shows that in this as in other matters customary law was certainly not immutable, even though it was perceived or represented as such by those who were subject to it. In the sixteenth century the widespread practice seems to have been that the childless widow was to enjoy the revenues of her husband's property "for as long as she keeps his honor," while the widower was to retain a complete set of bedclothes (κρεβατοστρῶσι φουρνίδο) out of her goods, according to the "Romaic order" (τάξη ρωμαϊκή).[61] A common (but not universal) addition to this was that half of the property acquired after the marriage (τὰ ἀκίστα [It. *acquisti*]) would belong to the husband, and the other half to the wife.[62]

The major modification brought about during the following century is the weakening, if not the virtual abolition, of provisions for the widow's interest in her husband's property and a corresponding strengthening of the claims of the two partners' natal families. For example, we find no arrangements equivalent to the Byzantine τριμοιρία, by which, if a widower's children died after their mother, the surviving husband inherited one third of his wife's dowry.[63]

The course of the Naxian development cannot be traced with any accuracy because of gaps in the sources, but abundant evidence from the last thirty years of the seventeenth century shows that man and wife remained alien to the other's lineage throughout; the two united only in the new vertical line they themselves would create. If they produced no children, the property would be used by the collateral kin, perpetuating their separate vertical lines.

The separation of goods between the spouses had direct implications for women's lives, for it encouraged women as much as men to maintain close links with their respective families. As potential heirs, whose rights extended over four generations, the kin of the original couple had a lively if latent interest in the property of the latter; and, given the demographic situation, there were always good chances of the property's ending in the hands of parents and eventually siblings or, in the absence of these, an assortment of more distant relations.[64]

Acquired property is no longer specifically mentioned in the seventeenth-century contracts, but it seems that in most cases it was still considered to be jointly held, with each partner owning half.[65] There are many references to joint property, often accompanied by such remarks as, "bought through our joint efforts," or, "We worked together so that we could buy this." The inheritance of a peasant woman who died intestate was shared by her three children, but the widower kept his half of three bought fields. Moreover, he retained out of his children's portions the value of his wife's share of the debt that they had incurred in order to buy the land. In the town a woman of limited means left to her husband her share of the goods they had acquired together—a small house, six animals, and a few chattels.[66] These examples show how the picture of property relations between husband and wife that emerges from marriage contracts can be complemented by an examination of wills, in which the partners could make some choices within the customary limits.

Not many testators made provisions for general executors in their wills, but of those who did, wives often appointed their husbands, while in only two examples are women nominated as executors: a man appointed his wife, and a woman her husband together with one of her daughters. Men with young unmarried children, however, frequently left their spouses responsible for the administration of their property and the apportionment to offspring. Sometimes the usufruct of all or part of the property was left to the survivor for life or until remarriage. A gentlewoman left interest in a plot of land to her husband on condition that he should not take "either a legitimate wife or a mistress openly."[67]

Husbands and wives were often willing enough to leave something to their partner, but, as with every alienation of property to outsiders, the givers were anxious to stress that they were absolute masters or mistresses of the particular asset, free to do with it as they pleased. A detailed, although somewhat formulaic, justification would be given: special services were recalled, or the bequest was said to have been offered as repayment of debts or for the maintainance of the donor. Thus a peasant left to his second wife a field, some bees, his oxen, and all his chattels because after they had married they had worked together and with her labor and toil had repaid a debt that he had contracted with his first wife.[68] In cases like this, one can often discern behind the formulas a sense of genuine companionship in marriage, no doubt encouraged by the wife's material contribution to it.

Although parents were under a strong customary obligation to transmit the family property to their children and furthermore to every one of them (unless there was justified dissatisfaction), they were free to determine the relative value of each portion.[69] An examination of wills in which people apportioned to all their unmarried children will show whether there were gender-related patterns in the allocation of shares.

A notable tendency was to follow the practice whereby female property was inherited by females and male property by males, even though not in absolute terms, as it ran counter to the custom that each child had rights to a share of the property of both parents. In all social classes we find testators who bequeathed little or nothing at all (sometimes with the expressed consent of the affected parties) to children of the opposite sex.[70] An example is the wills of two craftsmen's wives who made identical provisions: all their modest property (house, fields, chattels) would go to the only daughter, except for a plot of land that would be the son's portion of the maternal estate.[71]

Clearly an ideal of basic equality among offspring existed in matters of inheritance, but we have seen that when limited resources or social constraints made choices inevitable, priority would be given to the female over the male children. Furthermore preferential treatment was often awarded to the eldest daughter—and most probably to the eldest son, too, but the evidence is less conclusive here.

This preference was closely linked to the idea not simply that firstborn sons will continue the family (i.e., paternal) line, which is common enough in many societies, but also that first daughters will continue the mother's—or more accurately the female—line. The perpetuation of the lines was materialized through two interlinked processes—the transmission of property and the transmission of baptismal name. The custom of Naxos was that the first daughter should be named after her maternal grandmother and the first son after the paternal grandfather. The next boy and girl would create secondary lines, taking the name of the maternal grandfather and paternal grandmother respectively. This system, reflecting a strongly bilateral ideology of descent, was consistently adhered to.

A grandchild was expected to inherit some of the property that originally belonged to the grandparent whose namesake she or he was. Thus, the mother's dowry house, passed on to her by her own mother, would be ideally transmitted to the first daughter, named after her maternal grandmother, and the same two names would alternate in the house from one generation to the next as the female line continued.[72]

It is impossible to say how far back the Naxian pattern goes, but it is still common in the Cyclades and the Dodecanese.[73] It contrasts with that prevalent in most parts of Greece, where both female and male first children are named after the paternal grandparents and only the subsequent two after the maternal ones. In these basically patrilineal societies daughters have traditionally had limited inheritance rights; the family house passes on from father to son, and it is the son's wife, not the daughter, who looks after the aged parents.[74]

Female Rights: Some Implications

Will-making is a good example of female legal rights because the evidence suggests that women were as likely as men to dispose of their property in this way. In all, 98 of the surviving wills were made by women, as against 100 made by men and 11 made jointly by couples.[75]

More importantly, there is no suggestion of distinctive "female" traits in most of the basic aspects of will-making. Variants in our documents are principally linked to factors unrelated to gender (such as the testator's age or class), and an interesting possibility is that, even within the restrictive framework of a patriarchal society, the equal property rights of women, involving similar obligations and interests to those of men, mitigated some traditional "female" attitudes and patterns of behavior.

A case in point concerns the testators' preoccupation with salvation. While considerably more women (75% as against 65% of men) made specific provisions for their soul (e.g., donations of chattels or cash in exchange for memorial services), the difference is slighter when it comes to alienations of real estate to the church, which involve 34 percent of the female and 31 percent of the male testators (among the childless, 50% and 47%, respectively; among those with children, 11% and 8%). The preponderance of female donors, while consistent, seems to be less significant than that suggested for his Western European model by Goody, who considers women's bequests to the church to have been a primary factor in the accumulation of ecclesiastical property.[76]

As property holders, women participated actively in economic life. A good proportion of landsellers were female—slightly over 40 percent, and more than half of the total sellers, if sales by a couple (or brother and sister, mother and son) are taken into account. The figures are not exact, because it is not always clear who had the main or sole responsibility for the transaction. Nevertheless two characteristics already discussed stand out: first, the strength of women's property rights, and second, the concept of a fund that was administered by the husband but to which every member of the family had claim.

The data for land buyers are contrastingly different. A mere 7 percent of the total were women, and not all of them necessarily acted on their own.[77] The strictly observed custom of preemptive rights for owners of adjacent property and close relatives meant that if a man wanted to buy land to which his wife had rights of preemption, she would appear as the buyer, whatever the actual situation.[78]

Nevertheless we know of a few widows who made transactions in their own right and even seemed intent on accumulating land. A good example is Kali Mostratou, a sea captain's widow, who bought land on three separate occasions between 1671 and 1673, paying the not inconsiderable total of 451 reals. She subsequently bestowed the second best of them on her granddaughter Aneza, together with another piece of land, some jewelry, chattels, and 200 reals in bills of credit.[79]

Apparently Kali invested not only in land but also in moneylending, but in this last she was not an exception. Women were often involved in the lending, as well as borrowing, of money. In fact they would appear as the person responsible any time the security offered for a loan was part of their own property. They also frequently acted as guarantors for their husbands' debts, but—at least in theory—they were not obliged to do so. Thus a widow asked a witness to testify that she had never pledged anything for her husband's debts, while a peasant woman entering a second marriage states that all debt incurred by her first husband will be charged to their son who had inherited the paternal property. On the other hand a woman from the town, who had been guarantor for the sum of 30 reals that her husband had borrowed, sold—after his death—a vineyard to pay the money back.[80]

A good example of a small-scale borrower in the town is Kalitsa Sandorinaia; she is often mentioned in transactions on her own, but when a debtor approached to inquire whether she was willing to have her husband receive some money owed to her, her answer was that her husband was her attorney, that she had made him master of her property, and that whatever he did with it was well done.[81] Her response in all probability reflects the actual experience of the majority of women, despite their professed rights and the separate status of their property.

The Naxian Model in a Wider Perspective

A question of particular interest is whether the feature of the Naxian system that appears to the modern student to be original to the island—namely the male dowry—is actually so. Only a tentative answer can be given at present, mainly because so little has been written about inheritance customs in any Greek region from the Middle Ages to the last century. What we know about regional variations in Western European customary law and also of later Greek custom as it appears on the basis of nineteenth- and twentieth-century investigations makes it extremely implausible that uniform practices were ever prevalent.

In the Byzantine period, legislative texts (the only source in abundance) define in detail the dowry brought by the woman into the marriage and the forms of dower (προγαμιαία δωρεά, ὑπόβολον, θεώρετρον) settled on her by the groom.[82] Analyses of marriage payments (either by the Byzantines themselves or by modern scholars) are generally made within this framework, but what we can glimpse of the actual situation is less clear.

Even though the evidence is scant and often difficult to interpret, in many cases a marriage portion was settled on a man when he married. Early references date from at least the tenth century, and the father's legal obligation to provide a προῖκα to both sons and daughters is legislated in the *Basilika* (28.4.11).[83] The reciprocity of settling property at marriage is also reflected in a gold bull of Michael Doukas for Robert Guiscard (end of the eleventh century), setting out the gifts which each party was to give upon the marriage of their children.[84]

In Byzantine Italy a bridegroom's parents might make settlements not only of a dower on the bride but also of a share (μοῖρα) of the family property on the groom himself,[85] and in the East a later marriage contract includes a similar settlement for the man: he is promised as a dowry (προῖκα) one third—"that is the ἀδελφομοίριον,"—of all paternal and maternal property.[86]

The importance of male dowry emerges with particular clarity in late formularies concerning adoption and stipulating that the adoptive parents will marry the son, make a dowry contract for him, and give him a προῖκα. Finally, the custom of a man's endowment is confirmed in a number of patriarchal decisions from the fourteenth century.[87]

In addition, the sources provide some interesting insights into the organization of the family, which is linked to the property rights of young married couples. A formulary of dowry contracts stipulates that the son will continue to live under his parents' roof after marriage; the bride will be ἐσώνυμφος and will bring her dowry into her husband's family, while the bridegroom will receive his inheritance only after his parents' death.[88] It is interesting to note that the reverse was stipulated in the case of a bridegroom who was to enter his bride's family and live with her mother.[89]

Further investigation of this specific problem is required before patterns of residence can be discerned and their links with social and economic factors traced. We may observe tentatively that cohabitation with the older generation was not always the norm, and that there is evidence of young couples having set up an independent household. For example, this is suggested by a son's gratitude toward his father for providing a home for him and his wife for a year, while the case of a man of twenty-five who could not leave his father's home and marry because the father refused to give him his προῖκα, emphasizes the role of dowry in enabling a man to marry and the concomitant notion that young bridegrooms were not necessarily expected to live under their father's roof, supported by him.[90]

There is no evidence in the sources that the male dowry enjoyed any special status, but this is not surprising, in view of the man's dominant position and the relative freedom that the Byzantines had in the disposition of family property. On the basis of several accounts it would seem that Byzantine men—and widows—enjoyed a freedom over the patrimony that was unknown to the people of seventeenth-century Naxos, although it is possible that the constraints imposed by the presence of children have been underestimated: examples quoted to support the view of "female ownership and control of wealth" or of women as "independent property owners" primarily concern childless widows.[91]

Nevertheless it is very probable that at least in the late Byzantine period economic circumstances led to the lifting of some customary restrictions. One indication is that the woman's dowry was usually appraised, and, as Diane Hughes has noticed for the West, "the *dos estimata* . . . was more easily alienable, since only its assessed worth had to be restored."[92] Another is the custom that we encounter, in the fourteenth century, of offering part of the dowry to the bridegroom κατὰ λόγον ξενίου, as a gift.[93] It should be stressed, however, that such tendencies may have been only a limited, urban phenomenon.

Too many aspects of the system remain unknown—such as, the evolution of the custom of male dowry, how widespread it was at any time, or how a woman's marriage portion rated in relation to those of her brothers. It is nevertheless clear that the idea of dowry representing the inheritance rights of both female and male children was well known and often acted upon, and that the great similarity in function between the man's and the woman's dowry offers an exciting prospect for future investigations.

A review of the patchy evidence on dowry systems in the seventeenth-century Greek world shows a considerable range of local variations. Marriage portions for men do not appear in dowry contracts from the Ionian islands, where we find some indication of male inheritance effected post mortem.[94] They are also absent in the admittedly late evidence from mainland Greece. It is very plausible that in most cases people followed the patrilineal practices that were so prevalent in recent times. Thus in a rare eighteenth-century example of a will from Mani (a region notorious for its rigid patriarchy to this day), we see a well-off man leaving one field and three olive trees to his daughter, while the remaining property went "to his children" (meaning the males).[95]

The one recorded exception on the mainland is some late Athenian marriage contracts that include male dowries. One such example has perhaps a wider significance. Half of the dowry settled on the bride by her foster parents was presented to the groom as a gift "to have as his own," and in return he was to put down whatever he possessed so that they might hold it together with his wife.[96] This once more suggests that the absence of a male portion in marriage settlements did not necessarily mean that the groom had not received his inheritance; it could simply mean that to have the property bound by a dowry contract was not considered necessary or even desirable, because the marriage, if not the woman, would thus gain claims on it.

Male dowry was often encountered in Crete, while in the villages of Chios only in 20 percent of the contracts examined is a marriage portion settled on the man. As if to counterbalance this, 60 percent of all contracts include a settlement on the bride—by the bridegroom or his family—of property which would be hers both during the marriage and in widowhood.[97]

The region in which the custom of male dowry seems to have been general and well-established is the Cyclades. The marriage arrangements of Syros and Santorini show that their system was almost identical to that of Naxos, and the dowering of sons is also attested for Andros, Paros, Serifos, Sifnos, Mykonos, Ios, Kimolos, Sikinos, Milos, and Kea.[98]

Since the mapping of the Greek dowry system is far from complete, only some general thoughts may be advanced as a conclusion. One of the features of dowry as usually conceived (i.e., the female marriage portion) is that it is a woman's legal property, to which, however, her rights are dormant for the duration of the marriage. Concomitantly, the dowry is protected, that it may fulfill its function (the maintenance of the woman and transmission to the next generation). None of these aspects is of comparable importance in the case of a man's portion, since he is both the owner and manager of his property and has moreover much wider scope to fend for himself. It is therefore possible (and much of the evidence quoted suggests this) that transfers of property at marriage essentially similar to a woman's dowry (in their origin, composition and function) were settled on men as well, much more often than has been realized; and this would obviously have implications for the organization of the household and the structure of the family.

In light of the combined evidence presented, it is clear that male dowry was part of an old tradition whose local variations and stages of evolution are largely untraced. The system of Naxos (and of the other Cyclades) cannot be considered unique, despite its peculiar emphasis on the preservation of the patrimony as a means of protecting not simply the woman but the whole family, or perhaps the established order of things in general. After all, two important factors contributing to the full-fledged form in which the Cycladic institution appears are the well-developed notarial tradition and the survival of adequate material in which the preoccupations of the people in this respect and the solutions that they adopted are laid down in a large number of neat and detailed arrangements.

Some Concluding Remarks

Female social inferiority has often been associated with or even attributed to the limited access of women to property. In the case of Naxos, however, we have seen that in legal terms female and male property rights were virtually identical and restricted by customary norms applied to both sexes. The overall evidence suggests that the women of Naxos were probably reckoned with in a way unknown to societies in which women were generally considered as perpetual minors. They were as actively involved in the management of dowry lands and in the transfer of property to the children as the peasant women of modern Greece, whose "informal power" within the family Ernestine Friedl has highlighted.[99]

Nevertheless none of this could transform either the structure of real power or the prevalent image of the woman's proper place. In short, the existence or absence of property and other legal rights offers only a partial explanation for the universality of the patriarchal structure and of woman's subordinate position. Much wider and further-reaching factors should also be taken into account, including the dominant role of the males in production and their greater access to experience, education, and political power, reinforced by a deeply rooted ideology that transcends the limits of space and time.

Notes

My grateful thanks to Catia Galatariotou, who read an earlier draft of this paper and offered a number of references, constructive suggestions, and comments; also to Ruth Babington, Lina Kasdagli, and Katerina Krikos-Davis for much valued help in matters of research and presentation.

1. June 30, 1689 (*Genika Archeia tou Kratous*, Athens [hereafter cited as *GAK*], cod. 86, fol. 435). It is clear that the husband did not have the power to stop his wife's action but issued the warning on his children's behalf, expecting them to set up claims against her when they came of age. The idea that the man is the head of the wife was a Byzantine topos (Angeliki E. Laiou, "The Role of Women in Byzantine Society," *Jahrbuch der österreichischen Byzantinistik* 32/1 [1982]: 260).

2. For the view that "historiography serves in the self-celebration of man: it is the record of his deeds and the gratification of male values," see Marielouise Janssen-Jurreit, *Sexism: The Male Monopoly on History and Thought*, trans. Verne Moberg (London: Pluto Press, 1982), 15–34. For an illuminating review of the method "to adopt gender system as a fundamental category of historical analysis," see Elizabeth Fox-Genovese, "Placing Women's History in History," *New Left Review* 133 (May–June 1982): 5–29.

3. On the question of Byzantine sources with regard to women, see Judith Herrin, "In Search of Byzantine Women: Three Avenues of Approach," in *Images of Women in Antiquity*, ed. Averil Cameron and Amélie Kuhrt (London and Canberra: Croom Helm, 1984), 167–89. On the legal position of Byzantine women, see Joëlle Beaucamp, "La situation juridique de la femme à Byzance," *Cahiers de civilisation médiévale* 20 (1977): 145–76. For a balanced overview see José Grosdidier de Matons, "La femme dans l'Empire byzantin," *Histoire mondiale de la femme* (Paris: Nouvelle Librairie de France, 1966), 3:11–43, and for social practice in the late period Laiou, "Role of Women."

4. Rosemary E. Bancroft-Marcus, "Women in the Cretan Renaissance," *Journal of Modern Greek Studies* 1 (1983): 19–38; Chrysa A. Maltezou, "E gynaika ste Benetokratoumene Krete me base tis notariakes peges," *Archaiologia* 21 (Nov. 1986): 37–40.

5. Most information by the foreign visitors cited here dates from the sixteenth and seventeenth centuries and is taken from the collection by Kyriakos Simopoulos, *Xenoi taxidiotes sten Ellada: Demosios kai idiotikos bios, laikos politismos, ekklesies kai oikogeneiake zoe apo ta periegetika chronika*, vol. 1, 333 m. Ch.–1700 (Athens, 1970). The women of Chios received special notice by numerous travelers (ibid., 488–96 and passim).

6. Ibid., 297–98 (Buondelmonti, ca. 1408).

7. Ibid., 412–13 (De Fresne Canaye, 1573). In the description of the ceremony, Simopoulos finds similarities with the Byzantine nuptial custom of *apokalypteria*.

8. Ibid., 612–13 (La Guilletière, 1668) and 709–11 (Sauger, 1698). Both authors are contemptuous of and disgusted with the ritual aspect of lament and the excessive and often violent reactions of the mourning women, who (as we now know) were continuing an unbroken tradition going back to Byzantium and ancient Greece. See Margaret Alexiou, *The Ritual Lament in Greek Tradition* (Cambridge: Cambridge Univ. Press, 1974).

9. Simopoulos, 565 (Thévenot, 1655). A similar observation was made by De Moncoy in 1645 (ibid., 525).

10. Ibid., 688 (Randolph, 1686).

11. The most up-to-date and comprehensive history of the period is B. J. Slot, *Archipelagus Turbatus: Les Cyclades entre colonisation latine et occupation ottomane c1500–1718*, 2 vols. (Leiden: Nederlands Historisch-Archaeologisch Instituut te Istanbul, 1982).

12. Iakovos T. Visvizes, "To problema tes istorias tou metabyzantinou dikaiou," *Epeteris Kentrou Ereunes Ellenikou Dikaiou* 6 (1955): 131–53. Comparisons made with Byzantine law refer particularly to the late period and its de facto formulated law, which was mostly based on *Novels*, imperial decrees, court decisions, and the like. See Dieter Simon, *E eurese tou dikaiou sto anotato byzantino dikasterio*, trans. I. M. Konidare (Athens: Ant. N. Sakkoulas, 1982). A good basis of comparison is the *Hexabiblos*, which exercised an enormous influence on post-Byzantine Greek law (Konstantinos Armenopoulos, *Procheiron nomon e Hexabiblos*, ed. Konstantinos G. Pitsakes [Athens: Dodone, 1971]). For the Orthodox Church, see N. J. Pantazopoulos, *Church and Law in the Balkan Peninsula during the Ottoman Rule* (Thessaloniki: Institute for Balkan Studies, 1967).

13. An example is the *ahdname* of 1646 published by Demetrios S. Gines, *Perigramma istorias tou metabyzantinou dikaiou* (Athens: Grapheion Demosieumaton Akademias Athenon, 1966), doc. 130. The importance of the concessions for the islands is discussed by Elene E. Koukkou, *Oi koinotikoi thesmoi stis Kyklades kata ten Tourkokratia* (Athens: Istorike kai Ethnologike Etaireia tes Ellados, 1980).

14. On the application of the Assizes to Naxos see David Jacoby, *La féodalité en Grèce médiévale, Les "Assises de Romanie": Sources, application et diffusion* (Paris and the Hague: Mouton, 1971), 116–23 and 271–93. On post-Byzantine customary law see Iakovos T. Visvizes, "Tina peri ton nomikon ethimon apo tes Tourkokratias mechri tou B. D. tes 23 Februariou 1835," *Athena* 53 (1949): 228–56. The legal system in seventeenth-century Naxos and several other themes mentioned in this paper are dealt with in detail in my doctoral dissertation, "The Island of Naxos in the Seventeenth Century: Some Aspects of the Economy and Society from the Notarial Sources," submitted to the University of Birmingham, School of History, in 1991.

15. Eva C. Topping, "Patriarchal Prejudice and Pride in Greek Christianity: Some Notes on Origins," *Journal of Modern Greek Studies* 1 (1983): 7. For attitudes within the Byzantine Church see Catia S. Galatariotou, "Holy Women and Witches: Aspects of Byzantine Conceptions of Gender," *Byzantine and Modern Greek Studies* 9 (1985): 55–94. More generally, on Byzantine stereotypes about women, see Vern L. Bullough, Brenda Shelton, and Sarah Slavin, *The Subordinated Sex: A History of Attitudes towards Women*, rev. ed. (Athens and London: University of Georgia Press, 1988), 102–12; translated excerpts of relevant Byzantine sources in Julia O'Faolain and Lauro Martinez, *Not in God's Image* (London: Virago, 1979), 89–99.

16. Agapiou monachou tou Kretos [= Agapios Landos], *Biblion oraiotaton kaloumenon Amartolon Soteria, syntethen eis koinen ton Graikon dialekton*, new ed. (Venice, 1851); for the first edition see Emile Legrand, *Bibliographie hellénique du dix-septième siècle ou description raisonnée des ouvrages publiés par les Grecs*, vol. 1 (Paris, 1894), no. 300. The book is

mentioned in a monk's will of October 30, 1673 (*GAK*, cod. 85, fols. 507–9) and in a list of books that a priest donated to his monastery ([November] 8, [1680], *GAK*, cod. 86, fols. 55–56).

17. In the twelfth century Kekaumenos used similar language and urged his son to be cautious and never familiar whenever he spoke to a woman, since her appearance, words, and nature posed a triple danger (*Cecaumeni Strategicon*, ed. B. Wassiliewsky and V. Jernstedt (1896; rpt. Amsterdam: Adolf Hakkert, 1965), 52.21–26.

18. V. Laurent, "La mission des Jesuites à Naxos de 1627 à 1643," *Echos d'Orient* 33 (1934): 218–26, 354–75, and 34 (1935): 97–105, 179–204, 350–67, 473–81 (esp. 359).

19. Simopoulos, 397 (Vormbser, 1556), 572 (Thévenot, 1655), 414 (De Fresne Canaye, 1573).

20. Phaidon Koukoules, *Byzantinon bios kai politismos*, 6 vols. (Athens: Institut Français d'Athènes, 1948–55), 2.2:166–68 cites many examples of adherence to the custom by the Byzantines. But even if the ideal of women's seclusion was ever applied to the majority of the female population in Byzantium (which is to be doubted), it certainly did not reflect social realities in the late period. See Laiou, "Role of Women," 249 ff.

21. July 17, 1669 (*GAK*, cod. 85, fol. 44).

22. Mourning and lamentation were an exclusively female domain, as seen in the detached account (by a man) of his dead son's wake, in which "many good ladies had gone to keep the grieving women company, according to the custom of our land" (August 16, 1687, *GAK*, cod. 86, fols. 387–88).

23. See Frances Rothstein, "Women and Men in the Family Economy: An Analysis of the Relations between the Sexes in Three Peasant Communities," *Anthropological Quarterly* 56 (1983): 10–23. For the idea of peasant women "heavily involved in socially productive labor," see Christopher Middleton, "The Sexual Division of Labour in Feudal England," *New Left Review* 113–14 (January–April 1989): 165. The same was probably true of the poorer urban strata.

24. On Santorini, Simopoulos, 533 (Richard, 1650). In 1571 nearly seven thousand Cretans served in the galleys, and some three thousand of them never returned (I. G. Giannopoulos, *E Krete kata ton tetarto benetotourkiko polemo [1570–1571]* [Athens: Privately published, 1978], 59, 94–95, 105–13).

25. Laiou, "Role of Women," 245–47; Rodney H. Hilton, "Women Traders in Medieval England," *Women's Studies* 2 (1984): 139–56. In both cases women were particularly active in the trading of foodstuffs.

26. On Chios see Simopoulos, 491. Most stages in the process of cloth production were accomplished everywhere by women, and it is perhaps because this was something ubiquitous that it is not often mentioned. We hear, however, that the women of Aegina and Santorini engaged in spinning and weaving, while those of Mykonos worked on local cotton and silk imported from Andros (ibid., 533, 673, 691). On Romylia and Icaria see ibid., 573 (Sieur de Poullet, 1657) and 486 (Lithgow, 1609), respectively.

27. Maltezou. That the range of female activity in Naxos was much wider than the sources allow is seen in the promise that a village widow made to her son to help him in the building of a house with her own physical labor (July 1, 1687, *GAK*, cod. 86, fols. 377v–378).

28. Refined courtesans were a category of their own and, in contrast with respectable women, shared much of the upper-class male world of culture and entertainment (Bancroft-Marcus, 21–23).

29. Laurent, 181–82; Maltezou.

30. Examples of Cretan marriage contracts in Wim Bakker and Arnold van Gemert, eds., *Manolis Varouchas: Notariakes praxeis—Monasteraki Amariou (1597–1613)* (Rethymno:

Panepistemio Kretes, 1987). It is worth noting that the *Hexabiblos* (IV, 1, 3, 6) stipulates that the future spouses should give their consent for both engagement and marriage but adds that a father considers a daughter who does not openly contradict as having given her consent, and that she may contradict only if the man proposed to her is worthless and profligate.

31. Thus in the town a widow of middling means who had given property to a grand-daughter stipulated that the girl should marry a particular young man, and that, in the event of either partner's dying before the wedding, another match should be arranged between other children of the two families, so that the relationship might be maintained (January 28, 1673, *GAK*, cod. 85, fol. 437v).

32. March 23, 1689 (Rome, *Cod. Vat. Gr. 2638*). The Byzantine epic *Digenes Akrites* provides illuminating insights into the ideal of female submission and passivity. See Catia Galatariotou, "Structural Oppositions in the Grottaferrata *Digenes Akrites*," *Byzantine and Modern Greek Studies* 11 (1987): 29–68, especially the abduction of the girl, who follows the man without questioning, and the interesting modern Greek parallel with abduction among the Sarakatsanoi (51 ff.).

33. November 5 and 20, 1664 (*GAK*, cod. 85, fols. 145–47).

34. The "monache Terziarie di S. Domenico," who resided at home, are mentioned by papal visitors (Giorgio Hofmann, "Vescovadi Cattolici della Grecia, IV: Naxos," *Orientalia Christiana Analecta* 115/4 [1938]: 83, 113, 142). Within the Koronellos family we find two examples of women (in both cases one of four sisters) destined to become nuns (January 21, 1683, *GAK*, cod. 86, fol. 496, and July 20, 1697, Athens, National Library, Mss. Ξ [hereafter *NL*]).

35. For the Byzantine evidence see Catia Galatariotou, "Byzantine Women's Monastic Communities: The Evidence of the *Typika*," *Jahrbuch der österreichischen Byzantinistik* 38 (1988): 263–90. A plausible explanation for the decline of female monasticism in the Ottoman period is that a conspicuous community of Christian women in a Muslim state would be exposed to intolerable risks, and this was one of the reservations of Roman Catholic missionaries, who in the course of the seventeenth century made several furtive attempts to establish a convent in Naxos.

36. The education of many upper-class men extended to Italian and even French; all Greek priests and many members of the urban middle classes were literate, while the schools run by the Jesuits and the Capuchins seem to have drawn Greek (male) pupils from both the town and the villages. Nuns employed as teachers are recorded in notarial documents of Venetian Crete (Maltezou), but female illiteracy was almost universal in Ottoman Greece. In the late Byzantine period we find a significant proportion of literate women, but they all belonged to the high aristocracy (Laiou, "Role of Women," 253–57).

37. The two figures suggest a higher life expectancy for women or a significant age difference at marriage, but an additional factor may be that men were still marriageable at a more advanced age than women.

38. Laurent, 367–68.

39. N. G. Polites, *Eklogai apo ta tragoudia tou ellenikou laou*, 3d ed. (Athens: Paraskeua Leone, 1932), no. 190.

40. Laurent, 358, 359.

41. Ibid., 180. Although Benetina is not referred to by name, the identification is confirmed from other sources. See also the belated dowry that her mother settled on her years later, with the unusual condition that the property be passed on to the children that Benetina had had with her husband, and not "any previous ones" (May 31, 1685, *NL*).

42. May 24, 1683 (*GAK, Mikres sylloges*, 81a).

43. Simopoulos, 670 (De Barres, 1674).

44. Ibid., 676. The information refers to the year 1673 and the source (Jean Giraud, French consul at Athens) is exceptionally reliable. The imposition of fines by the Ottoman authorities for illicit affairs is also encountered in Naxos. Byzantine law provided for very severe punishments for liaisons outside marriage, but it applied blatantly double standards in favor of the men (Beauchamp, "Situation juridique," 156–57).

45. Regarding the bedsheets, see Simopoulos, 500 (Sandys, 1610). This "test of virginity," common in many parts of Ottoman Greece, was also performed in Byzantium (Koukoules, 4:117). On the tax, see Simopoulos, 400 (Nicolay, 1551). The suggestive name of this due, mentioned by several travelers, is *argomouniatiko*, and it may have originated in a relative scarcity of women.

46. Most evidence comes from the very few—and late—ecclesiastical court proceedings that have survived. See B. B. Sphyroeras, "Gamoi kai diazygia en Naxo ton IZ' kai IH' aiona," *Kykladika* 1 (1956): 5–33. All these grounds for divorce were established in Byzantine times. See Angeliki E. Laiou, "Contribution à l'étude de l'institution familiale en Epire au XIIIème siècle," *Fontes Minores* 6 (1984): 275–323.

47. October 20, 1707 (Sphyroeras, doc. 9).

48. March 1, 1664 (Naxos, *Istoriko Archeio Naxou*, "Cancellaria Arcivescovile di Naxia"); May 28, 1683 (*GAK*, cod. 86, fol. 187).

49. March 2, 1664 (*GAK, Sylloge Zerlente-K43*). A vivid example of a Byzantine's idea of a shrew wife who had also recourse to violence is given in one of the satirical vernacular poems of the twelfth century attributed to Ptochoprodromos. See *Poèmes prodromiques en grec vulgaire*, ed. D.-C. Hesseling and H. Pernot (1910; rpt. Amsterdam: Martin Sandig, 1968), esp. lines 26–34.

50. Laurent, 193.

51. Goody's and Tambiah's concept of diverging devolution (i.e., transmission of property to heirs of both sexes) is a useful analytical tool in the case of Naxos, provided that the assumptions made with regard to dowry and the ensuing conclusions are applied to both the female and male contributions to the marriage—a divergence which singles out the specific local practice without invalidating the model altogether. See Jack Goody and S. J. Tambiah, *Bridewealth and Dowry* (Cambridge: Cambridge Univ. Press, 1973).

52. The same tendency appears in the figures for agricultural implements: 22% of all men received these as part of their dowry (40% in the case of peasant bridegrooms), as against 8% of all women.

53. Diana Owen Hughes, "From Brideprice to Dowry in Mediterranean Europe," *Journal of Family History* 3 (1978): 282. For late Byzantine evidence regarding the protected and separate status of female dowry, see N. P. Matses, *To oikogeneiakon dikaion kata ten nomologian tou Patriarcheiou Konstantinoupoleos ton eton 1315–1401* (Athens: N.p., 1962). Cf. the relevant clauses in a seventeenth-century legal code, the *Nomokriterion*: Gines, *Perigramma*, doc. 100.

54. May 28, 1683 (*GAK*, cod. 86, fol. 187). The term *siderokephalo* was more commonly used in connection with agreements for animals farmed to peasants, in which case it meant that the owner was guaranteed return of the original number of animals, irrespective of damages.

55. November 18, 1655 (*GAK*, cod. 85, fol. 548).

56. June 21, 1669 (Naxos, *Archeio Katholikes Archiepiskopes Naxou*, "Register of Filoti," fol. 685); March 31, 1673 (*GAK*, cod. 85, fol. 374v); January 9, 1679 (*NL*).

57. July 26, 1687 (*GAK*, cod. 86, fol. 381).

58. July 17–19, 1669 (*GAK*, cod. 85, fols. 44–45).

59. Goody and Tambiah, 62.

60. When there were children these were in effect considered co-owners of the patrimony

among people of all social classes, as is made clear by the fact that they were often required to give their consent—presumably when they were old enough—for the alienation of family property. A similar concept is encountered in Byzantium (Matses, 88; Herrin, 177).

61. Most of the surviving sixteenth-century marriage contracts have been published by Iakovos T. Visvizes, "Naxiaka notariaka engrapha ton teleutaion chronon tou doukatou tou Aigaiou (1538–77)," *Epeteris tou Archeiou tes Istorias tou Ellenikou Dikaiou* 4 (1951): 1–166. According to Visvizes (141–42), the "Romaic order" assigning the bedding to the widower was a Byzantine custom. In fact it is found in the late Byzantine formulary published by K. N. Sathas, ed., *Mesaionike Bibliotheke*, 7 vols. (Venice, 1872–94), 6:608, in which the same term, *kravvatostrosion*, is used.

62. An example of 1540 in Visvizes, "Naxiaka notariaka engrapha," doc. 40. Visvizes (141–43) believes that the community of goods between the spouses and the sharing of acquisitions in Naxos originated in Frankish law. For parallels in the Assizes of Romania, see Peter Topping, "Feudal Institutions as Revealed in the Assizes of Romania, the Law Code of Frankish Greece," in Peter Topping, *Studies on Latin Greece, A.D. 1205–1715* (London: Variorum Reprints, 1977), 155 and article 35.

63. The principle of *trimoiria* that we encounter in Ottoman Greece at a later date (see Pantazopoulos, 69–91) was apparently imposed by the church; the earliest example in Gines, *Perigramma*, dates from ca. 1710–14 (doc. 266). In a court case of 1682 from Mykonos, a husband is assigned a third of his late wife's goods but only for life; the *Novel* of Andronicus Palaeologus (*Novel* 26) is explicitly mentioned, but it is clear that the decision, made by a judge who was an outsider, was at variance with local custom (Iakovos T. Visvizes, "Dikastikai apophaseis tou 17ou aionos ek tes nesou Mykonou," *Epeteris tou Archeiou tes Istorias tou Ellenikou Dikaiou* 7 [1957]: 20–154 [47 and doc. 26]). On the Byzantine institution, see Matses, 95.

64. There are many references to people having inherited from uncles, nieces, or cousins, and in such cases the inheritance was called *xepesma*, rather than *kleronomia*.

65. What part of the actual purchases were classed in this category is not clear, because assets acquired with money or in exchange for property belonging to one partner would be written in his or her name. For the same principle in Byzantium see Matses, 93–94.

66. November 8, 1670 (Athens, Historical and Ethnological Museum, Department of Manuscripts, *Naxiako Archeio* [hereafter *NA*]); April 21, 1669 (*GAK*, cod. 85, fol. 25v).

67. July 28, 1682 (*GAK*, cod. 86, fol. 143v). In Venetian Crete, where the appointment of executors seems to have been the norm, female relatives (mostly wives) were frequently chosen for this role; examples in Sathas, 654–92. For an example of a Byzantine woman whom her husband named as his executor, see Herrin, 176–77.

68. February 20, 1682 (*GAK*, cod. 86, fol. 171v).

69. The rights of children to the patrimony were strong and ideally satisfied by means of the dowry, so that the children already endowed (*xoproukismena*) had no other claim, although parents could choose to leave them something extra by will. We find the same concept and term (*exoproika*) in the late Byzantine period (Matses, 180–81).

70. This is what anthropologists call "homoparental" practice or, according to Goody, "homogeneous" inheritance (Goody and Tambiah, 21). This tendency was probably the basis of a somewhat impressionistic report from the late Ottoman period concerning inheritance customs in the Archipelago, which have been considered to be "a remarkable survival or revival" of matriarchy (George Thomson, *The Prehistoric Aegean*, 3d ed. [London: Lawrence and Wishart, 1978], 202–3).

71. December 24, 1682 and May 18, 1688 (*GAK*, cod. 86, fols. 164v and 424v).

72. Examples include a nobleman who left property to all three namesakes among his grandchildren, and a mother who, when dowering her daughter, entailed one of the lands

on the granddaughter who would have her name (January 10, 1620, *Cod. Vat. Gr. 2638*; June 1, 1682, *GAK*, cod. 86, fols. 131–33).

73. An example from the Cyclades in Margaret E. Kenna, "Houses, Fields and Graves: Property and Ritual Obligation on a Greek Island," *Ethnology* 15 (1976): 21–34. The custom reaches its extreme in Karpathos, where the two children—normally the eldest—named after the maternal grandmother and paternal grandfather take all property originating in their namesakes (Bernard Vernier, "Putting Kin and Kinship to Good Use: The Circulation of Goods, Labour, and Names on Karpathos [Greece]," in Hans Medick and David Warren Sabean, eds., *Interest and Emotion: Essays on the Study of Family and Kinship* [Cambridge: Cambridge Univ. Press, 1984], 28–76). We do not, however, know the exact form of the system before the nineteenth century.

74. See for example Juliet Du Boulay, *Portrait of a Greek Mountainous Village* (Oxford: Clarendon Press, 1979) and Ernestine Friedl, *Vasilika: A Village in Modern Greece* (New York: Rinehart and Winston, 1962).

75. In contrast, social status was important in determining who made written testamentary provisions. The members of the nobility and landed upper classes in general, although they were few in real terms, make up 28% of all testators, the townspeople of all economic gradations 47%, and the villagers a mere 14%, while the status of the remaining 11% cannot be established.

76. Jack Goody, *The Development of the Family and Marriage in Europe* (Cambridge and New York: Cambridge Univ. Press, 1983), esp. 67; also 256, 261. The proportion of people donating real property to the church is illustrative of the very strong commitment to the rights of children as heirs: on the whole, half of the childless but less than 15% of the others made such legacies.

77. About 45% of all sellers and 78% of all buyers were men, and the remaining buyers and sellers were ecclesiastical institutions. The difference between sales by couples (12%, not counting the many cases of husbands who are simply said to have given their consent to the alienation without appearing as co-sellers) and purchases by couples (5%) also suggests that while men had an active role in the disposition of female property they were not equally prepared to have their wives share in newly acquired property.

78. On the right to preemption, see the essay by Speros Vryonis, Jr., in the present volume.

79. November 9, 1671, December 12, 1672, January 28, 1673, January 28, 1673 (*GAK*, cod. 85, fols. 253v, 357r+v, 437, 440).

80. November 15, 1673 (*GAK*, cod. 85, fol. 416v); May 23, 1662 (*NA*); March 21, 1646 (A. Ph. Katsouros, "Naxiaka dikaiopraktika engrapha tou 17 [sic] aionos," *Epeteris Etaireias Kykladikon Meleton* 7 [1968]: doc. 57).

81. February 4, 1682 (*GAK*, cod. 86, fol. 169v).

82. The *Hexabiblos* provides details for most aspects of Byzantine marriage payments (IV, 3–14). The *theoretron* had sometimes the meaning of "virginity price" (ibid., IV, 13, 3). Its characterization by Herrin (174) as "brideprice" is not accurate, because the *theoretron* was a settlement by the groom (or his family) on the bride herself (what is sometimes called "indirect dowry"), whereas the brideprice is not handed to the wife but goes to her male kin (Goody and Tambiah, 1–3, 61). For an illuminating discussion of the institution and a distinction between the three payments, see Stavros Perentides, "Pos mia synetheia mporei na exelichthei se thesmo: E periptose tou 'theoretrou,'" in *Aphieroma ston Niko Svorono*, 2 vols. (Rethymno: Panepistemio Kretes, 1986), 2:476–85.

83. I thank Ruth Macrides for this and other references, as well as for fruitful discussions about the Byzantine material and its interpretation. I also thank her for letting me read her paper "Dowry and Inheritance in the Late Period: Some Cases from the Patriarchal Regis-

Gender and Social Practice in Naxos

ter," to be published in Dieter Simon, ed., *Proceedings of a Colloquium on Family Property Law (Ein Fleisch, Ein Gut? Vermögensgemeinschaft vermögen im byzantinischen Familienguterrecht)*, Munich, July 1989.

84. Koukoules, 4:87. On the Byzantine male dowry see also Matses, 126–29. Any overall study of the concept and function of the forms of male contribution to the marriage must also take into account their relative value to the woman's dowry; for such an interpretation of the *hypobolon* see Joëlle Beaucamps, "Proikohypobolon—hypobolon—hypoballo," in *Aphieroma ston Niko Svorono*, 2:153–61.

85. F. Trinchera, *Syllabus Graecarum Membranum* (Naples, 1865), e.g., doc. 170 (of A.D. 1166). For an analysis of the Byzantine marriage contracts in Italy and comparisons with the Byzantine East, see Giannino Ferrari, "I documenti greci medioevali dei diritto dell'Italia meridionale e loro attinenze con quelli bizantini d'oriente e coi papiri greco-egizi," *Byzantinisches Arkhiv* 4 (1910; rpt. 1974).

86. Manouel I. Gedeon, "Byzantina symbolaia," *Byzantinische Zeitschrift* 5 (1886): 112–17, doc. A, according to Visvizes written in 1466/7: Iakovos T. Visvizes, "Tina peri ton proikoon engraphon kata ten Benetokratian kai ten Tourkokratian," *Epeteris Kentrou Ereunes Ellenikou Dikaiou* 12 (1965): 39. Both the term (*aderfomoiri*) and the concept of a "sibling portion" of paternal and maternal goods were central in the customary arrangements of Naxos.

87. Macrides, "Dowry and Inheritance." The formularies were published in Sathas, 628–31 (docs. 18 and 19, twelfth to thirteenth century); Dieter Simon and S. Troianos, "Dreizehn Geschaftsformulare," *Fontes Minores* 2 (1977): 262–95 (docs. 7, 8, late fourteenth to early fifteenth century).

88. Sathas, 607–9, doc. 1. At the time of division the groom will receive an equal share with his brothers.

89. Giannino Ferrari dalle Spade, "Registro vaticano di atti bizantini di diritto privato," *Studi bizantini e neoellenici* 4 (1935): 261 and docs. 7, 10.

90. Macrides. The prevalent practice among peasants in fourteenth-century Macedonia was for the wife to move in with her husband or his family (Angeliki E. Laiou-Thomadakis, *Peasant Society in the Late Byzantine Empire: A Social and Demographic Study* [Princeton: Princeton Univ. Press, 1977], 96–98).

91. Herrin, 175–77; Laiou, "Role of Women," 239–41. To check the range of regional variations, see André Guillou, "Il matrimonio nell'Italia bizantina nei secoli X e XI," *Settimani di Studio* 24 (1977): 869–86.

92. Hughes, 282. Appraised dowry was virtually unknown in Naxos, but it was the norm in Venetian territories like Crete and Zakynthos. The *Hexabiblos* (IV, 10, 1–5) makes a clear distinction between assessed and unassessed dowry and the implications of each.

93. Matses, 129–31; Macrides. See also Laiou, "Role of Women," 240, where the gradual change in the function of dowry is highlighted. We find an exact equivalent in the ubiquitous *charisma* to the bridegroom encountered in Venetian Crete. See examples in Bakker and van Gemert, docs. 76, 142, 315, 451, 638, 828.

94. In a document of 1698, four brothers from a village of Cephallonia made the decision to divide the patrimony *and* their acquisitions twelve years after their father's death, when the youngest was already a priest (Georgios Petropoulos, *Notariakai praxeis Kephallenias tes sylloges E. Blessa, ton eton 1701* [sic]–*1856* (Athens, 1962). The complete bibliography of printed sources is too long to be listed here, but see Gines, *Perigramma*, with two supplements in the *Epeteris Etaireias Byzantinon Spoudon* 38–40 (1972–73): 201–46, and 43 (1977–78): 152–87.

95. Before 1782: Stauros Ch. Skopeteas, "Diathekai ek tes Dytikes Manes," *Epeteris tou Archeiou tes Istorias tou Ellenikou Dikaiou* 6 (1955): 100–121. The custom, which persists in

93

some places, of reserving the word *child* for the male offspring was also present in Byzantium (Koukoules, 2.2:165).

96. October 27, 1801 (Visvizes, "Peri proikoon engraphon," doc. 23). The groom also settled a dower (*pro gamou dorea*, or "prewedding gift," of cash and chattels) found in all Athenian marriage contracts, while a man's dowry was not common.

97. Documents published in K. N. Kanellakes, *Chiaka analekta* (1890; rpt. Chios: Yioi N. Chaviara, 1983) and Iakovos T. Visvizes, "Ai metaxy ton syzygon periousiakai scheseis eis ten Chion kata ten Tourkokratian," *Epeteris tou Archeiou tes Istorias tou Ellenikou Dikaiou* 1 (1948): 1–164.

98. A. Th. Drakakes, "E Syros epi Tourkokratias: E dikaiosyne kai to dikaion," *Epeteris Etaireias Kykladikon Meleton* 6 (1967): 63–492. I have examined only briefly the unpublished material in the archives of the Catholic bishopric of Santorini. Evidence on the other Cyclades has been collected from a large number of printed sources.

99. Ernestine Friedl, "The Position of Women: Appearance and Reality," *Anthropological Quarterly* 40 (1967): 97–108.

BYZANTINE MUSICAL TRADITIONS AMONG THE SLAVS

Miloš Velimirović

A MONG THE NUMEROUS aspects of Byzantine influence on the Slavs, one that has received considerable attention among scholars in the last few decades is the relationship of Byzantine liturgical music and that of the East and South Slavs. As is well known, the East Slavic ethnic groups consist of various Russian branches—that is, Great Russians, Ukrainians, and Byelorussians. Of the South Slavs, the Serbs and Bulgarians accepted Christianity from Byzantine missionaries and embraced Eastern Orthodoxy, as opposed to the Croats and Slovenes, who, together with the West Slavs (Czechs, Slovaks, and Poles), became Roman Catholics. Another common trait among the Eastern Orthodox Slavs is their use of the Cyrillic alphabet, which is derived from the modified forms of the Greek alphabet. With these points in mind, it can safely be stated that the earliest traces of Byzantine musical traditions among these Slavs date from the second half of the ninth century, the period of activities of the Apostles to the Slavs, the "Holy Brothers" Constantine-Cyril and Methodius, who, in transmitting Christianity to the Moravians, must have chanted the ritual hymns singing Byzantine melodies of their own time. With this truly momentous missionary event, enhanced a century later by the conversion of the Kievan ruler Vladimir and his followers, written documentation came into being that provides us with definite proof of the close relationship of Byzantine religious practices and those of the Slavs.[1]

To start with, liturgical books demonstrate that the texts of the services are identical in meaning, the Slavic texts being exact translations from Greek into Old Church Slavonic. Furthermore, the very same musical notation that emerged in Byzantium in the mid-tenth century was in the eleventh century transmitted to the Slavs—more specifically, to the

Russians. This is amply documented in still extant musical manuscripts of Kievan and Novgorodian provenance. We do not have to follow this process through the centuries to realize that the roots of Russian church music are to be found in the melodies of Byzantine origin.[2]

Throughout the following centuries until 1453, when Constantinople fell into Turkish hands, there were periods of active exchanges involving additional translating and copying of musical manuscripts, as well as participation by Greek clergy in Slavic church services, despite the difference of language. There were also periods when these contacts were considerably reduced, as after the conquest of Constantinople in 1204 by the Crusaders and during the existence of the so-called Latin Empire, which lasted until 1261. During these decades, the Tartar invasion of Russian lands, which crested around 1240, further hampered access by some of the Slavic churches to the Byzantine musical traditions. As a result, scholars have to delineate the extent of the contacts and the types of relationships with Byzantium that were cultivated by the various Slavic states. The basic point, however, that has to be kept in mind for purposes of orientation is that, once accepted, melodies were repeated and maintained in use in the church services. At the same time, almost inevitably, they must have undergone some stylistic changes in actual performance, even if written records do not always reflect these changes as faithfully as one might wish.

In short, we are accepting as our basic premises that the foundations of Slavic church music are Byzantine, and that the contacts between Byzantium and the Slavs continued regardless of political events. Needless to say, due to geographical and political circumstances each Slavic ethnic group gradually developed its own musical traditions.

Curiously enough, although the Bulgarians are the closest neighbors of Byzantium, we have no written record of musical practice among them until rather late: the earliest known record of indigenous musical practice dates from the seventeenth century. Yet the proximity of Bulgarian lands to the thoroughly Greek culture of Constantinople is reflected in the fact that when the quite prominent school of musicians and chanters from the Rila Monastery was established in the late eighteenth century, it retained the Greek musical notation being used at that time, a notation that is considerably modernized and removed from the earliest forms of musical notation employed in the Middle Ages. This suggests that, regardless of historical circumstances, Bulgarians relied on such technical tools for the writing of music as were available in the more advanced Greek musical practice. In fact, we find even Bulgarian folk songs written down in the nineteenth century in the type of Neo-Greek neumatic notation which the Greeks of that time were using for their church music.[3] Western musical notation (using the five-line staff and clefs) penetrated into Bulgaria only in the mid-nineteenth century, and from that time on there are no further records of reliance on Byzantine principles. The earliest documented examples of the so-called *Bolgarski raspev*, or Bulgarian Chants, can be found in Russian musical manuscripts. Yet the script and notation follow Russian musical practices, which by that time—the seventeenth century—had evolved and reached a new stage, quite removed from their Byzantine roots. In sum, Bulgarian records are far from serving as satisfactory witnesses for Byzantine musical traditions among the Slavs, even in the period immediately after 1453.

The picture that emerges regarding the musical traditions of the various Russian peoples places us in an unenviable position. In the very year in which we celebrate the millennium of the Christianization of Kievan Rus', we simply have to write off the first half of that millennium as a period that remains enigmatic as far as the sound of the melodies is concerned. The reason for this state of affairs requires some discussion of the musical notation itself.

On the basis of musical manuscripts, it would appear that in Byzantium musical notation was viewed as a "tool" and that it evolved continuously through the centuries. While the earliest form of this notation, in use until the late twelfth century, cannot be read or transcribed into modern Western musical notation, from the end of the twelfth century onward the so-called Middle Byzantine musical notation is readable and can be transcribed easily into the notation commonly used in the West.[4]

It has already been pointed out that Byzantine notation penetrated into Russian usage by the eleventh century. Yet instead of being viewed as a tool subject to evolution, the notation was treated by the Russian copyists of manuscripts as being as inviolable as the text—that is, it was copied for centuries without any attempt at modernization. Thus the Russian musical documents reflect the early, unreadable stage of the Byzantine notation, which cannot be transcribed into our notation.

There are at present no fewer than fifty musical manuscripts of Russian origin and with musical notation written between the eleventh and fifteenth centuries. While this notation is clearly Byzantine in origin, there is at present no way in which these melodies can be reconstructed and brought to life. Given the present state of scholarship in this area, only some fragments of melodies may be transcribed, and there are enormous difficulties that have to be overcome before this music can be heard again.

There is some evidence that in the fifteenth century the process of change had begun, and by the sixteenth century had attained a new stage, in which a notation based on different principles from those of Byzantium came to be used. Even so, this notation becomes readable only in the seventeenth century. By that time, however, the melodies, while observing occasionally some patterns of structure that may be of Byzantine origin, display melodic outlines that strongly suggest the penetration of folk-song tunes into liturgical practice. This interrelationship of folk and liturgical music requires further study before anything more definitive can be stated.

There is, however, one aspect of liturgical and musical practice which the Russians certainly borrowed from Byzantium, and which seems to have enjoyed a moderate degree of use in some of the cathedrals, and that is the so-called ἀκολουθία τῆς καμίνου, or "Play of the Furnace," which is documented in several fifteenth-century musical manuscripts of Byzantine origin. This liturgical drama (and we shall use this term even though most Greeks object to it!) became quite popular and was profusely elaborated in Russian practices of the sixteenth and seventeenth centuries, when it was known to the Russians as *Peshchnoe deistvo*. Performed at Matins on the Sunday before Christmas, its theatrical appeal was great, and the Russian documentation of its staging may serve as a testimony to the process of adaptation of an originally modest Byzantine ritual that was chanted, as was any element of a religious service.[5]

This drama was a reminder of the steadfastness of the three children in the fiery furnace (as recounted in the Book of Daniel, chapter 3). The Byzantine version of this "Play of the Furnace" is rather simple, with mere hints of theatricality. In Russia its performance is documented from the first half of the fifteenth century through 1648, when it ceased to be a part of the services. The Russian rendition abounds with so many theatrical effects and stage props that it truly deserves to be viewed as a liturgical drama.

Subsequent developments of Russian religious music in the eighteenth century reflected musical practices that flourished because of the ever-stronger presence of foreign musicians, particularly Italian opera composers, and the schooling of Russians in Western Europe. The polyphonic music that emerged in Russia in the mid-seventeenth century gradually received a strong dose of Italian musical influence and was marked by the formation of an Italianate musical style, especially during the rule of Catherine the Great. This was the time of the growth of music for several choirs, each of which consisted of several parts (i.e., voices). Russian music came to be known for its use of deep basses and harmonic singing. The latter was absent in the Byzantine musical tradition. Byzantine chant from the outset was monophonic, consisting of a single melodic line. It is curious to note in passing that at the beginning of the twentieth century the inheritors of Byzantine musical traditions in Greece felt impelled to try to adopt Russian polyphonic models for experimentation in choral singing, a practice that is frowned upon by the majority of Greeks and is to this day restricted in Greece to a few churches only.

My reference to monophonic chant as being *the* Byzantine way of singing requires some additional comment. The term *monophonic* (i.e., singing in unison) properly applies to the type of practice found in the West in Gregorian chant. Yet as anyone who has attended a service in a Greek church knows, in addition to a melody there is a drone that the choir intones and chants, while on top of that drone a melody is being woven. The drone is known as ἴσον. What is the age of the "ison" and of its use? The best answer is, we do not know! The "ison" was never written down, and the earliest record in score is to be found only in the nineteenth century. Yet witnesses heard it in the sixteenth century: Martin Crusius, in his *Turcograeciae libri octo* (Basel, 1584), mentions reports of having heard the drone sound. It is a practice that parallels some folk music idioms in more than one part of the world, suggesting that it is not an isolated phenomenon. Further investigation is needed into the possibility of the use of the drone in periods when no written records support its existence.

For the time being we will defer the discussion of the musical traditions among the Serbs and the Rumanians (who, while not Slavs, by location belong to the sphere of Byzantine influence). Before we glance at those geographical areas, I shall try to depict, as succinctly as possible, the state of the art of Byzantine music and its practices in the mid-fifteenth century, so that the extent and examples of this art may be more easily grasped.

By the mid-fifteenth century the religious services in Byzantium were well established and quite elaborately developed.[6] Contrary to the superficial impression of some writers who claim that Byzantine liturgical rites were ossified and unchanged for centuries, any thorough study of musical manuscripts containing the vast body of hymns of all types used all over the Greek-speaking world, as well as among the Slavs, demonstrates quite clearly that as time went by the services *did* change and become enriched

with the availability of a constantly growing number of musical compositions. This is not to say that in actual practice some of the services could
not be abridged, as some of them undoubtedly were. The point, however,
is that from the fourteenth century onward there is a growing number of
new settings of hymns, copied side by side with the earlier melodies. Thus
on any specific feast day in the church calendar, singers could be faced by
an embarrassment of riches when having to decide which one of the many
settings of the same text, some old and some recent, they would chant
during a particular service. Therefore the celebration of the same type of
service could vary from day to day, each time using a different tune, in
addition to whatever traditional melodies were prescribed for specific
segments of the service.[7]

Furthermore, chanters in the fourteenth and fifteenth centuries, and
later as well, were often persons of considerable renown. Some attained
high positions in the church hierarchy. As we talk of these musicians, we
should stress that most of them were not only poets, but composers and
probably performers. Seldom does one encounter a division of labor
whereby a composer was only a composer, or a poet only a poet. There are
known instances in which a poet's text was set to music by another person,
a professional musician. We also know, particularly in later centuries (the
seventeenth and eighteenth), that there was a conscious attempt by some
professional musicians to recompose the whole church music repertory;
and we can only guess at this time why such an endeavor was undertaken.
Perhaps this huge project was prompted by a change in musical taste.
There may have been a desire to provide additional melodic embellish-
ments in order to make the sound of the music more attractive, or to purify
it from such accretions as were considered unsuitable for the deeply emo-
tional experience that a religious ceremony was supposed to be.

Let me also mention that names of musicians are known in great
numbers. While for earlier centuries their number is rather small, and
within certain periods there are occasional instances of anonymity such as
we encounter among painters of icons, from the fourteenth century onward, names of musicians are recorded in always increasing numbers, and
not necessarily with modesty. Some twenty years ago I published a study
dealing with the list of names of musicians in a rather ample musical
anthology dating from 1453 (MS 2406, National Library of Athens), with
a nice colophon recording the fall of Constantinople. In that manuscript
alone I found more than one hundred names of musicians and composers
to whom the melodies of hymns were attributed.[8] That is an impressive

number, especially if one compares it to the number of musicians known by name in all of Western Europe in the same period. Among these musicians were a few Slavs, although their number, compared to that of the Greeks, is quite small.

One curious point with reference to these earliest Slavic musicians (disregarding the famous hymn-writer John Koukouzeles, who was probably half Slav!) is that until the mid-fifteenth century they never used Slavonic texts but wrote music with Greek texts. Only in the fifteenth and sixteenth centuries do we encounter bilingual manuscripts that contain a single melody, yet with texts both in Greek and in Slavonic translation. One such source is a manuscript, small in size but significant for its content, no. 928 in the National Library of Athens, which contains a number of examples of chants with identical musical notation and two different texts, indicating that either text, Greek or Slavonic, could be sung to the same melody.

Rather unusual is the so-called Yale Fragment of the late eighteenth century. Written at the request of the metropolitan Serafim of Bosnia, the musician Peter of the Peloponnese, then very famous, set music to the Slavonic text.[9] The inscription at the beginning of the manuscript reads, "With [the help of] Holy God—[this] anastasimatarion[10] was set to music in the Slavonic dialect by the most learned musician, Kyr Peter Lampadarios of the Peloponnese, according to the order of the old anastasimatarion, at the request of the Very Reverend and Holy Metropolitan of Bosnia, Kyr Serafim, for the use of the Slavs and for the memory of his soul." Yet the whole manuscript is written in Greek transliteration of the Slavonic words.

Some fifty years ago there was rejoicing at the discovery of the first name of a Serb musician—Kyr Stefan the Serb—a musician of the fifteenth century. At present we know more names of musicians who called themselves Serbs and who may have been active in the fifteenth century, among them Nicolas the Serb and Isaiah the Serb. The case of the monk Joachim of the Harsianites Monastery in Constantinople, who had the title "domesticus of Serbia," is moot about his nationality, as he might have been either a Greek or Serb, a distinction that was, after all, irrelevant at that time. We also know that one of the most famous musicians of the period, the "lampadarios" Manuel Chrysaphes (whose autograph anthology—MS 1120—in the Iviron monastery on Mount Athos is dated 1458) resided in Serbia at one time. We have no idea why or when he did so, but we do know that one of his compositions is recorded in several manuscripts as a work which he "composed while in Serbia." This suggests that the musical traditions of Byzantium were being cultivated in Serbia at the time of the fall of Constantinople and beyond.[11]

Besides syllabic chants of psalms and various hymns and other more elaborate versions, there were highly melismatic chants in use. One such example from approximately the middle of the fifteenth century is a hymn sung at the Liturgy of the Presanctified, the Greek text starting with the words Νῦν αἱ δυνάμεις, or in Slavic, "Ninje sili nebesnija." (In English the text reads, "Now the Celestial Powers minister with us invisibly for lo, the King of Glory entereth now. Alleluia!") This hymn appears to be the best-known work of Kyr Stefan the Serb, and it has been located in a handful of manuscripts from the fifteenth and sixteenth centuries. This example of the creativity of a Serbian composer is currently accessible in a modern transcription by the Serbian scholar Dimitrije Stefanović, who has also recorded it in a performance by the Study Choir of the Musicological Institute in Belgrade.[12]

After the Turkish conquest of Serbia, in 1459, there are no records of Serbian composers until the late seventeenth and the eighteenth centuries, when some works appear in manuscripts, still retaining the basic Byzantine principles of the structuring of melodies and written in the contemporary Byzantine musical notation.

For sources pertaining to the sixteenth century, our attention has to shift from Serbia to a more distant territory, the very northern borders of present-day Rumania, and to the monastery of Putna, which was founded in the early years of the sixteenth century. In the next several decades Putna became a significant center for the copying of musical manuscripts and for the training of singers. Its most prominent musician was Eustathius the Protopsaltes, who composed a number of hymns and was renowned throughout the Balkans. Like his predecessors, he composed works that could be sung in either Greek or Slavonic. It is difficult, however, to assign a nationality to him, although Bulgarians and Rumanians have both claimed him for their own. In the last two decades no fewer than ten manuscripts have come to light illustrating the activities of Eustathius and of the Putna scriptorium. Of Eustathius' numerous compositions one might single out the most impressive setting of the Trisagion Hymn, a hymn which had existed in more than a dozen different versions, and to which he added his own version.[13]

If one were to listen to the musical compositions of Kyr Stefan the Serb and those of Eustathius, one might wonder what it is that is Byzantine in them. On what grounds can we claim the persistent presence of Byzantine artistic ideas in the musical style and the creativity of non-Greek musicians at a time when there was no longer in existence a Byzantine Empire that might have ensured by its power the acceptance of Byzantine influence?

We can examine this question by observing some rather obvious points: these compositions were written down using the contemporary Byzantine musical notation, and they can be found only in manuscripts containing the chants of the Eastern Orthodox rite and the texts that are used in that ritual. One may try to counter this point by suggesting that non-Byzantine melodies could just as well have been written down in Byzantine musical notation; we do have one example of a Roman Catholic *Kyrie eleison* recorded in a Byzantine manuscript.[14] But there are other aspects of this music that have to be considered as well. These are the use of rather specific modes and the presence of melodic formulas. A brief attempt at explaining these concepts is in order.

In Western European music of the Roman Catholic rite the whole body of chants is organized according to what is usually called a system of church scales, or modes. Each of these Western modes refers to a pitch-range (for example, from d to d^1, or from e to e^1), or an "octave-species," amounting to the eight basic scales. The Byzantine system of eight modes, known as *Oktoechos*, is different. What we translate as *mode* is in Greek designated as an ἦχος (or, as Slavs call it, a "glas"), and the important point to keep in mind is that the Byzantine *echos* is not a scale but a repertory of melodic formulas.[15] Thus one of the essential traits of Byzantine music is that it is *formulaic* and that each *echos* contains a set of melodic formulas. The Byzantine melodic formulas are not an ossified body of melodic turns, but only a skeleton, and each formula can be expanded and varied, while retaining its basic outline, which can be distinguished in the chanting. In short, the use of the formulaic principle in the structuring of the musical aspect of a hymn reveals the individual composer's degree of skill in using and interweaving these formulas. There is nothing comparable, to my knowledge, in the Western European tradition of chanting. Thus even if we disregard the musical notation, we can claim Byzantine origin and Byzantine influence when these traits appear.

The duration of Byzantine influence on the music of the Slavs varies. I have pointed out that in the case of Russian church music Byzantine influence ceases to play any significant role as early as the fifteenth century, by the time of the fall of Constantinople, when the new Muscovite state begins to take shape. I also stated that at present, at least, evidence of Byzantine influence on the musical traditions of Bulgaria is minimal, basically due to an almost total lack of documentation until rather late in the history of Bulgarian church music.

Serbian musical manuscripts of the eighteenth century still reflect a close adherence to Byzantine musical principles. Then suddenly, in the nineteenth century, the Serbian chant tunes collected by such a scholar as Stevan Mokranjac seem to show no resemblance whatsoever to Byzantine models. To make things even more curious, it was while studying these "new" melodies, as I call them, that Egon Wellesz discovered the principle of formulaic structure and then applied it to the examination of the Byzantine tradition.[16] Thus Wellesz established the basic premises for the investigation of Byzantine music. In a way this discovery by Wellesz, made during the period of the First World War, based on his examination of Mokranjac's edition of the *Osmoglasnik* (i.e., the Serbian *Oktoechos*), was a step toward the closing of a circle that began with the penetration of Byzantine influence into Slavic culture. The latter, as we know now, was shaped in a multitude of ways by Byzantine models.

It is a curious irony of history that the investigation and study of Byzantine music and its practice were neglected and ignored for so long by Western European scholars, and that the rediscovery of some of the basic and truly essential aspects of this musical tradition would take place, and find its key, in the study of the music of one of the inheritors of the Byzantine tradition other than Greece. It was in a country the culture of which was an offshoot of Byzantium's that the Byzantine way of thinking and of putting ideas together had been retained as the guiding principle. Needless to say, we are still studying this process of cultural adoption and hope to understand it even better in the years to come.

Notes

1. For a comprehensive survey of the state of present knowledge about the history of the church chants among the Slavs, see my entry in the *New Grove Dictionary of Music and Musicians*, ed. Stanley Sadie (Washington, D.C.: Grove's Dictionaries of Music, 1980), s.v. "Russian and Slavonic Church Music."

2. *New Grove Dictionary*, "Slavonic Neumatic Notations," s.v. "Neumatic Notations."

3. "Russian and Slavonic Church Music," 342–43.

4. *New Grove Dictionary*, "Byzantine Neumatic Notations," s.v. "Neumatic Notations."

5. Miloš M. Velimirović, "Liturgical Drama in Byzantium and Russia," *Dumbarton Oaks Papers* 16 (1962): 349–85.

6. The best discussion of the developments of Byzantine chant in Greek-speaking areas has just been published by Dimitri Conomos: "Sacred Music in the Post-Byzantine Era," in *The Byzantine Legacy in Eastern Europe*, ed. Lowell Clucas (Boulder, Colo.: East European Monographs, 1988), 83–105.

7. Documentation of this practice is presented by me in "The Prooemiac Psalm of Byzantine Vespers," in *Words and Music: The Scholars' View; a Medley of Problems and Solutions Compiled in Honor of A. Tillman Merritt by Sundry Hands*, ed. Laurence Berman (Cambridge: Harvard University, Department of Music, 1972), 317–37.

8. Miloš Velimirović, "Byzantine Composers in MS Athens 2406," in *Essays Presented to Egon Wellesz*, ed. Sir Jack [Allan] Westrup (Oxford: Clarendon Press, 1966), 7–18.

9. Dimitrije Stefanović and Miloš Velimirović, "Peter Lampadarios and Metropolitan Serafim of Bosnia," *Studies in Eastern Chant* 1 (London: Oxford Univ. Press, 1966): 67–85. The manuscript has no call number. It consists of eleven sheets of paper glued into a binding containing two Greek printed books (ibid., 67 n. 1). For the inscription in the original Greek and in English translation see ibid., 68.

10. The word *anastasimatarion* does not appear in older sources. It refers to the book containing ordinary hymns sung at Vespers on Saturday and Matins of Sunday services. The most comprehensive study of the anastasimatarion is that of Adriana Şirli, *The Anastasimatarion: The Thematic Repertory of Byzantine and Post-Byzantine Musical Manuscripts* (Bucharest: Musical Publishing House, 1986 [bilingual edition in Rumanian and English]).

11. Miloš Velimirović, "Joakeim Monk of the Harsianites Monastery and Domestikos of Serbia," in *Recueil de travaux de l'Institut d'Etudes Byzantines*, 8/2: *Mélanges Georges Ostrogorsky* (Belgrade: Naučno Delo, 1964): 451–58.

12. For basic data about Stefan the Serb, see *Leksikon jugoslavenske muzike*, 2 vols. (Zagreb: Jugoslavenski Leksikografski Zavod "Miroslav Krleza," 1984), 2:375–76. The modern transcription by Stefanović was published for the first time in Josip Andreis, Dragotin Cvetko, and Stana Djurić-Klajn, *Historijski razvoj muzičke kulture u Jugoslaviji* (Historical development of musical culture in Yugoslavia) (Zagreb: Školska knjiga, 1962), 564.

13. The late Anne Elizabeth Pennington, of Oxford University, devoted no fewer than six studies to the musical activities at the Putna monastery, and these are assembled in a posthumous tribute to her, entitled, *Music in Medieval Moldavia: 16th Century* (Bucharest: Musical Publishing House, 1985 [bilingual edition in Rumanian and English]). This volume includes Dimitri Conomos's study "The Monastery of Putna and the Musical Tradition of Moldavia in the Sixteenth Century" (221–66), which is published also in *Dumbarton Oaks Papers* 26 (1982): 15–28.

14. See the reference in the report by Michael Adamis, "An Example of Polyphony in Byzantine Music of the Late Middle Ages," in *Report of the Eleventh Congress, Copenhagen 1972* (Copenhagen: International Musicological Society, 1974), 2:737.

15. For more information about *Echos* and *Oktoechos*, see *New Grove Dictionary*, s.vv.

16. Egon Wellesz's first study on this subject was "Das serbische Oktoechos und die Kirchentöne," *Musica Sacra*, 50th year, fasc. 2 (1917): 17–19, followed by, "Die Struktur des serbischen Oktoechos," *Zeitschrift für Musikwissenschaft* 2 (1919–20): 140–48. His long series of studies culminated in his magisterial *A History of Byzantine Music and Hymnography*, 2d ed. rev. and enl. (Oxford: Clarendon Press, 1961). On the significance of Wellesz's work, see my "Egon Wellesz and the Study of Byzantine Chant," *Musical Quarterly* 52 (1976): 265–77.

THE BYZANTINE TRADITION IN THE CHURCH ARCHITECTURE OF THE BALKANS IN THE SIXTEENTH AND SEVENTEENTH CENTURIES

Charalambos Bouras

THE FALL OF Constantinople in May 1453 marked a sudden, violent interruption of the political life of the Christian peoples of the Balkans, but not of their religious life. Under the Sacred Muslim Law of the Ottoman state, the Christians assuredly became second-class citizens, but they were allowed to retain their religion, culture, administration of justice, and language.[1] Art and architecture, therefore, both of which served mainly their religious needs, continued to be practiced, and in some cases, when circumstances permitted, even underwent noteworthy development.

Today we find a rich and varied architecture, with hundreds of churches built after the middle of the fifteenth century, scattered virtually throughout the territories of the former Byzantine Empire. In any ambitious study of this architecture, it would be necessary to determine where and when the prevailing conditions were favorable for its creation, who took the initiative and financial responsibility for the erection of the buildings, and, finally, who were the builders. Unfortunately we are far from knowing the answers to these questions in regard to the great majority of the monuments.

Elsewhere in this volume others have described the social and administrative situation in the period of Turkish rule and the major role played by the church as the representative of the Christian nationalities within the Ottoman Empire. In matters of culture, as well, including art and architecture, the church's role remained a fundamental one, exercised largely through a well-organized system of metropolitan sees, bishoprics, and communities, and through the numerous monasteries.

As will become apparent later in this essay, architecture, as it evolved, kept the Byzantine tradition alive at least until the end of the seventeenth century. This means that it preserved to a significant degree the Greco-Roman architectural heritage of Late Antiquity. The patriarchate of Constantinople, which was naturally inclined to maintain the Byzantine modus operandi, preserved its Greek character, retained Greek as the official language, and continued to use the medieval Greek administrative and legal institutions that had been formed before the fall of Constantinople to the Ottomans. In other spheres, too, the Greeks, for a variety of reasons, retained a privileged position vis-à-vis the other subject Christian populations in the Ottoman system, until about 1830.[2]

But the patriarchate did not have any direct influence on architecture. This was due to the special conditions prevailing in the capital, a city to which the ambitious building projects of the sultans very quickly gave an impressive Turkish character. Nor was painting cultivated there by the church.[3] The earlier Byzantine churches in the city, chief amongst them Hagia Sophia, were converted into mosques, and the new churches, built under a discouraging and restrictive legal system, were few in number and deliberately humble in appearance. These churches were certainly not suitable as models for imitation outside the capital.

The models were supplied mainly by the monasteries. As an institution, the monasteries had changed hardly at all during the transition from Byzantine to Ottoman rule. Far from the cities, with their dense Turkish populations, the monasteries were relatively lightly taxed; and those that were patriarchal *stauropegia*—that is, under the immediate jurisdiction of the patriarchate and therefore independent of the local bishops—evolved into economically self-sufficient units, as well as religious and cultural centers. Under the peaceful conditions in the Balkans, particularly in the sixteenth century, old monasteries and also newly founded ones flourished, the former as never before. In the islands, in Thessaly (mainly at Meteora), in the Fruška Gora region of Serbia, and on Mount Athos large catholica[4] were erected at this time, adorned with brilliant wall paintings and portable icons and endowed with lavish incomes. Mount Athos, in particular, continued to enjoy an international reputation as a monastic center in the sixteenth and seventeenth centuries and exercised a direct influence on the entire Orthodox monastic world. The architecture of Mount Athos thus became very well known,[5] and Athonite buildings (churches but also other monastic structures) served as models throughout the Balkan peninsula for almost the next three centuries.

During the years of foreign domination, it was around the church that the Balkan Christians rallied in their great effort to survive. In order to live up to its role, the church turned to the established values of the past and became extremely conservative. This conservatism was a means of preserving the church's identity within the Turkish system and of resisting penetration by Western culture and the spirit of Roman Catholicism. The church thus retained, on the one hand, the scholarly tradition based on Greek theological literature, and on the other hand the artistic tradition inherited from Byzantium. In the latter case the promotion of Byzantine models kept quality at a high level and prevented the corruption of the arts through the adoption of a popular style, although this could not be avoided later, in the eighteenth and nineteenth centuries. Many of the ecumenical patriarchs were conscious of the role played by the church and were men of outstanding authority and intellectual repute. In Serbia, the patriarchate of Peć, which was reestablished during the period 1557–1600, played the same role by fostering a turn to the medieval style in the churches built there.[6]

Among the institutions connecting the period under examination with the Byzantine past was that of patronage. It was a long-standing religious and social custom to found monasteries, build churches, and adorn the churches with wall paintings, icons, and precious liturgical vessels. In Byzantium, the patrons had usually been the emperors, the aristocratic families, and state officials. After 1453 they were high church officials or the humbler members of congregations, either priests or entire communities. Later, beginning in the seventeenth century, the patrons included the Phanariot princes of Wallachia and Moldavia, the professional city guilds, and, finally, wealthy individuals, who usually founded monasteries. As in Byzantine times, acts of architectural patronage were commemorated by founders' inscriptions carved or painted above the entrances to the churches (fig. 1.1), and occasionally by donor portraits. Hundreds of these inscriptions have survived, comprising valuable source material for scholars studying the art and architecture of the period after 1453.

As we have already seen, the erection of churches was not forbidden by Turkish law. But it was systematically discouraged.[7] The necessary permits usually sanctioned the construction of a church only on the site of, and no larger than, an earlier church that had been destroyed, and these permits were valid for only a very short period of time. Some exceptions were tolerated on extraordinary occasions of general celebration, however, such as at the birth of a successor to the sultan or a royal marriage.[8] Also it was difficult for the authorities to check permits in the provinces; and less oppressive rules obtained in areas where the Christians had been granted special privileges, such as Mount Athos and the majority of the Aegean Islands.

The seventeenth century was not selected by chance as the chronological terminus for this survey. The Treaty of Karlowitz, in 1699, by which large areas of Greek territory were ceded by the Ottomans to Venice, was of great importance for the Greeks; but even more important was the gradual change in the predominant economic and social conditions after 1700, which produced a deep rift in the culture of the Balkans. Architecture and also painting changed in character after this date. One might claim that it was at this time that the post-Byzantine period ended and the modern period began.

In quantity and in quality the churches built in the sixteenth and seventeenth centuries differ greatly from one area to another, although invariably within the context described above. In the cities, such as Thessaloniki, Larissa, and Sofia, there are very few churches from this period, and these are architecturally insignificant. By contrast, in Attica and Epirus dozens of new churches were built, usually as the catholica of small monasteries. This uneven distribution is, of course, not unconnected to the settlement of Turkish populations in certain areas, such as Thrace, where comparatively few churches have survived.

The new flowering of the monasteries also had some indirect results. It is possible to detect the repopulation and revival of abandoned Byzantine complexes, like that of Hosios Loukas in Phocis, and the maintenance or even expansion of the prestige of other ancient complexes that were imperial foundations, such as the Great Lavra on Mount Athos, the monastery of St. John the Theologian on Patmos, the Nea Moni on Chios, and the distant monastery of St. Catherine in the Sinai. The use of the old catholica of these monasteries as architectural models, and the erection of new buildings within the ancient complexes themselves, restored the architectural link with the Byzantine past, through repetition of the traditional types and forms on a larger scale. As we shall see, foreign architectural elements, of Western or Ottoman origin, were admitted only to a limited extent, despite their impressiveness and accessibility.

The reluctance to admit foreign elements was not universal. In areas like Crete and the Ionian Islands, which remained under the suzerainty of Venice during this period, Western models—Gothic at first and Renaissance later—gradually met with acceptance, and in these regions the result was a radical and irrevocable break with the Byzantine architectural tradition.[9] At the same time, the local "schools" that had crystallized at an earlier date, like that of Serbia, continued to develop independently and produced some impressive buildings, in which the Byzantine tradition is evident to a lesser degree, as in Novo Hopovo and Mesić (figs. 1.2, 1.3).

Scholarly studies of the vast wealth of monuments surviving from the Turkish period in the Balkans are still very few and mostly unsystematic in their approach to the material. This is due to a reluctance on the part of many scholars to study a period that was not a "glorious" one in the history of the Balkans, and also to the indifference of foreign scholars to an art that did not contribute to the evolution of the arts in Western Europe during this period. In Greece, where the most numerous and important monuments of the period are to be found, there has never been a systematic inventory, documentation, or publication of them.[10] Many individual scholarly studies have appeared, however. We may note those of the churches of the Meteora by Soteriou;[11] of Kastoria, Athens, the island of Paros, and the Pindus by Orlandos;[12] of the prefectures of Pella and Florina by Moutsopoulos;[13] and of Attica and Boeotia by Lazarides.[14] For the monuments of Serbia up to 1690, one may turn to the excellent book by Šuput, which appeared in 1984.[15] Nevertheless a vast number of other monuments, in Yugoslavian Macedonia and other regions of the country, remain unknown. The Bulgarian churches of the centuries of Turkish rule have been studied by Mijatev and Koeva, and recently a broad, comprehensive study has been devoted to them by Kiel.[16] For Rumania, the gap is partially filled by the old, general survey by Ionescu.[17] The Cypriot monuments are known only from their wall paintings. In Albania, finally, the initial part of a first inventory and documentation has been published by Meksi and Thomo, in the periodical *Monumentet*.[18] A major comprehensive work covering all of the Balkan churches of this period remains a desideratum.

We may now quickly examine, by geographical area, some of the more important churches of the period. These form only a very small portion of the existing wealth of monuments, but an introduction to them is essential if we are to gain a direct knowledge of the subject.

Six of the largest catholica on Mount Athos belong to the sixteenth century and are in an excellent state of preservation.[19] They are those of the monasteries of Iviron (1514), Dionysiou (1539), Koutloumousi (1540), Stavronikita (1542), Xenophontos (1544), and Docheiariou (1568). A great number of other churches, in smaller Athonite foundations, such as hermitages, and also many utilitarian buildings, belong to the same or to the following century, the seventeenth.

Eastern Macedonia and Thrace have very few monuments,[20] but in central and western Macedonia they are both numerous and important. We may note the catholicon of St. Nikanor at Zavorda (unpublished; fig. 1.4), dating from 1534 (with superb wall paintings by Frangos Katelanos);[21] St. Zacharias, in the region of Kastoria; St. Demetrios at Vergina (1570); and the large catholicon of St. Anastasia near Thessaloniki (unpublished; fig. 1.5), which was restored in the nineteenth century.

Thessaly too is rich in post-Byzantine churches. The catholica of the monasteries of the Meteora, built in an awe-inspiring natural setting, are the most important: they are at the Great Meteoron (ca. 1550; fig. 1.6), Holy Trinity (1476), Barlaam (1517; fig. 1.7), and St. Stephen (1536; subsequently restored).[22] Thessaly, however, also has Dousiko, founded by St. Bessarion (1522; fig. 1.8), St. Panteleimon at Aghia (1580), the monastery of Petra (1550), and the monastery of Flamouri (1602), all of them monuments of exceptionally fine architecture and with excellent wall paintings, and all clearly influenced by Mount Athos.[23] The region of Phthiotis and Phocis to the south is of similar importance, with the monastery of Agathonos and the large catholicon of the monastery of Antinitsa, now in ruins, which was built at the end of the fifteenth century.[24] The islands of Euboea and the northern Sporades also have a number of monuments, smaller in scale but equally important, such as St. George "of the Castle" (*tou Kastrou*) on Skyros (fig. 1.9), the Galataki Monastery (1547), and St. George Arma (1637; fig. 1.10).[25]

In Attica there are the monasteries of Asteri, Pendeli, and Daou Pendeli, and in Athens numerous small basilicas, among which we may note St. Dionysios on the Areopagus, the ruins of which were discovered during an excavation by the American School of Classical Studies.[26] In the Peloponnesos are a number of important monasteries, such as Agnous (fig. 1.11), the Taxiarchai near Aighion (1620; fig. 1.12), the Aghia Lavra near Kalavryta, and those at Levidhi (fig. 1.13), Monemvasia (fig. 1.14), and Zerbitsa; and many small churches are preserved in the Mani (fig. 1.15).[27]

In western Greece, in Epirus, Aetolia, and Acarnania, as we have noted, a large number of monasteries have survived, usually with small catholica of local importance, dating from the seventeenth century. The catholica of the monasteries of Philanthropinoi and of St. John Prodromos on a small island in the Lake of Ioannina, and those of the monasteries at Sosinos and Zitsa, are among the most important.[28] On the Aegean Islands, the Cyclades (as on Thera, fig. 1.16), and the Dodecanese, many churches, most of them small, survive, harmoniously incorporated into the architectural complexes of the settlements, as on Mykonos, Paros, Siphnos, and Naxos. Outstanding monuments here include the Chotzoviotissa on Amorgos, the Paraportiani on Mykonos, the Meghali Panaghia on Samos (1596), the small church of the Holy Apostles on Patmos (1603) (a dependency of the monastery of St. John the Theologian), and the monasteries of Meghali Panaghia (fig. 1.17), Hypapanti (fig. 1.18), and Zoodochos Pighi (1617), also on Patmos.[29] On Cyprus, finally, there are at least ten churches built in the fifteenth or sixteenth centuries, and incidentally possessing wall paintings of high quality; these churches are all of the same plan, that of an aisleless basilica with a pitched wooden roof.[30]

The picture we have seen in western Greece, with small seventeenth-century catholica, may be extended unchanged to northern Epirus, the southern portion of modern Albania,[31] as for instance in the church of the Birth of the Virgin in Elbasan (fig. 1.19). The notable monuments here include the catholica of the monastery of the Timios Prodromos (Holy Forerunner) at Moschopolis (1632), St. Nicholas at Sarakinista (1630), and the Koimesis at Zervati (1583). In Bulgaria, the ecclesiastical monuments of the sixteenth and seventeenth centuries are usually small, aisleless basilicas, like that of Dobursko (1600–1614; fig. 1.20), or small three-apsed churches like the catholicon of the Trun Monastery (fig. 1.21).[32] It is only in the cases of the Panaghia at Bačkovo (figs. 1.22, 1.23) and the two basilicas at Arbanassi (Nativity and Archangels), that somewhat larger churches are met with in Bulgaria.

In Serbia, too, many ecclesiastical monuments survive from after the Ottoman conquest. We note, on the one hand, buildings attesting to an extension of the so-called Morava school of late Byzantine times, with aisleless domed churches (such as Remeta) or cross-domed churches (such as those at Krušedol or Novo Hopovo [fig. 1.2]); and on the other hand, a turn towards the medieval style of Raška, as we see at Mlado Nagoričino. Aisleless basilicas are very widely found, as far afield as Macedonia and Kossovo, without any typological variations.[33]

In order to detect similarities or differences between the church-building of the period of Turkish rule and that of the preceding period, it is necessary to make some analysis of the plans, architectural forms, and methods of construction that were predominant after 1453. A thorough analysis is, of course, not possible in a brief survey, especially in view of the large number of examples to be studied.

No architectural types occur among the churches of the sixteenth and seventeenth centuries that did not exist before 1453.[34] One cannot explain this fact on the grounds that the plans follow the Orthodox liturgy, which did not change in any significant respect after the fall of Byzantium in 1453. This explanation overlooks the large variety of church plans created by Byzantine architecture in every phase of its history. The repetition of earlier types should therefore be regarded as a symptom of the conservatism characteristic of the times.

The domed cross-in-square church, which formed the most common type in the middle and late Byzantine periods, continued to be a favored solution in the period that concerns us, from the Peloponnesos (as in two churches at Chrysapha, Laconia) and Attica (as in the two churches of the Koimesis at Oropos [fig. 1.24] and Sykaminon), to Bosnia (e.g., Gomionica) and Dalmatia (Krka).[35] The most widely found type, however, invariably used as a catholicon, is the cross-in-square domed church with apses added to the cross-arms—that is, the plan that is usually known as Athonite. And in fact the earliest examples of this type were built on Mount Athos, at the monasteries of the Great Lavra and Vatopedi.[36] It was from these buildings that this monastic plan par excellence, characterized also by a deep narthex of the kind usually called a λιτή, acquired its prestige and attraction. Churches of the Athonite type were built in Greece right up to the eighteenth century (catholica of Philotheou and Grigoriou on Mount Athos, fig. 1.25) and even the nineteenth century, as seen at Perivoli, Grevena (1803).[37] Characteristic examples from the sixteenth century are those of Dousiko in Thessaly (1522), the monastery of Agathonos in Locris, the monastery of Koroni in the Pindus (1587), Bačkovo in Bulgaria (figs. 1.22, 1.23), the Annunciation at Papraca in Serbia, and the six important Athonite catholica already mentioned. The idea of the two side apses housing the two groups of choristers in monastic churches of this type was adopted in many cases for smaller, aisleless churches, domed or not, as in Bulgaria (fig. 1.21) and some small monasteries on the Pindus.[38]

Other plans, deriving directly from Byzantium, continued to be employed. There are, for example, many small hall churches with domes (such as St. Athanasius in Selenitsa, fig. 1.26), domed free-cross churches (such as Prophet Elias at Koropi, Attica), and trefoil churches (such as the

Hypapanti on Hydra, and St. Nicholas at Kontra, Attica).³⁹ Basilicas also continued to be built, both timber-roofed, as in many examples in Kastoria, and barrel-vaulted, such as the Chrysopighi on Siphnos and some churches in Athens, a typical example of which is in the dependent monastery of the Holy Sepulchre there.⁴⁰ One building type of Byzantine origin that was now more widely used than before was the three-aisled basilica with dome, which can be seen at Kritsini, at the Phaneromeni Monastery on Salamis,⁴¹ and in many locations in northern Epirus, now southern Albania (at Vrachgoratzi, 1622, for example, and Magouleoi). Transverse vaulted basilicas were also common, as in the late Byzantine period, and examples can be cited from Epirus (St. Menas at Monodendri) and Euboea (e.g., the church of the Koimesis in Amarynthos [fig. 1.27], and the Panaghitsa at Vatheia).⁴²

We may note, finally, the revival of earlier, rare types. A very rare type was revived at St. Menas on Chios, a stauropegion of the patriarch Jeremiah II, of about 1580. This church features a domed octagon laid on a square plan, built in imitation of an eleventh-century Byzantine monument of great renown, the catholicon of the Nea Moni, on the same island.⁴³

I conclude this typological review with the observation that foreign influences in church-building were limited. While it is true that in the islands under Venetian occupation—Crete and the Ionian Islands—simple timber-roofed halls gradually displaced the Byzantine types, Turkish buildings were almost never imitated by the local craftsmen. I say "almost," because in a single example, the catholicon of the monastery of Daou Pendeli, near Athens, the curious hexagonal system of support for the dome is believed to be an imitation of the system seen in some Turkish mosques of the period.⁴⁴

We may now, again briefly, analyze some of the monuments from the point of view of style and architectural form. The division into local "schools" that is observable in the Balkans as early as the thirteenth century, chiefly in Serbia, continued to hold true. This does not mean, however, that these schools did not have a common origin, albeit a distant one, in Byzantium.

The symbolism that served the Orthodox faith and found expression in the domes, in the inscribed-cross plan, and in the iconographic program of the interior was continued in the period of Turkish rule. In this respect, too, the Byzantine monuments in continuous use served as models. It is clear, moreover, that some of the forms that were charged with symbolism did not find favor with the local Turkish governors, and were forbidden. It is no coincidence, for example, that from the fall of Constantinople until the late nineteenth century, not a single church with a dome was built, and not a single bell tower, either in Constantinople or in Thessaloniki.

In the articulation of their exterior surfaces, the large catholica of the fifteenth and sixteenth centuries, such as those at Antinitsa and Dousiko, employ the blind arches of the Byzantine churches of Macedonia, a form that is later confined to the exterior surfaces of the bema apse.[45] The Byzantine custom of incorporating previously used sculptures into the facades was also continued in the fifteenth and sixteenth centuries. These ancient Greek, early Christian, or Byzantine spolia not only adorned the facades but gave them a diachronic character and conveyed a sense of history such as had apparently been popular with the Byzantines. Sculpture somewhat similar to that incorporated into the exterior surfaces of the famous small twelfth-century Metropolis church in Athens is to be found on St. George Arma and the Panaghitsa at Vatheia, both on Euboea, and at Episkopi, Ano Volos.[46] The articulation of the roofs with gables at the facades, which, in the well-established Byzantine manner, gives external emphasis to the form of the cross, is still clear in the large catholica of the period. The masonry, finally, depending on the economic means available, either represents a continuation of Byzantine methods or, more usually, a simpler, rubble construction. On Mount Athos we have masonry consisting of rows of ashlar blocks alternating with bands of bricks, and in Serbia, imperfect cloisonné masonry (e.g., Jašunje),[47] features reminiscent of Byzantine practice; but these are rather unusual.

The Byzantine form of the dome on a high drum recurs in the major monuments of the period. There are many-sided domes with cornices conforming to the arches of the windows, in imitation of Constantinopolitan domes (as at Koutloumousi and Esphigmenou on Mount Athos, and the monastery of Petra), and also imitations of the so-called Athenian domes with level cornices, up to the end of our period (as in the Phaneromeni on Salamis).[48] In Serbia there are purely Byzantine domes (as at Ovcar) and domes that have Romanesque elements, reviving the local tradition (as at Mesić, fig. 1.3, where they have a corbel table frieze).[49] The exterior articulation of both the bema apse and the side apses by means of blind arcading also follows Byzantine models in countless examples.

The disposition and shape of the openings is related both to the form of the church and to the requirements of the interior space with regard to natural lighting. In the larger churches there was no fundamental change after 1453, except that the doors and windows became perceptibly smaller and fewer. There was a gradual but ultimately radical reduction in the number of marble elements, such as the colonnettes framing windows and doors. These elements were to reappear much later, in churches of the eighteenth century, in a completely new form, influenced by Turkish decoration (e.g., the church of St. Nicholas in Sora, on Andros, fig. 1.28). The decline in the earlier marble-carving techniques is also apparent in the abandonment after 1453 of the marble bema screens and their gradual replacement with carved wooden iconostases, as in Dobursko (fig. 1.20) and Dousiko (fig. 1.8). This new form, of decisive importance for the aesthetic impression conveyed by the interior of an Orthodox church, evolved mainly in Venetian Crete,[50] whence it spread to Patmos[51] and the Ionian Islands, later becoming general throughout the Balkans.

The interiors of the churches in the Turkish period were dimly illuminated, for the most part, on account of the limited number of openings and the increased height of the iconostasis. The darkness of these interiors has been explained as indicative of a desire on the part of the Christians to isolate themselves from a hostile environment, particularly in the cities, and as an expression of the climate of mysticism inherited from the theological movements of the Palaeologan era. It is more likely, however, that the true reasons were simpler and more practical in nature, although they must remain a matter of conjecture. The interior space was, in any case, affected by the increased number of iconographic subjects adorning the walls. In contrast with Byzantine churches, in which the painted figures or scenes had a certain grandeur and monumentality, in the sixteenth and seventeenth centuries the interior surfaces were divided amongst a large number of subjects, clearly with the aim of making the programs as didactic as possible for the congregations. A later example of this tendency is furnished by the profusely historiated interior of the monastery church of the Phaneromeni on Salamis.[52]

We now turn, again very briefly, to matters of construction. Naturally enough, in an area as large as the Balkans, the local methods of construction were affected by the different materials used and the availability of local craftsmen in each area. Even before 1453, therefore, the earlier style inherited from Byzantium, although unified, had distinct local variations. This continued to be the case under Turkish rule, during which time, because of the small size of the churches, no serious problems of statics presented themselves and, consequently, no adventurous constructional solutions were advanced.

The masonry of the churches has already been mentioned. Vaults were usually constructed of slablike stones, although in some of the larger monuments, such as the catholica of the monasteries of Flamouri, of Petra, and of the Metamorphosis at Meteora, one finds light, well-built brick vaults, recalling the best periods of Byzantine architecture.[53] In the roofing of small, poorer churches, however, some innovations were made, in the attempt to meet structural requirements with the aid of materials and techniques available locally—as in the use of enormous natural stone slabs (St. Nicholas at Kechrovouni on Tinos, of 1662) or in the mixed system of a cheap wooden roof supported on transverse masonry arches (St. Athanasius at Kouvara, in Attica).[54] The vaults might be covered externally with tiles, slabs of schist, or flat, accessible terraces, as in the Cyclades and Dodecanese.

In matters of construction it is possible to detect the adoption of a few methods and forms that were common in the Ottoman architecture of the period. The supporting of semidomes on squinches, for example, found in some barrel-vaulted basilicas in Athens, is an Ottoman idea, unknown in Byzantium. The preference for roofing spaces with small blind domes of hemispherical section without regard to the relative importance of the space beneath, is again an idea in general application in the porticoes of mosques and in Turkish buildings of a utilitarian nature. The same is true of the half-cloistered vault that is found later in the basilicas of Moschopolis in northern Epirus.[55] Clearly these structures were not regarded as inappropriate or improper in churches, despite their derivation from a different tradition. We know, moreover, that the same groups of craftsmen worked on the erection of both mosques and churches.

With the exception of marble-working, then, the decline of which has already been mentioned, Byzantine construction techniques survived into the sixteenth and seventeenth centuries. Their gradual abandonment came later, after 1700, and was caused by the widespread use of wood, rather than masonry, for the roofs, walls, columns, and other structural elements, a technique that was originally employed in houses and utilitarian structures and subsequently became common in churches.

I hope that this analysis, albeit very hasty, of types, architectural forms, and methods of construction has provided adequate support for the views on Balkan church architecture of the sixteenth and seventeenth centuries that were expressed earlier in this essay. I summarize these views here: (a) This architecture is represented by a large number of monuments of high quality; (b) it displays continuity with Byzantine church architecture until the end of the seventeenth century; and (c) it retained its independence and made very little use of foreign elements.

The question that arises if we wish to give an overall evaluation of these impressive phenomena is whether this was a great chapter in the history of architecture. Historians differ in their opinions on this point, depending upon their frames of reference. Orlandos and Kiel, probably having in mind the historical conditions under which the architecture was produced, value it highly and regard the period as an important one. Richard Krautheimer, on the other hand, perhaps with the achievements of the Byzantines as his measure, writes, "The after-life of Byzantine culture in the Ottoman Empire is limited in the realm of art largely to painting. Architecture dwindles into insignificant repetitiousness."[56]

Adherence to the medieval models, repetition, and the consequent decline in creativity were precisely the results of the conservatism and isolationist spirit developed by the Orthodox Church in those difficult times. The church may have had no other choice, however, if it was to preserve its identity, than to cultivate isolation from the Turks and a distrust of the artistic culture of Europe. We should not forget that in the islands ruled by Venice, in a much more "progressive" climate, at least in regard to architecture, the adoption of foreign elements resulted in the loss by Greek church architecture of its very identity.

During the last years of the Byzantine Empire the two tendencies of modernization and conservatism, as expressed by two great intellects of the time, Gemistos Plethon (d. ca. 1450) and Gennadios Scholarios (d. 1459), found themselves in confrontation. During the fourteenth and fifteenth centuries, important new ideas were hatching in Byzantium, but the fall of the empire to the Turks resulted in the predominance of the most conservative forces within the Orthodox society of the Balkans. For architecture, the results were such as we have seen: great intentions and high quality, but an absence of the forces that might have led to internal renewal and external prestige.

Notes

1. Denis A. Zakythinos, *E Tourkokratia: Eisagoge eis ten neoteran istorian tou Ellenismou* (Athens: N.p., 1957); Apostolos E. Vakalopoulos, "E these ton Ellenon kai oi dokimasies tous ypo tous Tourkous," *Istoria tou ellenikou ethnous*, 15 vols. (Athens: Ekdotike Athenon, 1971–78) (hereafter cited as *IEE*), 10:22–91; idem, *Istoria tou neou Ellenismou*, vol. 2A,

Tourkokratia 1453–1669: Oi istorikes baseis tes neoellenikes koinonias kai oikonomias (Thessaloniki: N.p., 1964).

2. André Grabar, *L'art du Moyen âge en Europe oriental* (Paris: A. Michel, 1968), 87.

3. Manolis Chatzidakis, "E zographike sten Pole meta ten Alose," *Deltion tes Christianikes Archaiologikes Etaireias* 5 (1966–69): 186; idem, "Peri scholes Konstantinoupoleos oliga," *Archaiologikon deltion* 27A (1972): 121–37.

4. A catholicon is the principal church of a monastery. In a *skete*, which is a kind of dependent house, this church is called a *kyriakon*.

5. Paul M. Mylonas, "L'architecture du Mont Athos," *Thesaurismata* 2 (1963): Supplement, 18–48; idem, "E architektonike tou Agiou Orous," *Nea Estia*, 74, no. 875 (Christmas 1963): 189–207.

6. Sreten Petković, *The Patriarchate of Peć* (Belgrade: Serbian Patriarchate, 1982), 6.

7. G. A. Soteriou, "Istorika semeiomata," *Athena* 37 (1925): 161–66.

8. Information on such cases in the capital is found in the historical account of Athanasios Komnenos Ypselantes, *Ekklesiastikon kai politikon ton eis dodeka biblion H', Th' kai I', etoi Ta meta ten Alosin, 1453–1789*, ed. G. Aphthonides (Constantinople, 1870), 377, 388, 552–53.

9. Georgios A. Soteriou, *Christianike kai byzantine archaiologia* (only one vol. published) (Athens: N.p., 1942), 1:502–5.

10. Three general but not extensive articles on the Greek monuments of the Turkish period are A. Orlandos, "L'architecture religieuse en Grèce pendant la domination turque," *L'Hellénisme contemporain* 7 (1953): 179–91; [Manolis Chatzidakis], "E metabyzantine techne (1453–1700) kai e aktinobolia tes," *IEE* 10: 410–37; and Charalambos Bouras, "E ekklesiastike architektonike sten Ellada meta ten Alose (1453–1821)," *Architecture in Greece* 3 (1969): 164–72.

11. G. A. Soteriou, "Byzantina mnemeia tes Thessalias ig' kai id' aionos (Symbole eis ten byzantinen architektoniken tes teleutaias periodou): 4. Ai monai ton Meteoron," *Epeteris Etaireias Byzantinon Spoudon* 9 (1932): 382–415.

12. Anastasios K. Orlandos, "Ta byzantina mnemeia tes Kastorias," *Archeion ton byzantinon mnemeion tes Ellados* 4 (1938): 165–88; idem, "Ai kamaroskepastoi basilikai ton Athenon," *Epeteris Etaireias Byzantinon Spoudon* 2 (1925): 288–305; idem, "Oi metabyzantinoi naoi tes Parou," *Archeion ton byzantinon mnemeion tes Ellados* 9 (1961) and 10 (1964); idem, "Stachyologemata ek monon tes Pindou," *Archeion ton byzantinon mnemeion tes Ellados* 5 (1939–40): 167–97.

13. Nikolaos K. Moutsopoulos, *Ekklesies tou nomou Pelles* (Thessaloniki: Etaireia Makedonikon Spoudon, 1973) and *Ekklesies tou nomou Florines* (Thessaloniki: Etaireia Makedonikon Spoudon, 1964; abridged trans.: *The Churches of the Prefecture of Florina* [Thessaloniki: Institute for Balkan Studies, 1966]).

14. P. Lazarides, in the annual reports of the First Ephorate of Byzantine Monuments, *Archaiologikon deltion* 16–28 (1960–73).

15. Marica Šuput, *L'architecture serbe pendant la domination ottomane 1459–1690* (Belgrade: Académie Serbe des Sciences et des Arts, 1984) (Serbo-Croatian with French summary).

16. Krăstju Mijatev, *Die mittelalterliche Baukunst in Bulgarien*, trans. Michail Matlieu (Sofia: Verlag der Bulgarischen Akademie der Wissenschaften, 1974), 195–210; Margarita Koeva, *Pametnitsi na kulturata prez bulgarskoto Vuzrazhdane: Arkhitektura i izkustvo na bulgarskite tsurkvi* (Sofia: Izdatelstvo Septemvri, 1977); Machiel Kiel, *Art and Society of Bulgaria in the Turkish Period: A Sketch of the Economic, Juridical and Artistic Preconditions of Bulgarian Post-Byzantine Art and Its Place in the Development of the Art of the Christian Balkans, 1360/70–1700: A New Interpretation* (Maastricht and Assen: Van Gorcum, 1985).

17. Grigore Ionescu, *Istoîria arhitecturii in Rominia*, 2 vols. (Bucharest: Editura Academiei Republicii Populare Romîne, 1963, 1965).

18. Aleksandër Meksi and Pirro Thomo, "Arkitektura pasbizantine në Shqipëri," (Post-Byzantine architecture in Albania), *Monumentet* 11 (1976): 127–45; 19 (1980): 89–115; 20 (1980): 45–68; 21 (1981): 99–148 (Albanian with French summaries).

19. See above, n. 5; also Sotiris Kadas, *Mount Athos: An Illustrated Guide to the Monasteries and Their History*, trans. L. Turner (Athens: Ekdotike Athenon, 1984).

20. For eastern Macedonia, see M. Chatzidakis, "Post-Byzantine Art 1430–1830: Architecture," in Miltiades B. Hatzopoulos et al., eds., *Macedonia: 4000 Years of Greek History and Civilization* (Athens: Ekdotike Athenon, 1983), 410–14.

21. Myron Michaelides, " O naos tou Aghiou Zacharia Kastorias," *Archaiologikon deltion* 22A (1967): 77–86 and pls. 43–54.

22. Soteriou, "Ai monai ton Meteoron" (see above, n. 11).

23. John T. Koumoulides and Christopher Walter, *Byzantine and Post-Byzantine Monuments at Aghia in Thessaly, Greece: The Art and Architecture of the Monastery of St. Panteleimon* (London: Zeno, 1975). P. M. Mylonas, "The Monastery of Petra on Southern Mount Pindus," *Churches in Greece, 1453–1850* (Athens: Spoudasterio Istorias tes Architektonikes tou Ethnikou Metsobiou Polytechneiou, 1979–), 2:138–49. (All of the articles cited hereafter in this series are written in Greek, with an English summary.) Yannis Kizis, "The Monastery of Flamouri in Magnesia," ibid., 151–66.

24. Agathonos: G. A. Soteriou, "Byzantina mnemeia tes Thessalias ig' kai id' aionos (Symbole eis ten byzantinen architektoniken tes teleutaias periodou): 2. E Mone tes Panagias kai tou ag. Demetriou para to Tsagezi (Komneneion-Konomeio)," *Epeteris Etaireias Byzantinon Spoudon* 5 (1928): 361–63 and ill. 10; P. Lazarides, "Byzantine kai mesaionika mnemeia Phthiotidos," *Archaiologikon deltion* 20.B2 (1965): 308–10. Antinitsa: A. K. Orlandos, "E epi tes Othryos mone tes Antinitses," *Epeteris Etaireias Byzantinon Spoudon* 7 (1930): 369–81.

25. Galataki: Soteriou, "E Mone tes Panagias" (see above, n. 24), 361, 363, and figs. 11, 12. St. George Arma: Paulos Lazarides, "Mesaionika Euboias," *Archaiologikon deltion* 21.B1 (1966): 238–41.

26. Heaton Comyn, "Church of the Ruined Monastery of Daou-Mendeli, Attica," *Annual of the British School at Athens* 9 (1902–3): 388–90 and pls. 14–17; J. Travlos and A. Frantz, "The Church of St. Dionysios the Areopagite and the Palace of the Archbishop of Athens in the 16th Century," *Hesperia* 34 (1965): 157–202.

27. G. Soteriou, "To katholikon tes Mones Lauras tou Agonos," *Emerologion tes Megales Ellados* for 1925, 183–98; Amalia Androulidakes, "Mone Zerbitsas," *Peloponnesiaka* 15 (1982–84): 161–83; Ramsay Traquair, "The Churches of Western Mani," *Annual of the British School at Athens* 15 (1908–9): 198 ff., 204, 207, 208, 210, 213.

28. Andreas Xyngopoulos, "Mesaionika mnemeia Ioanninon," *Epeirotika chronika* 1 (1926): 55–60 (St. John Prodromos). Rea Leonidopoulou-Stylianou, "The Katholikon of the Monastery of Sosinos in Pogoni, Epiros," *Churches in Greece*, 2:67–86. Heleni K. Makri, "The Katholikon of the Monastery of Profitis Elias at Zitsa, Epiros," ibid., 87–98.

29. Paraportiani: D. Basileiades, *Metabyzantine aigaiopelagitike ekklesiastike architektonike: To acheiropoieto symplegma tes Paraportianes Mykonou* (Athens: N.p., 1961; offprint from *Architektonike*, 5, no. 27). Holy Apostles: K. Ch. Fatouros, *Patmiake architektonike: E ekklesia ton Hagion Apostolon os deigma charakteristikes Patmiakes technotropias* (Athens: Archaiologikon Deltion, 1962).

30. Georgios Angelos Soteriou, *Ta byzantina mnemeia tes Kyprou* (Athens: Academy of Athens, 1935).

31. Meksi and Thomo (cited above, n. 18).

32. Kiel, 256–70 passim.

33. Šuput, 43–99 passim.

34. On church typology, see Orlandos, "L'architecture religieuse."

35. Chrysapha: Moschoula Chryssoulakis and Maria Karyotou, "The Church of Aghios Demetrios at Chrysapha, Laconia," *Churches in Greece*, 2:287–398; Maria Karyotou, "The Church of the Dormition at Chrysapha," in *Anastelose—Synterese—Prostasia mnemeion kai synolon* (Athens: Greek Ministry of Culture, 1984), 49–64. Oropos and Sykaminon: Anastasios K. Orlandos, "Mesaionika mnemeia Oropou kai Sykaminou," *Deltion tes Christianikes Archaiologikes Etaireias* 4 (1927): 31–45; Evangelia Kambouris, "The Koimesis tis Theotokou at Sykamino, Attiki," *Churches in Greece*, 2:231–40. Gomionica and Krka: Šuput, fig. 36.

36. Paul M. Mylonas, "Le plan initial du catholicon de la Grande Lavra au Mont Athos et la genèse du type du catholicon athonite," *Cahiers archéologiques* 32 (1984): 89–112.

37. Miltiadis D. Polyviou, "The Church of Haghios Nicolaos at Perivoli in the Area of Grevena," *Churches in Greece*, 1:83–92.

38. Bulgaria: Mijatev, 204–8. Pindus: Orlandos, "Stachyologemata," 184–97.

39. Koropi: C[haralambos] Bouras, A. Kaloyeropoulou, and R. Andreadi, *Churches of Attica* (Athens: N.p., 1970), 16, 17, 19 and ills. 66–69. Kontra: ibid., 85, 86, 97 and ills. 70–74.

40. Tasos Tanoulas, "Aghioi Anargyroi of Kolokynthi at Athens," *Churches in Greece*, 2:179–90.

41. Georgios A. Soteriou, "E en Salamini Mone tes Phaneromenes (Symbole eis ten exelixin tou architektonikou typou tes basilikes meta troullou)," *Epeteris Etaireias Byzantinon Spoudon* 1 (1924): 109–38.

42. A. K. Orlandos, "Stauropistegoi naoi Batheias Euboias," *Archeion ton byzantinon mnemeion tes Ellados* 7 (1951): 111–30.

43. Charalambos Bouras, "The Catholicon of the Monastery of Aghios Menas on Chios," *Churches in Greece*, 2:241–48.

44. Comyn, "Daou-Mendeli."

45. Antinitsa: Orlandos, "Mone tes Antinitses." Dousiko: Kiel, 149–50.

46. St. George Arma: Lazarides, "Mesaionika Euboias," 238–41, figs. 2–5. Vatheia: Orlandos, "Stauropistegoi naoi Batheias Euboias," 114–16, figs. 3–5. Episkopi, Ano Volos: unpublished.

47. Šuput, pls. 53, 54.

48. See above, n. 41.

49. Šuput, pls. 31 (Ovcar) and 10–13 (Mesić).

50. Manolis Chatzidakis, "Ikonostas," *Reallexikon zur byzantinischen Kunst*, 3:349–53.

51. Charalampos M. Koutelakes, *Xyloglypta templa tes Dodekanesou mechri to 1700* (Athens and Ioannina: Dodone, 1986).

52. See above, n. 41.

53. Flamouri: Kizis, figs. 17–19. Petra: Mylonas, "Monastery of Petra," fig. 17.

54. Kechrovouni: D. Basileiades, *Ai epipedostegoi metabyzantinai basilikai ton Kykladon* (Athens: G. D. Kypraiou, 1962; offprint from the *Epeteris tes Etaireias Kykladikon Meleton* 2 [1962]), 94 and 95; figs. 42 and 43. Kouvara: Bouras, Kaloyeropoulou, Andreadi, 161, pl. 21, fig. 181.

55. Stilian Adhami, "Tri bazilika të mëdha të ndërtuara në Voskopojë brënda katër vjetëve" (Three large basilicas constructed at Voskopoje in the space of four years), *Monumentet* 14 (1977): 145–68; 15–16 (1978): 89–100 (Albanian with French summaries).

56. Orlandos, "L'architecture religieuse," 191; Kiel, 256–71 (in reference to the churches of Bulgaria); Richard Krautheimer, *Early Christian and Byzantine Architecture*, 3d rev. ed. (Harmondsworth, 1981), 439.

Fig. 1.1. Moschopolis (Albania). Church of St. Athanasius. Founder's inscription over the entrance. (Photo: Author)

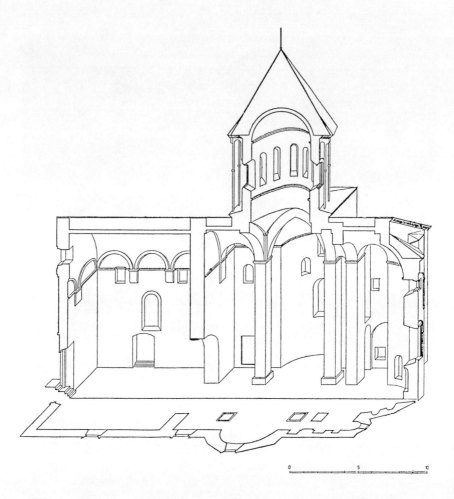

Fig. 1.2. Monastery of Novo Hopovo (Yugoslavia). Church of St. Nicholas. Axonometric section. (Drawing: after Marica Šuput, *L'architecture serbe pendant la domination ottomane 1459–1690* [Belgrade: Académie Serbe des Sciences et des Arts, 1984], ill. 14)

Fig. 1.3. Monastery of Mesić (Yugoslavia). Church of the Forerunner.
(Photo: after Šuput, *L'architecture*, pl. 11)

Fig. 1.4. Zavorda (Greece). Monastery of the Metamorphosis (Transfiguration). Church of St. Nikanor (catholicon). (Photo: Author)

Fig. 1.5. Monastery of St. Anastasia, near Thessaloniki. Catholicon. (Photo: Author)

Fig. 1.6. Meteora (Greece). Monastery of the Metamorphosis (Transfiguration), or Great Meteoron. Catholicon. (Photo: Author)

Fig. 1.7. Meteora (Greece). Monastery of Barlaam. Catholicon. (Photo: Author)

Fig. 1.8. Monastery of Dousiko (Greece). Catholicon. Interior. (Photo: Author)

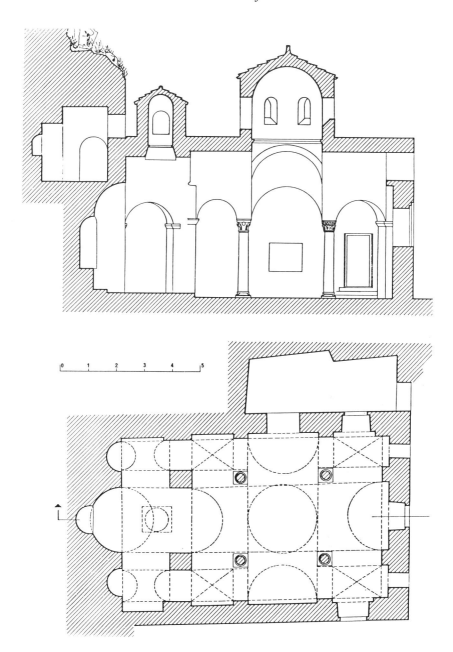

Fig. 1.9. Skyros (Greece). Church of St. George "of the Castle" (*tou Kastrou*). Plan and section. (Author)

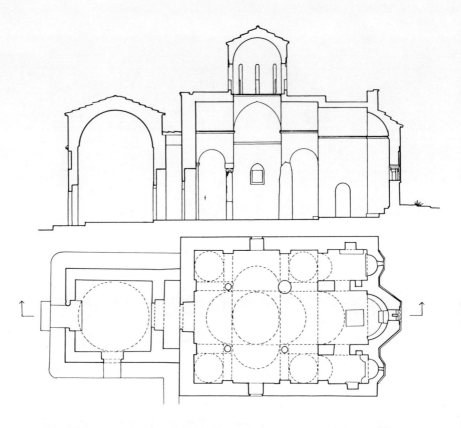

Fig. 1.10. Euboea (Greece). Monastery of St. George Arma. Catholicon. Plan and section. (Adapted from Paulos Lazarides, "Mesaionika Euboias," *Archaiologikon deltion* 21.B1 [1966], ills. 1, 3)

Fig. 1.11. Monastery of Agnous, Argolid (Greece). Catholicon. (Photo: Author)

Fig. 1.12. Aigialeia (Greece). Monastery of the Taxiarchai. Catholicon.
(Photo: Author)

Fig. 1.13. Levidhi (Greece). Church of the Dormition of the Theotokos.
(Photo: Author)

Fig. 1.14. Monemvasia (Greece). Church of St. Nicholas. (Photo: Author)

Fig. 1.15. Prasteion, Western Mani (Greece). Church of St. Theodore.
(Photo: Author)

Fig. 1.16. Oia, Thera (Greece). Church of the Anastasis. (Photo: Author)

Fig. 1.17. Patmos (Greece). Church called "the Meghali Panaghia." (Photo: Author)

Fig. 1.18. Patmos (Greece). Church of the Hypapanti (Presentation of Christ in the Temple). (Photo: Author)

Fig. 1.19. Elbasan (Albania). Church of the Birth of the Theotokos. North arcade. (Photo: Author)

Fig. 1.20. Dobursko (Bulgaria). Church of the SS. Theodore. Interior. (Photo: after Machiel Kiel, *Art and Society of Bulgaria in the Turkish Period* [Maastricht and Assen: Van Gorcum, 1985], p. 265)

Fig. 1.21. Trun (Bulgaria). Monastery of the Archangels. Catholicon. (Photo: after Kiel, *Art and Society*, p. 263)

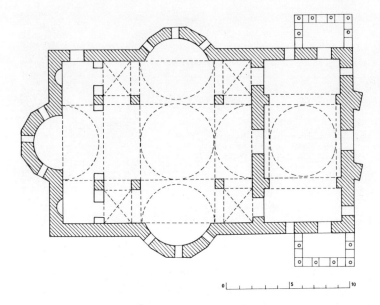

Fig. 1.22. Bačkovo (Bulgaria). Church of the Theotokos (catholicon).
Plan. (Adapted from Krăstju Mijatev, *Die* mittelalterliche Baukunst in
Bulgarien, trans. Michail Matliev [Sofia: Verlag der Bulgarischen
Akademie der Wissenschaften, 1974], fig. 265)

Fig. 1.23. Bačkovo (Bulgaria). Church of the Theotokos (catholicon).
(Photo: after *Kratka istoriia na bulgarskata arkhitektura*, [Sofia: Bulgarskata Akademiia na Naukite, 1965], fig. 170.)

Fig. 1.24. Oropos, Attica (Greece). Church of the Dormition of the Theotokos.
(Photo: Author)

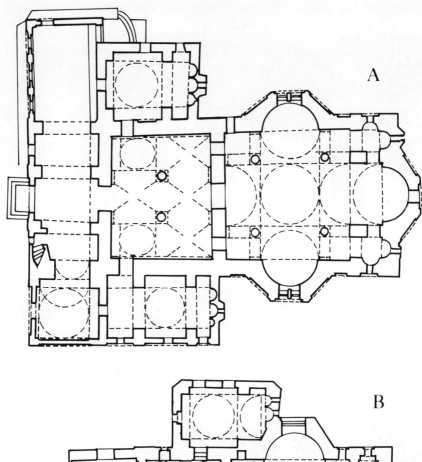

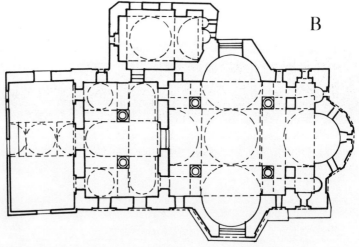

Fig. 1.25.
A. Monastery of Philotheou, Mount Athos (Greece). Catholicon, 1746.
Plan. (Paul M. Mylonas)
B. Monastery of Grigoriou, Mount Athos (Greece). Catholicon, 17th c.
Plan. (Paul M. Mylonas)

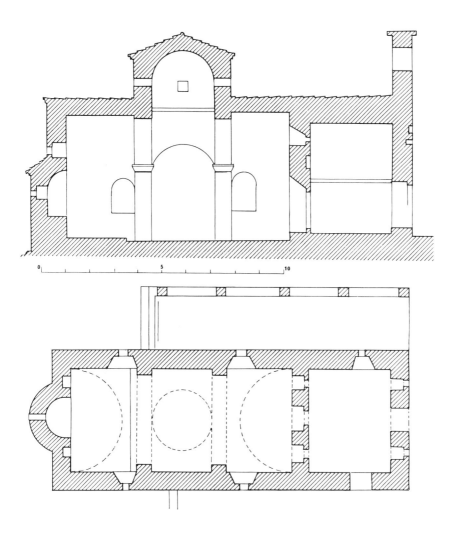

Fig. 1.26. Monastery at Selenitsa (Albania). Church of St. Athanasius (catholicon). Plan and section. (Adapted from Aleksander Meksi and Pirro Thomo,
"Arkitektura pasbizantine në Shqipëri: Kishat një nefshe," *Monumentet* 19
[1980]: 113)

Fig. 1.27. Amarynthos, Euboea (Greece). Church of the Dormition of the Theotokos. (Photo: Author)

Fig. 1.28. Sora, Andros (Greece). Church of St. Nicholas. Doorway. (Photo: Author)

THE ICON AS A CULTURAL
PRESENCE AFTER 1453

Thalia Gouma-Peterson

As the God-inspired Basil, who was learned in things divine, says,
"The honor [shown] to the image is conveyed to its prototype."

St. John of Damascus (ca. 730)

When I enter a Latin church, I do not revere any of the [images of]
saints that are there because I do not recognize any of them.

Gregory Melissenos (1438)

IN HER ROOM my grandmother, Stavroula Gouma, born in the southern
Peloponnese in 1878, had a large case enclosed by glass doors in which
were images of the Virgin, Christ, and various saints. She called it her
iconostasis, and in front of it she kept an oil lamp burning day and night. To
these images she prayed several times a day, crossing herself, genuflecting,
and kissing them. For her the icons were living presences identical with the
saintly figures whom they represented. They were friends to whom she
confided her joys and sorrows and whom she asked for help and solace.
Her most intimate friend was the *Panaghia* (the Holy Virgin), and in her
lengthy monologues she frequently uttered "*Panaghitsa mou*," a diminu-
tive term of endearment. When in the early 1950s I was leaving for the
United States, she offered to give me one of her icons for my journey. I
chose one of the Virgin and Christ Child. This icon has been with me ever
since and continues to remind me of Stavroula's deep faith and trust in the
Theotokos (the one who bore God), with whose maternal anxiety and
suffering she identified, as had women in Greece for centuries.

Such acts of devotion, strange though they may seem to modern
Western women, would have seemed perfectly normal to a woman living
in the Byzantine Empire any time from the fifth century onwards, and
especially so after the Iconoclastic Controversy (726–843), when the

validity of sacred images was hotly contested and fiercely fought for and against. In the final triumph of icons women played as active a role as men, both on an official and unofficial level. Though their activities are less well documented than are those of men, there are accounts of female devotion to icons in Byzantine texts. Furthermore, it was two empresses who restored the official worship of icons: Irene in 787 and Theodora in 843. Also, historical and textual accounts indicate that through the worst of Iconoclasm, the women of the imperial family continued to worship sacred images, against their husbands' explicit orders, as did women throughout the empire. For these women, as well as for a segment of the male population, especially the monks, the validity of image worship did not need official sanction. Sacred images had been an integral part of their daily life for centuries; and, since women were excluded from the official church structure, portable icons, which people brought into their homes, encouraged a private and personal form of devotion. As mediators between heaven and earth they provided direct access to the divine. By the twelfth century this personal belief in the icon as protector, friend, and intercessor, shared by men and women, in both private and public life, had spread to neighboring lands, such as the Serbian and Bulgarian kingdoms, and to more distant Russia. The high regard accorded to icons and their active presence in private and public life visibly identified these cultures as Orthodox and differentiated them from the Catholic West. In short, icons became significant carriers of a tradition that, in parts of Eastern Europe, has continued uninterrupted into the twentieth century.

The fall of Constantinople to the Turks in 1453 did not reduce the importance of sacred images in private devotion and in the liturgy, and there continued to be a demand for icons. However, as the social and financial structure of the Byzantine Empire broke down, the market for these objects of devotion in what had been the centers of the empire declined. This trend, which started in the fourteenth century and accelerated in the fifteenth, forced painters to move to foreign and provincial centers in search of work. Crete with its substantial Greek Orthodox population drew the largest number of these refugee artists. The large island was especially attractive because, under Venetian rule since 1204, it had by the fourteenth century come to provide a prosperous and open environment where painters could freely practice their trade. By the mid-fifteenth century the main city, Candia (modern Herakleion), became the residence for teachers of painting and a training ground for those wishing to learn to paint in a Byzantine style.

Recent research in the notarial registries in the Venice State Archives has revealed that the colony of painters grew rapidly: from 38 in the fourteenth century, to 128 in the fifteenth, and 160 in the sixteenth.[1] The documents, primarily legal acts, have also furnished information about the lives of these artists and, when signed works have been known, have established with greater accuracy the dates of activity of the most important painters. As a result, we now have some information about three of the leading painters of the fifteenth century: Angelos Akotantos, Nicholas Philanthropenos, and Andreas Ritzos.

Angelos Akotantos (active 1438–50) taught painting in Candia with his brother John (active 1435–77) and has signed, with his first name, a substantial number of icons of excellent quality (fig. 2.1).[2] This body of work, with its characteristic elegance and refinement, its classicizing ideal beauty, and its expression of tenderness and humanity, can now be securely dated to the second quarter of the fifteenth century. As such it can be seen as a continuation of the classicizing and emotionally appealing style of the Palaeologan period (1261–1453). It therefore gives some sense of the character and quality of Constantinopolitian work of the second quarter of the fifteenth century, of which little survives. It is known that both Angelos and John visited the capital and therefore were in touch with its art. It may even be possible that the brothers had originally come from Constantinople, as was the case with Nicholas Philanthropenos (active 1375–1440), who also was a teacher of painting in Candia. No signed works by Philanthropenos have been identified so far, but much is known about his activities from the notarial registries.[3] He worked both for noble Venetian patrons, for whom he painted altarpieces, and for Greeks residing in the villages of Crete, for whom he painted smaller icons. Around 1419 he returned to Constantinople to buy color pigments and silver leaf, and in 1435 he worked on the mosaics of San Marco in Venice. This extraordinary versatility suggests that the Cretan painters could work in a variety of media and for patrons with different tastes. This is borne out by the activities of painters during the sixteenth century.

Andreas Ritzos (active 1451–92) was a member of a family of painters active in Candia from about 1420 to 1570 (his father Maneas, a goldsmith and painter, is noted in 1423; his son Nicholas, a painter, was born in 1460 and died before 1507; his grandson Maneas, a painter, lived from 1528 to 1571).[4] Andreas, best known for his large and very popular icons of the Virgin of the Passion (fig. 2.2), also painted two large and impressive icons of the Enthroned Virgin and Christ Child and the Enthroned Christ for the Monastery of St. John at Patmos. His style and that of his son Nicholas, to whom the handsome icon of the Enthroned Virgin and Child with Angels and Scenes from Christ's Life (fig. 2.3) is generally attributed, is very close to that of Angelos, though more linear, severe, and restrained. The stylistic resemblance is not accidental, for a document of 1477 indicates that John Akotantos, Angelos's brother, was the teacher of Andreas Ritzos, and that he agreed to sell to him his "54 examples of various figures of saints" (i.e., models and sketches) that he had inherited from his brother. This direct transference from one painter to another gives some insight into how the Byzantine tradition was preserved over the centuries.

The market for devotional images painted in the *maniera greca* (i.e., the Greek manner, or Byzantine style) rapidly expanded during the second half of the fifteenth century. The registries establish both the size of the commissions and the role of merchants in this large-scale production.[5] In 1499, in three related documents (July 4), two merchants, one a Venetian and the other a Greek from the Morea, ordered from three painters of Candia a total of 700 icons of the Virgin, 500 to be painted *alla latina* and 200 *alla greca*. In another document (May 18, 1499), Antonio Tajapiera and his apprentices contracted themselves to the painter Michele Focà for two months, to paint seven pictures of the Virgin every day, a total of 350 pictures. In a related document of July 1499, the wood carver Giorgio Sclavo agreed to provide Michele Focà with one thousand wooden panels of three specified sizes. Clearly, by the end of the fifteenth century such devotional images were being mass produced to meet the demands of a Greek and Italian clientele in Crete, Venice, Dalmatia, and elsewhere. Both Andreas and Nicholas Ritzos worked for this market, as did most of the other 128 painters known by name from the registries, many of whom did not sign their work. A large proportion of the new clientele was Catholic and wanted panels in a Gothic style (*alla latina*), which the Cretan painters were able to emulate successfully, as shown by the surviving examples of the Virgin Madre della Consolazione (fig. 2.4), the *Pietà*, and Christ the Man of Sorrows.

The expanding Italian market for devotional images in a Byzantine style was stimulated by the continued and increasing presence of Greeks in Venice and elsewhere in Italy. These Greeks regarded Venice not merely as a place of refuge, but as "another Byzantium," as Bessarion, archbishop of Nicaea, phrased it in 1468, in a letter to the doge of Venice in which he bequeathed his private library to the city.[6] (Bessarion's collection, containing 500 Greek manuscripts, was the largest collection of its kind in the West.) Bessarion had come to the West in 1438–39 in the retinue of the Byzantine emperor John VIII Palaeologus who, together with the patriarch of Constantinople and some seven hundred Greek clerics and laymen, attended the council in Ferrara and Florence for the union of the churches. This large group of Greeks stayed in Italy for eighteen months and participated in what was probably one of the most elaborate and sumptuous ecclesiastical and political spectacles of the century. Bessarion, who returned to the West in 1440 and also became a cardinal of the Roman Church, remained there till his death, in 1472.[7] He became a central figure in the flowering and study of Greek letters.

More important than the temporary presence of the emperor and 700 Greeks in Italy was the permanent presence of the Greek colony in Venice, which grew rapidly in the fifteenth century and soon became one of the largest and most significant contingents of foreigners in the city (15,000 by 1580). By 1514 it was granted permission by the Council of Ten to erect an Orthodox church and cemetery, the (still extant) church of San Giorgio dei Greci. In the early sixteenth century Venice also became the principal European center for Greek studies. In this revival of classical scholarship Cretan men of letters played an important role.[8] The distinguished Marcos Musuros was for years editor of Aldus Manutius's Greek Press, and professor of Greek at Padua (1503–9) and at the Ducal Chancery School in Venice (1512–16). In short, the flourishing market, during the same period, for devotional images painted in the "Greek manner" appears to be related to the general admiration for Greek culture and the growing presence of Greeks in the West.

By the mid-sixteenth century the demand for devotional panel paintings in a Byzantine or late Gothic style had, however, subsided. No large-scale commissions like those of the late fifteenth century are recorded in the notarial acts. This probably reflects a shift of taste in Italy, even among more conservative patrons. Other markets for Byzantine icons in Venice, Crete, the Balkans, and elsewhere in the Near East held up, however. Major clients were the large monastic foundations in central and northern Greece. In 1499, for example, Nicholas Ritzos (fig. 2.3) was commissioned by Jerasimo Cipreo Calojero, a monk from Cyprus and treasurer of the Sinaite dependency in Candia, to paint a total of twenty-four icons: two for the monastery of St. John of Patmos, seventeen for St. Catherine's monastery at Mt. Sinai, two for the monastery of Dionysiou on Mt. Athos, and one for the monastery of Strophadia on the island of Amor-

gos.[9] During the sixteenth century, various important monastic foundations undertook ambitious programs of renovation and employed a larger
number of painters. Most important of these was the Cretan monk Theophanes Strelitzas (d. 1559), surnamed Bathas, who worked at Meteora in
the late 1520s and came to Mount Athos in 1535 to paint the frescoes of
the Great Lavra and a set of at least twelve icons for the new iconostasis.[10]
Theophanes, a very prolific painter (there are records of over 100 icons by
him at Candia, Mount Athos, and Mount Sinai), exercised a significant
influence into the seventeenth century, both through the iconographic
types he created and through his severe, sober, and firmly modeled figure
style.

Private individuals also continued to be a major source of employment for the Cretan painters. Wills and lists of inventories of portable
property in Candia show that by the second half of the sixteenth and early
seventeenth century most citizens owned at least one icon, and that the
wealthier Candiotes owned as many as twenty or thirty.[11] Icons were
frequently included in dowry agreements, were listed in payments of
debts, and were willed to relatives or churches. In the homes of the wealthy
middle class and the nobility (both Cretan and Venetian) they hung in all
the rooms of the house (workrooms, bedrooms, reception rooms) together with paintings *all'italiana* and *alla fiamenga* (in a Flemish style) of
both religious and secular subjects. These icons represented a great variety
of traditional Byzantine subjects: the Virgin and Child, Christ, images of
various saints, and narrative biblical events, especially of Christ's Passion.
The evidence gathered for Candia suggests that similar patterns may have
existed among Greeks and some Italians in Venice.

Icons continued to be commissioned for and willed to churches as
acts of devotion and piety by both men and women. Two especially
impressive examples were given as gifts to the Church of San Giorgio dei
Greci, in Venice. In 1546 "the servant of God John Manesi and his brother
George," according to an inscription in Greek and Latin, commissioned a
large icon of the *Deësis* (fig. 2.5).[12] Manesi is represented twice, once at the
feet of Christ and a second time, together with his brother, in a landscape
setting that functions like a predella below the main image. Here the
brothers are dressed in miltary attire, hold weapons, and are accompanied
by their horses, which shows that they were *stradiotes* (mercenary soldiers)
in the service of the Venetian Republic. Some years later an especially
impressive icon of the Virgin in Glory Exalted by the Prophets was given
as a gift to the church of San Giorgio dei Greci by John Mourmouris.[13]

Mourmouris himself is represented among the row of prophets (fig. 2.6, *extreme right*) below the enthroned Virgin and Christ Child, and in the background are inscribed two prayers, one above his own portrait and the other above the figure of John the Baptist (*extreme left*). The first is addressed by Mourmouris to the Baptist (his namesake) and implores him to intercede on his behalf to the Virgin. In the second, St. John asks the Virgin to intercede on behalf of Mourmouris to Christ. These elaborate prayers for a double intercession show that in the mid-sixteenth century the religious function of the icon within a more secular society had not changed. Mourmouris was an educated man, a copyist from Nauplion, who resided in Venice between 1550 and 1563.

Not all such icons were commissioned by Greeks. In 1661 John Mengano Kydonio, a Venetian nobleman of Candia, ordered an icon of the Virgin *Kardiotissa* (fig. 2.7) from one of the most important seventeenth-century Cretan painters, Emmanuel Tzanes Bounialis, active in Crete and Venice (1655–90). The icon is signed and dated and bears both a dedicatory inscription, asking for the Virgin's protection in this life, and the donor's coat of arms. Mengano, who asked Tzanes to paint a characteristically Cretan type, the *Kardiotissa*, in a Byzantine style and with a Greek dedicatory inscription, belongs to the group of noble Venetians who absorbed the customs of the Greek population of Crete.[14]

Tzanes's icon gives us an excellent opportunity to observe how the style of Cretan painters changed in spite of their adherence to traditional iconographic types. His *Kardiotissa* is an almost exact copy, in reverse, of Angelos's *Kardiotissa* (fig. 2.1), painted about 200 years earlier, and it illustrates the common Cretan practice of working from outline sketches taken directly from other images. These sketches the painters passed on to their students, as John Akotantos's sale to Andreas Ritzos also documents. But the close similarities between the two images highlight the differences. The outlines are identical, but in Tzanes's icon the linear patterns are harder and the solidly modeled faces and hands have an unreal fleshiness. This ponderous fleshiness is an intrusion from Tzanes's Western style, for he, like other sixteenth- and seventeenth-century Cretan painters, also worked in a style derived from Italian Renaissance painting. This was inevitable, since the Cretan painters were exposed to Western art both through their trips to Venice and through paintings and engravings that reached Crete. A striking example of this stylistic duality is provided by two signed icons by Michael Damaskinos, one of the major Cretan painters of the sixteenth century (active 1570–91).[15] The linear and frontal bust of St. Anthony (fig. 2.8) is representative of his severe Cretan style, which influenced many of his contemporaries. The St. Michael (fig. 2.9), on the other hand, is one of Damaskinos's more successful examples in a Western style, indebted to Venetian Renaissance painting. Damaskinos lived in Venice for several years, where he remained till 1583 and participated in the decoration of San Giorgio dei Greci.

During the second half of the sixteenth century the presence of Western stylistic elements in Cretan painting increased. This may reflect both the painters' desire to renew their art and the wishes of some patrons for a more contemporary style. Most Cretan painters, however, did not entirely transform their way of painting. Had they done so, their images would have ceased being recognizable likenesses of the sacred prototypes.

Out of these cross-currents one distinctive artist emerged who was able to combine organically the Byzantine aesthetic with a Western idiom. There can no longer be any doubt that when Domenikos Theotokopoulos (El Greco, 1541–1614) left for Venice he was about twenty-six years old (according to a notarial act he was still in Candia in 1566) and that he was a fully trained icon painter.[16] The recent discovery of an icon of the Dormition of the Virgin (fig. 2.10) in the Church of the Dormition in Ermoupolis, on the island of Syros, signed in Greek ΔΟΜΗΝΙΚΟΣ ΘΕΟΤΟΚΟΠΟΥΛΟΣ Ο ΔΕΙΞΑC and executed in a style reminiscent of Palaeologan painting, firmly places him within the context of the Cretan School.[17] In this early work Theotokopoulos demonstrates a true understanding of the classicizing essence of Byzantine art, which most of his contemporaries had lost. He was able to use elements of the classical tradition, as it had survived in Palaeologan art, to give a believable ideal structure to his dematerialized figures. For him this Byzantine structure was an operative principle, not a schematic formula. Because of this, he was able, after only a brief apprenticeship in Venice, to absorb the Venetian Renaissance style of painting. By 1570 he was in Rome, and, unable perhaps to find commissions, he moved to Spain in 1577. There he remained for the rest of his life.[18] In his late style, which he developed in Spain between 1586 and 1595, and to which he adhered till his death, he reverted to painting devotional images that could be called icons (fig. 2.11). He restricted the range of his subjects and focused on specific iconographic types that he repeated with little variation. Boldly disregarding normality of proportions and physical beauty, he proceeded to elongate, dematerialize, and spiritualize his figures, which progressively became bodiless visions illuminated from within by a divine source.

The Cretan style of icon painting, in its purest amd most severe form, survived into the seventeenth century in the work of Emmanuel Lambardos, whose signed icons span the years 1593–1647. Lambardos, who was born in Rethymnon, does not seem to have worked in Venice. His beautifully painted and technically flawless traditional images of the Virgin and Child are both elegant and remote. But in spite of their remoteness they retain some of the melancholy humanity of Angelos's work. They were popular in Crete, the Balkans, Dalmatia, and Italy. They evidently had wide appeal because of their authentically Byzantine character. Their popularity is suggested by a large icon of the Virgin *Hodegetria* (fig. 2.12), the style and technique of which leave no doubt that it was painted in the early seventeenth century either by Lambardos himself or a member of his workshop, and which bears a dedication by Timotheos Gonemis, his wife Reggina Aninou, and their daughter Marigoula. It is known from documents that Timotheos, from Corfu, married Reggina, from Kefallonia, in 1794, a date that provides a *terminus post* for the dedicatory inscription.[19] Nothing is known about the previous owners or the circumstances of the rededication, but clearly the icon was still highly prized 150 years after it had been painted.

The war of Crete (1645–69) and the subsequent Turkish occupation severed the ties between Venice and Crete and destroyed the financial and cultural life of the island. It also ended the movement of painters between Crete and Venice. Large numbers of Cretan artists fled to Venice and to the Ionian Islands (still under Venetian rule), especially Corfu, and there carried on the tradition of icon painting.[20] These painters had to rely on their own ability to maintain a connection with the Byzantine past. Some were able to hold on to the severe Cretan style of the mid-sixteenth century. Others reverted to an increasing eclecticism and worked in several styles with various degrees of admixture of Western elements.

One of the most imaginative painters of this traumatic period of transition was Theodore Poulakis. Born in Crete in 1622, he moved to Corfu and then to Venice, where he worked from 1644 to 1655 and from 1670 to 1675. He died in Corfu in 1692, having presumably worked there during the times when he was not in Venice.[21] His icon of St. Spyridon with Scenes of His Life (fig. 2.13) incorporates elements of both his Byzantine and Western styles. Painted in bright, luminous colors, it is constructed on the basis of the Byzantine schema of a large central figure framed by smaller scenes. The tension between the flowing garments, derived from the engravings of the Flemish painter Sadeler, and the flattened and frontal saint with his severe Byzantine face informs the whole composition. Throughout the narrative scenes, purely Byzantine passages alternate with mixed spatial references and flowing drapery. In spite of these admixtures, the bodies of the figures do not acquire weight and the overall composition remains planar and flat. In keeping with the characteristic Byzantine de-emphasis of corporeality, Poulakis's system of drapery does not cover a solid body.

The eighteenth century was a turning point for the Greeks under Turkish domination. The conquest of the Peloponnese by the Turks in 1715 and the relative peace in the Balkans allowed Western commerce to penetrate into the East. This fostered the emergence of a Greek merchant class—since local commerce throughout the Balkans was almost exclusively in the hands of Greeks—and created a new clientele for icons.[22] The greater wealth and the formation of commercial companies of craftsmen and farmers organized on the principle of collaborative capital in the villages of Chalkidiki, Epirus, the Peloponnese, and the islands resulted in a middle class that participated directly in the economic and adminstrative system. As a result, purely local centers acquired greater importance. A parallel phenomenon was that of itinerant painters, especially from Macedonia and Epirus, who became increasingly more important during the second half of the eighteenth century. These groups of painters, related by family ties or place of origin, organized themselves into traveling companies that moved to villages, towns, and monasteries, painting frescoes and icons for churches and private donors and decorating the houses of the new merchant class. Their activity spread from Epirus and Macedonia to Mount Athos and Thessaly, and to the Peloponnese and the islands. Their work acquired more the character of folk art. The stylistic elements of folk art and its spontaneous realism gave the Byzantine style a new breath of life. Many painters active during this period are known by name, and their productivity as well as their mobility are very impressive: e.g., Anthony Skordilis at Milos, Seriphos, and Siphnos; Michelis the Cretan at Amorgos; Christodoulos Kallergis at Mykonos and in the Peloponnese; the monk Jeremiah at Nauplion; Panagiotis of Yannina in Corinthia; and George Markos from the Peloponnese in Attica.[23]

Within this more diversified milieu the Orthodox Church, since 1453 centered around the patriarchate in Constantinople, remained a strong unifying force and continued to be the major sustaining religious and cultural institution. The fact that Greek was the official language of the church also helped to preserve the group consciousness of the Greeks.

How vital the church and religious beliefs still were in the eighteenth century is illustrated by the account of the activities of the monk Auxentius, recorded by the historian Kaisarios Dapontes, an eyewitness. Auxentius, a popular preacher in the villages of Nicomedia (ca. 1750), drew crowds of thousands, who came to hear him from every part of the country. Dapontes tells us that this audience was composed not only of "common people . . . but high class people too and teachers and priests and bishops." He also reports that among the religious objects owned by Auxentios the most important was an icon of the Virgin. Dapontes describes this icon in reverential terms and states that it helped immensely to enhance Auxentius's reputation, because "the people were stricken by the love of the icon."[24]

This characteristically Orthodox reaction to an icon as to a living human being was also expressed in seventeenth- and eighteenth-century descriptions of icons in letters and *proskynetaria* (devotional books for pilgrims) in which they are referred to as *empsychos* (having a soul) and *holozontanos* (completely alive).[25] It is, in fact, clear that the central Iconophile concept of the icon as sacred because "the honor [shown] to the image is conveyed to its prototype," survived into the eighteenth century, as illustrated by Dionysius of Fourna, who quotes it in his *Hermeneia*, or *Painter's Guide*, written between 1728 and 1733. Dionysius, a monk and painter of icons and frescoes who was active on Mount Athos (1711–34), also urged the student of painting to emulate the great examples of early Byzantine painters. For his own work, Dionysius used as prototypes the magnificent Palaeologan frescoes of the Protaton (ca. 1300), which local tradition attributed to the legendary painter Panselinos from Thessaloniki.

The return to earlier prototypes advocated by Dionysius is characteristic of much eighteenth-century work. It was part of the struggle of a cultural and religious minority under foreign domination to retain the ties to their past. But this conservatism did not prevent indigenous elements of folk art from being absorbed into the Byzantine context. This is illustrated by two lively and colorful icons by Constantine Kontarinis (fig. 2.14) and Laskaris Leichoudis (fig. 2.15). Kontarinis, a native of Crete active in Corfu (1715–32), painted in both a Byzantine and Western style, and in a most interesting autobiographical icon of the Miracle of St. Luke and St. Eleutherios, of 1718 (fig. 2.14), combined these styles and also introduced elements of folk art. The icon represents an event that occurred on October 18, 1718, the feast day of St. Luke, when the painter's son Nicholas was miraculously saved from drowning in a well, near the church of St. Eleutherios, in Corfu (*inscription bottom left*).[26] Kontarinis, believing St. Luke and St. Eleutherios to have been responsible for his son's salvation, painted the icon as a sign of gratitude and dedicated it to the church. He represented himself, dressed in the contemporary attire of a gentleman and wearing a sword, kneeling in front of St. Eleutherios, under whose feet he has placed his signature. The story of the drowning is shown immediately below, in front of the church. In this lively and original icon, Kontarinis painted the heavenly apparition of St. Luke in a Western manner, St. Eleutherios in a Byzantine manner, and the church and human figures in a folk-art style. These stylistic differentations, which are well integrated and add to the vitality of the painting, also correspond to the hierarchical importance of the figures. Kontarinis here used stylistic modes as a means of symbolic differentiation in a manner reminiscent of early Byzantine painting.

In Laskaris Leichoudis's St. Nicholas with Scenes of his Life, of 1733 (fig. 2.15), which is related to Poulakis's St. Spyridon (fig. 2.13) both in layout and iconography, folk art permeates the whole composition. It is especially evident in the scenes from the life of the saint, full of lively action, ornate architectural fragments, and a profusion of ornamental patterns.[27] The schematic figures in their direct expressiveness and eloquence lack any pretensions to classical gracefulness. They come out of a different context, in which the classical refinement of Constantinople was but a distant memory. The colorful icon of St. Gregory the Theologian and St. Artemios, of 1770 (fig. 2.16), is an example of the more strictly traditional eighteenth-century icon in both iconographic types and composition, but here too the painter enlivened the two saints with a profusion of decorative detail.[28] St. Gregory's wonderfully rich vestments, in shades of pink and white with contrasting flowers, are reminiscent of the floral panels decorating the wealthy merchant homes. This very vital influence of folk art survived the Greek revolution of 1821 and continued as an important force in the nineteenth century.

The icons here discussed span a period of four hundred years, from the fall of Constantinople to the emergence of modern Greece. What is so remarkable is that throughout these centuries they remain essentially Byzantine in form and content and in function and meaning. They are holy images and recognizable portraits of protectors to whom prayers would be addressed and through whom these prayers would be conveyed to the prototype.

Notes

I am indebted to the College of Wooster for a Luce Research Grant that enabled me to complete the work for this article. I thank Dr. Myrtali Acheimastou-Potamianou, director of the Byzantine Museum, Dr. Angelos Delivorrias, director of the Benaki Museum, and Mrs. Sophia Papageorgiou, librarian of the Gennadios Library of the American School of Classical Studies for permission to use photographs of works in their respective collections. Professor Carl A. Peterson, of Oberlin College, I thank for his editorial advice and critical insight and Dr. Maria Constantoudaki-Kitromilides, of the University of Athens, for help in obtaining photographs of icons in the collection of the Hellenic Institute in Venice. I am grateful to the late Dr. Laskarina Bouras, Curator of Byzantine Collections of the Benaki Museum, for her friendly and helpful collegiality.

This article appeared first in Gary Vikan, ed., *Icon* (Washington, D.C.: The Trust for Museum Exhibitions, and Baltimore: The Walters Art Gallery, 1988) and is reprinted here, with some changes, by kind permission of the Trust for Museum Exhibitions.

My epigraphs are from Cyril Mango, *The Art of the Byzantine Empire 321–1453*, (Englewood Cliffs, N.J.: Prentice Hall, 1972), 169, 254. Gregory Melissenos, a member of the Greek delegation at the Council of Ferrara, is quoted by Sylvester Syropoulos in *Vera historia unionis non verae* (see Mango, 254).

1. Mario Cattapan, "Nuovi documenti riguardanti pittori cretesi dal 1300 al 1500," *Pepragmena tou B' Diethnous Kretologikou Synedriou 1966*, 4 vols. (Athens: Philologikos Syllogos o Chrysostomos, 1968–69), 3:29–46; idem, "Nuovi elenchi e documenti dei pittori in Creta dal 1300 al 1500," *Thesaurismata* 9 (1972): 202–35; idem, "I pittori Andrea e Nicola Rizo da Candia," *Thesaurismata* 10 (1973): 238–82; Maria Constantoudaki, "Oi zographoi tou Chandakos kata to proton emisy tou 16ou aionos oi martyroumenoi ek ton notariakon archeion," *Thesaurismata* 10 (1973): 291–380.

2. Maria Vassilakes-Mavrakakes, "O zographos Angelos Akotantos: To ergo tou kai e diatheke tou," *Thesaurismata* 18 (1981): 290–98; Nano Chatzidakis, *Icons of the Cretan School (15th–16th Centuries): Exhibition Catalogue* (Athens: Benaki Museum, 1983), 17–28.

3. Maria Constantoudaki-Kitromilides, "A Fifteenth Century Byzantine Icon-Painter Working on Mosaics in Venice," *Jahrbuch der österreichishen Byzantinistik* 32/5 (1982): 265–72.

4. Cattapan, "I Pittori," 238–82; Thalia Gouma-Peterson, "The Dating of Creto-Venetian Icons: A Reconsideration in the Light of New Evidence," *Allen Memorial Art Museum Bulletin* 30 (1973): 12–22; Manolis Chatzidakis, "Essai sur l'école dite 'Italogrecque,'" *Venezia e il Levante fino al secolo XV*, 2 vols. in 3 (Florence: Leo S. Olschki Editore, 1973, 1974), 2:69–124; N. Chatzidakis, 28–30; Manolis Chatzidakis, *Ellenes zographoi meta ten Alose (1450–1830)* (Athens: Kentro Neoellenikon Ereunon, 1987–), 1:73–92.

5. Cattapan, "Nuovi Elenchi," 202–35.

6. Deno J. Geanakoplos, *Byzantine East and Latin West: Two Worlds of Christendom in Middle Ages and Renaissance: Studies in Ecclesiastical and Cultural History* (New York: Barnes and Noble, 1966), 114–22, and idem, *Greek Scholars in Venice: Studies in the Dissemination of Greek Learning from Byzantium to Western Europe* (Cambridge: Harvard Univ. Press, 1962), 125–58.

7. Geanakoplos, *Byzantine East*, 84–111; Thalia Gouma-Peterson, "Piero della Francesca's Flagellation: An Historical Interpretation," *Storia dell'arte* 28 (1976): 217–33.

8. Geanakoplos, *Byzantine East*, 112–37.

9. Cattapan, "I pittori," 238–82.

10. Manolis Chatzidakis, "Recherches sur le peintre Théophane le Crétois," *Dumbarton Oaks Papers* 22–23 (1969–70): 311–52; idem, *Ellenes zographoi*, 82–85; Andreas Xyngopoulos, *Schediasma istorias tes threskeutikes zographikes meta ten Alosin* (Athens: Archaiologike Etaireia, 1957), 94–112.

11. Maria G. Constantoudaki, "Martyries zographikon ergon sto Chandaka se engrapha tou 16ou kai 17ou aiona," *Thesaurismata* 12 (1975): 35–136.

12. Manolis Chatzidakis, *Icônes de Saint-Georges des Grecs et de la collection de l'Institut* (Venice: Neri Pozza, [1962]), 21–22.

13. Ibid., 23–27.

14. Chryssa Maltezou, "Agnoste eikona tou Emmanouel Tzane (1661): E Panagia e Kardiotissa kai o aphierotes tes Ioannes Menganos," *Thesaurismata* 10 (1973): 283–90.

15. Chatzidakis, *Icônes*, 51–73; idem, *Ellenes zographoi*, 90–91; Xyngopoulos, *Schediasma*, 136–59.

16. Marie Constantoudaki, "Domenicos Theotocopoulos (El Greco) de Candie à Venise: Documents inédits (1566–1568)," *Thesaurismata* 12 (1975): 292–308.

17. *From Byzantium to El Greco* (Athens: Greek Ministry of Culture and the Byzantine Museum of Athens, 1987), 133, 190–91.

18. Harold E. Wethey, *El Greco and His School*, 2 vols. (Princeton: Princeton Univ. Press, 1962), 1:3–75.

19. K. Milanou, "E technike ton Byzantinon eikonon," *Archaiologia* 22 (1987): 49–52.

20. Thalia Gouma-Peterson, "The Survival of Byzantinism in 18th Century Greek Painting," *Allen Memorial Art Museum Bulletin* 29 (1971): 25–59; Xyngopoulos, *Schediasma*, 191–351; Chatzidakis, *Ellenes zographoi*, 93–99.

21. Gouma-Peterson, "Survival of Byzantinism," 36–37; Chatzidakis, *Ellenes zographoi*, 94; idem, *Icônes*, 143–46; Xyngopoulos, *Schediasma*, 248–56.

22. Gouma-Peterson, "Survival of Byzantinism," 36–37; Chatzidakis, *Ellenes zographoi*, 99–128.

23. Gouma-Peterson, "Survival of Byzantinism," 40–44.

24. Steven Runcimann, *The Great Church in Captivity: A Study of the Patriarchate of Constantinople from the Eve of the Turkish Conquest to the Greek War of Independence* (London: Cambridge Univ. Press, 1968), 348, 383–84; T. H. Papadopoullos, *Studies and Documents Relating to the History of the Greek Church and People under Turkish Domination* (Brussels: N.p., 1952), 129–39, 147–49, 203–16 (for the activities of Auxentios in Nicomedia).

25. Gouma-Peterson, "Survival of Byzantinism," 44–46; Xyngopoulos, *Schediasma*, 275–76, 279.

26. Xyngopoulos, *Schediasma*, 318; idem, *Sylloge Elenes Stathatou: Katalogos perigraphikos ton eikonon* (Athens: Archaiologike Etaireia, 1951), 19–20; Gouma-Peterson, "Survival of Byzantinism," 48–51.

27. Ibid., 52–53; A[ndreas] Xyngopoulos, *Katalogos ton eikonon, Mouseion Benaki, Athenai* (Athens: [Benaki Museum], 1936), 85–87.

28. Gouma-Peterson, "Survival of Byzantinism," 11–25.

Fig. 2.1. Angelos, Virgin *Kardiotissa*. Mid-15th c. 121 × 96 cm. Byzantine Museum of Athens.

Fig. 2.2. Andreas Ritzos, Virgin of the Passion. Second half of the 15th c. 102 × 85 cm. Florence, Galleria dell'Accademia. (Photo: Alinari/Art Resource)

Fig. 2.3. Nicholas Ritzos (attributed), Enthroned Virgin and Child with Angels and Scenes from Christ's Life. Second half of the 15th c. 87 × 65 cm. Benaki Museum, Athens.

Fig. 2.4. *Virgin Madre della Consolazione*. Second half of the 15th c. 63 × 45 cm. Benaki Museum, Athens, Stathatos Collection.

Fig. 2.5. *Deësis*. 1546. 119 × 89 cm. Venice, Collection of the Hellenic Institute. (Photo: after Manolis Chatzidakis, *Icones de Saint-Georges des Grecs et de la collection de l'Institut* [Venice: Neri Pozza, [1962], pl. 6)

Fig. 2.6. Virgin and Child with Prophets, detail. Mid-16th c. 68 × 87 cm. Venice, Collection of the Hellenic Institute. (Photo: after Chatzidakis, *Icones*, pl. 9)

Fig. 2.7. Emmanuel Tzanes Bounialis, Virgin *Kardiotissa*. 1661. 104 × 77 cm. London, private collection. (Photo: after Chryssa Maltezou, "Agnoste eikona tou Emmanouel Tzane (1661): E Panaghia e Kardiotissa kai o aphierotes tes Ioannes Menganos," *Thesaurismata* 10 [1973]: pl. 9)

Fig. 2.8. Michael Damaskinos, St. Anthony. Second half of the 16th c. 86 × 67 cm.
Byzantine Museum of Athens.

Fig. 2.9. Michael Damaskinos, St. Michael. Second half of the 16th c. 104 × 75 cm. Present location unknown. (Photo: Sotheby's)

Fig. 2.10. Domenikos Theotokopoulos (El Greco), Dormition of the Virgin. Second half of the 16th c. 61.4 × 52.2 cm. Syros, Ermoupolis, Church of the Dormition of the Theotokos. Byzantine Museum of Athens.

Fig. 2.11. Domenikos Theotokopoulos (El Greco), Christ. Ca. 1600. 72 × 57 cm.
National Gallery of Scotland.

Fig. 2.12. Emmanuel Lambardos or his workshop, Virgin *Hodegetria*. First half of the 17th c. 122 × 89 cm. Benaki Museum, Athens.

Fig. 2.13. Theodore Poulakis, St. Spyridon with Scenes of His Life. Second half of
the 17th c. 50 × 45 cm. Benaki Museum, Athens.

Fig. 2.14. Constantine Kontarinis, Miracle of St. Luke and St. Eleutherios. 1718. 42 x 62 cm. Athens, Gennadius Library of the American School of Classical Studies, Stathatos Collection.

Fig. 2.15. Laskaris Leichoudis, St. Nicholas with Scenes of His Life. 1733. 65 × 53 cm. Benaki Museum, Athens.

Fig. 2.16. St. Gregory the Theologian and St. Artemios. 1770. 26 × 18 cm. Allen Memorial Art Museum, Oberlin College General Acquisitions Fund, 1970.

WALTERS LECTIONARY W.535 (A.D. 1594) AND THE REVIVAL OF DELUXE GREEK MANUSCRIPT PRODUCTION AFTER THE FALL OF CONSTANTINOPLE

Gary Vikan

A S THE ILLUMINATED manuscript ranks among the foremost witnesses to the Byzantine artistic legacy, so the illustrated Gospel lectionary ranks among Byzantium's most impressive types of illuminated manuscript.[1] For although chronologically confined to the Middle Byzantine period, the illustrated lectionary, by virtue of its integral role in the Divine Liturgy, reached a unique level of iconographic richness among Byzantine manuscripts. Indeed, its subtly orchestrated pictorial response to the Orthodox calendar of major and minor feasts mirrors in miniature a portion of the grand cosmological scheme of sacred images characteristic of Middle Byzantine mural cycles and icon screens. Through an intermixing of historiated initials, unframed marginal vignettes, single-column scenes (in what are characteristically large, two-column codices), and full- or nearly full-page elaborately framed miniatures, the movable and fixed liturgical calendars unfold in a narrative panorama drawn, like the lections themselves, primarily from the Gospels, with occasional additions from the apocrypha and saints' lives. Inevitably, the most important holidays in the Byzantine church year dominate the lectionary's decoration, with emphasis falling especially on those sacred events associated with Holy Week.

The high point of the illustrated Gospel lectionary was reached during the later decades of the eleventh century, in such extraordinary manuscripts as Dionysiou 587 (fig. 3.60), Morgan Library M639, San Giorgio dei Greci 2, and Vatican Library *graecus* 1156. But although such service books continued to play a central role in the liturgy of the Orthodox—as the embodiment of Christ's divine wisdom in the "Little Entrance," and as an ever-present, often luxuriously bound altar implement—and although many technically fine manuscripts of this type continued to be produced over the centuries, the illustrated lectionary as it had developed during the Middle Byzantine period effectively disappeared as a genre in East Christian art. Indeed, it seems to have been revived only once, and then only very briefly, around 1600, as an outgrowth of the broader *Byzance après Byzance* efflorescence of Orthodox ecclesiastical arts fostered, above all, by the voevods of Rumania; as the only lay Christian rulers left within the old empire, these Balkan princes had become leaders in reviving and perpetuating the cultural and political heritage of Byzantium.[2] Perhaps nothing is more evocative of their cultural leadership than the famous painted churches of Moldavia, such as those at Voroneţ (fig. 3.1; A.D. 1547) and Suceviţa (A.D. 1601), whose exterior fresco cycles are at once firmly rooted in the Byzantine iconographic and stylistic past, and yet distinctly post-Byzantine and Rumanian in their innovative synthesis of images and architecture.[3] But there was a parallel though much less well known post-Byzantine renaissance in book art as well,[4] and it is this revival, but more specifically, its reflection in an extraordinary illustrated lectionary in the Walters Art Gallery that is the topic of this study.

The Manuscript

Some time in the 1920s Henry Walters acquired in Paris from Léon Gruel, one of the foremost bookbinders of the day, a large, copiously illustrated Greek lectionary on paper (W.535; figs. 3.2–19) which, until shortly before, had been in the possession of the Greek patriarchate in Jerusalem (*Anastaseos* 4).[5] Although known to scholars since the turn of the century through Athanasios Papadopoulos-Kerameus's comprehensive catalogue of the Greek manuscript holdings in Jerusalem, and subsequently published in the United States by the New Testament text critic Kenneth W. Clark, Walters manuscript 535 has never received the attention that its ambitious picture cycle and fascinating history deserve. Its main interest has been its dated scribal colophon—1594: "Luke from Cyprus"—and its fine calligraphy. Overlooked by Maria Vogel and Victor Gardthausen (*Die griechischen Schreiber*), who cite just two of now at least twenty-eight known manuscripts by this accomplished scribe, it has more recently figured peripherally in several studies (by Politis, Gratziou, and Vikan) devoted to "Luke from Cyprus" or, more generally, to Greek calligraphy in the Orthodox East around 1600. But nowhere has its substantial illustration received more than passing comment, and its fascinating history—involving the most powerful of all Rumanian voevods, Michael the Brave, and Tsar Theodore Ivanovich, son of Ivan the Terrible—has been explored only in the most summary way.[6]

Executed on fine imported paper probably of French or north Italian manufacture, Walters lectionary W.535, at about 40 × 27 centimeters, ranks with the largest manuscripts extant from the post-Byzantine period, and in fact it is significantly larger than its Middle Byzantine lectionary counterpart (e.g., Morgan Library M639 measures 33.5 × 23.4 centimeters).[7] Consisting of a *synaxarion* with daily readings through the Orthodox movable year from Easter to Easter, followed by a full *menologion* for the Byzantine fixed calendar beginning September 1, it is 850 pages long. The title of each lection is rendered in gold, and each *incipit* is set off by a large gold letter—either the customary tau for Τῷ καιρῷ ἐκείνῳ (In that day), or alternatively, an epsilon for Εἶπεν ὁ Κύριος (The Lord said). The four successive sections of the *synaxarion*, comprising readings drawn mainly from John, Matthew, Luke, and Mark, are set off by elaborate gold and polychrome headpieces above stylized Slavonic style titles; each faces a full-page Evangelist portrait executed in gouache against a gold background (figs. 3.2, 3.9, 3.14, 3.17).

Unusual size, fine calligraphy, and elaborate portraits place this manuscript among a very select group of deluxe post-Byzantine lectionaries, but what makes it virtually unique is its picture cycle, consisting of fifty-seven framed marginal miniatures. Seventeen miniatures fall within the John readings, sixteen are found in the Matthew section, twenty in Luke, and four in Mark; but surprisingly, there are no illustrations in the *menologion*, and those in Mark break off about a third of the way through the readings. Each picture is proximate to the text passage it illustrates (fig. 3.13), but in no case does it physically impinge on the writing column. Interestingly, toward the beginning of the manuscript most of the miniatures (75% in John) are found on the recto of the folio, whereas further into the book more appear on the verso (60% in Luke). Apparently special care was taken with the appearance of the forward portion of the book, as one would expect with a deluxe, presentation copy. And indeed, this notion is confirmed by the number and location of the lections chosen for illustration, for while the first week of John has a picture for each daily reading, Mark, comprising the Lenten and all-important Holy Week lections, has just four miniatures in toto, ending with Palm Sunday—an anomalous situation when compared with the Middle Byzantine lectionary, whose picture cycle will mirror Orthodoxy's devotional preoccupation with the events leading up to the Crucifixion and Anastasis.[8] This, coupled with the fact that W.535 has no *menologion* (fixed calendar) miniatures, means that such important feast days as the Annunciation, Nativity, Presentation in the Temple, Baptism, Transfiguration, Crucifixion, and *Koimesis* of the Virgin are not represented.[9]

Iconographically more striking still is the narrative density with which many of the readings are illustrated, however obscure they might be liturgically, for among the fifty-seven miniatures in Walters W.535 there are nearly 140 individual narrative episodes. This ratio of image to text is higher, for many passages, than that of the most copiously illustrated Middle Byzantine Gospel books, Paris *graecus* 74 and Florence *Laurentiana* VI,23. A case in point is the miniature devoted to the Parable of the Prodigal Son, the reading for the eighteenth Sunday in the Luke section (fig. 3.16). Just twenty-two verses (Luke 15.11–32) provide the basis for ten distinct actions evoking the following eight narrative episodes, all of which are remarkably detailed, and accurate to the biblical account:

1. The father gives his younger son his inheritance (15.12; upper left).
2. The son journeys to a far country (15.13; top left).
3. The son wastes his inheritance through riotous living (15.13; top center).
4. The son is forced to work among the swine (15.15, 16; top right).
5. The father welcomes his prodigal son home and provides him with new clothing (15.20–22; bottom left).
6. A fatted calf is slaughtered, and father and son celebrate the reunion (15.23, 24; bottom center).
7. Returning from the fields and hearing the celebration, the elder son asks a servant for an explanation (15.25–27; lower right).
8. The father goes out to entreat the angry elder son (15.28–32; middle right).

In Paris *graecus* 74 the same passage is illustrated with seven distinct actions representing six episodes, while in *Laurentiana* VI,23 at most four actions can be discerned.[10]

Three artists are identifiable among the sixty-one miniatures in Walters 535. Clearly the foremost of the three (Hand I: figs. 3.2–5, 3.8–12, 3.14, 3.17), by virtue of the prominence of his work, is that responsible for all four Evangelist portraits and twenty-two of the marginal miniatures, including all of those up through folio 20r (Monday of the second week in John) and each of the three that is coupled with a headpiece to a major section of readings. Except for portraits of Luke and Mark, and one headpiece miniature, this artist disappears after folio 125, in the Matthew section. Each of his miniatures was executed in gouache and gold, and his background architecture is at once highly detailed and fantastic, with a multiplicity of lancet windows and hatched silver roofs with sagging rooflines. This miniaturist's figures are puppetlike in their proportions, with large, round heads and narrow, sloping shoulders. They are characterized by striding poses, and by dramatic gestures and glances. Drapery clings to the body, except for occasional stylized darts of hem jutting out into space. In contrast with the third miniaturist, this one preferred narratively simple compositions, with the action concentrated in the foreground (contrast figs. 3.9 and 3.16).

The second identifiable artist in Walters 535 (Hand II: figs. 3.6, 3.7) was responsible for just four miniatures, which fall between folios 25 and 40 in the John readings. He used a watercolor technique distinguished by strong, contrasting shades of red and green (mostly in drapery), by a variety of thin, earth-tone washes, and by broad areas of uncolored paper (mostly in faces). Yet these are apparently finished miniatures, for such final touches as the cross and inscription in Christ's halo are in evidence; this miniature technique is an otherwise familiar one in the Orthodox East during the later sixteenth century (compare figs. 3.7 and 3.52; and see below). The second artist was an accomplished draftsman, whose figures are solemn in demeanor and statuesque in proportions; their hands, head, and feet are small, and their drapery refined and angular.

Much as the first miniaturist was given pride of place, presumably as a reflection of his greater reputation or authority, the third identifiable miniaturist in W.535 was literally relegated to the back—and yet given the most work. He was responsible for thirty-two miniatures (and the one preparatory drawing),[11] but only three of those, buried in the middle of the Matthew readings, fall before folio 125. This artist was given no Evangelists to portray, and was denied the headpiece miniature in the Luke readings, even though he accounts for all the marginal miniatures in the manuscript beginning thirty folios before that point and continuing to the end of the cycle (i.e., from the thirteenth week of Matthew, through Luke and Mark). He, too, used the technique of watercolor, but in at least two perceptibly different states of completion (contrast figs. 3.15 and 3.18), the more finished of which (fig. 3.18), because it includes facial tones, should probably be understood as completed, even though Christ's halo is still without its inscribed cross. Thin salmon and earthy yellow washes predominate. The figural proportions are taller and more elegant than those characteristic of Hand I, but they do not achieve the grace and monumentality of Hand II; moreover, the draftsmanship is generally simpler than that of the second artist, whereas the narrative complexity of each composition, especially in the upper background, is much greater than that common to either of the other two artists. Finally, this miniaturist has a clearly distinguishable approach to background architecture, which he treats as so many thin, stage-set divisions for the narrative action (contrast figs. 3.8 and 3.16). For the contrast in style between Hands I and III, as they rendered the same narrative event with virtually the same iconography, see figures 3.12 and 3.13: the Parable of the Talents.[12]

The Scribe

Covering nearly all of folio 422r is an elaborate scribal colophon (fig. 3.19): "The present divine and sacred holy εὐαγγέλιον [lectionary] was finished by my hand, lowly and worthless bishop of Buzău Luke, from Cyprus, in the days of our most pious master John Michael Voevod. The year from the incarnation of our Lord Jesus Christ 1594, indiction 7, June 4, day 3 [Tuesday]."

The identity of "Luke from Cyprus" may be reconstructed on the basis of Greek and Slavic archival documents, as well as from more than two dozen known manuscripts by his hand, and from a short notice in a chronicle of the Wallachian voevods (covering 1602 to 1618) composed by Matthew, metropolitan of Myra: "Luke, the most holy metropolitan of Hungro-Wallachia, good and faithful man, from childhood turned to the monastic mode of life, and became highly skilled in calligraphy. He drew his origins from Cyprus."[13]

That Luke was a Cypriot is confirmed by the fact that in many of his colophons, as in W.535, he signs τοῦ Κυπρίου. Yet, it is equally certain that he spent most of his life in the principality of Wallachia (the southeastern portion of what is modern Rumania); indeed, his presence there is documented from 1583 until his death in 1629. Although no direct evidence can be cited, it may be supposed that Luke, as a boy or young man, was among the many Greeks who emigrated to the Balkans when the Turks captured Cyprus in 1571.

Luke the Cypriot initially settled in Buzău, about 110 kilometers northeast of Bucharest, and over several decades was primarily responsible for the creation of the nearby Monastery of Izvorani. The first documentation of Luke as bishop of Buzău, a post vacant from early 1581, is a charter issued by Voevod Petru Cercel in September 1583, naming "the very honest and saintly archbishop, Luke of Buzău." Before that, he signed at the rank of deacon in the colophon of an illustrated Joseph romance datable around 1580 (San Francisco, Greeley Collection), and as ἱερομόναχος in a Psalter now on Mount Athos dated 1583 (St. Paul Skiti 806). From that year until 1601 Luke's tenure as bishop is reflected in more than a half-dozen manuscript colophons, as well as in a series of archival documents relating his ecclesiastical, juridical, and diplomatic activities. A charter issued in late 1603 by Voevod Radu Şerban identifies Luke the Cypriot as metropolitan of Hungro-Wallachia, the highest post in the Wallachian Orthodox Church, vacant since August 1602. Luke's activities as metropolitan, which necessarily drew him to the capital Tîrgovişte, about 80 kilometers northwest of Bucharest, are recorded in a series of documents extending from 1603 until his death and burial at the Izvorani Monastery in 1629. As metropolitan, Luke was the dominant figure in the Wallachian Church, and he enjoyed the continuing protection and patronage of the highly cultivated, westernizing voevod Radu Mihnea, who ruled intermittently from 1601 to 1623. He was closely acquainted with Anastasie Crîmca, metropolitan of Moldavia, who was also a well-known manuscript illuminator, and with the famous Calvinist patriarch Cyril Loukaris; among his friends was another important scribe and ecclesiastic, Matthew, metropolitan of Myra, who from 1609 was abbot of the Dealu Monastery near Tîrgovişte, and the chief chronicler of the Wallachian court.[14]

Despite his high ecclesiastical rank and considerable diplomatic achievement (see below), Luke was evoked in Matthew's chronicle specifically because he was "highly skilled in calligraphy"; indeed, Anthimos of Adrianople, the future patriarch, wrote in a dedicatory notice that "he [Luke] has surpassed, in our time, all others in the art of calligraphy."[15] Twenty-eight known manuscripts, certainly only a portion of his oeuvre, testify to the high sophistication and unfailing quality of his work. Luke seems never to have lessened his dedication to calligraphy, even as metropolitan and after having reached old age; his dated works span more than forty-five years. And it is clear from his generous use of gold, ornament, and illustration, his large, ornate script, and the high proportion of his manuscripts that are liturgies or lectionaries, that Luke's scribal career was primarily devoted to the production of deluxe service books for presentation to important monasteries and churches; at least three of his manuscripts may be directly associated with the patronage of Wallachian voevods.[16]

Over the last few decades the various identities of Luke the Cypriot—as scribe, illuminator, miniaturist—have been defined with substantial precision. In an article in the 1958 *Byzantinische Zeitschrift* Linos Politis identified Luke as one of the most skilled, productive, and influential post-Byzantine practitioners of a tradition of ornate and highly refined liturgical script traceable back at least three centuries to a Palaeologan scribal school centered in the Hodegon Monastery in Constantinople.[17] Luke's link to that tradition may well have been by way of the scribe Ambrosios, abbot of the Monastery of St. Andrew (Nicosia) (fig. 3.36; A.D. 1552), who was practicing Hodegon school calligraphy on Cyprus at precisely the time when Luke would have received his training there.[18] Over nearly half a century Luke's calligraphic style remained more or less constant; his letter forms are large, round, and elegant, becoming, with time, only slightly freer and more expressive. On the other hand, Luke's ornament style, which has been the subject of two independent studies within the last several years (Vikan, 1988; Gratziou, 1989), periodically took quite new directions, though all the while retaining formulas and various elegant mannerisms that unmistakably betray their authorship.[19] Early in his career Luke preferred traditional carmine decoration, with fretwork filler for initials and simple interlace headpieces. These motifs were common among Hodegon school manuscripts two centuries earlier, but show as well a continuous tradition throughout the Orthodox East, including Cyprus, from the Middle Byzantine period down to the seventeenth century. Also evident early, and conspicuous right up to the end of Luke's career, are complex interlace headpieces in gold and colors that conform closely to contemporary and earlier printed books and manuscript illumination of the South Slavic regions just north and west of Wallachia. Unlike Matthew of Myra, however, Luke only rarely revived the traditional Middle Byzantine flower-petal style, although like Matthew, he was much influenced, especially later in his career, by Western engravings as adapted and popularized in the East through Slavonic printed books.[20] And finally, as I sought to demonstrate in my 1976 dissertation, it is likely that Luke left Cyprus a fully-trained painter, as well as a scribe and illuminator.[21] This is clearly implicit in his two earliest manuscripts, the *Life of Joseph/Romance of Joseph and Aseneth* in San Francisco (Greeley Collection; figs. 3.37, 3.38) and the *Joasaph and Barlaam* in Athens (Senate Library 11), which together contain more than one hundred watercolor miniatures.[22] Not only are these illustrations physically integral to and contentually dependent upon their accompanying text—as no other miniatures are in Luke manuscripts—they are in a Westernizing style clearly derived from that current on Cyprus at the time when Luke would have received his training there (fig. 3.39).[23]

How does the Walters lectionary fit into the manuscript oeuvre of Luke the Cypriot? It is distinguished as extraordinary among an unusually fine series of books by its large format, luxurious headpieces, elaborate colophon, and most of all, by its ambitious miniature cycle.[24] For after the early Joseph and Joasaph manuscripts (with, respectively, eighty and twenty-three miniatures), and a few Gospel books and liturgies with simple author portraits, there is just one other Luke manuscript incorporating pictures: an *Akathistos Hymnos* at Princeton (University Library Garrett 13) with twenty-five full-page miniatures in Cretan style illustrating the hymn's prelude and twenty-four stanzas.[25] As for the script and ornament in W.535, the former, at once more decorative and expressive than that of the decade-earlier *Life of Joseph/Romance of Joseph and Aseneth* (contrast figs. 3.2 and 3.37), is representative of Luke's early maturity as a calligrapher, whereas the latter, for the most part, is an elaborate though characteristic manifestation of his fully developed "Slavic interlace style."[26] It parallels the ornament in a roughly contemporary liturgy, signed by Luke in the Barlaam Monastery (fig. 3.40), while at the same time recalling specific headpieces of earlier Slavic manuscripts upon whose tradition Luke clearly depends (fig. 3.41; A.D. 1469).[27] On the other hand, the simpler initials in Walters 535 (fig. 3.13) are virtually identical to those used throughout the *Life of Joseph/Roman of Joseph and Aseneth* (fig. 3.37), while the manuscript's Mark headpiece (fig. 3.17) is a polychrome version of the sort of carmine fretwork headpiece characteristic of Luke's early manuscripts (fig. 3.42)—and is in turn remarkably like the Ambrosios headpiece reproduced in figure 3.36.[28] The latter bond, and the identity of decorative initial style between Ambrosios and Luke (compare figs. 3.13 and 3.37 with 3.36), substantially strengthen the possibility of a direct teacher-student link between these two Cypriot scribes.

Clearly, the headpieces and initials of the Walters lectionary are by Luke the Cypriot, but the miniatures are just as clearly not. This itself is characteristic of Luke, for neither the various author portraits nor the *Akathistos* miniatures referred to in the previous paragraph were executed by the calligrapher himself.[29] Luke the Cypriot was first and foremost a scribe and illuminator, and only secondarily, and apparently only early in his career, a miniaturist.[30]

Walters 535 and *Anastaseos* 5

Who added the miniatures to the Walters lectionary? When were they added, and where? The answer lies in another lavishly illustrated Greek lectionary—one signed and dated in Moscow in 1596 by "Arsenios, bishop of Elasson"—which Papadopoulos-Kerameus catalogued beside the Walters lectionary in the Greek patriarchate in Jerusalem in 1897 as *Anastaseos* codex 5 (figs. 3.20–32).[31] Indeed, *Anastaseos* 5 was apparently taken with *Anastaseos* 4, and other manuscripts, to Damascus in 1918 as collatoral on a loan.[32] But while *Anastaseos* 4 went on from there to Paris and then Baltimore, *Anastaseos* 5 returned to Jerusalem—without its four Evangelist portraits, which were acquired in the 1930s by the Morgan Library (M654), and three (perhaps four) of its sectional *incipit* pages, two of which ended up in the Art Museum of Princeton University in the 1950s (54.67, 68), while another made its way, via the Lillian Malcove Collection, to the University of Toronto in 1982 (M82.446). Not only is *Anastaseos* 5, like Walters 535, a large-format daily lectionary with Evangelist portraits and more than four dozen individual lection miniatures, its illustrations are clearly by the first of the three artists identifiable in the Walters manuscript (compare figs. 3.2–5, 3.8–12, 3.14, 3.17 with 3.20–29). This miniaturist executed all fifty of the Jerusalem manuscript's lection miniatures and possibly all four of its figurative sectional headpieces, though he did not do its Evangelist portraits, which betray a grander, more somber sensibility, closer to the style of the Russian icon painter Dionisy (contrast figs. 3.2 and 3.20).[33]

The familial bond between these two otherwise highly individualistic books goes beyond an identity of artist to include iconographic matches through their first nine miniatures (W.535: 9r–20r; *Anastaseos* 5: 2r–14r), extending from Easter Sunday through Monday of the second week after Easter (compare figs. 3.2–5 with 3.20–23).[34] Their respective compositions are virtually identical, save for the fact that those in the Walters manuscript are significantly larger—8.3 × 7.7 centimeters versus 5.0 × 3.2 centimeters for figures 3.4 and 3.22—and, accordingly, somewhat richer in detail. And there is yet another suggestive point of iconographic contact between these two books; namely, that immediately following the nine matches (W.535: fols. 21r–38r; *Anastaseos* 5: 15r–39r), where *Anastaseos* 5 continues to show miniatures for each daily lection but W.535 no longer does, the latter bears a series of short inscriptions—presumably guides for the illustrator(s)—which indicate where its counterpart miniatures were to be placed.[35] The thirteen instances of this picture-to-inscription linkage substantially strengthen the notion that the histories of these two unusual manuscripts were closely intertwined.

Before proceeding to the question of whether one of these two books was copied from the other, and to the critical historical information for both supplied by the dedication notice in the Jerusalem codex, it will be useful to characterize in more depth their general similarities and differences.

In addition to parallels in page size, figure style, individual lection iconography, and overall decorative program, these two manuscripts parallel one another in calligraphy, insofar as the scribe Arsenios was also a practitioner—though certainly a less skilled one than Luke—of the post-Byzantine tradition of liturgical script traceable back to the Hodegon Monastery school of the Palaeologan period.[36] The *Anastaseos* 5 headpieces, however, are clearly different from those of W.535 (contrast figs. 3.2 and 3.20); and, because the former are readily attributable to the hand of the manuscript's main miniaturist (Hand I) through their *Deësis* medallion portraits, this further corroborates the attribution of the headpieces in the Walters lectionary to Luke himself. Unlike the Walters manuscript, and Middle Byzantine lectionaries generally, the Jerusalem manuscript was written in a single column. Moreover, in *Anastaseos* 5 the miniatures were set into the writing column, supplanting the *incipit* letter, whereas those of W.535 were without exception placed outside the writing column (contrast figs. 3.2 and 3.20). And finally, there are clear iconographic divergencies between these two books after their string of nine matches, for while Walters 535 from that point on essentially reverts to Sunday lection illustration, all the way into the Mark section, *Anastaseos* 5 illustrates nearly all the daily readings through the remainder of the John section, but after that is virtually without pictures. Specifically, it has forty-seven miniatures in John, but just two in Matthew, one in Luke, and none in Mark (and none in the *menologion*). So even more than Walters 535, *Anastaseos* 5 departs programmatically from Middle Byzantine lectionary decoration, which, while it typically will favor the John section, never shows such a dense series of pictures for that or any other section, and never so totally neglects Holy Week and the major feasts of the fixed calendar.

In terms of the ratio of image to text, *Anastaseos* 5 appears, prima facie, to offer impressive statistics, for it is fully twice as rich in illustration through John as, for example, the eleventh-century lectionary Dionysiou 587. In fact, it is in this section every bit as dense iconographically as are the two most fully illustrated Middle Byzantine Gospel books, Paris *graecus* 74 and Florence *Laurentiana* VI,23.[37] But the statistics are misleading, for although *Anastaseos* 5 has fifty framed lection miniatures—just seven fewer than Walters 535—they encompass only about thirty distinct iconographic episodes, as compared to about 140 episodes in the Walters lectionary. This is due in part to the fact that the miniaturist responsible for the whole of *Anastaseos* 5, Hand I, generally seems to have preferred monoscenic compositions. But mostly it was the result of a formulaic iconographic approach applied consistently in *Anastaseos* 5 (after folio 14), but almost never in Walters 535. Thirty-one (60%) of the fifty miniatures of *Anastaseos* 5 are in fact nothing more than slight variations on a single simple compositional formula for showing Christ addressing a group of men. In seventeen cases it is Christ addressing the Jews (fig. 3.25) and in eleven cases it is Christ addressing his disciples (fig. 3.29); so inevitably the iconography is often only marginally appropriate to the text it accompanies.[38]

Beyond these thirty-one "Christ addressing" scenes, there are a few miniatures in *Anastaseos* 5 that were apparently concocted from appropriated iconography. For example, for Wednesday of the fourth week in John, wherein the story is recounted of (the adult) Christ teaching in the Temple (John 7.14), the iconography (fig. 3.26) is that of the twelve-year-old Christ disputing with the doctors in the Temple (Luke 2.41–50), down to the inappropriate detail of Christ's depiction as a beardless youth.[39] Then, seven folios further on, for the Tuesday reading in the sixth week in John, wherein the Pharisees are described as growing increasingly concerned about Jesus as he teaches the throngs in Jerusalem (John 12.19), the miniature (fig. 3.28) consists of two stock elements: a standard "Christ addressing" scene (fig. 3.25) and the previously misappropriated scene of Christ disputing with the doctors (fig. 3.26).[40] A paucity of narrative detail in the middle chapters of John's Gospel, inattention by the miniaturist to the specific story lines of the individual lections, and, presumably, insufficient iconographic models for obscure portions of the Gospels, seem to have conspired in the creation of a remarkably monotonous set of miniatures. In this respect, above all, *Anastaseos* 5 differs fundamentally from Walters 535.

Was Walters 535 the model for *Anastaseos* 5? Or was it the other way around? Or was neither copied from the other?[41] The relative dates of the books, 1594 and 1596, would suggest the first scenario, as would the fact that the iconography in *Anastaseos* 5 becomes monotonous precisely from the point where there are no counterpart miniatures in Walters 535. But if this were so, then why are there inscriptions for just those miniatures in W.535, the supposed model; and, more importantly, why does *Anastaseos* 5 subsequently diverge so clearly from W.535, both through its rendering of the same event differently (contrast figs. 3.8 and 3.27: Christ Restores Sight to the Man Born Blind), and through its illustrating of the same lection on the basis of a different narrative segment in its text (contrast figs. 3.6 and 3.24: Sunday III in John)?[42] And how could one then account for the fact that several of the nine *Anastaseos* 5 miniatures with W.535 "model" counterparts are, in being smaller and iconographically simpler, at the same time more accurate to the text? Most telling are their respective versions of the Road to Emmaus (Luke 24.13–28): that of *Anastaseos* 5 correctly shows just the two disciples whom Christ is described as meeting (fig. 3.21), whereas W.535 incorrectly shows Christ encountering a group of men (fig. 3.3). The prospect of the latter manuscript correcting the former (that is, Hand I correcting himself), while not impossible, is doubtful.[43]

Disregarding for the moment the difficulty posed by their respective colophon dates of 1594 and 1596, could Walters 535 have been copied from *Anastaseos* 5? In toto, obviously not, for there are many miniatures in W.535, beginning with the Anastasis accompanying Easter Sunday (fig. 3.2), which have rich, substantive iconography but no counterpart miniatures in *Anastaseos* 5; unlike the formulaic scenes in the latter manuscript, these clearly presuppose specific models. But still, the prospect of a partial genealogical dependency of W.535 on *Anastaseos* 5 is an attractive one. For not only is there an extraordinary level of stylistic, iconographic, and programmatic coincidence between these two otherwise unusual books, but in those cases where the Walters manuscript does diverge iconographically from *Anastaseos* 5 through the course of their nine initial matches, it does so seemingly as a natural consequence of Hand I adapting a small model to suit a relatively larger format. Compare, for example, their respective miniatures accompanying the first Friday lection in John, wherein Christ is shown driving the merchants from the Temple: the background architecture has clearly been expanded from *Anastaseos* 5 (fig. 3.22) to W.535 (fig. 3.4), and in the latter manuscript sheep have been added in the right foreground, seemingly with the twofold intention of filling in the space and enriching the narrative. Yet even if a partial model-copy relationship between *Anastaseos* 5 and W.535 could somehow be proved, the puzzle would still remain as to why the copying process was not continued after the second Monday reading in John. And of course, there is the more immediate problem of reconciling Rumania 1594 with Moscow 1596, and providing a scenario that will eventually place both books in Jerusalem.

Moscow 1596

On folio 515v of *Anastaseos* 5 is a scribal colophon, written in the formula, if not the controlled liturgical script, characteristic of Hodegon school calligraphers (fig. 3.31): "The gift of God, and the labor of Arsenios, and bishop ('chief sacrificer') of the throne of Elasson."[44]

Arsenios, bishop of Elasson, later a saint in the Russian Church, is known from a rich variety of sources.[45] Born in 1549 to an ecclesiastical family in northern Greece, Arsenios quickly rose in rank and authority within the church, first under the protection of the metropolitan of Larissa, and later under Patriarch Jeremiah II. After study in Constantinople, he was successively deacon, priest, and bishop of Elasson, a town on the slopes of Mount Olympus. After a visit to Russia in 1585, Arsenios taught Greek for two years in the Orthodox confraternity of L'vov. There, in 1588, he met Jeremias II, who asked that he accompany him back to Russia as his interpreter during the negotiations which, in 1589, raised Moscow to the status of a patriarchate. Arsenios stayed on there until his death in 1625, enjoying the protection of Job, patriarch of Moscow, as well as of Tsars Theodore Ivanovich, Boris Godunov, and Michael Romanov, whom he served as advisor. Occasionally a scribe and sometimes a chronicler (of Jeremias's negotiations, first in a poem and later in his *Memoirs*), Arsenios was throughout his life a patron of the ecclesiastical arts, most notably on behalf of the monasteries of his native Thessaly.[46] Successively archbishop of Archangel, Tver, and finally Suzdal, he was so revered in his adopted country that after he died the Russians venerated his relics for their reputed miracle-working properties, and later canonized him as a saint.[47]

According to a dedicatory poem on the page facing the colophon (fol. 516r; fig. 3.32 [translation in note 31]), *Anastaseos* 5 was completed in Moscow on March 6, 1596, as a gift of the scribe to the Monastery of St. Saba, near Jerusalem, in memory of his father Theodore the priest and his mother Christodoule, and his brothers Joasaph, bishop of Stagai, Mark, bishop of Demetrias, and the ἱερομόναχοι Athanasios and Pachomios. But this was not the only manuscript by Arsenios to travel that route. In the same year another large, deluxe Greek lectionary was written and illuminated in Moscow for dedication in the Holy Land (Greek Patriarchate, Treasury 1; figs. 3.33–35), and although unsigned, it, too, is clearly by the hand of Arsenios (compare figs. 3.20 and 3.34).[48] More luxuriously illuminated than either Walters 535 or *Anastaseos* 5, but without lection illustrations, Treasury 1 is bound in gem-encrusted gold covers showing, appropriately for its dedication, the Anastasis and the Adoration of the Cross, along with the Evangelists (fig. 3.33); inside are four gouache Evangelist portraits which, although iconographically nearly identical to those of *Anastaseos* 5, are by the hand of an even more refined miniaturist (contrast figs. 3.20 and 3.34). According to a donor notice rendered in both Greek and Russian, this lectionary was dedicated in the year 1596 to the Church of the Holy Sepulchre in Jerusalem on behalf of Boris Godunov and Tsar Theodore Ivanovich; however, nonscribal notes inside reveal that it was in fact delivered to Jerusalem only in 1600, "from the hands of Boris" (Theodore having died in 1598), via the Archimandrite Theophanes, future patriarch of Jerusalem.[49]

The miniatures and ornament in Arsenios's two lectionaries of 1596 reflect the most sophisticated levels of contemporary Russian book art, as one would expect from the imperial dedication of Treasury 1 and the scribe's long-standing position of influence among the topmost ecclesiastical and political circles in Moscow. Reference has already been made to the dependency of the *Anastaseos* 5 Evangelist portraits on the stylistic tradition of the great Russian icon painter Dionisy. Similar connections may be drawn between the unusually complex Evangelist portrait iconography shared by *Anastaseos* 5 and Treasury 1, and that current in the finest Moscow manuscripts (compare figs. 3.30 and 3.35 with 3.43; A.D. 1531), and between their title page decoration and that found in deluxe Russian Gospel books and lectionaries of the period (compare figs. 3.20 and 3.34 with 3.44 and 3.45).[50]

This was the mise-en-scène for Arsenios of Elasson and *Anastaseos* 5 in Moscow, 1596. And it was into this setting that Luke the Cypriot arrived during the early months of that year as part of a diplomatic mission from Voevod Michael the Brave (1593–1601) to Tsar Theodore Ivano-vich.[51] In his ambitious and initially successful campaign to unite the three Rumanian principalities of Wallachia, Moldavia, and Transylvania in a crusade against the Ottomans, Michael was seeking the support of Russia (most immediately, against the Poles and the Tartars), and toward that end he called on the proved diplomatic skills of an influential Slavic-speaking Greek ecclesiastic from Wallachia, his friend and confidant: Luke, bishop of Buzău.[52]

The pieces to the puzzle of Walters 535 now rapidly begin to fall into place. Luke brought with him to Moscow in 1596 a lectionary that both textually and aesthetically was complete and ready for use two years earlier. (It was not at all uncommon at the time for richly illuminated lectionaries, Gospels, Psalters, and liturgies to be dedicated without author portraits, or for manuscripts once completed to receive their dedication only months or even years later.)[53] It is known that Tsar Theodore sent gifts back with Luke to Voevod Michael,[54] and it may safely be assumed that gifts were initially taken north to Moscow as well. Perhaps Walters 535 was a gift of the Rumanian voevod to the tsar or the new patriarch, or perhaps it remained a personal possession of Luke. Its deluxe format and the pro-tocol of the state occasion would suggest the former scenario, but the absence of an explicit dedication notice—either from Luke to the voevod, or from the voevod to the tsar or patriarch—more strongly favors the latter.[55] And so, too, does the evidence of an illuminated *Akolouthia* in the Dionysiou Monastery on Mount Athos (cod. 429), signed and dated by Luke in Wallachia in 1588, "in the days of" but apparently neither specifi-cally for nor on behalf of the then current voevod, John Mihnea.[56] Later additions of both text and ornament by two other itinerant Greek scribes known to have converged in Moscow in 1596/7 leave no doubt that this book, too, was brought north by Luke on his diplomatic mission—and in this instance, almost certainly as the scribe's private possession. Dionysiou 429 is instructive as well for the "model" it provides of a textually and aesthetically complete book—in this case, one eight years old—receiving subsequent embellishment in Moscow.

One of the two scribes having a hand in Luke's *Akolouthia* of 1588 was Matthew of Myra, fellow calligrapher and illuminator, and longtime friend of Luke, who was in Moscow from 1596 to at least 1597/8 in his capacity as πρωτοσύγκελλος of the Great Church.[57] Moreover, Matthew is explicitly named as the recipient of a signed but undated liturgy by Luke now in the Panteleimon Monastery on Mount Athos (cod. 426):

"These divine and holy liturgies are the property of my brother in Christ, ἱερομόναχος Matthew, and let whosoever would take them from him be excommunicated and cursed by me, Archbishop Luke."[58]

Because the formula in which Matthew added his own colophon at the end of the book ("[By the] hand of Matthew, monk and πρεσβύτερος from Pogoniani") is that characteristic for the scribe in 1599, when he was in L'vov, and because the two calligraphers are not known to have met before 1599, except in Moscow, it may safely be assumed that Panteleimon 426, like Walters 535 and Dionysiou 429, was brought along by Luke to Russia in 1596. And like those other books, this one was to receive significant additions, for while the first two liturgies (fols. 2–99), those traditionally attributed to John Chrysostom and Basil, are in Luke's hand, the Liturgy of the Presanctified (fols. 101–120) was clearly added by Matthew.

Interestingly, Matthew also made additions to *Anastaseos* 5—or more precisely, a single addition, in the form of the initial tau marking Monday in the fourth week of the Matthew readings (fol. 83v; fig. 3.46). Clearly distinct from and much finer than the manuscript's other initials (fol. 441r; fig. 3.47), which match those of Treasury 1 and thus may be attributed to Arsenios himself, this *T* is decorated with stylized dragon heads and tulips closely matching those of the initials in a liturgy in the Tatarna Monastery, signed and dated by Matthew in Moscow on February 16, 1596 (fig. 3.48).[59] Completed just three weeks before *Anastaseos* 5, this manuscript was presented by Matthew as a gift to Arsenios, "in gratitude for his good services to us." Arsenios, in turn, gave it to the Tatarna Monastery, along with an icon and a silver gilt casket, in 1602, but not before a local Moscow painter had added a *Deësis* watercolor miniature at the head of the Chrysostom liturgy, in an area left blank by the scribe (fig. 3.49).[60] Thus the Tatarna liturgy not only provides a parallel for the subsequent embellishment of a Greek manuscript by a Russian painter but also graphically documents the intimate working relationship of local and visiting Greek scribes, and the indigenous community of Moscow manuscript illuminators. This is the formula of collaboration—with Luke, Arsenios, and Matthew in close contact—that is implicit in Walters 535 and *Anastaseos* 5, just as it is in Dionysiou 429, Panteleimon 426, and Treasury 1.

Common sense alone suggests that the paths of Luke and Arsenios would have crossed in Moscow during the later winter or spring of 1596, and of course the iconographic bond of W.535 and *Anastaseos* 5 substantially confirms it. Yet it is noteworthy as well that Panteleimon 426, the manuscript begun by Luke and then given to and completed by Matthew, bears two nonscribal, marginal additions in the intercessory prayer sections of the two liturgies in Luke's hand; one (fol. 33v) asks that the Lord remember "Arsenios ἀρχιερέως and Seraphim the monk," and the other (fol. 80v; fig. 3.50) invokes the same blessing on "Arsenios ἀρχιερέως and Philotheos the monk, and their parents." Noting that the names do not match those listed in the *Anastaseos* 5 dedication (Ioasaph, Mark, Athanasios, and Pachomios), Olga Gratziou has argued that a different Arsenios was involved, whereas Linos Politis had favored an identification with Arsenios of Elasson.[61] What both failed to note, however, is that the invocations are in the hand of an accomplished if not brilliant calligrapher distinct from both Luke and Matthew, and that their letter forms are strikingly similar to those of Arsenios of Elasson in his two lectionaries, *Anastaseos* 5 and Treasury 1 (figs. 3.20 and 3.34), and on the back of a Transfiguration icon he dedicated in 1594 (fig. 3.51b; on which, see below).[62]

Clearly, all the miniatures in Walters 535 were added in Moscow by Russian painters.[63] The first miniaturist (Hand I), already linked to Moscow through his participation in *Anastaseos* 5, worked in a style much like that of the panel painter responsible for a small Transfiguration icon presented by Arsenios to the Monastery of St. Catherine at Mount Sinai in 1594 (figs. 3.51a & b).[64] In addition to similar figural proportions and facial types, the icon shows tufts of tall grass growing from the mountainside that are very much like those appearing occasionally in the Hand I miniatures of W.535 and *Anastaseos* 5 (figs. 3.8, 3.9).[65] Similarly, the distinct though closely interrelated styles of Hands II and III are paralleled in the added *Deësis* headpiece in Matthew's Tatarna liturgy of 1596 (compare figs. 3.7 and 3.49), though even closer are some of the miniatures in a late sixteenth-century illustrated *Life of St. Sergius of Radonezh* in the Lenin Library, Moscow (figs. 3.52, 3.53).[66] Beyond the shared technique and color scheme, specific, sometimes striking parallels may be cited among the miniatures in that manuscript for the elegant proportions, reserved gestures, and "squinting eyes" characteristic of Hand II (compare figs. 3.7 and 3.52), and for the stagelike architectural scheme and dense, multi-tiered iconography of Hand III (compare figs. 3.13 and 3.53).[67] Interestingly, Hand I, unlike Hands II and III, took care to add appropriate Greek inscriptions to his miniatures, most notably on the open scrolls and books within the Evangelist portraits (figs. 3.2, 3.9, 3.14, 3.17; contrast the Russian in the *Anastaseos* 5 John portrait [fig. 3.20]). However, that his native language was Russian is clear from the Cyrillic-style angularity of his letter forms, especially his lambdas and mus (figs. 3.2, 3.17), and from his etas, which often look more like their Russian counterpart, with the inclined cross stroke (fig. 3.2). Much more clearly Cyrillic in style are the letters used to spell out the Greek inscription on the scroll held by Matthew in *Anastaseos* 5 (fig. 3.30). Indeed, the polyglot mélange of post-Byzantine nationalities that gave birth to manuscripts as rich and complex as Walters 535 and *Anastaseos* 5 is effectively epitomized in the elegant though linguistically ambivalent inscribed books and scrolls that their Evangelists hold.

As for the dedication of Walters 535, all evidence points toward Luke himself as the owner of the manuscript between 1594 and 1596, up to the point of its illustration. Should it be imagined that he then presented it to some local Moscow ecclesiastic (the new patriarch? Arsenios?), or perhaps to Ivan or Boris, and that this new owner in turn had it decorated and dedicated? Or would it not make more sense to suppose that this book followed roughly (perhaps exactly) the same path as *Anastaseos* 5; namely, that it was decorated and dedicated on behalf of the scribe himself?[68] The two books, otherwise so similar in their illustration, would then have gone together to the Holy Land, probably to the Monastery of St. Saba.[69] Logic suggests that both would have been finished by the time of Luke's departure from Moscow in the spring of 1596, and that they soon thereafter would have made their trip to the Holy Land. But it is also possible that they departed Moscow only some time later—perhaps in 1600, in the company of their sibling lectionary of 1596, Treasury 1, which, when Papadopoulos-Kerameus catalogued it, was still identified as codex *Anastaseos* 18.[70] But unlike that imperial dedication, no elaborate cover would have been necessary for Luke's gift, and none likely ever existed;[71] indeed, the original colophon of 1594 would still have been adequate, by Luke's standards, to convey appropriate honor to the donor.

Models

Two closely interrelated questions remain to be answered. What was (were) the specific iconographic source (sources) for the entity represented by W.535/*Anastaseos* 5? And what, precisely, is the relationship between these two books?

Ironically, the iconographic banality of some of these miniatures (fig.

3.25) and the extraordinary image-to-text accuracy and narrative density of others (fig. 3.16) could both be taken as symptoms of the same thing; namely, that the illustration was created from scratch, for without models, miniaturists will tend either to fall back on meaningless pictorial topoi or else read and illustrate the text de novo, in all of its fullness and detail.[72] Moreover, the stylistic and compositional heterogeneity of the illustration (contrast figs. 3.4 and 3.16) could be taken to support the same conclusion, since through successive generations of copying a picture cycle will inevitably become increasingly homogeneous, and it will inevitably enforce that homogeneity on each copy; conversely, in the absence of such a single model cycle, the individual stylistic and narrative approaches of the various miniaturists (or of course, the various models) will inevitably manifest themselves more clearly. Note was already made of significant programmatic differences separating W.535/*Anastaseos* 5 from Middle Byzantine illustrated lectionaries generally, and it is well known that Russian miniaturists of the second half of the sixteenth century were among the most creative and ambitious in the history of East Christian book art.[73]

But all of this does not add up to a de novo picture cycle, or anything close to it, for even if one dismisses the three dozen "Christ addressing" scenes, as well as those dozen or so miniatures like the Parable of the Prodigal Son (fig. 3.16), which by their unprecedented narrative density and extraordinary accuracy would presumably not have deep iconographic roots, if any, one is still left with a substantial proportion—perhaps half—of the W.535/*Anastaseos* 5 miniatures that presuppose specific models. Reference has already been made to the Anastasis in Walters 535 (fig. 3.2) and to the Christ Teaching in the Temple miniature in *Anastaseos* 5 (fig. 3.26) as both requiring access to traditional East Christian iconography. Similar though even more specific evidence is provided by the miniature of Christ healing a man of palsy in Walters 535 (fig. 3.10), insofar as the motif of lowering through the roof is not supported by the text of the accompanying Matthew lection (Matthew 9.1–8), though it is consistent with passages in Mark (2.1–12) and Luke (5.17–26) that recount similar healings. Obviously, this iconography was appropriated and not invented on the spot, but what is more significant is the fact that it (its source) falls squarely within the established Middle Byzantine tradition for portraying this event (fig. 3.54).[74] Moreover, there are many other miniatures in both manuscripts which, although completely faithful to their accompanying text, coincide iconographically with and therefore presumably drew upon much earlier Byzantine traditions. And significantly, these genealogical relationships transcend the iconic *dodecaorton* cycle, which one would expect to show iconographic continuity into the post-Byzantine period (compare figs. 3.18 and 3.55: Raising of Lazarus), to include such relatively obscure parables and miracle scenes as the Good Samaritan and Christ Feeding the Five Thousand (compare figs. 3.11 and 3.56).[75]

So clearly, the question is not whether pictorial models were available to the miniaturists responsible for W.535/*Anastaseos* 5; rather, it is whether their picture cycles represent more or less faithful copies from (or at least, exclusive dependency upon) some specific illustrated Middle Byzantine lectionary(ies), or whether they represent ad hoc assemblages from a multiplicity of visual sources—complemented by some pure invention, and perhaps inspired in a general way by the Middle Byzantine illustrated lectionary. Both opportunity and motivation for the former, "one-source," scenario were certainly there, for the Rumanians and the Russians of the sixteenth century were avid collectors of fine Byzantine manuscripts, many of which—including the famous Dionysiou lectionary—they rededicated with sumptuous new bindings, and some of which they copied.[76] But in fact, the evidence points in quite the opposite direction, for not only are there no direct iconographic links between these books and any single extant Byzantine lectionary, including Dionysiou 587, but their profound programmatic differences from Middle Byzantine illustrated lectionaries (mostly, their inattention to Holy Week and *menologion* illustration) also virtually preclude any such specific derivation. And there is the added evidence of the miniatures themselves, which in some instances (fig. 3.18) may be shown to descend from their Middle Byzantine sources (fig. 3.55) only indirectly, by way of a post-Byzantine variant (fig. 3.57; A.D. 1547).[77] There are even cases wherein the miniature has been derived from a specifically Russian reinterpretation of the medieval model. For example, the Women at the Tomb miniature in Walters 535 (fig. 3.6) clearly derives from the contemporary Russian version of the scene (fig. 3.58), which incorporates the *Noli me tangere*.[78] But not only is the *Noli me tangere* not part of the accompanying Mark lection text, the iconography has been corrupted in transmission, insofar as Mary Magdalene has here inappropriately been deleted from that portion of the composition, leaving Christ incongruously alone.

With what, then, is one left? One is left with two closely interrelated picture cycles made up in part from newly (or nearly newly) invented scenes, some of which are compositionally banal and some rich and dense, and in part from borrowed scenes, some of which could have been more or less contemporary with the likes of Dionysiou 587 and some of which are clearly post-Byzantine—or even post-Byzantine Russian. Moreover, what applies to the cycles as a whole applies to their constituent parts, for like the former, the latter (the individual miniatures), when they comprise multiple narrative episodes, represent a mixture of new and appropriated imagery. For example, the miniature in Walters 535 wherein Christ Restores Sight to the Man Born Blind (fig. 3.8) consists of four distinct episodes (Christ forms the clay; Christ applies the clay; the blind man washes off the clay; neighbors question the man about the miracle), only the core two of which (Christ applies the clay; the blind man washes off the clay) seem to derive from traditional Byzantine iconographic sources (fig. 3.59).[79] Were *podlinniki* (handbooks) used; was the technique of pouncing employed?[80] Neither manuscript provides any direct evidence of either, although close compositional interrelationships between the two miniatures of the Man Born Blind (figs. 3.8, 3.27) and the two miniatures of the Parable of the Talents (figs. 3.12, 3.13) suggest the availability in the workshop (scriptorium?) of iconographically rich and abundant models, even for the "nearly newly invented" scenes.[81]

The deluxe format of these two books and their general similarities to Middle Byzantine illustrated lectionaries in page layout and overall narrative conception (compare figs. 3.2 and 3.20 with 3.60 [Dionysiou 587]) together strongly suggest that the intention was indeed to emulate a revered book type of the Byzantine past—and of course, this is fully consistent with the Byzantinizing mentality of Luke the Cypriot and Arsenios of Elasson.[82] After all, these men were accustomed to handling fine Byzantine manuscripts, including lectionaries, and they were accustomed to transcribing and illuminating such service books in the traditional, deluxe format; it just seems that here, for once, the decision was made to go that final step and to revive a Byzantine book type in all of its original splendor.

What precisely is the relationship between the picture cycles of Walters 535 and *Anastaseos* 5? Although the miniatures in *Anastaseos* 5, unlike those in W.535, are integral to the writing column, they may not have been planned from the beginning, since the space they occupy is no greater than that of the *incipit* initials used throughout the remainder of the manuscript (compare figs. 3.20 and 3.34, 3.25 and 3.47). Indeed, it could be argued that they were *never* intended, since if they were, the initial letters for the lections' opening formulas (taus and epsilons) would have been integrated into the text proper; as it is now, they do not exist.[83] In other words, it is quite possible that when Luke the Cypriot arrived in Moscow, *Anastaseos* 5 had been written but not illuminated, and that Arsenios got the idea of illustrating it from Luke—even though he and not Luke would ultimately be the central player in that idea's realization, thanks to his contacts among local painters. There is much to recommend this scenario, since despite the fact that the two men were approximately equal in age, ecclesiastical rank, and political and diplomatic achievement, Luke was certainly the calligrapher of greater ability, reputation, and experience (notably, in collaborating with illustrators), and his manuscript, as already illuminated, was much the superior one. The two campaigns of illustration may then have proceeded more or less side-by-side, as the books' shared miniaturist, iconography, and history would otherwise suggest. Whether *Anastaseos* 5 might have been partially complete when the illustration of Walters 535 actually got underway, as the seeming dependent relationships among some of their nine sets of matches imply, is debatable. But what is unmistakably clear is that Walters 535, by virtue of its much greater iconographic richness and its more subtle and balanced relationship to its text, is by far the better realization of the idea of an illustrated lectionary. Indeed, to the extent that there was any conscious copying (exclusively by Hand I, of Hand I), it did not go on for long, since it is confined to the front portion of the Walters manuscript, and accounts for only about 15 percent of its completed cycle.

Why did not the copying continue (assuming it ever began); and why were the miniatures never executed in those dozen or so instances in which Walters 535 bears inscribed iconographic guides corresponding to miniatures in *Anastaseos* 5? The answer may lie in the possibility that Walters 535 was not simply *fortuitously* a better product than *Anastaseos* 5, but that it represents a conscious attempt to improve upon or surpass *Anastaseos* 5—either as the latter was actually executed or, more likely, as it was conceived. Certainly, the critical juncture came at the point where the two books diverge, in the readings for the second week after Easter. From that point on in *Anastaseos* 5, Hand I continued to plod through the daily John lections, ultimately creating a monotonous, imbalanced picture cycle, whereas just then in Walters 535 he and/or his collaborators began to take a freer and more creative hand with their project. Indeed, the catalyst for this sudden change may well have been the appearance in the W.535 project of the second illustrator, since after the first illustrator's miniature for Monday of the second week after Easter (fol. 20r), and the coincident change in the manuscript's iconographic program, Hand II executed the next four miniatures in succession (comprising three Sundays and one Wednesday reading); the first illustrator does not reappear until the sixth Sunday in John (fol. 48r), which more or less coincides with the end of the marginal iconographic guides. In any event, the break had been made, for from this point onward, targeting the more important Sunday lections, the W.535 miniaturists spread out their illustration—which under any circumstances they could not likely have sustained at the daily lection rate to the end of the book—and thereby at once more successfully integrated their picture cycle into the overall text, and sidestepped the many weekday lections in John for which few if any models could ever be found, and little inherent narrative action exists upon which to base new iconography. At that point, around folio 20, those in charge of illustrating Walters 535 seem to have reinterpreted their goals and redirected their energies; the proof lies not only in the divergent path they followed from *Anastaseos* 5, with its relatively greater ultimate success, but also in those dozen or so marginal iconographic guides (by and/or for Hand I?) that were then abandoned and erased.[84]

Conclusions

To what extent do Walters 535 and *Anastaseos* 5 attest to the survival of Byzantine culture after the fall of Constantinople? Unlike Voroneţ (fig. 3.1), which is one of an interrelated series of elaborately painted Moldavian churches extending over several generations, these two illustrated lectionaries represent an isolated "renaissance" phenomenon. Indeed, there is only one other illustrated Greek lectionary that may even be cited from the period—*Anastaseos* codex 1 of 1646/7—but its crude picture cycle is totally independent of W.535/*Anastaseos* 5 (compare figs. 3.16 and 3.61: The Parable of the Prodigal Son).[85] Moreover, by comparison with Voroneţ, which was functionally integrated into the Moldavian Orthodox community of its time and whose frescoes responded to local social and religious concerns, these lectionaries are "rootless." That is, there is little or nothing in their iconography that reflects Russian or Wallachian issues of the day, and the cycles themselves, because they substantially neglect the Great Feasts, are only marginally responsive to the liturgy as actually experienced. Clearly, by the nature and pattern of their decoration, these books were intended more for show than for use. But these truths notwithstanding, there is one way in which Walters 535 and *Anastaseos* 5 surpass even Voroneţ in their evocation of the post-1453 afterlife of

Byzantine culture so eloquently defined and described by Nicolae Iorga (*Byzance après Byzance*) and Sir Steven Runciman (*The Great Church in Captivity*). They are material, indeed aesthetic manifestations of that rich post-Byzantine Orthodox mélange—that thick, meaty soup of nationalities and languages—that under the encompassing umbrella of the Ecumenical Church was the very essence of Eastern Christianity after the collapse of the Byzantine state. Itinerant, multilingual Greek diplomat-scribes simultaneously in the service of patriarchs, voevods, and tsars, traveling unencumbered across national frontiers from the Mediterranean to the Slavic North, and drawing together, as they do, Constantinople, Moscow, and Jerusalem—this is what Walters 535 and *Anastaseos* 5 evoke. Luke the Cypriot and Arsenios of Elasson, writing in Byzantine style, collecting and reviving Byzantine books, helped to give an aesthetic voice to a world defined much less by shared ethnicity, nationality or language, than by shared belief, and by a shared Byzantine identity, at one remove, in the afterglow that was *Byzance après Byzance*.

Notes

Special thanks are due to John Nesbitt for help with the colophons, and to Mary-Lyon Dolezal for generously sharing her knowledge of Middle Byzantine lectionaries with me. For help with the Russian sources, I am indebted to Tatiana Blumenthal and Elana Klausner Vikan.

This article is a prolegomenon to a monographic treatment of Luke the Cypriot's manuscript production. My research on Rumanian manuscript illumination has been generously supported by the International Research and Exchanges Board and by the American Council of Learned Societies.

1. For the illustrated Byzantine lectionary, see the articles by Kurt Weitzmann collected in *Liturgical Psalters and Gospels* (London: Variorum Reprints, 1980), nos. 7–14; and, most recently, Mary-Lyon Dolezal, "An Eleventh-Century Lectionary (Vat. Lib. cod. gr. 1156) and Its Position in Byzantine Art and Liturgy" (Ph.D. diss., University of Chicago, 1990).

2. N[icolae] Iorga, *Byzance après Byzance: Continuation de l'"Histoire de la vie byzantine"* (Bucharest: Institut d'Etudes Byzantines, 1935), esp. chap. 6; Andrei Pippidi, *Tradiția politică bizantină în țările române în secolele XVI–XVIII* (Bucharest: Editura Academiei Republicii Socialista România, 1983); and Steven Runciman, *The Great Church in Captivity: A Study of the Patriarchate of Constantinople from the Eve of the Turkish Conquest to the Greek War of Independence* (London: Cambridge Univ. Press, 1968), esp. chap. 10.

3. Figure 3.1 = Voroneț, monastery church. See *Voroneț: 15th and 16th Century Frescoes* (Bucharest: Foreign Language Publishing House, 1959) and, more generally, George Oprescu, ed., *Istoria artelor plastice în România* (Bucharest: Editura Meridiane, 1968–), 1:366–82, 2:134–40. For an analysis of one salient compositional motif shared by most of the Moldavian fresco cycles, the Tree of Jesse, with special attention to its medieval iconographic roots and its contemporary, distinctly Rumanian additions, see Michael D. Taylor,

"Three Local Motifs in Moldavian Trees of Jesse, with an Excursus on the Liturgical Basis of the Exterior Mural Programs," *Revue des études sud-est européennes* 12/2 (1974): 267–75.

4. Linos Politis, "Un centre de calligraphie dans les principautés danubiennes au XVIIe siècle. Lucas Buzău et son cercle," *Dixième congrès international des bibliophiles, Athènes 30 septembre–6 octobre 1977*, ed. Francis R. Walton (Athens, 1979), 1–11; Gary Vikan, "*Byzance après Byzance*: Luke the Cypriot, Metropolitan of Hungro-Wallachia," in *The Byzantine Legacy in Eastern Europe*, ed. Lowell Clucas (Boulder, Colo.: East European Monographs, 1988), 165–84; and Olga Gratziou, *Die dekorierten Handschriften des Schreibers Matthaios von Myra (1596–1624): Untersuchungen zur griechischen Buchmalerei um 1600*, Soderheft der Zeitschrift *Mnemon*, 1 (Athens: K. Michalas, 1982).

5. Baltimore, The Walters Art Gallery, cod. W.535. Gospel lectionary with daily *synaxarion* readings (fols. 9r–379r) and complete *menologion* (fols. 380v–421v). In Greek on paper (watermarks: Charles Moïse Briquet, *Les filigranes*, 2d ed. [New York: Hacker Art Books, 1966], "raisin" [no. 13147; Le Puy, 1588] for flyleaves; "VP" for text [unidentified]). 425 folios (including 10 flyleaves: 1–7/423–425) measuring 39.5 × 26.5 centimeters. Fifty-four original Greek quire marks (alpha to nu-delta) beginning on folio 9r (preceded by a single leaf). All quires regular and complete except for 11, 14, 32, 39, 45 (7 fols.), 34 (9 fols.), 47 (2 fols.), 51 (5 fols.) 54 (4 fols.). Stylus-ruled with double vertical outer framing lines and single verticals in intercolumniations; horizontals contained. Minuscule script in two columns of twenty-one lines measuring 25.0 × 7.0 × 15.0 centimeters. Scribal colophon (fol. 422r) dated 1594 naming Luke from Cyprus, bishop of Buzău. Four Evangelist portraits, fifty-seven framed marginal miniatures plus one preparatory drawing, five headpieces, and numerous gold lection titles and *incipit* initials. Original(?) red brocade cover, in two layers, over wooden boards. Paper gilt edged and tooled.

Provenance: Written and illuminated in Wallachia (Rumania) in 1594; illustrated in Moscow, likely in 1596; sent as a gift to a church or monastery in the Holy Land (the Monastery of St. Saba?), probably in the same year; in 1897 catalogued by Papadopoulos-Kerameus in the Jerusalem Greek patriarchate; around 1918 put up as collateral on a loan in Damascus by the patriarch; acquired by Henry Walters in the 1920s in Paris, from Léon Gruel.

Bibliography: Athanasios Papadopoulos-Kerameus, *Ierosolymitike bibliotheke*, 5 vols. (St. Petersburg, 1891–99), 3:199 f. (*Anastaseos*, cod. 4); Caspar Réné Gregory, *Textkritik des Neuen Testamentes*, 3 vols. (Leipzig: J. C. Hinrichs, 1900–1909), 1:460, 3:1472; idem, *Die griechischen Handschriften des Neuen Testaments* (Leipzig: J. C. Hinrichs, 1908), 153, 340; Eudoxiu de Hurmuzaki, *Documente privitoare la istoria Românilor*, vol. 14, *Documente grecești privitoare la istoria Românilor*, N. Iorga, pt. 1, *1320–1716* (Bucharest, 1915), 100 (no. 178); Marcu Beza, "Urme romînești la Ierosalim," *Boabe de grîu* 4 (1933): 325; Seymour DeRicci and W[illiam] J[erome] Wilson, *Census of Medieval and Renaissance Manuscripts in the United States and Canada*, 3 vols. (New York: H. W. Wilson, 1935–40), 1:760; Ernst Cadman Colwell and Harold Rideout Willoughby, *The Four Gospels of Karahissar*, 2 vols. (Chicago: Univ. of Chicago Press, 1936), 2:74; Kenneth W. Clark, *A Descriptive Catalogue of Greek New Testament Manuscripts in America* (Chicago: Univ. of Chicago Press, 1937), 367–71; Viktor Brătulescu, *Miniaturi și manuscise din Museul de Artă Religioasă* (Bucharest: Imprimeria Națională, 1939), 10 (no. 9); Marvin Chauncey Ross, ed., *Early Christian and Byzantine Art*, Baltimore, the Baltimore Museum of Art (Baltimore: Trustees of the Walters Art Gallery, 1947), no. 742 (exhibition catalogue); N. Șerbănescu, "Mitropoliții ungrovlahiei," *Biserică ortodoxa romînă* 77 (1959): 772; David Diringer, *The Illuminated Book: Its History and Production*, (London: Faber and Faber, 1957), pl. II–27e; Dorothy Miner, "More About Medieval Pouncing," in *Homage to a Bookman: Essays on Manuscripts, Books and Printing Written for Hans P. Kraus on His 60th Birthday, Oct. 12, 1967* (Berlin: Gebr. Mann

Verlag, n. d.), 103–6; Gary Vikan, ed., *Illuminated Greek Manuscripts from American Collec-tions: An Exhibition in Honor of Kurt Weitzmann* (Princeton: The Art Museum, Princeton Univ., 1973), 210 (exhibition catalogue); Gary Vikan, "Illustrated Manuscripts of Pseudo-Ephraem's *Life of Joseph* and the *Romance of Joseph and Aseneth*" (Ph.D. diss., Princeton, 1976), 489 f., 622 f.; Ariadna Camariano-Cioran, "Contributions aux relations rumano-chypriotes," *Revue des études sud-est européennes* 15 (1977): 497; Politis, "Un centre," 4; Gratziou, *Matthaios von Myra*, 26, 29, 101; Gheorghe Buluță and Sultana Craia, *Manuscrise miniate și ornate din epoca lui Matei Basarab* (Bucharest: Editura Meridiane, 1984), 10; Vikan, "Luke the Cypriot," 169 f.; Olga Gratziou, "E diakosmese sta cheirographa tou Louka Oungroblachias, tou Kypriou," *Epeteris tou Kentrou Epistemonikon Ereunon* 17 (1988–89): 59–61, 65.

Illustration:

JOHN READINGS

8v	John Portrait = HAND I (fig. 3.2)
9r	EASTER SUNDAY: John 1.1 (fig. 3.2)
	Headpiece = Luke the Cypriot
	The Anastasis = HAND I
	John the Baptist Bears Witness to the Light = HAND I
10v	EASTER SUNDAY VESPERS: John 20.19
	Christ Appears to His Disciples behind Closed Doors = HAND I
11r	MONDAY OF WEEK I: John 1.18
	"The Voice of One Crying in the Wilderness" = HAND I
12r	TUESDAY: Luke 24.12 (fig. 3.3)
	Peter at the Tomb; The Road to Emmaus = HAND I
14r	WEDNESDAY: John 1.35
	"Behold the Lamb of God" = HAND I
16r	THURSDAY: John 3.1
	Christ Addresses Nicodemus = HAND I
17r	FRIDAY: John 2.12 (fig. 3.4)
	Christ Drives the Merchants from the Temple = HAND I
18r	SATURDAY: John 3.22
	Christ and John Baptizing = HAND I
19r	SUNDAY AFTER EASTER: John 20.19 (fig. 3.5)
	Doubting Thomas = HAND I
20r	MONDAY OF WEEK II: John 2.1
	The Miracle of Cana = HAND I
26r	SUNDAY OF WEEK III: Mark 15.43 (fig. 3.6)
	The Women at the Tomb = HAND II
31v	SUNDAY OF WEEK IV: John 5.1
	Christ Heals the Paralytic = HAND II
35r	WEDNESDAY: John 7.14 (fig. 3.7)
	Christ Teaches in the Temple = HAND II
39r	SUNDAY OF WEEK V: John 4.5
	Christ and the Samaritan Woman = HAND II
48r	SUNDAY OF WEEK VI: John 9.1 (fig. 3.8)
	Christ Restores Sight to the Man Born Blind = HAND I
58r	SUNDAY OF WEEK VII: John 17.1
	"Father, the Hour Has Come" = HAND I

MATTHEW READINGS

67v	Matthew Portrait = HAND I (fig. 3.9)
68r	MONDAY OF THE HOLY SPIRIT: Matthew 18.10 (fig. 3.9)
	Headpiece = Luke the Cypriot
	The Parable of the Lost Sheep = HAND I
73r	SUNDAY OF WEEK I: Matthew 10.32
	All Saints = HAND I
77r	SUNDAY OF WEEK II: Matthew 4.18
	Christ Calls Peter and Andrew, and James and John;
	Christ Heals the Sick = HAND III
82r	SUNDAY OF WEEK III: Matthew 6.22
	The Sermon on the Mount = HAND III
87r	SUNDAY OF WEEK IV: Matthew 8.5
	Christ Heals the Centurion's Servant = HAND III
92r	SUNDAY OF WEEK V: Matthew 8.28
	Christ Exorcises the Two Gergesene Demoniacs = HAND I
98r	SUNDAY OF WEEK VI: Matthew 9.1 (fig. 3.10)
	Christ Heals a Man of Palsy = HAND I
102v	SUNDAY OF WEEK VII: Matthew 9.27
	Christ Restores the Sight of Two Blind Men = HAND I
107r	SUNDAY OF WEEK VIII: Matthew 14.14 (fig. 3.11)
	Christ Feeds the Five Thousand = HAND I
113r	SUNDAY OF WEEK IX: Matthew 14.22
	Peter Attempts to Walk on Water = HAND I
125r	SUNDAY OF WEEK XI: Matthew 18.23 (fig. 3.12)
	The Parable of the Talents = HAND I
129v	SUNDAY OF WEEK XII: Matthew 19.16
	The Parable of the Rich Man Seeking Eternal Life = HAND III
134v	SUNDAY OF WEEK XIII: Matthew 21.33
	The Parable of the Wicked Husbandmen = HAND III
142r	SUNDAY OF WEEK XIV: Matthew 22.2
	The Parable of the King's Wedding = HAND III
148v	SUNDAY OF WEEK XV: Matthew 22.35
	Christ Addresses the Pharisees about the Great
	Commandment = HAND III
154v	SUNDAY OF WEEK XVI: Matthew 25.14 (fig. 3.13)
	The Parable of the Talents = HAND III

LUKE READINGS

158v	Luke Portrait = HAND I (fig. 3.14)
159r	MONDAY OF WEEK I: Luke 3.19 (fig. 3.14)
	Headpiece = Luke the Cypriot
	The Dance of Salome = HAND I
169v	SUNDAY OF WEEK II: Luke 6.31 (fig. 3.15)
	Christ Addresses His Disciples = HAND III
174v	SUNDAY OF WEEK III: Luke 7.11
	Christ Raises the Son of the Widow of Nain = HAND III
179v	SUNDAY OF WEEK IV: Luke 8.5
	The Parable of the Sower = HAND III

SCRIBAL COLOPHON

422r (fig. 3.19): "The present divine and sacred holy *evangelion* [lectionary] was finished by my hand, lowly and worthless Bishop of Buzău Luke, from Cyprus, in the days of our most pious master John Michael Voevod. The year from the incarnation of our Lord Jesus Christ 1594, indiction 7, June 4, day 3 [Tuesday]. And those reading [it] pray for me through the Lord."

6. The herein reconstructed scenario of this manuscript's decoration, illustration, and dedication, which I first sketched out in a paper delivered at the Second Annual Byzantine Studies Conference in Madison, Wisconsin, in 1976, was summarized from my typescript by Olga Gratziou in her excellent 1982 monograph on the scribe Matthew of Myra (see n. 2, above).

7. Although the precise watermark of the text paper ("VP") does not appear in Briquet (see n. 4, above), it is generally similar to those of several mid- to late sixteenth-century north Italian and French paper manufacturers that are otherwise documentable among manuscripts by Luke the Cypriot and his circle (see Vikan, "Illustrated Manuscripts," 614, n. 3). Sheets measuring about 40 × 27 centimeters (40 × 54 centimeters for the bifolia), apparently the largest "off-the-shelf" paper format then available, were reserved by Luke and his circle for the occasional, deluxe lectionary (see the lists of manuscripts in Vikan, "Illustrated Manuscripts," 620–30; and Gratziou, *Matthaios von Myra*, 145–72).

8. Of the eight one-column framed miniatures in Morgan Library M639, four fall within Holy Week, with the remainder in the *menologion*. It would not be unusual, however, for a Middle Byzantine lectionary to be disproportionately embellished in the John section. Of the thirty-six anthropomorphic initials and marginal miniatures found in Morgan Library M692, twelve appear in the John readings, just one in Matthew, three in Luke, six in Mark (all in Holy Week), and fourteen in the *menologion* section. See Vikan, *Illuminated Greek Manuscripts*, nos. 28, 35.

9. For the iconographic dominance of Major Feast scenes in the Middle Byzantine lectionary, see esp. Weitzmann, *Liturgical Psalters and Gospels*, no. 10.

10. H[enri] O[mont], *Evangiles avec peintures byzantines du XIe siècle* (Paris: Imprimerie Berthaud Frères, 1908), pls. 125, 126; Tania Velmans, *Le tétraévangile de la Laurentienne: Florence, Laur. VI. 23* (Paris: Editions Klincksieck, 1971), fig. 241; and, for the issue of their dense iconography, see Kurt Weitzmann, "The Selection of Texts for Cyclic Illustration in Byzantine Manuscripts," in *Byzantine Books and Bookmen* (Washington, D.C.: Dumbarton Oaks, Center for Byzantine Studies, Trustees for Harvard University, 1975), 76.

11. The drawing, on folio 236r, was begun in preparation for the miniature illustrating the fifteenth Sunday in Luke (i.e., Zacchaeus Climbs a Tree to See Christ). But because that lection only begins on the verso of the folio, the drawing was abandoned and the miniature executed instead in its proper location. See Miner, 103–6.

12. The miniatures on folios 35r (fig. 3.7) and 73r in Walters 535 provide a clear stylistic contrast between Hands I and II, for although the narrative episodes are not the same (the former is Christ Teaches in the Temple, whereas the latter is All Saints), their respective compositions are substantially alike. And for additional proof that Hand III is not simply Hand I "unfinished," as several scholars have suggested (e.g., Miner, 103), contrast our figures 3.15 and 3.29. The former is an unfinished miniature by Hand III in Walters 535, whereas the latter is an unfinished miniature by Hand I in *Anastaseos* 5 (on which, see below).

13. For a review of the evidence, see Vikan, "Luke the Cypriot," 165–67. The Greek documents appear in Hurmuzaki; the Slavonic documents were published by the Rumanian Academy during the 1950s in the series *Documente privind istoria României*, ed. Mihail Roller, beginning with *Veacul XVI: B. Țara românească*, vol. 5, *(1581–1590)* (Bucharest:

Editura Academiei Republicii Populare Române, 1952). The documents were organized and reviewed in 1959 by Şerbănescu (768–72).

Luke's Manuscripts:

Athens, Byzantine Museum, cod. 203
———, National Library, cods. 755, 836
———, Senate Library, cod. 11
Baltimore, The Walters Art Gallery, cod. W.535
Constantinople, Patriarchal Library (lost)
Durham, N.C., Duke University Library, cod. gr. 39
Jerusalem, Greek Patriarchate, Treasury, cod. 2
Leningrad, IAR, cod. 189
Meteora, Barlaam, cods. 34, 78
———, Metamorphosis, cods. 624, 654y
Mount Athos, Dionysiou, cod. 429
———, Iviron, cods. 1385, 1423m
———, ———, *Akathistos hymnos*
———, Lavra, cods. H148, W140
———, Panteleimon, cod. 426
———, St. Paul Skiti, cod. 806
———, Simonopetra (lost)
Mount Sinai, cods. 1480, Gospels
Naxos, Koimesis, cod. 1
Paris, Bibliothèque Nationale, cod. gr. 100A
Princeton, Princeton University Library, cod. Garrett 13
San Francisco, Greeley Collection, *Life of Joseph/Romance of Joseph and Aseneth*

For the chronicle of the Wallachian voevods, see Emile Louis Jean Legrand, ed., *Bibliothèque grecque vulgaire* (Paris, 1881), 231 ff.

14. G. Popescu-Vîlcea, *Anastasie Crimca* (Bucharest: Editura Meridiane, 1972); Runciman, chap. 8; and Gratziou, *Matthaios von Myra*, 99–102.

15. Politis, "Un centre," 4.

16. Vikan, "Illustrated Manuscripts," 620–30 (nos. 9, 11); and idem, "Luke the Cypriot," 172–74.

17. Linos Politis, "Eine Schreiberschule im Kloster *ton Hodegon*," *Byzantinische Zeitschrift* 51 (1958): 17–36, 261–87 (but esp. 282 f.); idem, "Un centre"; and Vikan, "Luke the Cypriot," 168.

18. Figure 3.36 = Paris, Bibliothèque Nationale, cod. gr. 872, fol. 1r. See Gratziou, "E diakosmese," 58–60, fig. 2; and Politis, "Schreiberschule," 280.

19. Vikan, "Luke the Cypriot," 168 f.; Gratziou, "E diakosmese," 57–80.

20. Gratziou, *Matthaios von Myra*, 27–31; idem, "E diakosmese," 62 f.; and Vikan, "Luke the Cypriot," 169.

21. Vikan, "Illustrated Manuscripts," 489–92; idem, "Luke the Cypriot," 169–78; and Gratziou, "E diakosmese," 65.

22. Figures 3.37, 3.38 = San Francisco, Greeley Collection, *Life of Joseph/Romance of Joseph and Aseneth*, fol. 21r: Joseph Is Taken to Egypt; fol. 35r: An Angel Appears to Joseph in Prison. See Vikan, "Illustrated Manuscripts," 90 f., 135 f.; and idem, "Luke the Cypriot," 176. Nonscribal inscriptional evidence in both codices leaves no doubt that they were destined for a Rumanian and not a Cypriot owner, and that the owner was likely a voevod, or a member of his family. See Vikan, "Luke the Cypriot," 172–74.

23. Figure 3.39 = Paphos, catholicon of the Monastery of St. Neophytos: Meeting of Joachim and Anna (*dodecaorton* icon). See Athanasios Papageorghiou, *Byzantine Icons of Cyprus: Benaki Museum* (Athens: Benaki Museum, 1976), no. 54 (exhibition catalogue); and, most recently, idem, "Syrie et les icones de Chypre: peintres syriens à Chypre," *Report of the Department of Antiquities, Cyprus* (1989): 175 f. Closely related to the St. Neophytos iconostasis icons and to the miniatures in Luke's *Life of Joseph/Romance of Joseph and Aseneth* are the tipped-in Evangelist portraits in a Middle Byzantine Gospel book at the University of Chicago (MS 131). See Clark, *Catalogue*, 235–38.

24. For a detailed though incomplete catalogue of Luke's manuscripts, see Vikan, "Illustrated Manuscripts," 620–30.

25. Vikan, *Illuminated Greek Manuscripts*, no. 63; and Gratziou, *Matthaios von Myra*, 164, no. 38. Dr. M. Aspra-Vardavaki of Athens is presently preparing her dissertation on this manuscript for publication.

26. Politis, "Un centre," 4; Gratziou, *Matthaios von Myra*, 26; and Vikan, "Luke the Cypriot," 168 f.

27. Figure 3.40 = Meteora, Barlaam, cod. 78, fol. 4r. See Nikos A. Bees, *Ta cheirographa ton Meteoron*, vol. 2, *Ta cheirographa tes Mones Barlaam* (Athens: Akademia Athenon, Kentron Ereunes tou Mesaionikou kai Neou Ellenismou, 1984), no. 78. Figure 3.41 = Zagreb, Académie Yougoslave des Sciences et Beaux-Arts, cod. IIIa, 47, fol. 534r. See Svetozar Radojčić, *Stare srpske minijature* (Belgrade: Naučna Knjiga, 1950), 48, pl. 35b.

28. Figure 3.42 = Athens, National Library, cod. 755, fol. 41r. See Gratziou, "E diakosmese," 58 f., fig. 1.

29. Among Luke's manuscripts are those with miniatures in Italo-Byzantine, Cretan, Russian, and Moldavian-Slavic style. See Vikan, "Illustrated Manuscripts," 489, 620–30; Vikan, *Illuminated Greek Manuscripts*, no. 63; Marcu Beza, *Byzantine Art in Roumania* (London: B. T. Bratsford, 1940), no. 41; Gratziou, *Matthaios von Myra*, 153, no. 13; and idem, "E diakosmese," figs. 21–23.

30. The collaborative working relationship characteristic of Luke's illustrated manuscripts obtains in paradigmatic fashion in the unpublished Sinai Gospel book cited above in n. 13; there, text and initials are by Luke but the Evangelist portraits and headpieces are by Anastasie Crîmca, Luke's counterpart scribe-illuminator-miniaturist in the northern Rumanian principality of Moldavia. This sort of collaborative relationship between scribe and miniaturist became a prominent feature of Greek manuscript production beginning in the Palaeologan period. See Hans Belting, *Das illuminierte Buch in der spätbyzantinischen Gesellschaft*, Abhandlungen der Heidelberger Akademie der Wissenschaften, Philosophisch-historische Klasse (Heidelberg: C. Winter, 1970), 3–17.

31. Jerusalem, Greek Patriarchate, *Anastaseos*, cod. 5. Gospel lectionary with daily *synaxarion* readings and complete *menologion*. In Greek on paper. 512 folios (in 1897; 499 now) measuring 40.2 × 26.5 centimeters (at least 8 folios were excised in modern times; many others are now out of order). Minuscule script in one column of eighteen lines measuring 24.0 × 13.5 centimeters. Scribal colophons (fols. 515v, 516r) dated 1596 naming Arsenios, bishop of Elasson. Four Evangelist portraits, fifty framed miniatures, five headpieces (four are figurative), and numerous illuminated *incipit* initials and gold lection titles. Modern(?) binding.

Provenance: Written, illuminated, and illustrated in Moscow in the spring of 1596; soon thereafter sent as a gift of the scribe to the Monastery of St. Saba near Jerusalem; in 1897 catalogued by Papadopoulos-Kerameus in the Jerusalem patriarchate; around 1918 put up as collateral on a loan in Damascus by the patriarch; all four Evangelist portraits acquired by the Pierpont Morgan Library by the early 1930s; John and Matthew *incipit* pages acquired by the Art Museum, Princeton University, in 1954; Luke *incipit* acquired by Lillian Malcove of New York City in 1963.

Bibliography: Papadopoulos-Kerameus, 3:200–203; Gregory, *Textkritik*, 1:460; idem, *Handschriften*, 153, 340; DeRicci and Wilson, 2:1479; Clark, *Catalogue*, 161; Kenneth W. Clark, *Checklist of Manuscripts in the Libraries of the Greek and Armenian Patriarchates in Jerusalem* (Washington, D.C.: Library of Congress, 1953), 15, 30; Parke-Bernet Galleries, New York, *Rare Near Eastern Pottery* (February 19, 1954), lot 43 (sale catalogue); W. H. Bond and C. U. Faye, *Supplement to the Census of Medieval and Renaissance Manuscripts in the United States and Canada* (New York: Bibliographical Society of America, 1962), 305; Vikan, *Illuminated Greek Manuscripts*, no. 62; Politis, "Un centre," 5; Gratziou, *Matthaios von Myra*, 25, 99, 153; Sheila D. Campbell, ed., *The Malcove Collection* (Toronto: Univ. of Toronto Press, 1985), no. 313; Vikan, "Luke the Cypriot," 169 f.

Illustration:
Note: Folios in *italics* are bound out of order.

JOHN READINGS

1v	John Portrait = New York, Pierpont Morgan Library, cod. M654, fol. 4 (fig. 3.20)
2r	EASTER SUNDAY (fig. 3.20)
	Headpiece with *Deësis* = Princeton, Art Museum, cod. 54.67
	John the Baptist Bears Witness to the Light
3v	EASTER SUNDAY VESPERS
	Christ Appears to His Disciples behind Closed Doors
4r	MONDAY OF WEEK I
	"The Voice of One Crying in the Wilderness"
5r	TUESDAY (fig. 3.21)
	Peter at the Tomb; The Road to Emmaus
9r	THURSDAY
	Christ Addresses Nicodemus
10v	FRIDAY (fig. 3.22)
	Christ Drives the Merchants from the Temple
11v	SATURDAY
	Christ and John Baptizing
12v	SUNDAY AFTER EASTER (fig. 3.23)
	Doubting Thomas
14r	MONDAY OF WEEK II
	The Miracle of Cana
15r	TUESDAY
	Christ Addresses His Disciples
15v	WEDNESDAY
	Christ Addresses the Jews
16v	THURSDAY
	Christ Addresses the Jews
17v	FRIDAY
	Christ Addresses the Jews
19r	SATURDAY
	Christ Retreats to the Mountains; Christ Walks on Water
20v	SUNDAY OF WEEK III (fig. 3.24)
	The Crucifixion; Joseph of Arimathea before Pilate; the Entombment

22r	MONDAY
	Christ Heals the Nobleman's Son
23r	TUESDAY
	Christ Addresses the Jews
23v	WEDNESDAY (fig. 3.25)
	Christ Addresses the Jews
24r	THURSDAY
	Christ Addresses the Jews
25r	FRIDAY
	Christ Addresses the Jews
25v	SATURDAY
	Christ Addresses His Disciples
27r	SUNDAY OF WEEK IV
	Christ Heals the Paralytic
28r	MONDAY
	Christ Addresses the Jews
29v	TUESDAY
	Christ Addresses His Disciples
30v	WEDNESDAY (fig. 3.26)
	Christ Teaches in the Temple
32r	THURSDAY
	Christ Addresses the Jews
33v	FRIDAY
	Christ Addresses the Jews
39r	SATURDAY
	Christ Addresses the Jews
45r	MONDAY OF WEEK V
	Christ Addresses the Jews
46r	TUESDAY
	Christ Addresses the Jews
47r	WEDNESDAY
	Christ Feeds the Five Thousand
48r	THURSDAY
	Christ Addresses the Jews
34v	FRIDAY
	Christ Addresses the Jews
40v	SATURDAY
	Christ Addresses the Jews
41v	SUNDAY OF WEEK VI (fig. 3.27)
	Christ Restores Sight to the Man Born Blind
36v	MONDAY
	The Jews Decide to Put Christ to Death
37v	TUESDAY (fig. 3.28)
	The Jews Plot against Christ; Christ Addresses the Jews
49r	WEDNESDAY
	Christ Addresses the Jews
55v	THURSDAY
	The Ascension
57r	FRIDAY
	Christ Addresses His Disciples

50r   SATURDAY
        Christ Addresses His Disciples
51r   SUNDAY OF WEEK VII
        "Father, the Hour Has Come"
52v   MONDAY
        Christ Addresses His Disciples
53v   TUESDAY
        Christ Addresses His Disciples
54v   WEDNESDAY
        Christ Addresses His Disciples
58v   THURSDAY
        Christ Addresses His Disciples
59v   FRIDAY (fig. 3.29)
        Christ Addresses His Disciples

MATTHEW READINGS

65v   Matthew Portrait = New York, Pierpont Morgan Library, cod. M654, fol. 2 (fig.
        3.30)
66r   MONDAY OF THE HOLY SPIRIT
        Headpiece with Angel and *Deësis* = Princeton, Art Museum, cod. 54.68
        Christ and the Little Children
71v   SUNDAY OF WEEK I
        Christ Addresses His Disciples

LUKE READINGS

173v   Luke Portrait = New York, Pierpont Morgan Library, cod. M654, fol. 3
174r   Headpiece with Lion and *Deësis* = Toronto, University of Toronto, Lillian Mal-
        cove Collection, no. M82.446
218r   SUNDAY OF WEEK VII
        Christ Raises the Daughter of Jairus

MARK READINGS

319v   Mark Portrait = New York, Pierpont Morgan Library, cod. M654, fol. 1
320r   Headpiece with *Deësis* = location unknown

MENOLOGION

441r   Headpiece

SCRIBAL COLOPHON

515v(fig. 3.31): "The gift of God, and the labor of Arsenios, and Bishop ['chief sacrificer'],
of the throne of Elasson. The hand that wrote this book is subject to decay, but this book
shall abide forever."

SCRIBAL DEDICATORY POEM

516r (fig. 3.32):
    This writing came to an end on the sixth of March,
    through the hand of Arsenios, presently the bishop ["chief sacrificer"]
    of the God-preserved city, I say, of Elasson,
    which continues and is to be found near Hellas.
    [In the year] seven thousand, one hundred and four [A.D. 1596],

In the city of Moscow [the capital] of Great Russia,
[In the reign of him] who holds the scepter of that kingdom,
Tsar Theodore, the great autokrator,
of Vladimir, Moscow, and all the North.
It was sent for commemoration of my parents,
and my brothers by blood, [who are] *archieromonachoi*.
The priest Theodore was my father,
and Christodoule, my mother, and my brothers,
Joasaph, [bishop of] Stagai [Thessaly], Mark [bishop of] Demetrias,
Athanasios, Pachomios, reknowned among *hieromonachoi*.
[Praise be] to the revered Monastery of the Hallowed Saba,
which is in Palestine near the Jordan,
Glory be to God, and the Son, and the Holy Spirit,
the thrice-bright, venerated, indissoluble Trinity.

32. Provenance notes are on file at The Walters Art Gallery. See also n. 31 for specific bibliographical citations. Walters Gospel book 532 (formerly *Anastaseos* 7) followed a similar path from Jerusalem to Damascus to Paris to Baltimore.

33. G[ennadii] V[iktorovich] Popov, *Zhivopis' i miniatiura Moskvy serediny XV-nachala XVI veka* (Moscow: "Iskusstvo," 1975), fig. 153. The manuscript's fourth figurative headpiece, for Mark, was noted by Papadopoulos-Kerameus but is now apparently lost.

34. Iconographic comparison, W.535 and *Anastaseos* 5:

W.535/A5	READING	
	John	
9r/2r	Easter Sunday	match (for one of two miniatures)
10v/3v	Easter Sunday Vespers	match
11r/4r	Monday I	match
12r/5r	Tuesday I	match
16r/9r	Thursday I	match
17r/10v	Friday I	match
18r/11v	Saturday I	match
19r/12v	Sunday after Easter	match
20r/14r	Monday II	match
21r/15r	Tuesday II	frame/formula*
25r/19r	Saturday II	guide**/
26r/20v	Sunday III	divergent
27v/22r	Monday III	guide/
28r/23r	Tuesday III	guide/formula
29r/23v	Wednesday III	guide/formula
29v/24r	Thursday III	guide/formula
30r/25r	Friday III	guide/formula
30v/25v	Saturday III	guide/formula
31v/27r	Sunday IV	divergent
33r/28r	Monday IV	guide/formula
34r/29v	Tuesday IV	guide/formula
35r/30v	Wednesday IV	divergent
36v/32r	Thursday IV	guide/formula
37v/33v	Friday IV	guide/formula
38r/39r	Saturday IV	guide/formula

48r/41v	Sunday VI	divergent
58r/51r	Sunday VII	divergent
	Matthew	
68r/66r	Sunday of Holy Spirit	divergent
73r/71v	Sunday I	divergent
	Luke	
195v/218r	Sunday VII	divergent

* = formulaic iconography for Christ addressing a group of men
** = illustrator's guide for miniature that was never executed

35. See n. 34. These inscriptions ("guides"), which for the most part were subsequently erased, extend from the second through the fourth week after Easter. In the first instance after the nine matches (Tuesday II), there is a frame and just the hint of a composition, but no visible inscription. In the miniature of the Women at the Tomb (fig. 3.6), the inscription was not erased, apparently because it was partially covered by the frame and watercolor of the completed miniature. Written in Russian (on which, see below), it indicates that this was to be, as it is, the miniature of the "myrrh bearers."

36. Politis, "Un centre," 4 f.

37. For John chapters 5 through 8, *Anastaseos* 5 has eighteen miniatures, Paris *graecus* 74 has eighteen miniatures, and *Laurentiana* VI,23 has sixteen miniatures. See Omont, *Evangiles*, pls. 152–59; and Velmans, figs. 277–83. Through the John readings *Anastaseos* 5 has forty-seven miniatures, whereas Dionysiou 587 has only about two dozen, ranging from simple figurative initials to elaborate two-column framed compositions. See S[tylianos] M. Pelekanidis, P. C. Christou, C. Tsioumis, and S. N. Kadas, *The Treasures of Mount Athos: Illuminated Manuscripts*, vol. 1 (Athens: Ekdotike Athenon, 1973), figs. 190–212.

38. Interestingly, the *incipit* formula accompanying many of these John lections in *Anastaseos* 5 indicates that Christ is addressing "the Jews," whereas the biblical account may stipulate only "the people." The miniature will then be accurate to the *incipit*, but sometimes, as on folio 23v, in explicit contradiction to the Bible text (which uses the word *autoi*, and clearly implies that more than the Jews were in attendance). It is also noteworthy that for six miniatures in succession, beginning with folio 30v, there is a single continuous narrative context which presupposes that the action takes place in the Temple, but in only the first miniature is this the case; for the others, the standard "Christ addressing" (in an open landscape) formula was used. Also, for six miniatures beginning on folio 57r there is a single continuous narrative context which presupposes that the action takes place around the table of the Last Supper, but in each instance the standard "Christ addressing" formula was used instead.

39. For the traditional Byzantine iconography for this passage as it appears in Paris *graecus* 74, see Omont, *Evangiles*, pl. 98.

40. For the central role of such formulaic, internally generated iconography in the illustration of Paris *graecus* 74, see Jean-Guy Violette, "The Order in Which Were Painted the Quires of the Paris gr. 74," *Ninth Annual Byzantine Studies Conference: Abstracts of Papers* (Durham, N.C.: The Byzantine Studies Conference, 1983), 21 f.

41. Although the two manuscripts are closely related textually, sharing the "Jews" *incipit* formula and unusual readings for (e.g.) weeks fourteen and sixteen in Matthew, they are not identical, a fact most clearly apparent in their *menologion* sections.

42. Both miniatures are accurate to the Bible text, though *Anastaseos* 5 follows the first half of the lection (Mark 15.43–47), whereas W.535 follows the second half (Mark 16.1–8).

43. For an overview of the principles and methodology upon which this supposition

depends (i.e., the supposed inherent momentum of iconographic "corruptions" in successive copies of a narrative picture cycle), see Gary Vikan, "Ruminations on Edible Icons: Originals and Copies in the Art of Byzantium," *Studies in the History of Art* 20 (1989): 47–49; and, for their applicability among post-Byzantine manuscripts, see Vikan, "Illustrated Manuscripts," especially iv f.

44. Politis, "Schreiberschule," 18 f.; and Vikan, "Luke the Cypriot," 168.

45. The evidence is succinctly reviewed in Gratziou, *Matthaios von Myra*, 23. See also B[oris] L['vovich] Fonkich, *Grechesko-russkie kul'turnye sviazi v XV–XVIIvv. (Grecheskie rukopisi v Rossii)* (Moscow: Nauka, 1977), 19 f., 56–59; and esp. William K. Medlin and Christos G. Patrinelis, *Renaissance Influences and Religious Reforms in Russia: Western and Post-Byzantine Impacts on Culture and Education (16th–17th Centuries)* (Geneva: Librairie Droz, 1971), 46 f.

46. He commissioned liturgical implements, textiles, icons, and manuscripts. See the references in Gratziou, *Matthaios von Myra*, 23 n. 27.

47. Medlin and Patrinelis, 47.

48. Jerusalem, Greek Patriarchate, Treasury, cod. 1 (formerly *Anastaseos* 18). Gospel lectionary with daily *synaxarion* readings and a complete *menologion*. In Greek on paper. 445 folios measuring 40.0 × 26.7 centimeters. Minuscule script in one column of eighteen lines. Four Evangelist portraits, five headpieces, and numerous illuminated *incipit* initials. Original binding in repoussé gold and semiprecious stones showing the Anastasis, the Adoration of the Cross, and the Evangelists; it carries a dedicatory notice in Greek and Russian dated 1596 (Greek: 1596/7; Russian: 1595/6) naming Tsar Theodore Ivanovich and Boris Godunov.

Provenance: Three colophons by Theophanes, archimandrite and later patriarch of Jerusalem, indicate that the book was delivered by him from Boris Godunov to the Church of the Holy Sepulchre in 1600 (Theodore Ivanovich died in 1598); catalogued there by Papadopoulos-Kerameus in 1897.

Bibliography: Papadopoulos-Kerameus, 3:219–23 (as *Anastaseos* 18); Clark, *Checklist*, 30; Vikan, *Illuminated Greek Manuscripts*, 207–10; Fonkich, 54–56; Gratziou, *Matthaios von Myra*, 25–27; Politis, "Un centre," 5 (with the attribution to Arsenios).

Illustration:
FRONT COVER Anastasis; Adoration of the Cross; the Evangelists (fig. 3.33)
iv   John Portrait (fig. 3.34)
2r   Headpiece (fig. 3.34)
53v   Matthew Portrait (fig. 3.35)
54r   Headpiece
140v   Luke Portrait
141r   Headpiece
265v   Mark Portrait
266r   Headpiece

49. Papadopoulos-Kerameus 3:220, 222 f.; and Gratziou, *Matthaios von Myra*, 25.

50. Figure 3.43 = Moscow, Lenin Library, Cod. M.8659: John. See A[leksei] N[ikolaevich] Svirin, *Drevnerusskaia miniatiura* (Moscow: Iskusstvo, 1950), 81, 87; and idem, *Iskusstvo knigi drevnei Rusi* (Moscow: Iskusstvo, 1964), 116 f., fig. 248. Figure 3.44 = Moscow, Synodal Library, cod. 267, fol. 93r. See T. V. Dianova, "Staropechatnyi ornament," *Drevnerusskoe iskusstvo: Rukopisnaia kniga* 2 (Moscow: Nauka, 1974), 330, plate opposite 320. Figure 3.45 = Moscow, Lenin Library, Cod. M.8644, fol. 13r. See Svirin, *Miniatiura*, plate opposite 64; and Gratziou, *Matthaios von Myra*, 26, with special reference

to the engraving-style floral ornament prominent in the headpieces of both Arsenios manuscripts. The stylistic and morphological differences between the headpieces in *Anastaseos* 5 and those in Treasury 1, their high level of sophistication in comparison with their individual lection initials (likely by Arsenios), and the attribution of the *Anastaseos* 5 headpieces to the miniaturist responsible for that manuscript's lection miniatures (as noted above), all militate against an attribution of the major ornament in either manuscript to Arsenios himself—who, in any event, seems to have been an avocational scribe-illuminator only.

51. P[etre] Constantinescu-Iaşi, *Relaţiile culturale romîno-ruse din trecut* (Bucharest: Editura Academiei Republicii Romîne, 1954), 89; *Istoria romîniei*, vol. 2, ed. A. Oţetea (Bucharest: Editura Academiei Republicii Romîne, 1967), 982 (and 999, for the second trip, in 1597).

52. From the 1580s until his death in 1629 Luke was a central player in the political and diplomatic life of Rumania; indeed, he and Michael probably met while the latter was himself still a diplomat. See Şerbănescu, 768–72 (esp. 770). For the career of Michael the Brave and his Russian negotiations, see Alexandru-Dimitrie Xénopol, *Histoire des Roumains de la Dacie trajane*, 2 vols. (Paris: Ernest Leroux Editeur, 1896), 1:344–99.

53. Vikan, "Illustrated Manuscripts," 620–30; Gratziou, *Matthaios von Myra*, 145–72 (most notably, nos. 4, 5, 10, 27, and 48, which are elaborate lectionaries without Evangelist portraits). Although completed in 1595/6, Treasury 1 did not reach its destination until 1600. See also the discussion of Matthew of Myra's Tatarna Monastery liturgy, below, which was written in 1596 but dedicated only in 1602, and Luke's *Akolouthia* of 1588 (Dionysiou 429), whose dedication came only some time after 1596.

54. Şerbănescu, 770; and Gheorghe Cront, "Le chypriote Luca, évêque et métropolite en Valachie (1583–1629)," *Praktika tou protou Diethnous Kyprologikou Synedriou*, 3/1 (Nicosia, 1973): 46. Although both are citing documents referring to Luke's 1597 trip, one can reasonably assume similar exchanges took place in 1596.

55. It was common practice for Luke and his circle of itinerant Greek calligraphers to dedicate deluxe manuscripts themselves—to friends, fellow ecclesiastics, monasteries, and lay authorities (see Gratziou, *Matthaios von Myra*, 145–72). The mere mention of the name of the reigning voevod (W.535) or tsar (*Anastaseos* 5) did not constitute any implication of patronage or dedication. Contrast the colophon of Walters 535 with that of a Luke liturgy of 1616 in the Iviron Monastery on Mount Athos (cod. 1423m), which was "bound over into the holy and splendid Monastery of Iviron, by the command of the most pious ruler, John Radu Voevod" (see S[tylianos] M. Pelekanidis, P. C. Christou, C. Tsioumis, and S. N. Kadas, *The Treasures of Mount Athos: Illuminated Manuscripts*, vol. 2 [Athens: Ekdotike Athenon, 1975], 335). On the issue of whether the cover of Walters 535 may have borne a dedicatory notice, like Treasury 1, see below.

56. Gratziou, *Matthaios von Myra*, 148, no. 6.

57. Ibid., 13 f., 19–31, 98–103. Matthew's arrival in Wallachia, were he lived more or less continuously until his death in 1624, may be dated to 1606. Born in Pogoniani (northern Greece) around the middle of the sixteenth century, Matthew was elevated to the status of metropolitan of Myra in 1605.

58. Gratziou, *Matthaios von Myra*, 153, no. 13.

59. Figure 3.48 = Tatarna Monastery, liturgy, fol. 25v. See Gratziou, *Matthaios von Myra*, 145 f., no. 2.

60. Figure 3.49 = Tatarna Monastery, liturgy, fol. 1r: *Deësis* with SS. John Chrysostom and Basil. See Gratziou, *Matthaios von Myra*, fig. 16.

61. Ibid., 153, no. 13; and Linos Politis, "Persistances byzantines dans l'écriture du XVIIe siècle," *La paléographie grecque et byzantine*, Colloques internationaux du Centre National de la Recherche Scientifique, no. 559 (Paris, 1977): 374.

62. On the pages facing the *incipits* of the two liturgies he had transcribed (fols. 1v, 42v), Luke added his own "Lord, remember . . ." invocations.

63. Occasional spilling of colors and the absence of any correlation between illustrator and gathering indicate that the book was bound when painted.

64. Figure 3.51a,b = Mount Sinai, Monastery of St. Catherine, icon 1533 (120): Transfiguration. Unpublished. Here published by permission of the Alexandria-Michigan-Princeton Expedition to Mount Sinai. "+[I,] The lowly Archbishop of Elasson and Demonikos, / Arsenios, send the present holy icon, the divine Transfiguration / of our Great God and Saviour Jesus Christ, to his revered / and great imperial [?] monastery, that one on the holy / mountain trod upon by God [?], Sinai. From the great orthodox city of Moscow, of / Great Russia. For my spiritual salvation. The month of June, indiction 7, 1594."

65. Compare also with our figure 8 and the Sinai Transfiguration panel a late-sixteenth-century icon in the Tretyakov Gallery (no. 12111): Christ Restores Sight to the Man Born Blind. See V[alentina] I[vanova] Antonova and N[adezhda] E[vgen'eva] Mneva, *Katalog drevnerusskoi zhivopisi XI-nachala XVIIIvv.* (Moscow: Iskusstvo, 1963), vol. 2, no. 549.

66. Figures 3.52, 3.53 = Moscow, Lenin Library, *Life of St. Sergius of Radonezh*, fol. 38v: Birth of St. Sergius; fol. 349r: The Praise-Hymn of St. Sergius, and the Parable of the Talents. See G. Georgyevsky, *Old Russian Miniatures* (Moscow: Academia, 1934), pls. 6, 96; Svirin, *Miniatiura*, 94–119; and idem, *Iskusstvo*, 124 f. For evidence that several painters contributed to the illustration of this manuscript, compare Georgyevsky's pls. 6, 8, 21, 23, and 96.

67. Note also the similarity between the inscriptions in the St. Sergius manuscript (fig. 3.52) and those in W.535 (fig. 3.6).

68. I had earlier assumed ([as cited in] Gratziou, *Matthaios von Myra*, 27, and Vikan, "Luke the Cypriot," 168) that W.535 was a gift of Voevod Michael to Tsar Theodore, and that the latter had it decorated and dedicated.

69. Like *Anastaseos* 5, *Anastaseos* codex 2, a lectionary by Matthew of Myra dated 1610, was originally dedicated and sent to the Monastery of St. Saba (in this case, directly from Wallachia). See Gratziou, *Matthaios von Myra*, 160, no. 27. Unfortunately this book, too, has been partially dismembered.

70. Arguing against the notion that *Anastaseos* 5 and Walters 535 traveled to the Holy Land with Treasury 1, in 1600, is the clear distinction in status between their respective donors, with the imperial gift perhaps requiring exclusive delivery by someone of Theophanes's status. Furthermore, their destinations were not precisely the same, and Theophanes, who wrote notes in the imperial donation in several locations (see n. 48, above), has left no trace in either *Anastaseos* 5 or W.535.

71. For Russian covers much like those on Walters 535, see Georgyevsky, pl. 99.

72. One of the basic tenets of Kurt Weitzmann's philological method of picture criticism (*Illustrations in Roll and Codex: A Study of the Origin and Method of Text Illustration* [Princeton: Princeton Univ. Press, 1947]) is that the archetype cycle is maximally rich in its breadth and accurate in its narrative detail. Over time, through multiple copies, the cycle as a whole will tend to shrink and iconographic misunderstandings will progressively "corrupt" the individual compositions. See Vikan, "Ruminations," 48 f.

73. Svirin, *Miniatiura*, 94–119 (esp. 110); and witness, for example, the *Life of St. Sergius of Radonezh* picture cycle (figs. 3.52, 3.53)

74. Figure 3.54 = Florence, Laurentian Library, cod. Plut. VI,23, fol. 112v: Christ Heals a Man of Palsy. See Velmans, fig. 198.

75. Figure 3.55 = Paris, Bibliothèque Nationale, cod. gr. 74, fol. 192r: Raising of Lazarus. See Omont, *Evangiles*, pl. 165. Figure 3.56 = Paris, Bibliothèque Nationale, cod. gr. 54, fol. 55v: Christ Feeds the Five Thousand. See Henri Omont, *Miniatures des plus*

anciens manuscrits grecs de la Bibliothèque Nationale du VIe au XIe siècle, 2d ed. (Paris: Librairie Ancienne Honoré Champion, 1929), pl. XCII/4. Note the twelve stacked baskets of leftover food; note Christ receiving and distributing the loaves and fishes at the upper left and center, and the generally similar way in which the Disciples move among the crowd.

76. For the Rumanians, see Vikan, "Illustrated Manuscripts," 493 f. Voevod Alexander II (1568–77), during whose reign Luke the Cypriot likely arrived in Wallachia, commissioned the Sučeviţa Gospel book (Bucharest, Museum of Art, cod. gr. 23), which was copied from a manuscript closely related to Paris *graecus* 74; moreover, he added covers to a number of Middle Byzantine manuscripts which he rededicated to the Monastery of St. Catherine at Mount Sinai (e.g., cod. 208), and briefly owned the Rockefeller-McCormick New Testament (Chicago, University Library, cod. 965). His father, Voevod Micea III (1543–54/1558–59), rebound and rededicated Dionysiou 587 (on which, see especially Weitzmann, *Liturgical Psalters and Gospels*, no. 12). For Byzantine manuscripts in Russia, see Medlin and Patrinelis, 48–50.

77. Figure 3.57 = Mount Athos, Dionysiou Monastery, catholicon: Raising of Lazarus. See Gabriel Millet, *Monuments de l'Athos relevés avec le concours de l'Armée française d'Orient et de l'Ecole française d'Athènes*, vol. 1, *Les peintures* (Paris: Librairie Ernest Leroux, 1927; only one vol. published), pl. 202.1. These frescoes were commissioned by Voevod John Peter.

78. Figure 3.58 = Moscow, Tretyakov Gallery, icon no. 22210: Women at the Tomb. See Antonova and Mneva, no. 527.

79. Figure 3.59 = Mount Athos, Iviron, cod. 5, fol. 405v: Christ Restores Sight to the Man Born Blind. See Pelekanidis et al., *Treasures*, vol. 2, no. 39. Among the most extreme examples of this augmentation of traditional iconography is the Good Samaritan miniature in Walters 535 (fol. 201v), only one of whose six or so individual iconographic episodes (i.e., the stripping and beating) seems to derive from traditional sources (see Velmans, fig. 221). In the case of the miniature in *Anastaseos* 5 wherein the Jews Plot against Christ and Christ Addresses the Jews (fig. 3.28), the appropriated portion, as already noted, derives from a different narrative context altogether (i.e., the youthful Christ disputing with the doctors in the Temple).

80. For the so-called Stroganov *Podlinnik*, which includes painters' models for the entire fixed calendar and dates to the period of W.535/*Anastaseos* 5, see *Ikonenhandbuch der Familie Stroganow* (Munich: Slavisches Institut, 1965).

81. Although Dorothy Miner (103–6) believed that she had found evidence of pouncing in the drawing for the unexecuted miniature on folio 236r in Walters 535 (Zacchaeus Climbs a Tree to See Christ), I can find no such evidence, and in fact, the drawing differs from the executed miniature on the opposite side of the same folio in composition, figural proportions, and in absolute dimensions. As for the circulation of (availability of models for) more or less newly invented iconography, a closely related variant on the Parable of the Talents appears in the *Life of Sergius of Radonezh*, cited above (compare figs. 3.12 and 3.13 with fig. 3.53); there is no evidence that any of the constituent elements of this iconography, in any of its permutations, derives from traditional Byzantine sources. But interestingly, both (Hand I) variants on the Man Born Blind (figs. 3.8, 3.27) are consistent with traditional Byzantine iconography (our fig. 3.59; and Velmans, fig. 284).

82. Figure 3.60 = Mount Athos, Dionysiou, cod. 587, fols. 1v, 2r: John portrait, and the Anastasis. See Pelekanidis et al., *Treasures*, vol. 1, nos. 189, 190.

83. This would make both *Anastaseos* 5 and Walters 535 illustrated lectionaries "after the fact," although the former, unlike the latter, was never first completed to the point of full illumination.

84. This "improvement-over-*Anastaseos* 5" scenario applies whether or not Hand I's formulaic daily lection miniatures were actually in place in *Anastaseos* 5 at the point when the

two illustration projects diverged. Initially, the intention was to illustrate those lections in W.535 as well, and toward that end the guides were added up through the fourth week after Easter (but interestingly, no further). Then something (someone?) changed. Either seeing those monotonous miniatures, or realizing even in their absence that no appropriate models or textual inspiration was likely to be found, that plan was abandoned.

85. Figure 3.61 = Jerusalem, Greek Patriarchate, *Anastaseos* cod. 1, fol. 139r: The Parable of the Prodigal Son. See Papadopoulos-Kerameus, 3:193–96; Beza, *Byzantine Art*, no. 44; and Gratziou, *Matthaios von Myra*, 106. Written in Wallachia by the scribe Isaiah, who may have been a student of Matthew of Myra, it measures about 42 × 28 centimeters. Interestingly, its picture cycle, which is even more ambitious than that of Walters 535, is much more equitably distributed up to and through the *menologion* section.

Fig. 3.1. Voroneţ, monastery church. (Photo: Author)

Fig. 3.2. Baltimore, The Walters Art Gallery, cod. 535, fols. 8v-9r: John and Pro-choros; headpiece, Anastasis, John the Baptist Bears Witness to the Light.

Fig. 3.3. Baltimore, The Walters Art Gallery, cod. 535, fol. 12r: Peter at the Tomb, Road to Emmaus.

Fig. 3.4. Baltimore, The Walters Art Gallery, cod. 535, fol. 17r: Christ Drives the Merchants from the Temple.

Fig. 3.5. Baltimore, The Walters Art Gallery, cod. 535, fol. 19r: Doubting Thomas.

Fig. 3.6. Baltimore, The Walters Art Gallery, cod. 535, fol. 26r: Women at the Tomb.

Fig. 3.7. Baltimore, The Walters Art Gallery, cod. 535, fol. 35r: Christ Teaches in the Temple.

Fig. 3.8. Baltimore, The Walters Art Gallery, cod. 535, fol. 48r: Christ Restores Sight to the Man Born Blind.

Fig. 3.9. Baltimore, The Walters Art Gallery, cod. 535, fols. 67v–68r: Matthew; headpiece, Parable of the Lost Sheep.

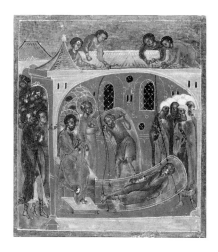

Fig. 3.11. Baltimore, The Walters Art
Gallery, cod. 535, fol. 107r: Christ
Feeds the Five Thousand.

Fig. 3.10. Baltimore, The Walters Art
Gallery, cod. 535, fol. 98r: Christ
Heals a Man of Palsy.

Fig. 3.12. Baltimore, The Walters Art
Gallery, cod. 535, fol. 125r: Parable
of the Talents.

Fig. 3.13. Baltimore, The Walters Art Gallery, cod. 535, fol. 154v: Parable of the Talents.

Fig. 3.14. Baltimore, The Walters Art Gallery, cod. 535, fols. 158v–159r: Luke; headpiece, Dance of Salome.

Fig. 3.15. Baltimore, The Walters Art Gallery, cod. 535, fol. 169v: Christ Addresses His Disciples.

Fig. 3.16. Baltimore, The Walters Art Gallery, cod. 535, fol. 247r: Parable of the Prodigal Son.

Fig. 3.17. Baltimore, The Walters Art Gallery, cod. 535, fols. 272v–273r: Mark; headpiece.

Fig. 3.18. Baltimore, The Walters Art Gallery, cod. 535, fol. 281r: Raising of Lazarus.

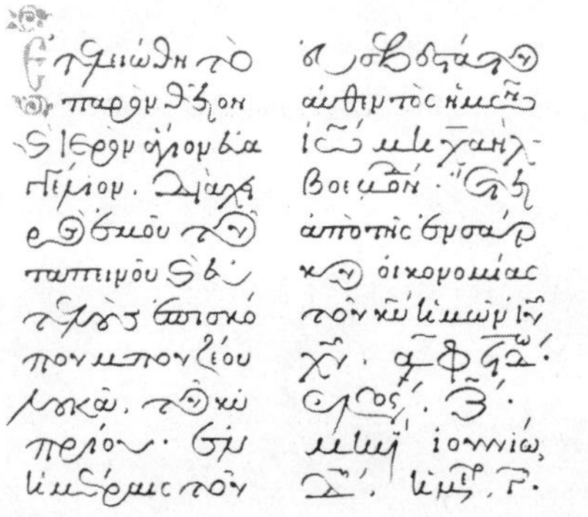

Fig. 3.19. Baltimore, The Walters Art Gallery, cod. 535, fol. 422r: scribal colophon.

Fig. 3.20 (*left*). New York, Pierpont Morgan Library, cod. M654, fol. 4: John and Prochoros.

Fig. 3.20 (*right*). Princeton, Art Museum, cod. 54.67: headpiece, *Deësis*.

Fig. 3.21. Jerusalem, Greek Patri-
archate, *Anastaseos*, cod. 5, fol. 5r:
Peter at the Tomb, Road to Emmaus.
(Photo: Library of Congress)

Fig. 3.22. Jerusalem, Greek Patriarchate, *Anastaseos*, cod. 5, fol. 10v:
Christ Drives the Merchants from the
Temple. (Photo: Library of Congress)

Fig. 3.23. Jerusalem, Greek Patriarchate, *Anastaseos*, cod. 5, fol. 12v:
Doubting Thomas. (Photo: Library
of Congress)

Fig. 3.24. Jerusalem, Greek Patri-archate, *Anastaseos*, cod. 5, fol. 20v: Crucifixion, Joseph of Arimathea be-fore Pilate, Entombment. (Photo: Li-brary of Congress)

Fig. 3.25. Jerusalem, Greek Patri-archate, *Anastaseos*, cod. 5, fol. 23v: Christ Addresses the Jews. (Photo: Library of Congress)

Fig. 3.26. Jerusalem, Greek Patri-archate, *Anastaseos*, cod. 5, fol. 30v: Christ Teaches in the Temple. (Photo: Library of Congress)

Fig. 3.27. Jerusalem, Greek Patri-archate, *Anastaseos*, cod. 5, fol. 41v: Christ Restores Sight to the Man Born Blind. (Photo: Library of Con-gress)

Fig. 3.28. Jerusalem, Greek Patriarchate, *Anastaseos*, cod. 5, fol. 37v: The Jews Plot against Christ, Christ Addresses the Jews. (Photo: Library of Congress)

Fig. 3.29. Jerusalem, Greek Patriarchate, *Anastaseos*, cod. 5, fol. 59v: Christ Addresses His Disciples. (Photo: Library of Congress)

Fig. 3.30. New York, Pierpont Morgan Library, cod. M654, fol. 2: Matthew.

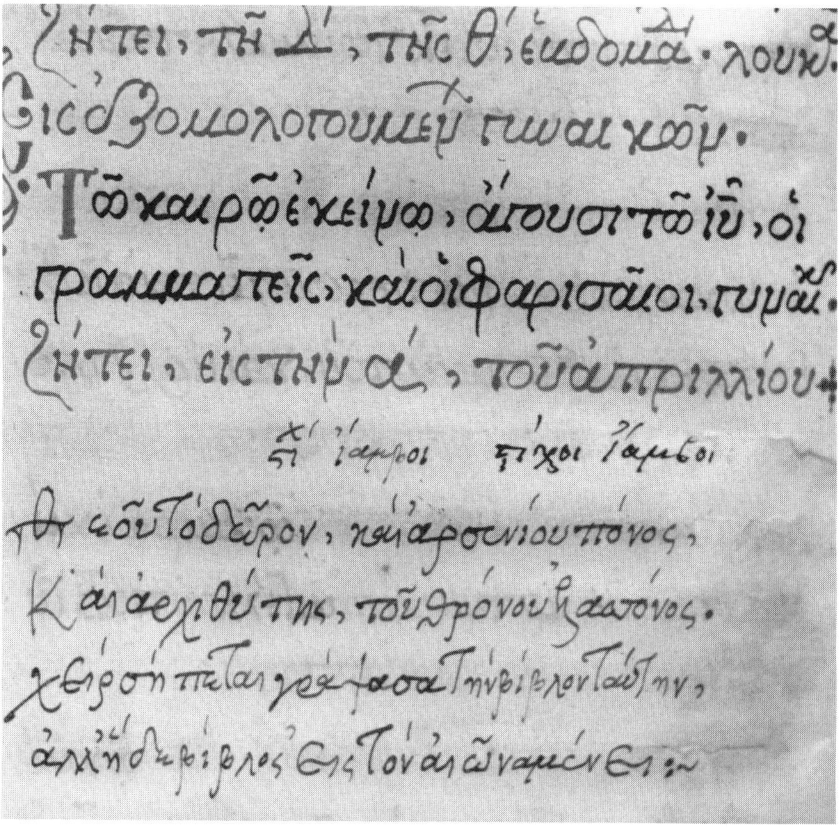

Fig. 3.31. Jerusalem, Greek Patriarchate, *Anastaseos*, cod. 5, fol. 515v: scribal colophon. (Photo: Author)

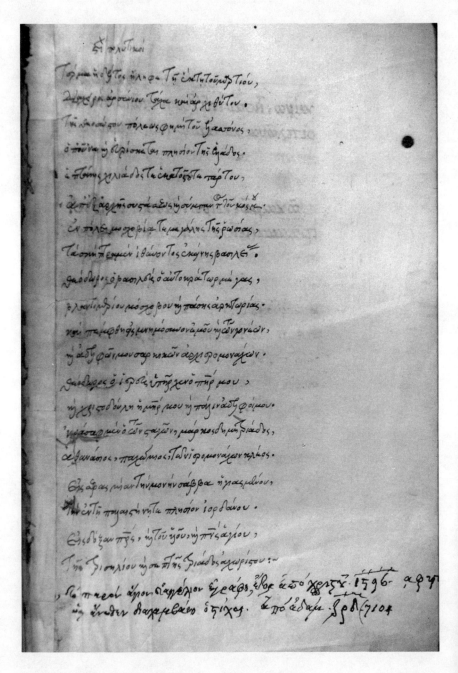

Fig. 3.32. Jerusalem, Greek Patriarchate, *Anastaseos*, cod. 5, fol. 516r: scribal dedicatory poem. (Photo: Author)

Fig. 3.33. Jerusalem, Greek Patriarchate, Treasury, cod. 1, front cover: Anastasis, Adoration of the Cross, Evangelists. (Photo: Library of Congress)

Fig. 3.34 (*left*). Jerusalem, Greek Patriarchate, Treasury, cod. 1, fol. 1v: John and Prochoros. (Photo: Library of Congress)

Fig. 3.34 (*right*). Jerusalem, Greek Patriarchate, Treasury, cod. 1, fol. 2r: headpiece. (Photo: after Athanasios Papadopoulos-Kerameus, *Ierosolymitike bibliotheke*, 5 vols. [St. Petersburg, 1891–99], 3: plate opposite 219)

Fig. 3.35. Jerusalem, Greek Patriarchate, Treasury, cod. 1, fol. 53v: Matthew.
(Photo: Library of Congress)

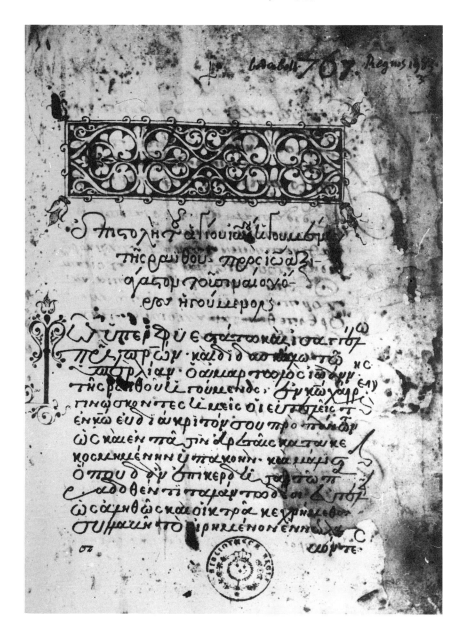

Fig. 3.36. Paris, Bibliothèque Nationale, cod. gr. 872, fol. 1r: headpiece.

Fig. 3.37. San Francisco, Greeley Collection, *Life of Joseph/Romance of Joseph and Aseneth*, fol. 21r: Joseph Is Taken to Egypt. (Photo: Author)

Fig. 3.38. San Francisco, Greeley Collection, *Life of Joseph/Romance of Joseph and Aseneth*, fol. 35r: An Angel Appears to Joseph in Prison. (Photo: Author)

Fig. 3.39. Paphos, Monastery of St. Neophytos, icon: Meeting of Joachim and Anna. (Photo: A. Papageorghiou)

Fig. 3.40. Meteora, Barlaam, cod. 78, fol. 4r: headpiece. (Photo: after Nikos A. Bees, *Ta cheirographa ton Meteoron*, vol. 2, *Ta cheirographa tes mones Barlaam* [Athens: Akademia Athenon, Kentron Ereunes tou Mesaionikou kai Neou Ellenismou, 1984], pl. 13)

Fig. 3.41. Zagreb, Académie Yougoslave des Sciences et Beaux-Arts, cod. IIIa, 47, fol. 534r: headpiece. (Photo: after Svetozar Radojčić, *Stare srpske minijature* [Belgrade: Naučna Knjiga, 1950], pl. 35b)

Fig. 3.42. Athens, National Library, cod. 755, fol. 41r: headpiece.

Fig. 3.43. Moscow, Lenin Library, cod. M.8659: John. (Photo: after A[lexei] N[ikolaevich] Svirin, *Drevnerusskaia miniatiura* [Moscow: Iskusstvo, 1950], 81)

Fig. 3.44. Moscow, Synodal Library, cod. 267, fol. 93r: headpiece.

Fig. 3.45. Moscow, Lenin Library, cod. M.8644, fol. 13r: headpiece.
(Photo: after Svirin, *Drevnerusskaia miniatiura*, plate opposite 64)

Fig. 3.46. Jerusalem, Greek Patriarchate, *Anastaseos*, cod. 5, fol. 83v: initial. (Photo: Library of Congress)

Fig. 3.47. Jerusalem, Greek Patriarchate, *Anastaseos*, cod. 5, fol. 441r: initial. (Photo: Author)

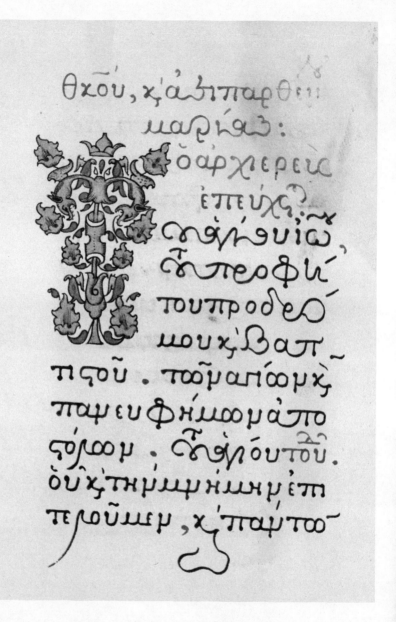

Θκ̄ου, κ̄ ἁγιπαρθεν
μαρίαϋ:
ὁ ἀρχιερεις
ἐπευχ̄
ϋιῶ
τῷ πεοφιλ̄
του προδ̄
μου κ̄ βαπ-
π σ̄ου . τῷ μ̄ α πίῳ μ̄
παν ευφ̄μων ἀπο
σ̄όλων . τ̄ ἁγ̄ ου του.
ὁυ κ̄ την μν̄μην ἐπ
π ρ̄ ουμεν , κ̄ παντω̄

Fig. 3.48. Tatarna Monastery, liturgy, fol. 25v: initial. (Photo: O. Gratziou)

Fig. 3.49. Tatarna Monastery, liturgy, fol 1r: headpiece, *Deësis*. (Photo: O. Gratziou)

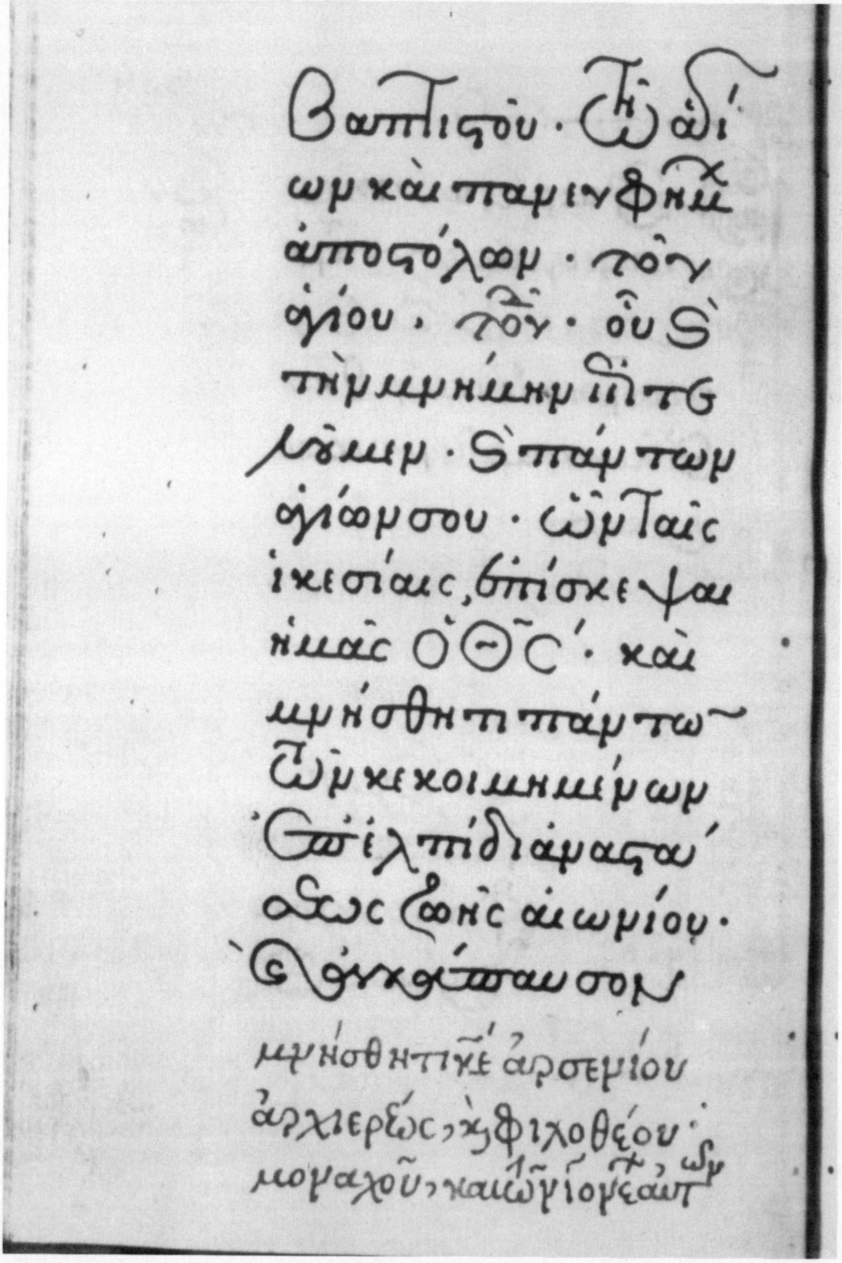

Fig. 3.50. Mount Athos, Panteleimon, cod. 426, fol. 80v: nonscribal invocation. (Photo: Thessaloniki, Patriarchal Institute for Patristic Studies)

Fig. 3.51*a*, *b*. Mount Sinai, Monastery of St. Catherine, icon no. 1533 (120): Transfiguration; dedication. (Photo: Alexandria-Michigan-Princeton Expedition to Mount Sinai)

Fig. 3.52. Moscow, Lenin Library, *Life of St. Sergius of Radonezh*, fol. 38v: Birth of St. Sergius. (Photo: after G. Georgyevsky, *Old Russian Miniatures* [Moscow: Academia, 1934], pl. 6)

Fig. 3.53. Moscow, Lenin Library, *Life of St. Sergius of Radonezh*, fol. 349r: Praise-Hymn of St. Sergius, Parable of the Talents. (Photo: after G. Georgyevsky, *Old Russian Miniatures*, pl. 96)

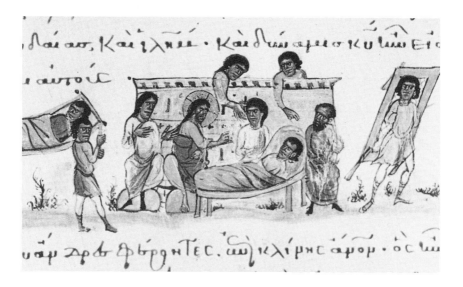

Fig. 3.54. Florence, Laurentian Library, cod. Plut. VI,23, fol. 112v: Christ Heals a Man of Palsy. (Photo: after Tania Velmans, *Le tétraévangile de la Laurentienne: Florence, Laur. VI. 23* [Paris: Editions Klincksieck, 1971], fig. 198)

Fig. 3.55. Paris, Bibliothèque Nationale, cod. gr. 74, fol. 192r: Raising of Lazarus. (Photo: after H[enri] Omont, *Evangiles avec peintures byzantines du XIe siècle*, [Paris: Imprimerie Berthaud Frères, 1908], pl. 165)

ⲟⲩ χ ρ ι α ψ ι χ ο ω ι ψ α π ι
Θ ∈ ι ψ δ ο π ι ά ψ τ ο ι ϲ Φ ϙ ∈ ι ψ·
ο ι δ ∈ μ ϙ ο ω ι ψ α ψ τ ω· ο ⲩ
Κ ∈ χ ο μ ∈ ψ ω δ ∈· ∈ ι μ ⲏ ⲡ
π ∈ ά ρ τ ο ι ϲ ⲕ α ι δ ⲩ ο ι χ θ ⲩ·

non habet neare ue
dare uos illis manducare·
Responderunt ei No
habemus hic nisi q̅q̅
panes et duos pisces·

Fig. 3.56. Paris, Bibliothèque Nationale, cod. gr. 54, fol. 55v: Christ Feeds
the Five Thousand.

Fig. 3.57. Mount Athos, Dionysiou Monastery, catholicon: Raising of Lazarus. (Photo: after Gabriel Millet, *Monuments de l'Athos relevés avec le concours de l'Armée française d'Orient et de l'Ecole française d'Athènes*, vol. 1, *Les peintures* [Paris: Librairie Ernest Leroux, 1927], pl. 202.1)

Fig. 3.58. Moscow, Tretyakov Gallery, icon no. 22210: Women at the Tomb.

Fig. 3.59. Mount Athos, Iviron, cod. 5, fol. 405v: Christ Restores Sight to the Man Born Blind. (Photo: after S[tylianos] M. Pelekanidis et al., *The Treasures of Mount Athos: Illuminated Manuscripts*, vol. 2 [Athens: Ekdotike Athenon, 1975], fig. 39)

Fig. 3.60. Mount Athos, Dionysiou, cod. 587, fols. 1v, 2r: John; Anastasis. (Photo: K. Weitzmann)

Fig. 3.61. Jerusalem, Greek Patriarchate, *Anastaseos*, cod. 1, fol. 139r: Parable of the Prodigal Son. (Photo: Library of Congress)

THE REFECTORY PAINTINGS
OF MOUNT ATHOS:
AN INTERPRETATION

John J. Yiannias

I F A VISITOR to Mount Athos finds himself in a monastery that is idiorrhythmic, one in which each monk regulates his own diet and eats in his room, he is likely to be served food in the guests' quarters. But if the monastery is of the coenobitic variety, enjoining the common meal, he will be asked to share the monks' simple fare in their refectory, or *trapeza*,[1] as they listen to a text read aloud. And there he may find that the walls are covered with paintings, as in a church (fig. 4.1).[2]

The refectory paintings of the Holy Mountain, as Athos is known to Orthodox Christians the world over (fig. 4.2), have received little scholarly attention, in part because most of them postdate the fall of Byzantium to the Ottomans, which puts them beyond the scope of interest of many Byzantinists, and in part because in any monastery a visitor's thoughts go first to the church. As a result, the majority of these paintings have remained unknown to the outside world.

Monastic dining halls were painted in the medieval and Renaissance West, as well as in Byzantium—as famous a work as Leonardo's *Last Supper*, after all, was done for a refectory. The trapeza paintings of the Holy Mountain come out of the Byzantine tradition of refectory art, although some of them incorporate elements of Western iconography; and they are all the more important because few refectory paintings, representative of scarcely more than a dozen monuments, remain from the Byzantine period proper (see Appendix I).

While the refectory paintings of Athos are in many instances of an arresting and somber beauty (figs. 4.3, 4.4), we will concentrate our attention here on the meaning that they acquire when assembled into programs. This meaning, and not their aesthetic qualities, or even their subjects taken individually, is what distinguishes them from paintings in other settings. For in point of style refectory paintings are only characteristic of their respective periods, while with rare exceptions the subjects treated in them are not confined to refectories.

Thirteen of the twenty ruling monasteries on Athos, and at least four of the dependent houses, have trapeza paintings. In only three or four of the monasteries do any of these predate the fall of Byzantium, and in every such case they are remnants of a program that was covered or replaced by a later one. Ironically this low rate of preservation of the early paintings is due in large measure to the attempts of the Athonites after the Ottoman conquest to keep the monasteries in decent repair. Unencumbered by antiquarian inhibitions, the monks renovated as the need arose and as money became available, leaving few of the old refectories, or their paintings, intact.

The oldest refectory painting on Athos is a fragment from the late twelfth century, preserved at Vatopedi and depicting the meeting of Sts. Peter and Paul.[3] Some paintings of the early fourteenth century have been found in the refectory of Chilandari, the Serbian monastery, on the gable of the apsidal wall, above the present ceiling; they represent Christ flanked by angels and, below this, three scenes with Abraham.[4] At the Great Lavra, a painting assignable perhaps to the Palaeologan period, depicting the monastery's founder, St. Athanasius the Athonite (d. ca. 1003), has been discovered in a space adjoining the south arm of the refectory.[5] Finally, at Docheiariou remains of paintings of standing figures, possibly predating the sixteenth century, have recently come to light directly below the present refectory, in a storeroom that seems to have served as the original trapeza.[6]

The bulk of the refectory paintings on Mount Athos, however, are post-Byzantine. Their dates are as follows:

Sixteenth century: the Great Lavra,[7] Philotheou (1539/40, although some of the paintings may be of later date),[8] Stavronikita (ca. 1546),[9] and Dionysiou (the north chamber, adjacent to the main entrance: *a* in fig. 4.5).[10]

Sixteenth or seventeenth century: Xenophontos, except for the apse and the immediately surrounding wall surface.[11]

Seventeenth century: Dionysiou (south chamber, 1602/3: figs. 4.1, *b* in 4.5),[12] Chilandari (all but the main apsidal wall; 1622),[13] and Docheiariou (the arm containing the apse, 1676: *a* in fig. 4.5).[14]

Eighteenth century: Docheiariou (the arm containing the main entrance, 1700: *b* in fig. 4.5),[15] Pantocratoros (1749),[16] Vatopedi (1786),[17] Chilandari (the apsidal wall, 1780),[18] and probably Xenophontos (the apse and the immediately surrounding surface).[19]

Eighteenth or early nineteenth century: the Skete of St. John the Forerunner (Prodromou), a dependency of the monastery of Iviron (1799 or shortly thereafter);[20] and most of Esphigmenou except the apsidal wall.[21]

Nineteenth century: the rest of Esphigmenou (the apsidal wall and a few scenes on the adjoining surfaces of the two long walls);[22] Xeropotamou (1859), where also an earlier, and thus far undated, layer of frescoes was recently exposed by falling plaster;[23] and the largest refectory of all, that of the Russian monastery of St. Panteleimon, also called "Rossikon" (1897).[24]

Late nineteenth or early twentieth century: St. Paul's;[25] the vast, inactivated Russian *skete* of St. Andrew, also called "the Saray";[26] and the *kelli*, once Russian but now Greek, of Bourazeri.[27]

Twentieth century: Pantocratoros (west wall, 1980).[28]

Much has been lost. From inscriptions and early travelers' accounts we learn that the refectories of Konstamonitou (Kastamonitou), Koutloumousi, Zographou, Iviron, Simopetra, and Karakallou had paintings; but these are either destroyed or plastered over. (See Appendix III.)

In the discussion that follows, the refectories painted after the mid-nineteenth century—St. Paul's, the Saray, Bourazeri, and St. Panteleimon—will be omitted. Their paintings reflect some notable departures from earlier practice, not only in style but also in thematic selection and layout, and would require separate treatment.

First, a word about the refectories as buildings. In the Athonite monasteries the trapeza is always to the south or west of the principal church, or catholicon, and is usually incorporated into the roughly quadrangular, multistoried construction that encloses the courtyard, in which stands the catholicon.[29] In five cases—the Great Lavra, Vatopedi, Esphigmenou, Iviron, and Koutloumousi—the refectory is free-standing, or nearly so, and is positioned opposite the entrance to the catholicon. Easy access from the catholicon is important, since meals always follow church services, and on important feast days are begun with a formal procession from the catholicon. In four monasteries—Dionysiou, Xenophontos, Docheiariou, and Xeropotamou—a roofed concourse connects the catholicon and the refectory.

As shown in figure 4.5, the ground plans of the refectories that we are considering describe three basic shapes: a more or less simple oblong with an apse at one end of the long axis (supplemented at Chilandari by a smaller apse at the other end); two oblongs joined to form a single space, each chamber with its apse; and a cross, either of the "Latin" type (Great Lavra and Vatopedi) or a tau (Docheiariou).[30] The refectory of Vatopedi has, in addition to the apse at the end of the long arm, an apse at the end of each lateral arm. The ceilings of the refectories are of wood and can be pitched or flat, and plain or ornamented. The reader on important feast days uses a pulpit, and on ordinary days a folding lectern. The table in front of the main apse in every refectory, reserved for the abbot and other notables, is used only on important occasions, such as major feast days. At the Great Lavra, Vatopedi, and Chilandari some or all of the tables are of stone, often rounded on one end, recalling the "sigma" tables seen in early images of the Last Supper (fig. 4.6).[31] The tables at the Great Lavra have attracted, ever since the seventeenth century, as much attention in the travel books as any other physical feature of the monastery.[32]

Early travel writers and students of Athonite life typically wrote that the subjects chosen for depiction in the refectories were those in which food plays a role in the narrative; and having made this seemingly unexceptionable observation they would move on to other topics. But in reality the paintings that answer to this description, such as those of the Last Supper, the Multiplication of the Loaves, or the Miracle at Cana, account for only a small fraction of the square footage of the decorated interiors. A different impression of the refectory programs is conveyed by a simple itemization of their subjects.

We will take as an exemplar the program in the trapeza of the Great Lavra (figs. 4.7, 4.8), a building the main parts of which may well date from the lifetime of St. Athanasius the Athonite.[33] This program is the largest in area of those preserved on Athos, except for the modern one at St. Panteleimon; and it is probably the oldest, although several times touched up. It may be the work of Theophanes the Cretan (surnamed variously Strelitzas and Bathas; d. 1559), a major representative of the Cretan school, who we know painted St. Nicholas Anapafsas, a small monastery church at the Meteora, in 1527; the catholicon of the Great Lavra in 1535; and (with the assistance of one or two sons) the catholicon, refectory, and tiny side-chapel of St. John the Forerunner at Stavronikita in 1545–46.[34]

In the conch of the apse at the Great Lavra is a *Last Supper* (fig. 4.10). The pediment of the wall overhead, which is pierced by three windows, has a *Prophets of Old*, consisting of an image of the Theotokos ("Bearer of

God") and infant Christ on the intrados of the central window and figures of ten prophets on the jambs of all three windows and in the spaces between them (figs. 4.11, 4.12).[35]

Occupying the zone between the Prophets of Old and the crown of the main apse, beginning at the left edge of the west wall and unfolding clockwise in the west arm, is the *Acathist Hymn* to the Theotokos (figs. 4.13–17). In common with other examples, this cycle has a separate scene for each of the poem's twenty-four stanzas, beginning with three representations of the Annunciation to the Theotokos and ending with several frames showing her and Christ with supplicants. A twenty-fifth frame shows the veneration of an icon of the Theotokos and Christ Child, an allusion to the historical events surrounding the composition of the hymn's famous proem, Τῇ ὑπερμάχῳ στρατηγῷ ("Unto [Thee] the Champion Leader").[36]

In the bottom zone of all three walls of this arm are standing saints holding scrolls with ascetical texts. The two niches in this zone that flank the apse contain figures of *St. John the Forerunner* and the *Theotokos* (fig. 4.13).

A *Menologion* cycle, an illustrated calendar in which are represented martyrdoms, the standard scenes associated with major feasts, and standing saints, also begins on the west wall of the long arm, but proceeds through the middle registers of the entire cruciform space (except for the end walls of the short arms) and into the corner chambers. Perhaps the largest in area of the Menologion cycles on Athos, this one spans the first six months of the Church year, September through February (figs. 4.13–21, 4.25). The sequence in which the walls comprising this cycle are read is indicated in figure 4.9.[37]

The two lateral arms of the cross contain, in addition to the Menologion entries in the middle zone of the side walls, a cycle each in the top zone: in the south arm, the *Early Life of the Theotokos* (figs. 4.20, 4.21), and in the north arm, the *Life of St. John the Forerunner* (figs. 4.18, 4.19).

The end walls of the lateral arms interrupt the progression of these two cycles, as well as of the Menologion. A *Tree of Jesse* occupies about forty square meters of the end wall of the south arm (fig. 4.22). Below the Tree itself, on both sides of the reclining form of Jesse, stand eleven "philosophers" and a sibyl.[38] In the lower zone is the story of *Cain and Abel*. The end wall of the north arm (fig. 4.23) has in the middle zone a *Dormition of St. Athanasius the Athonite*, and, in the gable above it, *Christ the True Vine*.

The walls of the lateral arms, except for the end wall containing the Tree of Jesse, have two large compositions each in the bottom zone. In the north arm are represented, moving clockwise, the *Spiritual Ladder of St. John Climacus*, illustrating that sixth-century treatise's account of the monk's perilous ascent to heaven, and the *Allegory of Death*, consisting of a monk looking at a scythe-bearing skeleton that stands atop a globe (west wall, fig. 4.18); then *St. Sisoës and the Tomb*, with the Egyptian ascetic contemplating a skeleton in a sarcophagus, a reminder of the passing of worldly greatness, and the *Life of the Solitary*, showing a monk in the wilderness, who is scorned by men but glorified by God (north wall, fig. 4.23); and then the *Death of the Just Monk*, with an angel standing on the deceased and receiving his soul, and the *Martyrdom of St. Ignatius Theophorus*, with the saint flanked by two devouring lions (east wall, fig. 4.19).[39]

In the south arm the bottom zone has, on the east, the *Prophet Elijah Fed by the Raven in the Wilderness* and the *Sacrifice of Abraham* (fig. 4.21), and on the west the story of *St. Gerasimus and the Lion* and the *First Ecumenical Council* (fig. 4.20). Six more Ecumenical Councils, making a complete series, are distributed evenly between the two corner chambers (fig. 4.25).

All three walls of the east arm, which contains the main entrance, are reserved for a large triptychlike *Last Judgment*, appropriately the final painting to confront the monks as they leave the refectory (fig. 4.24).[40] The corner chambers flanking the east arm have, in addition to the Menologion entries and Council scenes, figures of stylites and standing saints, and two additional scenes: in the north chamber, *St. Zosimus Giving Communion to St. Mary of Egypt*, and in the south chamber, *St. Pachomius Receiving the Angelic Habit from the Angel of the Lord* (for the locations, see fig. 4.25).[41]

Finally, paintings cover the upper half of the broad main facade from one end to the other. Those over the main entrance—an *Annunciation* at the summit of the gable, a *Theotokos and Infant Christ with Donors* beneath this, and the twelve *Apostles* around the arch of the doorway—and the two *Archangels* flanking the doorway are heavily repainted but presumably duplicate the sixteenth-century subjects. The remaining scenes appear to be contemporary with those of the interior. On the left half of the facade are discernible the *Multiplication of the Loaves and Fishes*, one or two unidentifiable scenes with Christ, several scenes from the *Life of St. Athanasius the Athonite*, the *Parable of the Publican and Pharisee* (fig. 4.26), and four standing saints. On the right half are more scenes from the life of St.

Athanasius, the *Parable of the Wise and Foolish Virgins*, the *Miracle at Cana*, and four more standing saints.[42]

Several subjects at the Great Lavra are represented in earlier programs, indicating that the planner drew at least in part on a Byzantine tradition of trapeza decoration, although differences in architectural plan and surface format imposed or allowed for variations in placement. The Last Supper, as we shall see presently, had already a long history in refectories. The Communion of St. Mary of Egypt, the Prophet Elijah Fed in the Wilderness, and the Miracle at Cana appear in the late thirteenth- or early fourteenth-century program at Apollonia (in present-day Albania); the last subject also appears in the Georgian cave monasteries of Bertubani and Kolaguiri (early and later thirteenth century, respectively). Two stylites are portrayed in another Georgian cave refectory, that of Udabno (early eleventh century). The Sacrifice of Isaac is the subject of one of the thirteenth-century fragments at Chilandari. The Multiplication of the Loaves is seen at Bertubani and in the thirteenth-century trapeza program of the monastery of St. John the Theologian on Patmos, which also has the Ecumenical Councils (depicted as disputations between Orthodox and heretical hierarchs) and the Death of the Just Monk.[43]

The links with later programs are even more numerous. While there is no typical refectory program on Athos, many of the subjects seen at the Great Lavra were repeated in other Athonite refectories, making for some continuity well into the nineteenth century—and incidentally suggesting that the program of the Great Lavra, impressive in many respects but also hallowed by association with the most prestigious monastery on the Holy Mountain, in all likelihood set some decisive precedents. The Acathist Hymn appears, always in the top register, and always beginning on or near the apsidal wall, at Stavronikita, Philotheou, Chilandari, Docheiariou, Xenophontos, and Esphigmenou.[44] The Prophets of Old is seen at Philotheou, in a large niche to the left of the apse, and at Xenophontos, where the waist-length figures of prophets framing the apse and the Theotokos with the Infant Christ in the conch form a single composition.[45] A Menologion covering most of September, October, and November was painted in 1602/3 at Dionysiou, and a greatly contracted one later at Esphigmenou.[46] A Tree of Jesse could be seen at Stavronikita as late as the early eighteenth century,[47] while an ingeniously modified Tree, incorporating a Prophets of Old, with the Theotokos and Christ enlarged to match in size their counterparts in church apses, occupies the conch of the main apse at Vatopedi, painted in 1786 (fig. 4.27).

A Spiritual Ladder was painted in 1602/3 at Dionysiou, where it is bent to fit the format (fig. 4.28), and in 1622 at Chilandari.[48] The Great Lavra's Last Judgment was copied on a smaller scale at Dionysiou in the sixteenth century,[49] Xenophontos in the sixteenth or seventeenth, and Pantocratoros in the eighteenth; and an example presumably along the same lines was seen by Didron at Karakallou in 1849.[50] The Communion of St. Mary of Egypt is repeated at Chilandari (1622), Docheiariou (1700), and Pantocratoros (fig. 4.30).[51] St. Pachomius Receiving the Angelic Habit is seen at Dionysiou (sixteenth century), Xenophontos, Docheiariou (1700), Esphigmenou, Pantocratoros (fig. 4.31), and Xeropotamou, and twice at Chilandari (east wall, 1622, and apsidal wall, 1780).[52] St. Sisoës and the Tomb appears at Xenophontos and Docheiariou (program of 1700). The Martyrdom of St. Ignatios Theophorus, a separately framed scene at the Great Lavra, is repeated at Xenophontos and Esphigmenou, although in both cases it is incorporated into the row of standing saints. In place of the Death of the Just Monk, Dionysiou has a Death of the Sinful Monk (1602/3).[53]

The Synaxis [Assembly] of the Bodiless Archangels, which at the Great Lavra appears as one of the entries for November in the Menologion,[54] is enlarged and placed next to the Spiritual Ladder at Dionysiou (fig. 4.29). The Synaxis signifies the Archangels' continued devotion to God after the fall of their colleague Lucifer; but it ordinarily depicts only the Archangels, holding an image of Christ.[55] To the example at Dionysiou are added Lucifer and his plummeting cohort, who bear a sobering resemblance to the falling monks in the adjacent Spiritual Ladder (fig. 4.28).[56] The more common type of Synaxis, without the falling angels, is repeated at Docheiariou and Xenophontos. At Chilandari— where, as at Dionysiou, it is accompanied by the Fall of Lucifer—the Synaxis forms part of a larger entourage of angels grouped around the Ancient of Days.[57]

Absent from the refectory of the Great Lavra but present in some others are an Apocalypse and an extensive series of Gospel scenes. A large Apocalypse cycle is painted in the covered space connecting the refectory and the church at both Dionysiou and Xenophontos (eighteen and thirteen frames, respectively), and in the main chamber of the refectory at Docheiariou (twenty-one frames). The compositions in this cycle are borrowed from sixteenth-century Western woodcuts, but the forms are Byzantinized.[58]

The presence or absence of a Gospel cycle (as distinct from Gospel scenes illustrating Great Feasts, which will be discussed presently) constitutes a major point of difference between refectories. The Great Lavra, Stavronikita, and Xeropotamou have each but a few Gospel scenes, such as the Multiplication of the Loaves, the Miracle at Cana, and of course the Last Supper.[59] The Great Lavra adds two parables, as we have seen; but its relegation of the Gospel scenes (except for the Last Supper) to the east facade, while putting them closer to the catholicon, also places them literally outside the rest of the program, somewhat as if they were afterthoughts. The refectories at Philotheou, Dionysiou, Esphigmenou, and Pantocratoros, on the other hand, have each about a dozen or more Gospel scenes, including several miracles of healing, all displayed prominently within the main body of the program, in the uppermost register.[60]

Of the Great Feasts, however—the christological and Marian events on which the church has traditionally placed the greatest liturgical emphasis—only the Annunciation is common.[61] The program at Vatopedi, of 1786, unusual in several respects, is the only one on Athos with more than two Great Feast images—the Nativity, Baptism, Crucifixion, and Descent into Hell; these are painted high on the apsidal walls of the lateral arms. At Xeropotamou, however, the older layer of paintings that has begun to appear includes what seems to be a Transfiguration, and it is possible that additional Great Feasts were represented there.

Some Byzantine refectories, also, had a Gospel cycle, while others did not; but the sampling is too small to yield statistics about the frequency of these subjects in the Byzantine period.[62] For the same reason, it is impossible to determine whether the Great Feasts were as rare in the Byzantine programs as in those we find on Athos. Two Great Feasts remain in the thirteenth-century program in the Monastery of St. John the Theologian on Patmos,[63] and it seems there were at least three in the undated, now vanished refectory of the Peribleptos Monastery in Constantinople, described by the Spanish ambassador Clavijo in 1403.[64] In the Palaeologan refectory at Apollonia, in Albania, where much of the program can be identified, the Great Feasts are absent. In the three published cave monastery refectories of Georgia, only one is represented—the Annunciation, at Udabno.[65] In the small, partially preserved refectory program at the Hermitage of St. Neophytos on Cyprus there are no Great Feasts, and indeed no Gospel scenes.

What are the reasons for the choice of subjects in the refectories of Athos? Is there a discernible meaning, a thematic unity, to these programs—or, for that matter, those of earlier date?

It was observed initially that the walls of a refectory bear a resemblance to those of a church simply by virtue of being covered with images. In the Byzantine tradition, which established the Orthodox norm, images are the usual and, indeed, indispensable means of marking a space for religious use. But theoretically paintings of any sacred subjects will serve this purpose. Allowance should therefore be made for the possibility that the selection for a refectory was, to some extent, arbitrary, or at least not determined by factors peculiar to a refectory.

Accordingly, we must inquire into the possibility of some specific resemblances to church programs, since these would have provided an obvious model for the decoration of a large interior. To what extent does the refectory program imitate that of a church? And do the dissimilarities between them point to any important differences in meaning?

The most appropriate candidate for the comparison is the catholicon, although whatever one observes about it in this regard is true also of other churches of similar plan, since church programs, as much after the Ottoman conquest as before, were fairly standardized. The usual Athonite catholicon employs a variant of the popular inscribed-cross plan worked out in the Middle Byzantine period. It is a squarish building on the first level, with a cruciform superstructure, a high central dome at the crossing, lower vaults over the corner spaces of the first level, a main apse fronted by a sanctuary in the east, side-apses (choirs) on the north and south, a spacious inner narthex (called the λιτή), and a shallower exonarthex. (For two examples, see fig. 1.25.) The paintings generally conform to the Byzantine principle of hierarchical arrangement, with an image's importance determining its height and its proximity to the main apse or to the center of the church.

The subjects depicted in churches proliferated from the twelfth century onward,[66] and by the sixteenth, as more scenes from Christ's life were promoted to the higher levels of the interior, a thematic entropy threatened to set in there; but the main lines of a hierarchical scheme always show through.[67] The eternal, static order, exemplified by the images of Christ Pantocrator and his celestial court, takes precedence over the temporal order, represented, for example, by the events in Christ's earthly life. Within the temporal order the Great Feasts outrank the events of lesser dogmatic and liturgical significance, such as Christ's parables and miracles of healing, as well as later historical events, such as martyrdoms, saints' miracles, and councils. Subjects making a universally valid statement, such as the Theotokos and St. John the Forerunner interceding with Christ (the

Deësis), outrank those of purely local reference, of which an example might be the donor as a supplicant presenting his church to Christ.

These "rules" were by no means observed with the scholastic precision that could govern the disposition of sculptures on a Gothic cathedral facade. But there is generally a dilution of value in predictable directions: outward from the center, with a secondary concentration in the main apse, where the Theotokos and Infant Christ are stationed; downward from the vaulted surfaces onto the flat supporting walls; and westward from the naos, or main part of the church, into the narthex.

Viewed in relation to this scheme, a refectory can be described as a space with images that are collectively of diluted value, more or less so depending on whether they include a Gospel cycle. But even when it includes Gospel scenes, the refectory does not compete with the catholicon, since it lacks both the celestial, timeless images that are reserved for a dome—the Pantocrator and his surrounding angels and prophets—and, for the most part, the Great Feasts, which in the church tend to be assigned to the naos when possible. In effect, as was observed a century ago by Brockhaus, the refectory draws from much the same set of subjects as the narthex.[68] The refectory program is less a recapitulation or adumbration of the church program than a selection of subjects from mainly its lower levels and western extremity, accented by a few images drawn from the higher levels. Sometimes, but by no means always, preference is given to subjects that for some reason or other do not appear in the catholicon.[69]

As is true of a narthex program, that of a refectory has its internal gradations of value. But whereas a narthex is a space of passage usually fitted with the vaults suitable for a vertically developed hierarchy of images, the refectory is a cul-de-sac on the order of a timber-roofed basilica, directing one's attention toward a vaulted space (the apse) at the end of the long axis. In a refectory, as in a church, subjects of greater importance are generally placed above those of lesser importance, a ranking most clearly expressed when the walls are divided into horizontal registers. At the same time, the images of greatest value gravitate horizontally, as it were, toward the apse.

Visual habit, if nothing else, ensured that the refectory would, to some degree, be decorated as if it were a church. To anyone accustomed to seeing church interiors, the bottom zone of a flat wall fairly cries out for figures of frontally posed standing saints, and accordingly every one of the Athonite refectories that we are examining has them. The saints are almost always monastics, and the majority hold opened scrolls displaying ascetical quotations. Most of them wear simple monastic garb, although in the few cases in which it is biographically suitable, their scrawny bodies are shown undraped (fig. 4.32). Even the church fathers in the apse, who in church apses are shown in liturgical vestments, in refectories are clothed as simple monks, generally with lowered cowls. Only in some later programs, as we shall see, do they wear liturgical vestments, in imitation of their counterparts in church apses.

The resemblances continue. The spandrels of the apsidal arch in a refectory invite an image of the Annunciation, since in churches Gabriel and the Theotokos occupy surfaces analogous to the spandrels, facing each other across the opening of the eastern arch under the main dome. In refectories these two figures are often accompanied by smaller ones of prophets holding scrolls foretelling the Incarnation (figs. 4.2, 4.34), as in the Prophets of Old. At Vatopedi, one of two Athonite monasteries dedicated to the Annunciation (the other being Philotheou), Gabriel and the Theotokos are made larger and transferred for emphasis to the niches flanking the main apse. At the Great Lavra, there is no separate image of the Annunciation on the interior of the trapeza, probably because, as we have seen, the subject appears in the three opening frames of the Acathist Hymn cycle.

In refectories the space over the crown of the apsidal arch often contains the Mandylion, or Holy Linen (which came to be known in the West as the "Veronica Veil"), an image affirming the circumscribable nature of Christ's person—that is, the physical reality of the Incarnation (fig. 4.33). The image's location in the refectory resembles its location in a church, where it typically occupies the small surface between the crown of the eastern arch and the drum of the central dome.[70]

We come now to the apse itself, the surface of greatest value in a refectory. In churches the main apse, second in importance only to the central dome, is given a representation of the Theotokos, usually enthroned, holding the Infant Christ. The temptation to follow this model and to paint the Theotokos with Christ in the apse of the refectory had to be weighed against the desire for an apsidal image that would call attention to the refectory's identity as distinct from that of the church. It is not surprising that this should have been a representation of the Last Supper.

The Last Supper had been represented in Eastern refectories since at least the Middle Byzantine period. The earliest published example appears in the Georgian cave monastery of Udabno, dated by Vol'skaia to the beginning of the eleventh century, depicting Christ in his traditional place of honor at the left edge of the table.[71] The painting is to one side of the apse. About fifty years later, a Last Supper of the same compositional type was painted in the lunette of the apse (which is actually a rectangular arched niche) in the refectory at Çarıklı Kilisse, in Cappadocia.[72] This would appear to be the oldest preserved example assigned to the apse, preceding by some three centuries in Byzantine art the compositional adjustment that might have seemed a prerequisite for the image's axial placement—the moving of Christ to the center of the far side of the table.

Fragments of a Last Supper apparently of the "new" compositional type are visible in the apse of the refectory at Apollonia, painted in the later thirteenth or early fourteenth century.[73] Clavijo in 1403 saw a mosaic Last Supper in the refectory of the Monastery of St. John Studion in Constantinople, and from his description it seems that it was either the only image in the refectory or the most prominently displayed. In 1648 De-Montconys saw another mosaic Last Supper in the refectory of the Peribleptos Monastery in Constantinople, and he specifies that it was in the apse. Unfortunately he gives no information about its date. The mosaic is not mentioned in Clavijo's brief description of the refectory.[74]

In the refectories of Athos we find the image jostling for the apsidal position with that of the Theotokos and the Infant Christ. The Last Supper prevails at the Great Lavra, Philotheou (fig. 4.33), the seventeenth-century program at Dionysiou (fig. 4.1), Pantocratoros, Esphigmenou, and Xeropotamou.[75] The Theotokos and Christ prevail in the older program at Dionysiou, where, surrounded by the appropriate ancillary figures, they constitute a Christmas Hymn,[76] and at Docheiariou (fig. 4.34), Xenophontos, and Vatopedi (fig. 4.27)—in the last instance as the central image of a modified Tree of Jesse, mentioned earlier. At Stavronikita a compromise was effected by dividing the conch between the two subjects, placing the Theotokos and Christ above and the Last Supper below (fig. 4.38); and this arrangement was copied in 1780 at Chilandari.[77]

Only in the small trapeza of the Skete of St. John the Forerunner (ca. 1799) was there recourse to a third subject. The apse contains a *Deësis*, which may be seen as a concession to a Georgian tradition exemplified at Udabno or as an acknowledgment of the skete's dedication.

At the Great Lavra, although a Last Supper was preferred for the conch, a way was found to fit the "displaced" image of the Theotokos and Christ onto the wall above the apse, as was observed earlier, by combining it with figures of prophets to form a Prophets of Old (fig. 4.11).[78] In sixteenth-century churches the Prophets of Old is commonly painted in a dome of the narthex.[79]

The refectory at Docheiariou provides an unusual and instructive example of a program that follows the church model closely in some respects and departs from it widely in others. Here the apsidal paintings bear a stronger resemblance to those in a church than do the apsidal paintings of any other refectory, and therefore they seem initially to deny the separate identity of the trapeza; yet these same paintings are explainable as an attempt to localize the program. Docheiariou is dedicated to the Archangels and to St. Nicholas. By depicting the enthroned Theotokos and Christ Child, rather than the Last Supper, in the conch, the planner was able legitimately to display the Archangels Michael and Gabriel full-length and in a prominent location (fig. 4.34), since in church apses they are commonly shown thus, flanking the Holy Pair. This choice, which has no parallel in the other refectories, led in turn to the clothing of the church fathers, in the zone beneath, in liturgical vestments (fig. 4.35), since, furnished with the full-length Archangels, the apse was already on the way to looking like that of a church. To complete the simulation, a *Melismos*, an image familiar in church apses from the thirteenth century onward, which makes reference to the sacrifice of the Eucharist by depicting the infant Christ lying on a paten, was painted above the apsidal windows (fig. 4.36).[80] Finally the inscription adjacent to the Melismos, giving the date for the paintings in this portion of the building (1676), was worded to refer to the refectory as the ἁγία τράπεζα ("holy trapeza"), a phrase normally denoting a church's altar table (fig. 4.37).

The "confusion" was now complete, the apse being virtually indistinguishable from that of a church. At some later date a monk erased the word ἁγία ("holy"), and with it the inscription's unintentionally irreverent equivocation.[81] The misleading phrase appears in no other refectory, to this writer's knowledge. But in some later programs, such as those of Vatopedi, Xenophontos (which is but a short walk from Docheiariou), and Esphigmenou, the church fathers in the apse are depicted, as here, in liturgical vestments. The fashion had caught on.

The rest of the program at Docheiariou, while also keyed to the monastery's dedication, stresses the refectory's identity as a space subordinate to that of the church and therefore appropriate for less exalted subjects. An Apocalypse cycle, which at Dionysiou and Xenophontos is painted in a space adjacent to but outside the refectory proper, is assigned here to the main space, which contains the apse; and this rather daring placement is to be explained, no doubt, by the fact that angels play a conspicuous role in all of the scenes. The monastery's dedication also determined the thematic choices for the hall forming the foot of the cross, painted a generation later, in 1700. Fourteen episodes from the Bible and sacred history in which the Archangels figure prominently (such as Jacob's Ladder and the Miracle at Chonae) are painted in the upper register of the long wall on the east, over the two main doorways (plan, fig. 4.5), while in the upper register of the wall opposite, with its final (sixteenth) frame pushed onto the adjoining end wall, is a Life of St. Nicholas. The upper register of the end wall goes on to illustrate, in five frames, a story associated with the early history of Docheiariou, the Boy and the Treasure Lost at Sea, according to which God saved from murder a boy in possession of some gold, who later became abbot of the monastery.[82]

It has been considered almost self-evident by some scholars that the central theme in Eastern refectory art is the Eucharist, since, in addition to the Last Supper, subjects are depicted that can be interpreted as prefigurations of that sacrament, such as the Hospitality of Abraham, the Wedding at Cana, and the Sacrifice of Isaac.[83] But it is well to remember that the refectory is emphatically *not* where the Eucharist is performed. A fundamental distinction must be drawn between the Eucharist as a sacramental rite and the many interrelated ideas that are associated with it in the biblical and liturgical texts, such as self-denial, unity in the faith, love for one's neighbor, and the anticipation of eternal life. If by looking for the "meaning" of refectory paintings we are looking for what they are supposed to make us "think of," it seems doubtful, for reasons that will follow, that the Eucharistic rite is our answer, in the case of either the Athonite refectories or any refectories painted in the Byzantine tradition.

Moved from one setting to another, subjects may, and often do, undergo a change of meaning. Although this observation may not occasion doubt, an example will be useful here. The *phiale* at the Great Lavra, the small domed structure by the entrance to the catholicon, containing a large marble basin used in the ceremony of the blessing of the waters, has on the interior surface of its dome some seventeenth-century paintings of St. John the Forerunner preaching and baptizing (fig. 4.39). Similar scenes appear in the north chamber of the refectory at Dionysiou, in the middle register of the north wall (fig. 4.40). But in the phiale they are intended to establish a mystical identity, some kind of effectual similarity, between the waters blessed in the basin and those sanctified by John's baptism of Christ, while at Dionysiou, which is dedicated to the Forerunner, they serve primarily to localize the refectory program, much as do the Archangel and St. Nicholas cycles at Docheiariou.

Since paintings of the Last Supper ostensibly make the most obvious reference to the Eucharist, we must ask what they in fact mean in a refectory. While the Last Supper marked the institution of the Eucharist, the Supper's sacramental and liturgical implications are given form, as students of Byzantine art know, in the Communion of the Apostles, which depicts Christ administering the bread and wine to two lines of approaching Apostles. This subject, common in the semicylinder of church apses, is represented in only two trapeza programs, to my knowledge, those at Patmos and the Monastery of Hosios Meletios on Mount Kithairon (the latter probably seventeenth century).[84] Perhaps the image was considered to be too evocative of the actual Eucharistic rite, and therefore better confined to a church.

The effectiveness of a Last Supper as an image evocative of the Eucharistic rite, on the other hand, is compromised by two facts. First, it is as much, if not more, an image of the prophecy of Judas' betrayal as of the institution of the sacrament. John rests his head on Christ's chest or lap and Judas reaches obtrusively across the table, a conflation of details from all four Gospel accounts of the prophecy of the betrayal (Matt. 26:21–23; Mark 14:18–20; Luke 22:21; John 13:21–27). Second, the Last Supper was, needless to say, a meal, which early in the church's history the Eucharist ceased to be. A Last Supper can serve as a biblical analogue to the monastic repast without placing much stress on the sacramental ideas made explicit in the Communion of the Apostles. The interest shown by Theophanes the Cretan in the creases of the tablecloth in his *Last Supper* for the refectory at Stavronikita (fig. 4.38), a detail not seen earlier in post-Byzantine Last Suppers, undoubtedly reflects his exposure to Western models;[85] but this degree of verisimilitude was probably made more acceptable by the painting's placement in a refectory, where some detraction from the supernatural, mystical character of the depicted event may have been considered excusable or even desirable.

The Last Suppers in refectories pose a complex and interesting problem of interpretation, which the foregoing remarks are intended merely to broach. Clearly, context—liturgical, spatial, theological—must be given its due in the interpretation of any Byzantine or post-Byzantine image. In analyzing refectory programs, we should consider what it is that takes place in the refectory, and what are the ideas associated with the building's function.

The reading of a text during the monastic meal is a common practice in the East as in the West.[86] Long ago, Heinrich Brockhaus surmised that the subjects of some refectory paintings on Athos correspond to those in the readings, and that their presence is to be explained, at least partly, on that basis; and he was surely correct.[87] Unfortunately, it is difficult, and usually impossible, to determine what was read in a given refectory at that point in time when its program was being planned. But even in the absence of such a tight and demonstrable correlation, some indications can be gleaned from the written sources. Since the refectory programs of Athos are to some extent a continuation of programmatic traditions rooted in other parts of the Byzantine world, it is justifiable to search the entire body of Byzantine monastic texts, whatever their provenance, for references to readings that may shed light on the choice of images.

Among the pertinent documents are the *typika* (rule books, ordinals), of both the "liturgical" and "foundational" variety, which occasionally designate the texts to be read in the refectory. A typikon written in 1162 for the Monastery of the Theotokos τῶν Ἡλίου βωμῶν, in Asia Minor, calls for the reading of "some [texts] or other from Scripture," (ἀπό τινος τῶν θείων γραφῶν), and thereby seems, at first, to provide a very efficient explanation for the presence of Gospel scenes in refectories. But the prescription is an unusual and curious one, if the choice of texts was in fact as arbitrary as it is made to sound, for it would mean that Gospel selections could be read out of their annual liturgical sequence. It is more likely that the typikon is referring to readings from scriptural books other than the Gospels.[88]

In other typika, among them some written for Athonite monasteries, texts of a pronouncedly ascetical nature are prescribed, including the lives of certain desert fathers and martyrs and the *Spiritual Ladder* of St. John Climacus.[89] St. Athanasius the Athonite, in one of his typika for the Great Lavra, the Ὑποτύπωσις, specified that the refectory readings were to be the texts left unfinished in church.[90] Since these could include biographical notices of saints, which are read during Matins, a Menologion cycle, illustrating such texts, would seem entirely suitable for a refectory. Of course, we should not imagine that the monks would search the walls to see which of the Menologion paintings corresponded to the *vita* of the day: the monastic meal must have allowed them scarcely enough time for real, let alone art-historical, rumination.

It is doubtful that any refectory program would be so recherché as to be explainable entirely on the basis of trapeza readings. But refectory ritual consists also of the processions into and out of the building, and a ceremony now seldom performed except in monasteries, the Elevation of the Panaghia. On important feast days a piece of the Eucharistic loaf, dedicated to the Theotokos, is elevated in the name of the Holy Trinity, on a small plate called a *panaghiarion*. The rite has certain features of a Eucharist but is not to be confused with it. The Elevation of the Panaghia is a ceremony in which the indissolubly connected ideas of the Trinity and of the role of the Theotokos in the Incarnation are given ritual affirmation. Its date of origin is unknown; in the fourteenth century it was being celebrated in the imperial palace in Constantinople, and in the fifteenth century Symeon archbishop of Thessaloniki wrote approvingly of its performance in monastic refectories.[91] The association of the Elevation with the trapeza must have been conducive to the inclusion in refectory programs of such subjects as the Tree of Jesse, the Acathist Hymn, the Annunciation, the Prophets of Old, and the Mandylion, all of which draw attention to the Incarnation as a physical fact.

Also of great importance for an understanding of refectory paintings, no less than of paintings in churches, is the annual festal cycle, since the meaning of the subjects is modulated by the liturgical use made of the texts from which they derive. It is not surprising to find that many of the paintings depict subjects associated with Lent. The Acathist is a Lenten hymn; the Ecumenical Councils are commemorated on the first Sunday of Lent; the *Spiritual Ladder* is read in church, as well as in the refectory, during Lent; and the Last Judgment (of which the Menologion, as well as the scene of Judgment itself, is evocative, with its commemoration of the saints in heaven) is a subject of meditation from the last day of meat-taking before Lent until Easter. The life of St. Mary of Egypt, too, is read during Lent. The Last Supper is of course commemorated on Great, or Holy, Thursday; and while the fast is broken on that day, the tone of the services is penitential, not festive. In short, many of the subjects are Lenten subjects, recalled in the texts that come to the fore during this season of sobriety and preparation.[92]

In his "Dinner-Party of the Seven Sages," Plutarch tells of an Egyptian custom of exhibiting mummies at dinner parties. He writes, "Even if it may not incite you to drink and enjoy yourself, it does incite to mutual liking and regard. For it urges that, *Life is short; do not make it long by vexations*."[93] In other words, if we are given only a brief span in which to live, why make it unpleasant?

Centuries later it was customary in some Italian monasteries to place skulls on the refectory table, one to each place setting, so that the hapless brethren would be reminded, while eating, that the appetites are transitory and the flesh corruptible. This very idea is expressed, usually in the form of an ethical or, better, soteriological, imperative on the majority of the scrolls held by the standing saints in the Athonite refectories. At Esphigmenou and Vatopedi St. Anthony warns, "Do not be led astray by a full belly, O monk." At Dionysiou, St. John Damascene reflects, "Whoever would taste of the things hoped for will throw off the present things, for he has emptied himself of all desire for these."[94]

Between the view of eating expressed in Plutarch and the one just described, there is obviously a world of difference—in germinal form the whole difference, it may be argued, between the culture of classical antiquity and that of the Christian postclassical era. Each warns of the passing away of material things; but each advocates a different response. In classical philosophical literature—we think of Plato—the meal is, under normative conditions, an occasion for the exchange of civilities and ideas. In Christian ascetical literature, on the other hand, it is an occasion for the exercising of self-limitation and abstinence. While the rational control of the appetitive part of the soul is a recurrent Platonic theme (and one which patristic theology was later to develop), in the *Symposium* a whole meal passes without any allusion on the philosopher's part to serious dietary restraint, except for a reference to the impropriety of drinking too much. The satirist Lucian, in his own *Symposium*, describes a dinner that ends with the philosophical participants intemperately pummeling each other.[95] This is the antithesis of the Platonic convivium. The antithesis of the Christian ascetical meal, on the other hand, is the lavish monastic banquet, satirized in many works of art.[96]

Beginning early in the history of the Church, ascetical writers warned that gluttony is a passion capable of rendering its victim susceptible to the whole range of vices. Abstinence, on the other hand, was deemed a sine qua non, a basic training for the withstanding of trials and temptations of every sort, as well as for the development of the interior discernment without which a virtuous life and salvation are impossible. Self-denial for the sake of union with God is exemplified commonly in fasting and supremely in the martyrdoms of the saints. It would be out of place here to provide a florilegium on the theological implications of ingestion, but it is interesting to note that St. Gregory Palamas, the great Athonite father of the fourteenth century, pointed out that the first fast was—or should have been—Eve's and Adam's abstention from the fruit of the Tree.[97]

The preponderance of subjects depicted in refectories are, on one level or another, exhortations to the disciplining of the passions, that "dying to the world" that is at the heart of the monastic ethos. The ideas behind a set of paintings of this kind can best be summarized in the form of a proposition. The refectory programs of Mount Athos are saying, as it were, that "the Incarnation of the second Person of the Trinity, effected through the Theotokos, has made possible our salvation, *for which we on our part must practice self-denial*." It is its emphasis on the final, ethical clause that distinguishes the Athonite refectory, the building and its paintings together, from the church and makes it an expression of the rigorously ascetical spirit of the Byzantine tradition of monasticism.

Appendix I

Byzantine Refectory Programs

This writer knows of eight refectories in which paintings of the Byzantine period proper are preserved, not counting that of Chilandari. They are at:

A. Çarıklı Kilise (Göreme, Cappadocia). Nicole Thierry, "Une iconographie inédite de la Cène dans un réfectoire rupestre de Cappadoce," *Revue des études byzantines* 33 (1975): 177–85, dates the single painting here, a Last Supper, to the end of the second quarter of the eleventh century.

B. The Absinthiotissa (or Apsinthiotissa) Monastery, Cyprus. Fragments in the apse depict four hierarchs and may date from the twelfth century, according to their discoverer, A. Papageorghiou (personal correspondence with the writer, March 8, 1967). See also A. Papageorghiou, "E Mone Apsinthiotisses," *Report of the Department of Antiquities, Cyprus,* 1963, 82–83.

C–E. The cave monasteries of Udabno, Bertubani, and Kolaguiri, of the David Garedjel complex, in Georgia. The paintings are dated to the beginning of the eleventh, beginning of the thirteenth, and second half of the thirteenth century, respectively, by Aneli Vol'skaia, *Rospisi srednevekovykh trapeznykh Gruzii* (Tbilisi: Izdatel'stvo "Metsniereba," 1974).

F. The Monastery of St. John the Theologian, Patmos. The paintings date from the twelfth and thirteenth centuries. Orlandos, *E architektonike*, 93–103, 175–272, and Kollias, *Patmos*.

G. The Hermitage of St. Neophytos, on Cyprus, with paintings dated by Cyril Mango and Ernest J. W. Hawkins to ca. 1200 and ca. 1500 ("The Hermitage of St. Neophytos and Its Wall Paintings," *Dumbarton Oaks Papers* 20 [1966]: 119–206).

H. The Monastery of the Panaghia, Apollonia, Albania. The paintings date from the later thirteenth or the early fourteenth century. See Heide and Helmut Buschhausen, *Die Marienkirche von Apollonia in Albanien: Byzantiner, Normannen und Serben im Kampf um die Via Egnatia* (Vienna: Verlag der Österreichischen Akademie der Wissenschaften, 1976), 183–232, and Djurić, "Peinture de Chilandar," 43–44, for further references. See also the present author's essay on this program, to appear in Ćurčić and Mouriki, (as in n. 72).

Appendix II

The Existing Programs of Athos:
Remarks on Chronology

A. The Great Lavra

The date and attribution of the paintings in this refectory have been a matter of argument and speculation. The problem is reviewed by Agape Karakatsane in Chrestos Patrineles, Agape Karakatsane, and Maria Theochare, *Mone Stauroniketa: Istoria, Eikones, Chrysokentemata* ([Athens]: Ethnike Trapeza tes Ellados, 1974), 51–56. Karakatsane argues against the traditional attribution to Theophanes the Cretan (although she believes that he may have taken part as an assistant) and in favor of a date of 1522. But to her observations must now be added those of Mylonas ("Trapéza," 150–54), who supports an attribution to Theophanes and a date early in the period between 1527 and 1535. The commonly cited date of 1512 (e.g., Millet, *Monuments*, page preceding pl. 115, and Charles Diehl, *Manuel d'art byzantin*, 2d ed., 2 vols. [Paris: Auguste Picard, 1925, 1926], 2:846) is based on an eighteenth-century source that is not reliable on this point. See Chatzidakis, "Recherches," 320; Mylonas, "Nouvelles recherches," 176–77 and "Trapéza," 150–54.

B. Philotheou

The donor portrait on the interior, near the main entrance, representing Leo, king of Kakhetia (one of the Georgian kingdoms), and his son Alexander bears the date *zeta-mu-eta*, transcribed by Millet, Pargoire, and Petit, 98–99 [nos. 303 and 304], as 1540. Because no month is indicated, this should be corrected to 1539/40. The inscription credits Leo and Alexander with the restoration of the building; presumably the project included some or all of the wall paintings. These are in poor condition, largely because of damage by fire. Yet differences in style can be seen within the program, suggesting that the paintings may not all be contemporaneous.

C. Stavronikita

The inscription over the main exit, which gives the date 1770 (Millet, Pargoire, and Petit, 64 [no. 211]), refers to a renovation, to which Chatzidakis assigns the Dormition of St. Nicholas painted on the south wall (*O Kretikos zographos Theophanes*, 60). The sixteenth-century paintings can be attributed on the basis of style to the artists who painted the catholicon—Theophanes the Cretan and, assisting him, his son Symeon and possibly also a younger son, Neophytos (ibid., 39–40).

D. Dionysiou

The paintings in the two chambers of this trapeza were not distinguished from each other chronologically by some early scholars, including Josef Strzygowski *(Byzantinische Denkmäler*, vol. 1, *Das Etschmiadzin-Evangeliar: Beiträge zur Geschichte der armenischen, ravennatischen und syro-ägyptischen Kunst* [Vienna, 1891], 38), Brockhaus (292), and Nikol'skii ("Istoricheskii ocherk," 54−55), who assigned all of them to the sixteenth century. Millet later dated those in the north chamber to 1547, (*Monuments*, page between pls. 194 and 195), perhaps on the basis of their resemblance to those in the catholicon (for which, see Millet, Pargoire, and Petit, 158 [no. 458] and Gabriel Millet, *Recherches sur l'iconographie de l'Evangile aux XIVe, XVe et XVIe siècles d'apr`es les monuments de Mistra, de la Macédoine et du Mont-Athos* [1916; repr. Paris: E. De Boccard, 1960], 660) and those in the south chamber to 1603 on the basis of the apsidal inscription (Millet, Pargoire, and Petit, 169−70 [no. 491]). These dates have gone unquestioned, although the former is accepted as only approximate. Nikol'skii read the inscription as *zeta-nu-delta*, or 7054 (= 1546) ("Istoricheskii ocherk," 54−55); Millet's reading, now the accepted one, gives *zeta-rho-iota-alpha*, or 7111, without a month (= 1603, according to Millet; in the absence of a month, I am giving it as 1602/3). I was unable in 1984 to decipher the faint vestiges of the last two letters, but since a date in the early seventeenth century for the paintings in the south chamber is not inconsistent with their style, I am accepting Millet's reading.

E. Xenophontos

The paintings have been variously assigned to the fifteenth, sixteenth, and seventeenth century: Komnenos, 84 (Montfaucon, 494) (a seventeenth-century date by implication); Porfirii Uspenskii, *Vtoroe puteshestvie po Sviatoi Gorie Afonskoi Arkhimandrita, nynie Episkopa, Porfiriia Uspenskago v gody 1858, 1859, i 1861, i opisanie skitov Afonskikh* (Moscow, 1880), 45 (1567; repainted in 1642); Nikol'skii, "Istoricheskii ocherk," 56−57 (accepts Uspenskii's dates); Gerasimos Smyrnakes, *To Agion Oros* (Athens, 1903), 622 (1475); Kosmas Vlachos, *E Chersonesos tou Agiou Orous Atho kai ai en aute monai kai oi monachoi, palai te kai nun: Melete istorike kai kritike* (Volos: Panthessalikon Typographeion Ath. Plataniotou, 1903), 296 (1575); Brockhaus, 85 n. 1 (sixteenth century) and 60, 281, 283 (seventeenth century, apparently contradicting himself); Fritz Fichtner, *Wandmalereien der Athos-Klöster: Grundsätzliches zu den Planungen der Bildfolgen des 14.−17. Jahrhunderts; Welt- und Lebensanschauung, Ritur, Architektur, Malerei* (Berlin: Dietrich Reimer, Ernst Vohsen, 1931), 46, 62 (1633−54). Much of the confusion, still not dispelled, has stemmed from the variety of readings given the inscriptional evidence. See recently Denise Papachryssanthou, *Actes de Xénophon: Edition diplomatique* (Paris: P. Lethielleux, 1986), 24 and n. 5.

Except for those in the apse and the narrow zone immediately surrounding it, which are clearly later, the paintings are in abysmal condition, despite a repainting in 1893 (reported in Nikol'skii, "Istoricheskii ocherk," 91, and Vlachos, 296), and it is doubtful that they can be dated conclusively on the basis of style.

F. Docheiariou

The apsidal inscription is published in Ktenas, 52. The date in this inscription is given as *zeta-rho-pi-delta*, without a month, and has been rendered as 1676 (e.g., Nikol'skii, "Istoricheskii ocherk," 72; Smyrnakes, 570; Oskar Wulff, *Altchristliche und byzantinische Kunst*, vol. 2, *Die byzantinische Kunst von der ersten Blüte bis zu ihrem Ausgang* (Berlin-Neubabelsberg: Akademische Verlagsgesellschaft Athenaion M. B. H., 1914), 599. I am tentatively accepting this reading, rather than 1675/6. The second inscription, over one of the doors in the chamber forming the foot of the tau, gives the month and day (September 9), and the year in Western reckoning but Greek numerals (*alpha-psi* [= 1700]): Smyrnakes, 570 and Ktenas, 54.

G. Esphigmenou

In 1701 Ioannes Komnenos reported that the refectory was decorated with paintings (Komnenos, 88; Montfaucon, 496), as did Vasilii Barskii after his visit of 1725 (*Stranstvovaniia*, 1:229). The refectory underwent some kind of restoration (*anakainisis*) in 1810 (inscription in Porfirii Uspenskii, *Pervoe puteshestvie v Afonskie monastyri i skity Arkhimandrita, nynie Episkopa, Porfiriia Uspenskago v 1845 godu*, 2 vols. and Supplement [Moscow, 1877–81], 2A:254). In the absence of an architectural study of the building, it is not clear that it was completely rebuilt in this year, although many modern scholars have assumed that it was. Hence we lack a firm *terminus post* for the present wall paintings, most of which have suffered smoke damage and are not easily dated on the basis of style. After his visit of 1839–40, Didron reported that the refectory had paintings "toutes nouvelles," although "déjà endomagées par l'humidité," (Ainé Didron, "Le Mont Athos [Suite]," *Annales archéologiques* 4[1846]: 226), which makes it likely that the entire refectory was painted after the restoration of 1810. (Pan. K. Chrestou, in his *To Agion Oros: Athonike politeia—Istoria, techne, zoe* [Athens: Epopteia, 1987], 362, gives the year 1811, presumably on the basis of some documentary evidence.) The paintings now on the apsidal wall and western end of each side wall, however, are clearly later in style than the others, although probably still assignable to the nineteenth century.

Appendix III

Sources for the Athonite Trapeza Programs That Are No Longer Extant

A. Konstamonitou

Uspenskii, *Vtoroe puteshestvie*, 261 (visit of 1859).

B. Koutloumousi

[Barskii], *Stranstvovaniia*, 1:235 (visit of 1725) and 3:163 (visit of 1744).

C. Zographou

[Barskii], *Stranstvovaniia*, 1:227 (visit of 1725). The refectory erected in 1494/5 by the voevod Stephen, son of the voevod Bogdan (inscription in Teodor T. Burada, "O călătorie la muntele Athos," *Revista pentru istorie, archeologie și filologie*, 1/1 [Bucharest, 1882], 401–2) was identified by Athelstan Riley, whether correctly or not, as the one he saw in 1883 (*Athos, or, The Mountain of the Monks* [London, 1887], 356). The present trapeza (interior photograph in Karl Eller, *Der heilige Berg Athos* [Munich-Planegg: Otto Wilhelm Barth Verlag GMBH, 1954], 157) is modern, built in 1896, according to [Monk] Alexander Lavriotes, *Odegos Agiou Orous Atho* (Athens: N.p., 1957), 151. Its main hall is similar in plan to that of the trapeza of the skete of St. Andrew.

D. Iviron

John Covel, quoted in F. W. Hasluck, "The First English Traveller's Account of Athos," *Annual of the British School at Athens* 17 (1910–11): 117–18 (based on Covel's visit of 1677); Komnenos, 53 (Montfaucon, 476); [Barskii,] *Stranstvovaniia*, 1:190–92 (visit of 1725); Ainé Didron, "Le Mont Athos," *Annales archéologiques* 18 (1858), 117–18 (visit of July 1839–January 1840); Uspenskii, *Pervoe puteshestvie*, 1B:191 (who says, without citing his source, that the wall paintings were executed in 1672 at the expense of the Georgian ruler Ashotan, during the abbacy of Damaskinos). The present refectory, a large barrel-vaulted hall, was built in 1848 (Millet, Pargoire, and Petit, 87–88 [nos. 275 and 276]), and no wall paintings are visible.

E. Simopetra

Komnenos, 72 (Montfaucon, 485); [Barskii], *Stranstvovaniia*, 3:353, 356 (visit of 1744); Ainé Didron, "Les couvents de Saint-Grégoire et de

Simo-Petra au mont Athos," *Annales archéologiques* 24 (1864): 188 (visit of July 1839–January 1840); Uspenskii, *Pervoe puteshestvie*, 1B:142–43 (visit of November 1845); Millet, Pargoire, and Petit, 179 (no. 526). The inscription seen by Uspenskii bore the date 1633 and stated that the paintings had been paid for by the abbot Ioasaph. According to Uspenskii, the monks were talking of renovating the paintings, which by his day were blackened with age.

F. Karakallou

[Barskii], *Stranstvovaniia*, 3:115 (visit of 1744); Ainé Didron, "Le Mont Athos: Caracallou," *Annales archéologiques* 20 (1860): 282 (visit of July 1839–January 1840). In 1859 Uspenskii saw an inscription with the date 1687 but could not determine whether this referred to the construction of the building or to its paintings, which were then still visible: *Vtoroe puteshestvie*, 243–44; Millet, Pargoire, and Petit, 104 (no. 322); cf. Smyrnakes, 579. The trapeza seen by these authors is presumably the one destroyed by fire in 1874. The present trapeza is dated by inscription to 1879: Millet, Pargoire, and Petit, 104 (nos. 322 and 323).

Notes

1. This is the term most often used in the Byzantine sources, as well as by the Athonites today. Also common in the Byzantine sources is *aristeterion* (Anastasios K. Orlandos, *Monasteriake architektonike*, 2d ed. enl. [Athens: N.p., 1958], 43 n. 2, for references). Derivatives are the Serbo-Croatian *trpezarija*, the Bulgarian *trapezariia*, and the Russian *trapeznaia*.

2. All twenty ruling monasteries—i.e., those the representatives of which comprise the Holy Community, the governing body of Athos—have refectories. Idiorrhythmic status does not indicate that a monastery has no refectory, since every ruling house on Athos has been coenobitic at one time or another, or that its refectory is not painted, but only that the space is not used except on major feast days. Nor may one assume that the paintings in a refectory could have been commissioned only when the monastery was coenobitic.

3. Gabriel Millet, *Monuments de l'Athos relevés avec le concours de l'Armée française d'Orient et de l'Ecole française d'Athènes*, vol. 1, *Les peintures* (Paris: Librairie Ernest Leroux, 1927; only one vol. published), pl. 98.1; Doula Mouriki, "Stylistic Trends in Monumental Painting of Greece during the Eleventh and Twelfth Centuries," *Dumbarton Oaks Papers* 34–35 (1980–81): 110 for further bibliography.

4. Vojislav J. Djurić, "La peinture de Chilandar à l'epoque du roi Milutin," *Recueil de Chilandar* 4 (1978): 41–53. Christ is at the apex, and below him are Abraham and the Angels near the Oak of Mambre, the Hospitality of Abraham, and the Sacrifice of Isaac by Abraham. Djurić dates these paintings on the basis of style to the latter part of the second decade of the fourteenth century.

5. Paul M. Mylonas, "La trapéza de la Grande Lavra au Mont Athos," *Cahiers archéologiques* 35 (1987): 146–47 and fig. 5a. Mylonas cautions that the style of the painting cannot be dated more precisely without closer study. From his photograph it is difficult to verify that the painting is Palaeologan rather than post-Byzantine. Mylonas sees as further evi-

dence for a Palaeologan trapeza program at the Great Lavra the indication of an earlier layer of plaster intended for wall paintings below the present one and the presence at the monastery of a Palaeologan fragment (attributed by A. Xyngopoulos to the famous Manuel Panselinos) depicting the head of St. Nicholas (ibid., 148–49).

6. At least they predate the present trapeza, constructed in the first half of the sixteenth century. See Ploutarchos L. Theocharides and Giannes E. Tavlakes, "Ereunes sten palia trapeza tes M. Docheiariou Agiou Orous," *Deutero symposio byzantines kai metabyzantines archaiologias kai technes: Programma kai perilepseis anakoinoseon* (Athens: [Christianike Archaiologike Etaireia], 1982), 29–30.

7. Millet, *Monuments*, pls. 140–51. See my Appendix II, A.

8. Millet, *Monuments*, pl. 95. See Appendix II, B.

9. Millet, *Monuments*, pls. 166 and 167.1, 2; Manolis Chatzidakis, *O Kretikos zographos Theophanes: E teleutaia phase tes technes tou stis toichographies tes Ieras Mones Stauroniketa* (Mount Athos: Iera Mone Stauroniketa, 1986), 26–27 (by Archimandrite Basil), 59–61 and pls. 201–10. See Appendix II, C.

10. Millet, *Monuments*, pls. 210, 212–13.3, 214. See Appendix II, D.

11. For a general view, see Karl Eller, *Der heilige Berg Athos* (Munich-Planegg: Otto Wilhelm Barth Verlag GMBH., 1954), 143; other views on 145, 147 (possibly taken at Dionysiou, notwithstanding the caption), 149, 195, 225. See Appendix II, E.

12. L[eonid] Nikol'skii, "Istoricheskii ocherk Afonskoi stiennoi zhivopisi," *Ikonopisnyi sbornik* 1 (1906): Supplement, two pls. between 54 and 55 (partial view of west wall and general view of apsidal wall); and Millet, *Monuments*, pl. 211. See Appendix II, D.

13. Millet, *Monuments*, pls. 99–114; Zdravko Kajmaković, *Georgije Mitrofanović* (Sarajevo: Veselin Masleša, 1977), 189–267. Dated by inscription.

14. Views in F. Dölger, E. Weigand, and A. Deindl, *Mönchsland Athos* (Munich: F. Bruckmann Verlag, 1943), ills. 70 and 158. For a diagram of the apse, see L. Nikol'skii, *Afonskie stenopisi*, vol. 2 (St. Petersburg, 1908), facing 126. See Appendix II, F.

15. Dölger, Weigand, and Deindl, ill. 71. See Appendix II, F.

16. Dated by inscription. See G. Millet, J. Pargoire, and L. Petit, *Recueil des inscriptions chrétiennes de l'Athos*, pt. 1 (Paris: Albert Fontemoing, 1904); only one part published), 58 (no. 191); Ainé Didron, "Le Mont Athos," *Annales archéologiques* 18 (1858): 76; Euthymios N. Tsigaridas, "Toichographies kai eikones tes Mones Pantokratoros Agiou Orous," *Makedonika* 18 (1978): 193 and pl. 12. The inscription names three ordained monks from Ioannina—Seraphim, Cosmas, and Ioannikios—as the painters, and the monk Timothy, of the island Limnos, as the donor.

17. Dated by inscription. See Ainé Didron, "Le Mont Athos," *Annales archéologiques* 4 (1846): 235–37; Millet, Pargoire, and Petit, 36 (no. 118). The painter is Makarios of Galatista, known also from other works (Phoivos I. Piompinos, *Ellenes agiographoi mechri to 1821*, 2d ed., rev. and enl. [Athens: Etaireia Ellenikou Logotechnikou kai Istorikou Archeiou, 1984], 229–30).

18. Dated by inscription. See Kajmaković, 255 and ills. 101 and 107. The Last Supper, in the apse, is illustrated in Robert Byron and David Talbot Rice, *The Birth of Western Painting: A History of Colour, Form, and Iconography, Illustrated from the Paintings of Mistra and Mount Athos, of Giotto and Duccio, and of El Greco* (London: George Routledge and Sons, 1930), pl. 40.i, where it is wrongly dated to 1621.

19. See Appendix II, E.

20. Not to be confused with the Rumanian skete of the same name, near the Great Lavra. Sotiris Vojadjis [Voyadjis], "The Kyriakon of the Skete of St. John the Baptist (Skete of Iviron) on Mount Athos," *Churches in Greece 1453–1850* (Athens: National Technical University, 1979–), 3:87–88 and personal correspondence with the author. There are a

Deësis (an enthroned Christ flanked by the Theotokos and St. John the Baptist) in the apse and additional paintings in the space connecting the trapeza to the west side of the church. (I thank Mr. Voyadjis for providing me with photographs.) All of these paintings seem close in style to those in the church, which are dated by inscription to 1799 (ibid., 76, 84). For a discussion of *sketes*, dependent monasteries that may be either coenobitic or idiorrhythmic, see R. M. Dawkins, *The Monks of Athos* (London: Allen & Unwin, 1936), 139–42.

21. Dölger, Weigand, and Deindl, ill. 69. See Appendix II, G.

22. See Appendix II, G.

23. Inscription of 1859. See Millet, Pargoire, and Petit, 188–89 (no. 556). See also below, n. 60.

24. The date is given in an inscription painted over the arch opposite the apse.

25. According to Millet, Pargoire, and Petit, 151 (no. 441), the present trapeza was part of the reconstruction project of 1894. The paintings are modern and confined to the apsidal depression of the longer arm (a Virgin and Christ Child Enthroned) and the apse and wall above in the shorter arm (a Holy Trinity and Last Supper, respectively).

26. This huge nineteenth-century refectory is in ruinous condition, now that the skete is inoperative. Its decoration never proceeded far: four paintings were executed, all in proximity to the main entrance, in a style typical of Russian church art at the turn of this century. They are Christ the Good Shepherd (Christ entering a sheepfold with a lamb cradled in his left arm), the Return of the Prodigal Son, the standing figure of a desert father, and a painting too badly damaged to be identified.

27. This refectory has an Old Testament Trinity in the apse, a *Pokrov* with Athonite saints on the wall surrounding the apse, and a Multiplication of the Loaves and Fishes and a Miracle at Cana on the opposite wall, flanking the exit. All bear Cyrillic inscriptions. A *kelli* is usually a small house inhabited by a few monks and dependent on a monastery (see Dawkins, *Monks of Athos*, 147–48). Bourazeri, however, about half an hour by foot from Karyes, has over a dozen monks and a physical plant large enough to accommodate three or four times that number.

28. The earlier paintings on this wall were destroyed long ago by an earthquake. An inscription records that those of 1980 (a row of standing saints) were executed by the monk Cyril of Pantocratoros and paid for by the archimandrite Stephanos of the island Limnos, also of Pantocratoros. Probably not coincidentally, the donor of the older program was also a native of Limnos (see above, n. 17).

29. Heinrich Brockhaus, *Die Kunst in den Athos-Klöstern*, 2d ed. (Leipzig: F. A. Brockhaus, 1924), 32–33.

30. Mylonas, "Trapéza," 145 and fig. 3.

31. One table at Chilandari (the abbot's) and another at Vatopedi are circular and lobed. Other stone tables are scattered about the courtyard of Chilandari, while at Esphigmenou a few are in a storeroom off the courtyard. The latter were seen in the refectory by Barskii in 1744, who counted four, and by De Nolhac in the nineteenth century ([Vasilii Grigorovich Barskii], *Stranstvovaniia Vasil'ia Grigorovicha-Barskago po sviatym mestam Vostoka c 1723 po 1747 g.*, ed. Nikolai Barsukov, 4 vols. [St. Petersburg, 1885–87], 3:224; Stasnislas de Nolhac, *La Dalmatie, les îles Ioniennes, Athènes et la Mont Athos* [Paris, 1882], 246).

32. See John J. Yiannias, "The Wall Paintings in the Trapeza of the Great Lavra on Mount Athos: A Study in Eastern Orthodox Refectory Art" (Ph.D. diss., Univ. of Pittsburgh, 1971), 79–85, for references to the descriptions given in the older travel books and pilgrim's guides.

33. Paul Mylonas, "Nouvelles recherches au Mont-Athos (Lavra)," *Cahiers archéologiques* 29 (1980–81): 176; idem, "Trapéza."

34. N. P. Kondakov reported early in this century that the trapeza paintings of the Great

Lavra had been renovated in 1860 and 1866 (*Pamiatniki khristianskogo iskusstva na Afonie* [St. Petersburg, 1902], 73), and most likely there have been other repaintings as well. A partial cleaning by the Greek Archaeological Service was completed in the 1960s (S. Pelekanidis, in *Archaiologikon Deltion* 16B [1960]: 230, and Manolis Chatzidakis, "Recherches sur le peintre Théophane le Crétois," *Dumbarton Oaks Papers* 23–24 [1969–70]: 319). On the date and attribution, see Appendix II, A; and Chatzidakis, "Recherches," 315–23, where this and the other attributions to Theophanes are discussed.

35. The prophets from left to right: Zechariah, Habakkuk, Jeremiah, Gideon, Jacob, Moses, Aaron, Isaiah, Ezekiel, and one whom I cannot identify. See also below, n. 79.

36. Yiannias, "Wall Paintings," 115; Kajmaković, 211–13. An icon was credited with thwarting the Persian siege of Constantinople in 626. In some Acathist cycles, this scene depicts a city under siege; in some others the scene is absent (Kajmaković, 214–15, 217).

37. The paintings in the corner chambers have not been published.

38. This Tree is derived, as are the many similar post-Byzantine examples in Rumania and elsewhere, from a Western prototype of the thirteenth century. See Michael D. Taylor, "A Historiated Tree of Jesse," *Dumbarton Oaks Papers* 34–35 (1980–81): 125–76.

39. For a study of the subjects of St. Sisoës and the Tomb and the Death of the Just Monk, see Rainer Stichel, *Studien zum Verhältnis von Text und Bild spät- und nachbyzantinischer Vergänglichkeitsdarstellungen: Die Anfangsminiaturen von Psalterhandschriften des 14. Jahrhunderts, ihre Herkunft, Bedeutung und ihr Weiterleben in der griechischen und russischen Kunst und Literatur* (Vienna: In Kommission bei Hermann Bohlaus Nachf., 1971).

40. For a recent study of this subject, see Miltiadis K. Garidis, *Etudes sur le Jugement dernier post-Byzantin du XVe à la fin du XIXe siècle: Iconographie, esthétique* (Thessaloniki: Etaireia Makedonikon Spoudon, 1985).

41. Both paintings follow the traditional iconographic types, which can be seen in our figures 4.30 (although there Zosimus and Mary are on separate surfaces) and 4.31.

42. For illustrations of the facade paintings see also Millet, *Monuments*, pls. 140.1, 141.1, 142.1, 143.1; and for a fuller description, Yiannias, "Wall Paintings," 20–25, 185–92, 297–98. An unidentifiable fragment at the south end of the facade may also not be by the artist who painted the interior (ibid., 33).

43. For references on all of these older programs, see Appendix I.

44. *Stavronikita*: Twenty-four frames, the first and last still visible on the apsidal wall; on the south wall frames 2–5 are visible (Chatzidakis, *O Kretikos zographos Theophanes*, pls. 201, 208–210). The frames on the north wall have been destroyed, presumably in the renovation of 1770, to which Chatzidakis dates the enlargement of that side of the refectory (ibid., p. 59). Omitted from the comparative table in Kajmaković, 214–15. *Philotheou*: Twenty-four frames, unpublished. Omitted from Kajmaković's table. *Chilandari*: Twenty-five frames, the first bisected by a window (Millet, *Monuments*, pls. 99–103 and Kajmaković, 192–221). *Docheiariou*: Twenty-four frames, in the chamber containing the apse (1676). See Dölger, Weigand, and Deindl, ill. 70, for the six frames on the east wall (stanzas 4–9). *Xenophontos*: Painted on one of the long walls (the western) and consisting of only the first sixteen frames, unpublished. Not in Kajmaković's table. *Esphigmenou*: Twenty-four frames, unpublished. Not in Kajmaković's table.

45. Both sets of paintings are unpublished. The example at *Philotheou* resembles a monumental icon, with the prophets that ordinarily frame the central image being placed on the jambs and soffit of the niche. The prophets here are Jacob, Gideon, Jeremiah, Zacharias (father of John the Baptist), Ezekiel, Moses, Micah (?), Aaron, Daniel, and Habakkuk. At *Xenophontos* they are Moses, David, Gideon, Ezekiel, Jeremiah, Daniel, Solomon, Jacob, Aaron, Isaiah, Habakkuk, and Zechariah. At *Stavronikita*, what amounts to the same subject

is seen in the placing of the prefigurative Jacob's Ladder and Burning Bush by the apsidal conch (Chatzidakis, *O Kretikos zographos Theophanes*, pls. 203–4).

46. *Dionysiou*: Partial views in Nikol'skii, *Istoricheskii ocherk*, ill. facing 54; Konstantinos D. Kalokyres, *Athos: Themata archaiologias kai technes epi te chilieteridi (963–1963)* (Athens: "Aster" Al. kai E. Papademetriou, 1963), pl. 6; and Paul Huber, *Athos: Leben, Glaube, Kunst* (Zurich and Freiburg im Breisgau: Atlantis Verlag, 1969), ills. 206, 207. *Esphigmenou*: Unpublished; about a dozen of the entries, representing dates in September, November, December, and February, can be identified.

47. Ioannes Komnenos, *Proskynetarion tou Agiou Orous tou Athonos*, 2d ed. (Venice, 1864; first published in 1701), 93 (also in Bernard de Montfaucon, *Palaeographia graeca* [Paris, 1708; rpt. Farnborough, England: Gregg, 1970]); F. Braconnier, "Mémoires pour servir à l'histoire des monastères du Mont Athos, par le père Braconnier, Jésuite (1706)," in Henri Omont, *Missions archéologiques françaises en Orient aux XVIIe et XVIIIe siècles* (Paris, 1902), 1012. This Tree must have resembled the one at the Great Lavra, since both Komnenos and Braconnier mention that it included philosophers and a sibyl (Braconnier: "des sibylles"). It could no longer be seen at the time of Villoison's visit in 1785 (E. Miller, "Voyage de Villoison au mont Athos," *Revue de bibliographie analytique* 5 [1844]: 851). Perhaps it was destroyed in the restoration project of 1770 (see Appendix II, C).

48. Chilandari: Dölger, Weigand, and Deindl, ill. 162; Kajmaković, ill. 120.

49. The main portion is on the east wall of the north chamber, opposite the apse: Brockhaus pl. 10 (line drawing) and Millet, *Monuments*, pl. 210.2. The portion depicting the kings of the earth and the punishments in hell is on the adjoining south wall (not shown in Brockhaus or Millet).

50. At both Xenophontos and Pantocratoros it is on the wall facing the apse. At Karakallou it was also opposite the apse, on the west wall. See Ainé Didron, "Le Mont Athos: Caracallou," *Annales archéologiques* 20 (1860): 282.

51. Chilandari: Kajmaković, ills. 104, 114, 115. Docheiariou: Dölger, Weigand, and Deindl, ill. 73; Huber, ill. 205.

52. Chilandari: Kajmaković, ills. 106, 107, 117.

53. Stichel, fig. 3.

54. Southern corner chamber, west wall, top zone (see our fig. 4.25), as the entry for November 8 (unpublished).

55. Hippolyte Delehaye, ed., *Synaxarium Ecclesiae Constantinopolitanae* (= *Propylaeum ad Acta Sanctorum Novembris*) (Brussels, 1902), cols. 203–4. On the iconography, see André Grabar, *L'Iconoclasme byzantine: Le dossier archéologique*, 2d ed., rev. and enl. (Paris: Flammarion, 1984), 253, 264, 265, 267.

56. The moral is in keeping with the likening of monks to angels in ecclesiastical parlance and in the ascetical literature. I cite only St. Basil (Migne, *PG* 31: 629D, 872B–C) and the "Barlaam and Ioasaph" (Migne, *PG* 96: 857–1250 passim). Also, the monk's habit is called the *angelikon schema*.

57. *Docheiariou*: east wall, lower zone in the program of 1700 (Dölger, Weigand, and Deindl, ill. 71). *Xenophontos*: west wall, bottom zone (unpublished), with the Archangels reduced to Gabriel and Michael. *Chilandari*: Millet, *Monuments*, pls. 110, 111 and Kajmaković, ills. 106, 122.

58. *Dionysiou*: Millet, *Monuments*, pls. 206.3, 207.2, 208, 209. *Xenophontos*: ibid., pls. 184.1, 185.1. *Docheiariou*: Dölger, Weigand, and Deindl, ill. 70 (showing only the east wall). On the borrowings, see Ludwig Heinrich Heydenreich, "Der Apokalypsen-Zyklus im Athosgebiet und seine Beziehungen zur deutschen Bibelillustration der Reformation," *Zeitschrift für Kunstgeschichte* 8 (1939): 1–40; Juliette Renaud, *Le cycle de l'Apocalypse de Dionysiou: Interprétation byzantine de gravures occidentales* (Paris: Presses universitaires de

France, 1943); H. Brunet-Dinard, "Le Maitre IF, Inspirateur des fresques de l'Apocalypse de Dyonisiou," *Gazette des Beaux-Arts*, ser. 6, vol. 44 (1954): 309–16 (Engl. trans.: 363–65); and Huber, 365–83 and ills. 212–19.

59. *Stavronikita*: Last Supper (apsidal conch), Multiplication of the Seven Loaves and Fishes, and Miraculous Draught of Fishes (both in the apse, below the Last Supper). *Xeropotamou*: Last Supper and Multiplication of the Five Loaves and Two Fishes, to which may have to be added some paintings that came to light on an earlier layer a few years ago. The exposed section of one of these, seen by me in 1984, appeared to belong to a Transfiguration.

60. Excluding the Last Supper and any Great Feasts, I count eleven Gospel scenes at Philotheou, twenty-three or twenty-four at Dionysiou (sixteenth-century program), twelve at Esphigmenou, and nineteen at Pantocratoros. Those appearing in three or more refectories are the Miracle at Cana (Great Lavra, Philotheou, Pantocratoros), the Multiplication of the Loaves and Fishes (five loaves and two fishes: Pantocratoros, Vatopedi, Xeropotamou; seven loaves and fishes: Stavronikita and Dionysiou; indeterminate: Great Lavra and Philotheou), Christ Stills the Tempest (Philotheou, Esphigmenou, Pantocratoros), Christ Heals the Man Born Blind (Dionysiou, Philotheou [?], Esphigmenou, Pantocratoros), Christ Appears to the Disciples on the Sea of Tiberias (Stavronikita, Dionysiou, Pantocratoros), and Christ Annointed in the House of Simon the Leper (Dionysiou, Philotheou, Esphigmenou).

61. I am counting as Great Feasts the twelve that came to comprise the *dodecaorton*: the Annunciation, Nativity, Presentation in the Temple, Baptism, Transfiguration, Raising of Lazarus, Entry into Jerusalem, Crucifixion, Anastasis (Descent into Hell), Ascension, Pentecost, and the Dormition of the Theotokos. A more liberal interpretation of the term to include a few more of the major feasts would not materially alter our conclusions.

62. Bertubani preserves four, Kolaguiri two, Patmos sixteen (with emphasis on the Passion), and Apollonia eleven. The Peribleptos refectory in Constantinople had an Annunciation, a Nativity, and scenes showing "how [Christ] went about the world with His disciples, with the various events of His blessed life until His crucifixion and death" (*Clavijo: Embassy to Tamerlane, 1403–1406*, trans. Guy LeStrange [London: George Routledge and Sons, 1928], 67–68; *Embajada a Tamorlán*, ed. Francisco López Estrada [Madrid: Consejo Superior de Investigaciones Científicas, Instituto Nicolás Antonio, 1943], 40). In 1648 DeMontconys saw there a mosaic Last Supper in the apse (Jean Ebersolt, *Constantinople byzantine et les voyageurs du Levant* [Paris: Editions Ernest Leroux, 1918], 133–34). The trapeza of the Monastery of St. John Studion, in Constantinople, was reported by Clavijo to have a mosaic Last Supper (*Embassy*, 69). Finally, a poem by Theodore Metochites describes the early fourteenth-century trapeza program of the Monastery of the Chora, in Constantinople, as displaying "the mysteries and miracles" of Christ (Paul Underwood, *The Kariye Djami*, 4 vols. [New York and Princeton: Bollingen Foundation and Princeton Univ. Press, 1966–75], 1:188).

63. A Crucifixion and Anastasis: Anastasios K. Orlandos, *E architektonike kai ai byzantinai toichographiai tes Mones tou Theologou Patmou* (Athens: Grapheion Demosieumaton tes Akademias Athenon, 1970), fig. 109 and Kollias, fig. 24. According to Orlandos (175), about half of the interior surfaces are still covered with plaster and may conceal additional paintings.

64. See above, n. 62.

65. Vol'skaia, ill. 12.

66. Suzy Dufrenne, "L'Enrichissement du programme iconographique dans les églises byzantines du XIIIème siècle," in *L'Art byzantin du XIIIe siècle: Symposium de Sopoćani, 1965* (Belgrade: Faculté de Philosophie, Departement de l'Histoire de l'Art, 1967), 35–45.

67. An example is the catholicon of Stavronikita, now magnificently published in Chatzidakis, *O Kretikos zographos Theophanes*; see esp. 43–59. For general discussions of the distribution of themes in the church programs of Athos, see Brockhaus, 60–84, and R. W. Dawkins, "The Arrangement of Wall-Paintings in the Monastery Churches of Mount Athos," *Byzantina Metabyzantina* 1 (1946): 93–105. These and other early analyses of Byzantine and post-Byzantine church programs have to be read now in the light of the principles advanced by Otto Demus in his discussion of the Middle Byzantine "classic" program (*Byzantine Mosaic Decoration* [1948; rpt. New Rochelle, N.Y.: Caratzas Brothers, 1976]). As compared with the latter, the typical Athonite church is indeed, in Demus's words, "apt to seem a more or less disorderly profusion of pictures, jumbled together haphazard" (77). But one can still discern a hierarchical order in the late programs (Chatzidakis, *O Kretikos zographos Theophanes*, 43–44.)

68. Brockhaus, 84.

69. The observation, made by Brockhaus and others, that the refectory accommodates subjects for which there is no room in the catholicon must not be construed as a general principle. There are many instances of both duplication and omission.

70. Examples of the Mandylion over the central apse: Philotheou, Chilandari, Esphigmenou. At Stavronikita it is over the apsidal window and below the Last Supper (see the remarks in Chatzidakis, *O Kretikos zographos Theophanes*, 70, 74, 84, 115). In the south chamber at Dionysiou (see my fig. 4.1), the Mandylion appears over the niche to the left of the apse and is counterbalanced by a Keramidion, or Holy Tile, over the right-hand niche, a pairing inspired by the fact that in churches the two images confront each other across the space under the central dome.

71. The table, however, is not of the sigma type but oblong with rounded corners (Vol'skaia, ills. 2, 6–9). The Last Supper was depicted early in Western refectories as well, judging from the eleventh-century example in the Monastery of San Paolo fuori le Mura in Rome (Guglielmo Matthiae, *Pittura Romana del Medioevo*, 2 vols. [Rome: Fratelli Palombi, 1965, 1966], 2:39, 80).

72. Thierry, fig. 1.

73. Buschhausen, 197 and figs. 23, 27, 28. For the date, see Appendix I. The Buschhausens' identification of the figure at the far right of this painting as Christ is questioned in my forthcoming essay on the program at Apollonia, to appear in *The Twilight of Byzantium*, ed. Slobodan Ćurčić and Doula Mouriki (Princeton: Princeton Univ. Press, 1991).

74. For the Studion and Peribleptos, see above, n. 62. Since Clavijo's visit preceded the fall of Constantinople by only an economically impoverished half century, it seems unlikely that any mosaics were installed in the Peribleptos refectory in the time between his account and that of DeMontconys.

75. *Great Lavra* (Millet, *Monuments*, pl. 145; in color in Kalokyres, pl. III). *Philotheou* (Millet, *Monuments*, pl. 95.1). *Dionysiou* (in color in Philip Sherrard, *Athos The Holy Mountain* [Woodstock, N.Y.: Overlook Press, 1985], ill. 148).

76. Millet, *Monuments*, pl. 210.1.

77. *Stavronikita* (Chatzidakis, *O Kretikos zographos Theophanes*, pl. 205); *Chilandari* (Byron and Rice, pl. 40.i).

78. Without a close examination of this image, one cannot determine to what extent it has been repainted. Nevertheless in this writer's opinion it stands comparison with the finest Palaeologan treatments of the subject.

79. Yiannias, "Wall Paintings," 112–13. See also D. Mouriki, "Ai Biblikai proeikoniseis tes Panagias eis ton troullon tes Peribleptou tou Mystra," *Archaiologikon Deltion* 25A (1970): 223; Manolis Chatzidakis, *Icônes de Saint-Georges des Grecs et de la collection de l'Institut* (Venice: Neri Pozza, n.d. [1962]), 23–27; G. and M. Sotiriou, *Icones du Mont*

Sinai, 2 vols. (Athens: Instituit Français d'Athènes, 1956, 1958), 2:73–75. The subject is described by Dionysius of Fourna: see *The "Painter's Manual" of Dionysius of Fourna*, trans. Paul Hetherington (London: Sagittarius Press, 1974), 51 (where the title, in Greek "Anothen oi prophetai," is mistakenly translated, "The Prophets from Above"). The title derives from a troparion. See A[ndreas] Xyngopoulos, *Katalogos ton eikonon, Mouseion Benaki, Athenai* (Athens: [Benaki Museum], 1936), 50. This subject is seen often in icons as well as in wall paintings, particularly in the Palaeologan period and later.

80. Dufrenne, 36–38.

81. Noted by Christophoros Ktenas, *E en Agio Orei Atho iera, basilike, patriarchike kai stauropegiake mone tou Docheiariou kai ai pros to doulon ethnos yperesiai autes (963–1921)* (Athens: K. G. Makrides and I. L. Aleuropoulos, 1926), 52 n. 3.

82. The story is retold in Dawkins, *Monks of Athos*, chap. 30.

83. Vol'skaia, 33, 100–104, 164, 165; Djurić, 45–47. See Chatzidakis, however (*O Kretikos zographos Theophanes*, 60–61), who states that refectory paintings (he seems to be speaking of Eastern, or perhaps Athonite, refectory programs in general) are distinguished from those of a catholicon by the *absence* of the Eucharistic theme, as well as of images of the major feasts.

84. For Patmos, see Orlandos, *E architektonike*, 186 (fig. 109) and pls. 18, 19 and Kollias, figs. 24, 34, 36. The Communion is on the vault, near the apse. For Hosios Meletios, see Anastasios K. Orlandos, "E Mone tou Osiou Meletiou kai ta paralauria autes, "*Archeion ton byzantinon mnemeion tes Ellados*, 5 (1939–40): 57. Here the painting is in the apse.

85. Chatzidakis, *O Kretikos zographos Theophanes*, 71–72.

86. John Cassian (d. 435) considered the practice to be derived from Cappadocia. (*Institutions cénobitiques*, trans. Jean-Claude Guy [Paris: Editions du Cerf, 1965], 143).

87. Brockhaus, 85–86.

88. The quoted passage is in Aleksei Afanas'evich Dmitrievskii, *Opisanie liturgicheskikh rukopisei, khraniashchikhsia v bibliotekakh Pravoslavnago Vostoka*, vol. 1, *Typika*, pt. 1, *Pamiatniki patriarshikh ustavov i ktitorskie monastyrskie tipikony* (Kiev, 1895), 733.

89. Yiannias, "Wall Paintings," 257–63 and Appendix C.

90. Philipp Meyer, *Die Haupturkunden für die Geschichte der Athosklöster* (Leipzig, 1894), 136. For the date of the *Hypotyposis*, see Hans-Georg Beck, *Kirche und theologische Literatur im byzantinischen Reich* (Munich: C. H. Beck'sche Verlagsbuchhandlung, 1959), 589.

91. John J. Yiannias, "The Elevation of the Panaghia," *Dumbarton Oaks Papers* 26 (1972): 225–36. For the palace ritual see ibid., 230 and Pseudo-Codinus, *Traité des Offices*, ed. J. Verpeaux (Paris: Centre National de la Recherche Scientifique, 1966), 204. For Symeon of Thessaloniki see Migne *PG*, 155:661.

92. For references, see Yiannias, "Wall Paintings," 110–237, passim; and idem, forthcoming article on the trapeza program at Apollonia, cited above, n. 73.

93. *Moralia* 148B: *Selected Essays of Plutarch*, trans. T. G. Tucker (Oxford: Clarendon Press, 1913), 30–31.

94. At Philotheou, to cite but one more, the scroll held by St. Nicholas reads, "Love [*agape*] and self-control [*enkrateia*] cleanse the soul, and undefiled [*kathara*] prayer makes bright the mind [*noun*]." Some of the texts are from the *Apophthegmata Patrum*.

95. The story ends with, "This much, however, I have at last learned, that it is not safe for a man of peace to dine with men so learned" (Lucian *Symposium* [or, *Lapiths*] 48, trans. A. M. Harmon [Loeb ed.] [London: William Heinemann; Cambridge: Macmillan, 1913], 462–63).

96. Including, in an Orthodox context, a painting of 1876 by Vasilii Perov, one of the *Peredvizhniki*, entitled, "Trapeza," and illustrated in A. K. Lebedev, *The Itinerants* (Leningrad: Aurora Art Publishers, 1974), pl. 11.

97. Migne *PG* 151:81C. Much information on the medieval ideas about the religious significance of eating, although with emphasis on the Western sources, can be found in Bridget Ann Henisch, *Fast and Feast: Food in Medieval Society* (University Park and London: Pennsylvania State Univ. Press, 1976) and Caroline Walker Bynum, *Holy Feast and Holy Fast: The Religious Significance of Food to Medieval Women* (Berkeley, Los Angeles, London: Univ. of California Press, 1987).

Fig. 4.1. Dionysiou, trapeza. South chamber. General view of apsidal wall. Paintings 1602/3. (Photo: Author)

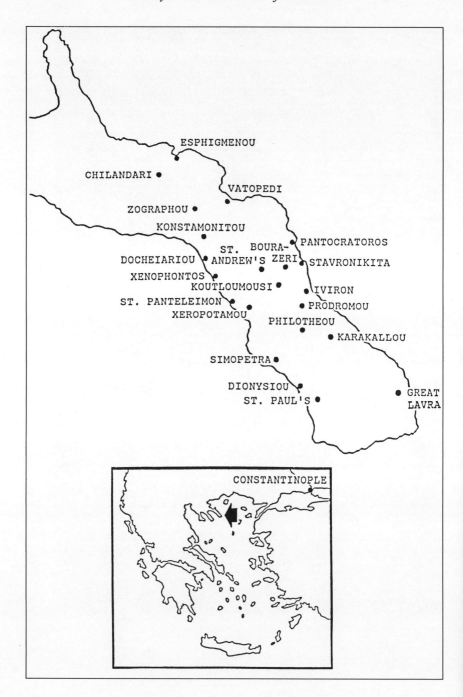

Fig. 4.2. Mount Athos, showing the approximate locations of the monasteries cited.

Fig. 4.3. Philotheou, trapeza. East wall, detail: St. Sabbas the Great and St. Euthymius the Great. 1539/40 (?). (Photo: Author)

Fig. 4.4. Esphigmenou, trapeza. North wall, detail: St. John the Kalybite. 1811 (?). (Photo: Author)

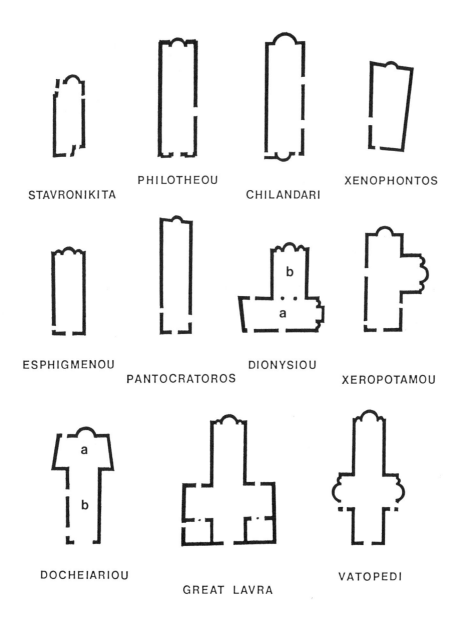

Fig. 4.5. Athonite refectories. Schematized plans, with windows omitted. (Adapted by the author from Paul M. Mylonas, "La trapéza de la Grande Lavra au Mont Athos," *Cahiers archéologiques* 35 [1987], fig. 3)

Fig. 4.6. Great Lavra, trapeza. West arm. Abbot's table. Length and width approximately 138 cm. (Photo: Author)

Fig. 4.7. Great Lavra, trapeza. Interior, looking west. (Photo: Benaki Museum, Athens, Photographic Archive)

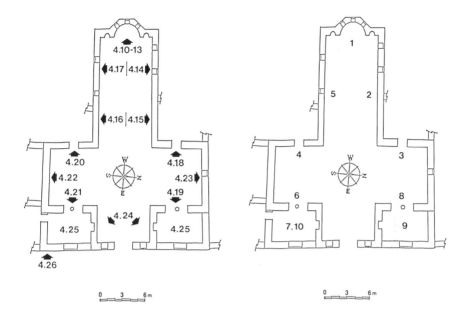

Fig. 4.8. Great Lavra, trapeza. Plan. The numbers refer to the illustrations in the present volume. (Plan adapted by the author from Paul M. Mylonas, "La trapéza de la Grande Lavra au Mont Athos," *Cahiers archéologiques* 35 [1987], fig. 4)

Fig. 4.9. Great Lavra, trapeza. Plan. The numbers indicate the sequence of walls in the Menologion cycle. For an analysis of the sequence in the corner chambers, see figure 4.25. (Plan adapted by the author from Mylonas, "La trapéza," fig. 4)

Fig. 4.10. Great Lavra, trapeza. Apse. Last Supper. (Photo: Photis Zachariou)

Fig. 4.11. Great Lavra, trapeza. West arm, west wall. Prophets of Old. (Photo: Author)

Fig. 4.12. Great Lavra, trapeza. West arm, west wall. Prophets of Old, detail: Theotokos and Christ. (Photo: Author)

Fig. 4.13. Great Lavra, trapeza. West arm, west wall. Top zone: Acathist Hymn, frames 1–5. Middle zone: Menologion, Sept. 1–6. Conch: Last Supper. Bottom zone: standing saints, with St. John the Forerunner and the Theotokos in niches.

(Photo: after Gabriel Millet, *Monuments de l'Athos relevés avec le concours de l'Armée française d'Orient et de l'Ecole française d'Athènes*, vol. 1, *Les peintures* [Paris: Librairie Ernest Leroux, 1927], pls. 145.2–3)

Fig. 4.14. Great Lavra, trapeza. West arm, north wall, west half. Top zone: Acathist Hymn, frames 6–10. Middle zone: Menologion, Sept. 7–14. Bottom zone: standing saints. (Photo: after Millet, *Monuments*, pl. 146.1)

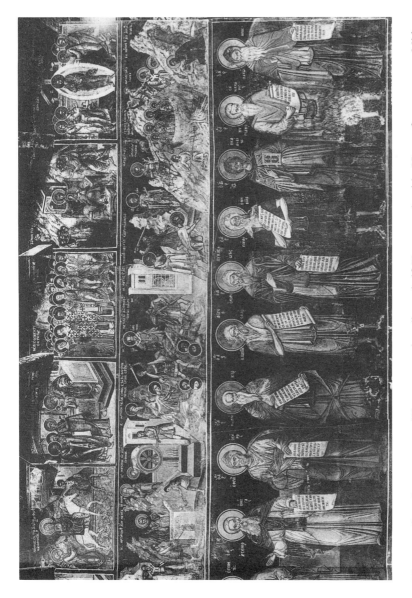

Fig. 4.15. Great Lavra, trapeza. West arm, north wall, east half. Top zone: Acathist Hymn, frames 11–15. Middle zone: Menologion, Sept. 15–21. Bottom zone: standing saints. (Photo: after Millet, *Monuments*, pl. 147.1)

Fig. 4.16. Great Lavra, trapeza. West arm, south wall, east half. Top zone: Acathist Hymn, frames 16–20. Middle zone: Menologion, Oct. 12–20. Bottom zone: standing saints. (Photo: after Millet, *Monuments*, pl. 146.2)

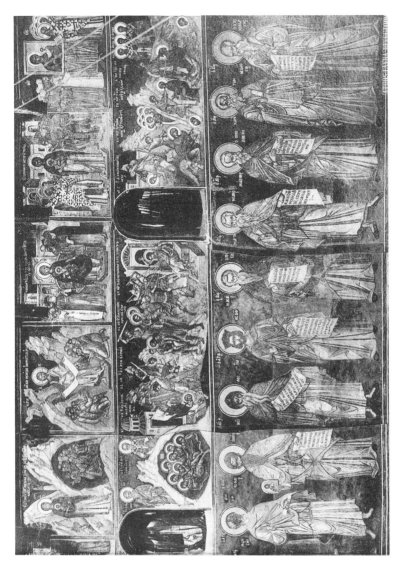

Fig. 4.17. Great Lavra, trapeza. West arm, south wall, west half. Top zone: Acathist Hymn, frames 21–25. Middle zone: Menologion, Oct. 21–31. Bottom zone: standing saints. (Photo: after Millet, *Monuments*, pl. 147.2)

Fig. 4.18. Great Lavra, trapeza. North arm, west wall. Top zone: Life of St. John the Forerunner, frames 1–5. Middle zone: Menologion, Sept. 22–30. Bottom zone: Spiritual Ladder and the Allegory of Death. (Photo: after Millet, *Monuments*, pl. 142.2)

Fig. 4.19. Great Lavra, trapeza. North arm, east wall. Top zone: Life of St. John the Forerunner, frames 6–10. Middle zone: Menologion, Dec. 1–10. Bottom zone: Death of the Just Monk and Martyrdom of St. Ignatius Theophorus. (Photo: after Millet, *Monuments*, pl. 143.2)

Fig. 4.20. Great Lavra, trapeza. South arm, west wall. Top zone: Early Life of the Theotokos, frames 6–10. Middle zone: Menologion, Oct. 1–11. Bottom zone: Story of St. Gerasimus and the Lion and the First Ecumenical Council. (Photo: after Millet, *Monuments*, pl. 140.2)

Fig. 4.21. Great Lavra, trapeza. South arm, east wall. Top zone: Early Life of the Theotokos, frames 1–5. Middle zone: Menologion, Nov. 1–6. Bottom zone: Prophet Elijah Fed by the Raven in the Wilderness and the Sacrifice of Isaac by Abraham. (Photo: after Millet, *Monuments*, pl. 141.2)

Fig. 4.22. Great Lavra, trapeza. South arm, south wall. Tree of Jesse, Story of Cain and Abel. (Photo: after Millet, *Monuments*, pl. 151.3)

Fig. 4.23. Great Lavra, trapeza. North arm, north wall. Christ the True Vine, Dormition of St. Athanasius the Athonite, St. Sisoës and the Tomb, and the Life of the Solitary. (Photo: after Millet, *Monuments*, pl. 150.2)

Fig. 4.24. Great Lavra, trapeza. East arm. Last Judgment. (Photo: after Millet, *Monuments*, pls. 149.1,2)

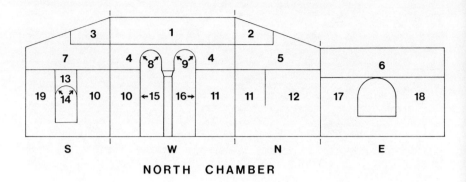

Fig. 4.25. Great Lavra, trapeza. Corner chambers. Arrangement of subjects. (Diagram: Author)

North chamber:

1–9: Menologion

1: Dec. 11–15/16

2: Dec. 16(?)–17(?)

3: Dec. 17/18–19/20

4: Dec. 20–27(?)

5: Dec. 28(?)–31(?)

6: Jan. 1–8

7: Jan. 9–15

8: Jan. 16–18

9: Jan. 19–23

10: Second Ecumenical Council

11: Third (?) Ecumenical Council

12: Fourth (?) Ecumenical Council

13: Unidentified saint

14: Unidentified saint (east); Melchizedek (west).

15: St. Maximus the Kausokalybite

16: Unidentified saint

17: Two unidentified standing saints (monks)

18: Three standing saints: ——, St. Patapius, ——.

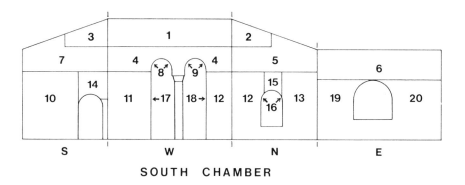

SOUTH CHAMBER

South chamber:
1–9: Menologion
1: Nov. 7–12
2: Nov. 13(?)-14(?)
3: Nov. 15–17/18
4: Nov. 18–24/25
5: Nov. 25–29/30
6: Feb. 1–9/10
7: Feb. 9/10–16
8: Feb. 17–19/20
9: Feb. 20/21–22
10: Fifth (?) Ecumenical Council
11: Sixth Ecumenical Council
12: Seventh Ecumenical Council
13: St. Zosimus Giving Communion to St. Mary of Egypt
14: St. Pachomius Receiving the Angelic Habit from the Angel of the Lord
15: St. Bessarion
16: St. Symeon Stylite (west) and St. Daniel (?) Stylite (east).
17: St. Onuphrius the Egyptian
18: St. Peter the Athonite
19: Two standing saints: St. Avramius and ———.
20: Three standing saints: ———, St. Theodore the disciple of St. Pachomius, St. Benedict.

Fig. 4.26. Great Lavra, trapeza. East facade. Above: two Miracles of St. Athanasius the Athonite. Below: Parable of the Publican and Pharisee. (Photo: Author)

Fig. 4.27. Vatopedi, trapeza. Main apse, conch. Tree of Jesse. 1786. (Photo: Author)

Fig. 4.28. Dionysiou, trapeza. South chamber, west wall. Spiritual Ladder. 1602/3.
(Photo: Author)

Fig. 4.29. Dionysiou, trapeza. South chamber, west wall. Synaxis of the Archangels, with the Fall of Lucifer. 1602/3. (Photo: Author)

Fig. 4.30. Pantocratoros, trapeza. East wall. St. Zosimus Giving Communion to St. Mary of Egypt. (*a*) St. Zosimus; (*b*) St. Mary. 1749. (Photo: Author)

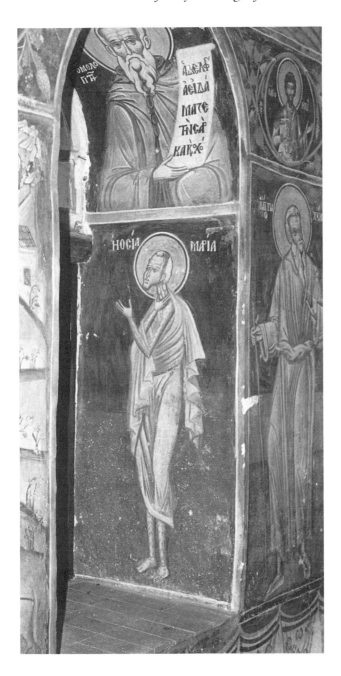

Fig. 4.31. Pantocratoros, trapeza. East wall. St. Pachomius Receiving the Angelic Habit from the Angel of the Lord. 1749. (Photo: Author)

Fig. 4.32. Chilandari, trapeza. East wall. SS. Onuphrius, Peter the Athonite, and Mark the Thracian. By George Mitrofanović, 1621. (Photo: Author)

Fig. 4.33. Philotheou, trapeza. Apsidal wall, detail. Above: Mandylion. Below: Last Supper. 1539/40 (?). (Photo: Author)

Fig. 4.34. Docheiariou, trapeza. Apse, conch. Above: Annunciation. Below: Theotokos with Christ and Archangels. 1676. (Photo: Author)

Fig. 4.35. Docheiariou, trapeza. Apse, detail. SS. Nicholas of Myra, Gregory the Theologian, and John Chrysostom. 1676. (Photo: Author)

Fig. 4.36. Docheiariou, trapeza. Apse, detail. Melismos. 1676. (Photo: Author)

Fig. 4.37. Docheiariou, trapeza. Apse, detail. Inscription. 1676. (Photo: Author)

Fig. 4.38. Stavronikita, trapeza. Apse, conch. Above: Theotokos with Christ. Below: Last Supper. By Theophanes the Cretan, ca. 1546. (Photo: Photis Zachariou)

Fig. 4.39. Great Lavra, phiale. Inner surface of the dome, detail: St. John the Forerunner Preaching and Baptizing. 17th c. (Photo: after Millet, *Monuments*, pl. 152.2)

Fig. 4.40. Dionysiou, trapeza, north chamber, north wall. Above: Miracles of Christ. Middle zone: St. John the Forerunner Preaching and Baptizing. 16th c. (Photo: Author)

CONTRIBUTORS

INDEX

CONTRIBUTORS

Sir Steven Runciman is a renowed medievalist and scholar of Byzantium and the Near East. He has written a magisterial three-volume *History of the Crusades* (1951–54) and over a dozen other books, including *The Emperor Romanus Lecapenus and His Reign* (1929), *The Medieval Manichee* (1947), *The Sicilian Vespers* (1958), *The Fall of Constantinople* (1965), *The Great Church in Captivity* (1968), and *The Last Byzantine Renaissance* (1970). An honorary Fellow of Trinity College, Cambridge, he lives in Scotland.

Speros Vryonis, Jr., was born in Memphis, Tennessee, and was educated at Southwestern College (B.A.) and Harvard (M.A. and Ph.D.). He has taught at Harvard, UCLA (where he was also director of the Von Grunebaum Center for Near Eastern Studies), the University of Chicago, and the University of Athens (Greece). Since 1988 he has been Director of the Alexander S. Onassis Center for Hellenic Studies at New York University. He has published over sixty articles in Byzantine, Balkan, and Near Eastern history of the medieval and modern periods and has written or edited fourteen books and monographs, including *Byzantium and Europe* (1967), *Individualism and Conformity in Classical Islam* (1977), *History of the Balkan Peoples* (in Greek; 1979), and *The Decline of Medieval Hellenism in Asia Minor and the Process of Islamization from the Eleventh through the Fifteenth Century* (1971).

John Meyendorff was born in Paris and received his doctorate at the University of Paris (Sorbonne). He is well known for his studies of Byzantine theology and history and Byzantino-Slavic relations. His books include *A Study of St. Gregory Palamas* (Engl. ed. 1964), *Byzantine Hesychasm: Historical, Theological, and Social Problems* (1974), and *Christ in Eastern Christian Thought* (Engl. ed. 1975). Father Meyendorff is Dean of St. Vladimir's Orthodox Theological Seminary and Professor of History at Fordham University.

Aglaia E. Kasdagli was born in Athens, Greece. She received her B.A. in history and archaeology at the University of Athens and her M.A. in medieval social history at the University of Birmingham. She is presently a doctoral candidate at the University of Birmingham, where she has also been a Research Associate in the Centre for Byzantine Studies. Her dissertation is on the economic and social history of the island of Naxos in the seventeenth century. She has written and translated in the areas of late Byzantine and modern Greek studies.

Miloš Velimirović is an internationally recognized authority on Byzantine and early Slavic music. Born in Belgrade and trained there as an undergraduate in both art history and the history of music, he subsequently earned an M.A. and Ph.D. in Music from Harvard. He taught at Yale and at the University of Wisconsin in Madison before accepting his present position as Professor of Music at the University of Virginia. He has written *Byzantine Elements in Early Slavic Chant* (1960) and about sixty articles and has served as editor of *Studies in Eastern Chant* (1966–1979). He is the recipient of numerous awards, including Fulbright Fellowships to Greece and Yugoslavia, Dumbarton Oaks Junior and Visiting Fellowships, and a Fellowship at the Institute for the Humanities at the University of Wisconsin.

Charalambos Bouras, a native of Preveza, Greece, earned an undergraduate degree in architectural engineering at the National Technical University of Athens and two Ph.D.'s, one at the University of Paris (History of Art) and another at the University of Thessaloniki (Architectural Engineering). He has written numerous books and articles on ancient, Byzantine, and post-Byzantine architecture. He is a member of several archaeological organizations in Greece, including the Central Archaeological Council and the Committee for the Preservation of the Monuments of the Acropolis, and is a corresponding member of the German Archaeological Institute. From 1966 until 1974 he taught architectural history at the University of Thessaloniki. Since 1974 he has held the chair of the History of Architecture at the National Technical University of Athens.

Thalia Gouma-Peterson, a native of Athens, Greece, received her A.B. and M.A. degrees from Mills College and her Ph.D. from the University of Wisconsin in Madison. She is the recipient of many scholarships and awards, including a Fulbright and a National Endowment for the Arts Grant. She has published not only in Byzantine and post-Byzantine art but also in Italian Renaissance painting, modern art, and feminist art criticism.

She has organized exhibitions and written several exhibition catalogues, including *Miriam Schapiro: A Retrospective, 1953–1980* (1980), *Sculpture Outdoors* (1982), and *Faith Ringgold: Paintings, Sculpture, Performance* (1985). She has served in various professional organizations, including the Nominating Committee of the College Art Association of America and the Women's Caucus for Art. She is the Museum Director of the College of Wooster and also Professor and Chair of that institution's Department of Art.

Gary Vikan received his B.A. at Carleton College and his Ph.D. at Princeton. He has published several articles on Byzantine metalwork, sculpture, icons, and illuminated manuscripts and has edited and contributed to, among other works, *Illuminated Greek Manuscripts from American Collections: An Exhibition in Honor of Kurt Weitzmann* (1973), *Medieval and Renaissance Miniatures from the National Gallery of Art* (1975), and *Silver from Early Byzantium* (1986). He has served in many editorial capacities, including that of Art Editor for the *Oxford Dictionary of Byzantium*. For several years associated with Dumbarton Oaks Center for Byzantine Studies, he is now the Medieval Curator at the Walters Art Gallery in Baltimore and an Adjunct Professor at Johns Hopkins University.

John J. Yiannias, Associate Professor of Art History at the University of Virgina, was born in Dubuque, Iowa. He received his B.A. in philosophy from the University of Michigan, his M.A. in General Studies in the Humanities from the University of Chicago, and his Ph.D. in Art History from the University of Pittsburgh, where he studied under William Loerke. He wrote his dissertation while on a Fulbright grant to Greece. He has published articles on Byzantine and post-Byzantine art and liturgy in various journals, including *Dumbarton Oaks Papers* and *Byzantinische Zeitschrift*. He is the organizer of the symposium on "The Byzantine Tradition after the Fall of Constantinople," for which most of the contributions to the present volume were written.

INDEX

The United Library
Garrett-Evangelical/Seabury-Western Seminaries
2121 Sheridan Road
Evanston, IL 60201